52 SIMPLE STEPS TO
Natural Health

Take charge of your life with the book that puts your health back into *your* hands! Discover a wealth of simple preventive measures and non-toxic solutions to common health-care problems with safe and proven natural techniques and therapies designed to extend and enhance your years.

YOU MIGHT BE SURPRISED TO LEARN THAT . . .

• Certain foods may save your teeth, including peanuts, cashews, and other nuts; sunflower and other seeds; and tea.

• Spending an extra 300 calories a day on work or an activity can keep 20 pounds of fat off your body in a year.

• You can build better bones by taking the herbs field horsetail or stinging nettle. Both herbs are rich sources of bone-building minerals like calcium, silicon, and magnesium.

• House plants such as spider plants, philodendrons, peace lilies, and orchids purify the air.

• Vitamin E, topically applied, can help promote healing and prevent scars from forming even for third-degree burns.

• Your hands and nails can indicate your state of health. Learn what to look for.

• Mushrooms can be medicinal. Shiitake mushrooms have long been used in Asia for their positive effects on aging and sexual dysfunction.

DISCOVER THE PATH TO GLOWING HEALTH
AND LONGEVITY NATURALLY WITH

52 SIMPLE STEPS TO *NATURAL HEALTH*

PRAISE FOR

The **Natural Health**

FIRST-AID GUIDE

By Mark Mayell and the Editors of *Natural Health* Magazine

"This is one terrific book. It's the only guide that combines state-of-the-art first-aid information with a broad array of natural healing techniques that help the body recover from injuries and prevent new ones. . . ."

—Michael Castleman,
coauthor of *Before You Call the Doctor*
and author of *The Healing Herbs*

"**The *Natural Health* First-Aid Guide** provides informed alternatives. . . . It should be on every bookshelf."

—Michael Tierra,
author of *The Way of Herbs*

". . . A treasure. . . . There is a wealth of information for the non-health professional to begin to feel at home in tackling everyday problems. . . ."

—Patch Adams, M.D.,
co-founder of the Gesundheit Institute
and author of *Gesundheit!*

"A lucid and comprehensive resource . . ." —Deepak Chopra, M.D.,
author of *Ageless Body, Timeless Mind*

". . . The first such book to include alternative as well as traditional treatments. The information is clear, concise, and comprehensive, and the author wisely makes a point of telling when a person should go to the hospital. **The *Natural Health* First-Aid Guide** should be in all libraries. . . ."

—*Library Journal*

". . . Hundreds of folk remedies and naturopathic, homeopathic, and acupressure techniques and remedies for common accidents and minor illnesses."

—Mike Maza, *Dallas Morning News*

"A comprehensive collection of first-aid remedies by the editors of *Natural Health* magazine . . . the leading national publication on alternative and natural health. . . . The guide covers a range of treatments unavailable elsewhere."

—Steve Hays, *The Light Connection*

The Editors of *Natural Health* Magazine

Mark Bittman, EDITOR
Bill Thomson, SENIOR EDITOR
Margaret Hanshaw, MANAGING EDITOR
Ellen Grimm, ASSOCIATE EDITOR
Tricia O'Brien, ASSISTANT EDITOR

52

SIMPLE STEPS

TO

Natural Health

A Week-by-Week Guide to More Healthful Living

MARK MAYELL
and the Editors of
Natural Health Magazine

POCKET BOOKS

New York   London   Toronto   Sydney   Tokyo   Singapore

An *Original* Publication of POCKET BOOKS

POCKET BOOKS, a division of Simon & Schuster Inc.
1230 Avenue of the Americas, New York, NY 10020

Copyright © 1995 by *Natural Health* Magazine

Library of Congress Cataloging-in-Publication Data

Mayell, Mark.
   52 simple steps to natural health : a week-by-week guide to more
   healthful living/Mark Mayell and the
editors of Natural Health magazine.
     p. cm.
   Includes index.
   ISBN 0-671-88061-6
   1. Naturopathy. 2. Health. 3. Mental health. I. Natural
health. II. Title. III. Title: 52 simple steps to natural
health.
RZ440.M39 1995
613—dc20   94-44712
                                           CIP

First Pocket Books trade paperback printing July 1995

10 9 8 7 6 5 4 3 2 1

POCKET and colophon are registered trademarks of Simon & Schuster Inc.

Front cover illustration by James Grashow

Text design by Stanley S. Drate/Folio Graphics Co. Inc.

Printed in the U.S.A.

CONTENTS

SIMPLE STEPS TO
NATURAL HEALTH
□
ACTIVITY AND EXERCISE

SIMPLE STEPS TO
NATURAL HEALTH
□
POSTURE

SIMPLE STEPS TO
NATURAL HEALTH
□
ENVIRONMENT

SIMPLE STEPS TO
NATURAL HEALTH
□
THE HEALING TOUCH

SIMPLE STEPS TO
NATURAL HEALTH
□
TAKE IT EASY

SIMPLE STEPS TO
NATURAL HEALTH
□
MIND AND SPIRIT

SIMPLE STEPS TO
NATURAL HEALTH
□
LONGEVITY

SIMPLE STEPS TO
NATURAL HEALTH
□
RELATIONSHIPS

SIMPLE STEPS TO
NATURAL HEALTH
□
ENJOY LIFE

ACKNOWLEDGMENTS

The Editors of *Natural Health* wish to thank the hundreds of writers, editors, interview subjects, and others who have expressed their ideas in the pages of the magazine over the past twenty-four years. They are the advance scouts whose in-depth reports from the frontiers of natural health served as the map for this book. In particular we thank Andrew Weil, M.D., Henry Dreher, Ronald Kotzsch, Gene Bruce, Mirka Knaster, Dan Seamens, Thomas Rawls, D. Patrick Miller, Craig Weatherby, Nathaniel Mead, Neal Barnard, M.D., Michael Castleman, Laurel Vukovic, Tom Monte, Judith Finn, Christopher Hobbs, Richard Leviton, Wendell Berry, John Belleme, Mary Walker, Jim Heynen, L. Larry McKinley, D.D.S., Bryan E. Robinson, Ph.D., Jeffrey Bland, Ph.D., Usha Lee McFarling, Joel Goodman, Jack Challem, Laura Taxel, Rita Robinson, Robert O. Becker, M.D., Elizabeth Frankl, Kirk Johnson, Larry Dossey, M.D., Norman Cousins, Kenneth R. Pelletier, Ph.D., Shari Lieberman, R.D., Patch Adams, M.D., John Bower, John Selby, and Bernie S. Siegel, M.D.

We also thank literary agent Nat Sobel, and at Pocket Books editor Claire Zion and assistant editor Amy Einhorn, for their continued advice and support.

PREFACE

52 Simple Steps to Natural Health began as an article idea for *Natural Health*'s twentieth-anniversary issue, which we published in May 1991. *Natural Health* magazine was founded two decades earlier with a simple but radical perspective on health. We believe that the average person can learn how to maintain well-being or even recover from illness without needing most of the high-tech interventions of modern medicine, and that by taking responsibility for your health and meeting the basic needs of your body, mind, and spirit, you can live in harmony and balance with humanity and nature. All of the magazine's articles since the premier issue have sought to show readers in various ways how to achieve such "natural health."

For the twentieth-anniversary issue we reviewed the previous two hundred and fifty or so issues of the magazine (then called *East West Journal*) and culled from them one hundred of the best natural-health ideas relating to diet, fitness, medicine, spirituality, and human potential. A number of brainstorming sessions and round-table discussions were necessary to filter out from the many possibilities the most timeless and essential ideas. This valuable winnowing led to an issue that was well received by readers, though space and other considerations limited the ultimate scope of the project.

We realized then that a book offers a better format for this type of material and so began working on *52 Simple Steps to Natural Health*. We trimmed the number of steps down from a somewhat unwieldy one hundred to fifty-two, a perfect number for encouraging readers to devote one week of the year to implementing each of the steps. Each step in this book thus summarizes some of the best, most direct techniques for achieving a quick and simple effect, whether it is to keep your back healthy or to increase your longevity.

The emphasis throughout has been on offering clear, eminently doable suggestions that anyone can put into practice in everyday life. You don't need the brain of Einstein, the strength of Hercules, or the patience of Gandhi to accomplish any of the fifty-two steps. All that you need are the inclination to give it a try and a few days to see its benefits begin to show.

No book, including this one, is an infallible prescription for perfect health. Illness, suffering, and death are a part of everyone's life. But for those who do embrace these simple steps to natural health, who do accept personal responsibility for their health and their life, the rewards will be significant. Even if you take only a few of these fifty-two steps to heart, they will help you to stay well, live long, and be happy.

> The Editors of *Natural Health*
> Brookline, Massachusetts
> Fall 1994

SIMPLE STEPS
TO
NATURAL HEALTH

FOOD
AND DIET

EAT FOR
OPTIMUM HEALTH

Some progressive nutritionists have begun to refer to the standard American diet by its acronym, SAD. The SAD diet emphasizes animal foods: most Americans derive over 50 percent of their calories and 72 percent of their protein from animal foods. This diet is also high in sugar: more than half of all carbohydrates the average American consumes are in the form of sweeteners such as sucrose and corn syrup. When grains are eaten, they're usually refined; vegetables are often canned. Worst of all, the SAD diet is rich in fat and oils: Americans' total dietary fat intake has increased from 32 percent of all calories at the turn of the century to 43 percent in 1985.

The SAD diet is appropriately named because of its long-term effects. Eating too much animal food, fat and oil, and sugar, and too few complex carbohydrates such as fresh vegetables and fruits, whole grains, and legumes, contributes to the development of degenerative diseases. These include Western societies' major killers: heart disease, diabetes, cancer, obesity, and strokes. It also includes a host of annoying if not fatal conditions, such as constipation, hemorrhoids, gout, osteoporosis, and tooth decay. According to the U.S. Surgeon General's 1988 *Report on Nutrition and Health,* diet-related diseases account for over two-thirds of all deaths in this country.

None of this is news to most nutritional experts. In the past decade it has become widely accepted wisdom that public health would greatly benefit if people consumed much less animal food and total fat. Population studies have repeatedly confirmed that a diet that is approximately 90 percent derived from plant sources and features a variety of fresh vegetables, whole grains, legumes, and fruits protects against most of the killer diseases common to industrialized societies.

Among the federal offices that are attempting to reform the SAD diet are the Surgeon General, the Food and Nutrition Board that develops recommended dietary allowances (RDAs), and the U.S. Department of Agriculture (USDA). A consensus has formed that fat should account for less than 30 percent of calories. Experts also recommend that people eat at least five servings of fresh vegetables and fruits per day and six or more servings of bread and cereals to obtain sufficient fiber and complex carbohydrates. You should also maintain an appropriate body weight and limit alcohol, sugar, and salt.

The USDA has embodied this message by discarding the "four food groups" model that it had developed in the mid-fifties. At that time the USDA started to recommend that people eat a variety of foods each day from among dairy, meat, fruits and vegetables, and breads and cereals. Unfortunately, it is easy enough to eat from all four groups but still have an unhealthy diet. For the most part, the four-food-groups model helps people avoid vitamin and mineral deficiencies in their diet, but it doesn't address the much more salient modern issue of too much fat, cholesterol, calories, and sugar.

In 1992 the USDA officially ditched the four food groups and adopted the pyramid, in which food groups are ranked by order of recommended number of daily servings. Bread and cereal form the base (8–11 servings). Vegetables and fruits are next up the slope (5–10 servings); then dairy and meat, expanded to include fish, dry beans, and nuts (4–6 servings total). Fats, oils, and sweets are at the top of the pyramid, to be used sparingly.

The USDA's modest endorsement of a plant-based diet and its deemphasis on meat and dairy products came in spite of loud objections from the American Dairy Association and the Cattlemen's Association. Nutritionists, on the other hand, have generally hailed the pyramid as a welcome change. Those who have criticized the pyramid have done so by charging that it is a useful first step though still flawed. Even using the pyramid, people can still eat too much total fat and too little fiber, according to the Physicians' Committee for Responsible Medicine (PCRM) in Washington, D.C. Some have

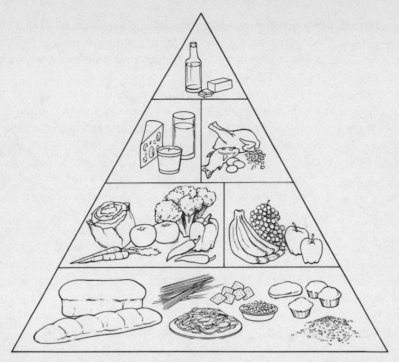

charged that the pyramid still overemphasizes the importance of meat and dairy foods, while others have questioned the categories—why are dry beans in the meat group?

Another shortcoming of the pyramid is that it doesn't encourage people to select nutrient-dense foods, says nutritionist Ellen Kamentsky, R.D. "Cucumbers, iceberg lettuce, and white pasta all count as servings, but they don't contain many nutrients. What you need are darker leafy greens and vegetables and beans and whole grains, or you are going to be losing out on a lot [of nutrients]."

The PCRM proposes sticking with a four-food-group model but changing the groups to grains, beans, vegetables, and fruits. Meat, poultry, dairy, and fish are optional, with small amounts to be eaten daily, weekly, or not at all. No foods are forbidden, but the basis of the diet is plant foods that are low in fat and calories yet rich in fiber and nutrients.

Everyday Steps to Natural Health

Whether you use the pyramid or the new four food groups as your model, here are some strategies that will help you make the transition to healthier eating habits.

Adjust your food planning and shopping habits. To eat more fresh foods and plant foods, incorporate some simple changes into how you stock your pantry and refrigerator as well as how you plan and prepare your meals.

You may need to make some adjustments in your regular food shopping habits. For instance, going to the supermarket once every two weeks allows you to stock up on limitless nonperishables, but frozen, canned, and prepared foods are often high in fat, salt, and sugar. These can't form the basis for a healthy diet. When you are trying to eat half a dozen servings of fresh vegetables and fruits every day, it is often more convenient to do shorter shopping trips every few days.

You can still use your main shopping trip to stock your pantry with pastas and sauces, dried or canned beans, whole grains, and quick-cooking grains such as bulgur and quinoa. These can serve as the foundation for large batches of grains, soups, sauces, and stews. Such dishes store well and lend themselves to a variety of planned leftovers. For instance, a grain that is used to make a Mexican dish one night can be used to make an Indian recipe the next.

Plan your meals to minimize total fat and, if necessary, cut back on animal foods. If you are in the habit of including animal foods in every meal, cutting back to only one serving of beef, chicken, or fish per day is a good first step. Thus, if you are eating at a restaurant for lunch, you may decide to have fish there and eat a plant-based breakfast and dinner. In your home, if you have a hamburger for lunch, prepare pasta as the dinner entrée.

Try to set aside a few more minutes for meal preparation, as well. It may take a few more minutes to cook a food that needs to be chopped and steamed, compared to a food that can be microwaved in its plastic container, but the end result of greater health is worth it.

Expand the range of foods from which you normally choose. Many people have the misconception that a healthy diet is an overly restrictive one. No hot dogs, potato chips, soft drinks, ice cream—what's left to eat? Actually, quite a bit. In many ways it is the SAD diet that is restrictive. A few types of meats, cheese and dairy products, baked goods, and a half dozen common vegetables comprise the bulk of the diet. By contrast, a moderately sized supermarket might offer three dozen types of vegetables, two dozen different fruits, a dozen each of legumes and beans, ten nuts, and a half dozen seeds. Within each category there is even more variety for those willing to look. For instance, within the fruit category your berry options include strawberries, blueberries, raspberries, black-berries, cranberries, and a few others.

By eating a wide variety of yellow and green fresh vegetables and fruits, grains, legumes, nuts, seeds, and other foods, you avoid high concentrations of toxins found in certain foods. These toxins may be either natural or synthetic, from aflatoxins (a natural carcino-gen found in trace amounts in peanuts and peanut butter) to the coal-tar dyes (artificial colors used in almost all processed foods). By not limiting your diet to only a few foods, you also decrease the risk that you'll miss out on some essential vitamins and minerals.

Tailor your new diet to your tastes and preferences, rather than to a dietary school such as vegetarianism. As the late scien-tist René Dubos noted, "A diet that is suitable for one person may be marginal, deficient, or even dangerous for another." Studies have found five- to sevenfold differences in the individual requirements for nutrients like calcium. Thus, one person may thrive on a strict vegetarian diet (no animal foods at all, including dairy products, eggs, and fish) while another on the same diet will lack energy. There are many dietary models competing for adherents, from vege-tarianism to high-protein weight-loss diets to natural-foods omni-vore. Nor are your choices restricted to these: you can always take what you like from one model and combine it with aspects of another.

Whether to eat animal foods is a major question for many people. Despite a sharp rise in the past two decades in the number of people who call themselves vegetarians, meat undeniably remains a popular food. Beef consumption in the U.S. fell 30 percent from 1976 to 1992 but is still over sixty pounds per person per year, and hamburg-ers remain the biggest single dietary source of saturated fat. "Most people are habitual meat eaters who have no interest in going vege-tarian—especially cold turkey," says Carol Gelles, author of *Whole-some Harvest,* a vegetarian cookbook for people who like the taste of meat dishes but want to cut back on them.

There is little question that adopting a varied plant-based diet will improve your chances of avoiding such chronic ailments as can-cer and heart disease. Animal foods can, however, still play a minor part in your diet, if you so choose. Even some longtime vegetarians have found that eating meat occasionally provides some health bene-fits. Anne Louise Gittleman, M.S., a nutritional counselor specializ-ing in women's health, says that strict vegetarianism has its limits.

It acts "as a good cleansing program for people who come from a diet heavy in animal foods and processed foods, and for a time it is therapeutic. But for some people, when it goes on too long, it seems to backfire." Gittleman says that some of her longtime vegetarian clients experience fatigue, protein deficiencies, and loss of hair.

Animal foods do have some nutritional advantages. They are relatively dense in nutrients such as zinc, iron, copper, and vitamin B_{12}. Some nutrients from animal foods are absorbed more easily than plant-based nutrients. If you do choose to eat animal foods, you can avoid their worst aspects (high fat, cholesterol, calories, and—for the average American—protein) by choosing lean cuts, trimming skin from chicken, and keeping portions small (three to four ounces of beef two or three times per week, for instance). A more difficult step is to avoid factory-farm meats, which usually have more fat than protein and often contain undesirable hormones. Healthier animal-food choices include seafood, organic or free-range chicken, and lower-fat meats such as beefalo and wild game.

If you want to eliminate almost all animal foods, by all means do so. In addition to the health considerations, there are important environmental and philosophical reasons for not eating animal foods. According to John Robbins, an heir to the Baskin-Robbins ice cream fortune who has become a leading spokesperson for animal rights and vegetarianism, "The reality is that most animal products are concentrated sources of saturated fat, cholesterol, pesticide and hormone residues, and other insults to the human body and spirit. . . . While it is certainly true that not everyone will function best on a diet totally void of any animal products, a substantial body of data indicates that, for the vast majority of people, the less animal products in the diet, the healthier the outcome is likely to be."

Make incremental changes to your diet over an extended period of time rather than radical changes overnight. Making a slow transition is not only easier but is more likely to be effective, whether your goal is to eat a diet that is 90 percent plant foods, to obtain only 20 percent of calories from fat, or just to give up meat two days a week.

If you're not sure where to start, as a first step you might identify and try to correct your worst eating habits. For instance, do you eat fatty cheese every day? Sugary pastries and coffee for breakfast on a regular basis? A half pound of butter a week? Animal foods at every meal? Rather than attempting to break all of your worst eating habits at once, focus on cutting back on total fats and increasing servings of fresh vegetables and fruits. For instance, to cut back on fat intake you might decide to

➤ switch to nonfat or low-fat dairy products and cheeses
➤ choose leaner cuts of meat
➤ throw out two of every three egg yolks (where almost all of an egg's fat and cholesterol are)
➤ make snacks and desserts an occasional treat instead of a regular event
➤ eat less at every meal, by always leaving at least a little food on your plate or not asking for seconds
➤ make butter an occasional food by switching from butter to apple butter or jam on your toast every other morning

Doing all of these things at once may be too much. If so, work on one at a time. Write out a simple resolution you decide to make and tape it to the refrigerator door as a reminder.

Making gradual dietary changes allows your taste buds to catch up with your good intentions. Put a plate of seaweeds, rice and beans, and kale in front of someone used to steak and potatoes and what happens? The food tastes "weird" and the person says, "Forget it—if living longer means eating this stuff, I'll choose an early death." A better option is to recultivate a taste for vegetables, grains, and other whole foods. At any meal, introduce only one new food at a time. Learn how to use simple cooking techniques to prepare richly flavored vegetarian recipes. For instance, traditional ethnic dishes are a good choice for richly flavored vegetarian fare, as are dishes that make use of pungent herbs and spices.

According to Rudolph Ballentine, M.D., author of *Making the Transition to Vegetarianism,* "I've found that a successful transition takes time. I think that people should make a move toward vegetarianism, but they should also be patient with themselves and base the process on developing self-awareness. . . . People who listen to what their body is telling them and who are willing to make a gradual transition tend to do better."

One all-too-common problem with making a drastic switch in your everyday food choices is that it causes cravings for what you are trying to give up. Strong cravings often result in binges. A young woman says, "I tried to give up all sweets overnight and ended up three days later going on a binge during which I polished off a whole package of Oreos in a single day. It worked much better when I broke the process down into a number of steps, first eliminating sweets before lunch, then after dinner, and so forth. Now I control my sweet tooth instead of the other way around."

Short Tips for Healthy Eating

❑ As you adopt new eating patterns, watch for signs in your body that your new diet is not working. Common signs of an inappropriate diet or nutritional deficiencies include lack of energy; hair that is dry, brittle, or falling out; menses that are irregular or nonexistent; gray or pasty complexion; skin that is dry, scaly, or rash-like; a tongue that is frequently discolored or coated; a constant sour taste in the mouth; tooth decay or bleeding gums; and split fingernails.

❑ Enlist the support of family and friends for dietary changes. The househusband who vows to change his diet, only to find he's cooking two sets of meals—one with healthy foods for himself and another for his resistant-to-change wife and children—is bound to fail. Make the education and adoption of a healthier way of eating a group project and it will go much further.

For More Information

For further information on healthy dietary choices:

The Healing Power of Foods by Michael T. Murray, N.D. (Rocklin, Calif.: Prima Publishing, 1993)

The Power of Your Plate by Neal Barnard (Summertown, Tenn.: The Book Publishing Company, 1990)

Cookbooks with excellent plant-based recipes:

Wholesome Harvest by Carol Gelles (New York: Little, Brown and Company, 1992)

The New Laurel's Kitchen by Laurel Robertson, Carol Flinders, and Brian Ruppenthal (Berkeley, Calif.: Ten Speed Press, 1986)

2

CONNECT TO
YOUR FOOD

"Tell me what you eat, and I will tell you what you are," claimed the nineteenth-century Frenchman and culinary commentator Anthelme Brillat-Savarin. To which may be added, "Tell me how you eat, and I will tell you who you are." Do you eat on the run with nary a thought about the morsel of food you are chewing? Are all of your foods grown and prepared for you by strangers? Do you consider food to be merely fuel for the body? Do all of your food choices support distant and unknown factory farms? If you answer yes to these questions, your basically one-dimensional view of eating may be limiting not only your physical health but your spiritual awareness.

Food touches upon virtually all aspects of our lives, from agriculture and ecology to family and religion. The tendency among some people in modern society is to separate food from many of these links and to reduce it to its calories and nutritional components. Yet food is also one of humanity's essential links to the sacred, notes writer Ronald Kotzsch. "One does not have to be religious to recognize that food ultimately is the gift of mysterious forces beyond our understanding and control," he says. "Indeed, all food is manna, bread fallen from heaven. To realize this is to begin a more healthful relationship with food. . . . Choose your food carefully, prepare it with love, eat it with consciousness and gratitude, and in moderation. Allow food to be a means of bonding with others."

Eating is also unmistakably an agricultural act, a fact many Americans are no longer aware of, claims Wendell Berry, poet, essayist, and Kentucky farmer. He says that eating responsibly is a necessary first step to reverse the decline in farming and rural life. Many eaters have become passive consumers, Berry notes, willing to ignore questions such as where food came from, how fresh it is, and how many artificial ingredients were added during production, storage, and shipping. Berry agrees with Sir Albert Howard on the need to understand "the whole problem of health in soil, plant, animal, and man as one great subject."

"A significant part of the pleasure of eating is in one's accurate consciousness of the lives and the world from which food comes," says Berry. "The pleasure of eating, then, may be the best available standard of our health. And this pleasure, I think, is pretty fully available to the urban consumer who will make the necessary effort."

Everyday Steps to Natural Health

Connecting to food in a positive way has beneficial effects on the physical, emotional, psychological, and spiritual quality of the person who eats it. Here are some ways to establish a positive relation with food.

Grow some of what you eat. Gardening connects you to all stages of the food cycle: planting, tending, reaping, and returning organic matter to the soil (if you make compost from leftovers and waste). Even people without a yard can start a small vegetable garden by using window boxes or containers. For those with only a tiny ten-by-twenty-foot plot, an average investment of $36 allows you to plant a vegetable garden that will yield $175 worth of vegetables.

"The pleasure of eating should be an *extensive* pleasure, not that of the mere gourmet," says Berry. "People who know the garden in which their vegetables have grown and know that the garden is healthy will remember the beauty of the growing plants, perhaps in the dewy first light of morning when gardens are at their best. Such a memory involves itself with the food and is one of the pleasures of eating. The knowledge of the good health of the garden relieves and frees and comforts the eater."

The positive effects of gardening are not limited to economics and the pleasures of eating. "I find gardening to be a healthy enterprise on many levels," says Andrew Weil, M.D., author of *Natural Health, Natural Medicine*. "It is a physical and mental challenge, a wonderful way to dissipate emotional tension, and a source of great satisfaction when you pick the fruits of your labor. I recommend gardening to many people who consult me for medical problems."

Perhaps most importantly, growing some of what you eat is a spiritual act, argues Sam Keen, author of *Fire in the Belly*. Growing things is an essential element of one of a dozen "rules of thumb, or rules of the road, for a spiritual journey in a troubled time," he notes. "More than anything we need to get the metaphor and experience of growing back into our lives. The ultimate truth about human life is not that we make it, but that there is something already alive that has intentionality. When we stop being in daily contact with growing things, we lose that experience and that implicit trust in life. Growing something that you eat is integral to the life of the spirit. It reminds us that we are not here primarily as makers and doers and shakers. We are here as created beings who must be responsive to life."

Learn more about the food you buy. An ignorant consumer is an easily cheated one. Various state and local officials do their best to assure that growers are fairly rewarded for their work and that foods are fresh and healthful. The job is immense, however (supermarkets often stock five to six thousand different items of food), and your help is needed. When you next shop, take a moment to ask the grocer, or the person behind the fish counter, where a product comes from, how it is grown and processed, how it is delivered to the store, and what the store's role is in getting the item from its source to you. Many food purveyors are eager to share their knowledge, though you may need to wait for a time when they are not faced with a backlog of customers.

You can also learn more about your food by visiting your local community farms, orchards, and farmers' markets. Support their efforts to supply people with food that hasn't been transported across the country at great expense in terms of energy costs and degree of freshness. Buying food grown or produced locally can eliminate costly middlepersons and allow you to eat foods most appropriate for your climate.

It is especially important to teach children the importance of learning more about their food, since many children in urban areas have no idea what is involved in creating a simple loaf of bread. Most of their information about food may come from television commercials. Children also often do not realize that many of the foods commonly eaten in America come from other countries (for example, bananas from the Philippines, sugar from Dominican Republic, coffee from Brazil, cocoa from Ghana) or distant parts of the U.S. (pineapples from Hawaii, raisins from California, beef from Nebraska, chickens from Maryland, oranges from Florida).

Make eating more than a pit stop. The increasing popularity of packaged goods and fast foods (7 percent of the American population eats at McDonald's each day) reflects and reinforces a cavalier attitude toward food. Prepared foods and the microwave can play a role even in a healthy diet, but when they become your normal mealtime habits, you are in danger of losing touch with eating. Here are some ways to stay connected.

❑ Invest some energy into your food. According to one survey, the maximum amount of time most American men say they want to spend putting a meal together is fifteen minutes. No doubt for some of these men, that fifteen minutes is meant to include both preparation and cooking time. Admittedly, people lead busy lives and fifteen minutes is all that can be invested in putting together some meals. On a regular basis, however, it is worthwhile to take the time and thought necessary to prepare a wholesome meal made from fresh ingredients. Choosing the right ingredients, washing and chopping vegetables, and carefully simmering a pot of rice invests some of your own energy, intelligence, and personality in the food. You can eat the dish and be assured that it contains healthful ingredients (even more so if you've grown some of it as well) that will sustain your body and mind.

❑ Share your meals with family or friends. The camaraderie and conversation that accompany a good meal can be as important to overall health as the food itself. A meal eaten alone while reading the newspaper, or shared with others while everyone stares at a television set, is likely to satisfy neither body nor soul. "To share food with others is to accept them and to enter a relation with them," says Kotzsch. "Conversely, to refuse to share food with someone creates alienation." Thus, it is not surprising that ethnic groups that value eating together have families that do better at staying together.

Kotzsch recounts the bizarre holiday gathering that resulted when, as an avid and newly converted vegetarian, he brought his own plate of brown rice, tofu, and seaweed to a relative's Thanks-giving dinner and announced he "would not eat turkey (putrefying, hormone-laden flesh), baked potatoes (from a deadly nightshade plant), nor cranberry sauce (sugar-laden)." The meal, he says, turned out to be a dour event for his awestruck family. It also left him feeling poorly afterward "despite my virtuous eating." Kotzsch notes that "because there is no better food than that cooked with love," his physical and spiritual health would no doubt have been better served by joining in with the others and sharing their food.

The late food writer M. F. K. Fisher observed, "It means a great deal to sit around the table, which is the center of life along with the bed, for warmth and love. Food and love are inexorably mixed."

❑ Add an element of ritual to your meals. Saying grace before a meal has become passé in our secular age, but the reason behind such blessings is as relevant today as it was when the custom developed thousands of years ago. A short prayer or statement of thanks ac-knowledges that animals or plants have sacrificed their lives so that we may continue to live. Unless the blessing is done by rote, it encourages the eaters to appreciate the work of all of those who made the meal possible, from the farmer or gardener who grew the produce to the cook who prepared it.

Offering a blessing can be overtly religious (such as the Catho-lics' "Bless us, O Lord, for these thy gifts . . ." or the Buddhists' "I reflect on the work of others, which brings this food to me . . .") or secular ("We thank the universe for the harmony that puts this food in front of us here today . . ."). Nor is a blessing the only way to add an element of ritual to a meal. Anything that contributes to a more mindful way of eating is useful. Try observing a moment of silence to reflect on the meal or expressing a few words on some special quality of the food being presented.

❑ Eat with consciousness. Try to fully savor the taste, smell, and texture of your food. Obviously, you can't expect to do this for every bite of the 1,400 pounds of food you'll consume on average in a year. On the other hand, if you never think about or really experience your food, you increase the likelihood that your relation-ship to food will become an addictive one. Absentmindedly or com-pulsively eating while driving, working at your desk, or watching television is a common problem that can lead to obesity and other health problems. Many young people, especially college-age women, suffer from bulimia, an eating disorder characterized by cycles of overeating and throwing up. Eating disorders can also affect athletes who want to lose or gain weight. Compulsive eating habits often result from emotional and spiritual imbalances. The food satisfies not the body but the spirit, albeit temporarily. Bringing more attention and awareness to eating can help break an addictive habit.

Short Tips for Connecting to Your Food

❑ Fast periodically to rest the digestive system and increase your appreciation of and gratitude for food (see Step 5).

For More Information

An excellent book of essays on the connections between food, health, and culture is:

Our Sustainable Table edited by Robert Clark (San Francisco: North Point Press, 1990)

3

SUPPLEMENT YOUR DIET

An estimated 120 million Americans spend more than $3 billion annually on vitamin and mineral supplements. About half of these people take supplements every day. Critics of nutritional supplements, including most doctors and government regulators, contend that many of these people are wasting their money. According to Stanley Gershoff, Ph.D., dean of the Tufts University School of Nutrition, "Most people in the United States get all the nutrients they need from the abundant food supply." Really?

A growing number of nutritionists and public-health experts disagree. They say that the typical American diet provides less than the RDA for various nutrients, especially vitamins E and B_6 and the minerals calcium, magnesium, and zinc. Even eating according to the latest federal guidelines and following the food-pyramid model (see Step 1) does not guarantee meeting the RDAs. A recent survey of ten of our staffers at *Natural Health,* an assortment of vegetarians and omnivores, found that eight consumed inadequate levels of vitamin A; five, too little vitamin C; and all ten, inadequate calcium. Larger surveys of the general public have garnered similar results. According to the Council for Responsible Nutrition (CRN), a Washington, D.C.–based association of the nutritional supplement industry, "One national government survey showed that not a single person out of more than 22,000 surveyed got 100 percent of the RDA for ten nutrients from diet alone."

Some nutrients are found in high levels only in food that are typically eaten infrequently. For instance, vitamin E is found mainly in oily nuts and seeds and vegetable oils, foods that many people are cutting back on to reduce their fat intake. Zinc is richest in oysters, wheat germ, and sesame seeds. When was the last time you ate any of those foods?

According to nutritionist Ellen Kamentsky, R.D., "To consistently get your RDAs from diet you have to do careful meal planning and select specific foods to cover nutrients like vitamin A and calcium. I know that there are plenty of days when it is hard for me to get all my vegetables. I take a supplement, and many dietitians I talk to generally take one just to cover the nutritional bases. I don't see how a RDA-level multiple supplement can hurt, and it can certainly help."

As if that is not enough reason to consider supplementing your diet, some nutritionists now say that the RDAs themselves are grossly insufficient to assure optimal health. The RDAs have changed little though they have been updated several times since they were first established in 1941 by the National Academy of Sciences' Food and Nutrition Board. RDAs are meant to be levels that are "adequate to meet the known nutrient needs of practically all healthy persons." The RDAs are not minimal but neither are they optimal. They were developed at a time when it was necessary to protect the public from severe, overt deficiency symptoms.

Today, relatively few people in the U.S. suffer from scurvy (from too little vitamin C) or beriberi (from a deficiency of thiamine). Yet preventing deficiency conditions is hardly the only benefit vitamins and minerals offer. Within the past decades a number of studies have confirmed that levels of nutrients beyond the RDA can help prevent many of the chronic diseases that plague industrialized societies, including cancer, heart disease, and diabetes. For example, a recent study performed by a team of researchers from China and from the U.S.'s National Cancer Institute involving thirty thousand people living in north-central China demonstrated that taking vitamin and mineral supplements can reduce the cancer death rate.

According to Alexander Schauss, Ph.D., nutritional researcher and the director of the American Institute for Biosocial Research, "Antioxidants, such as vitamin C, beta carotene, and vitamin E, may prevent the free-radical damage . . . associated with the most common form of cardiovascular disease, atherosclerosis. These vitamins may be required in much higher amounts than the RDA to prevent atherosclerosis than needed to prevent deficiency symptoms. Unless, of course, the development of atherosclerosis is a deficiency symptom of these vitamins!"

Calling RDAs "the nutritional equivalent of the minimum wage," Schauss says that what is needed is an entirely new perspective and a new scale for nutrient levels, one that can complement the "outmoded RDAs." He has developed a "suggested optimal nutrient allowance (SONA)" to help people maintain health over a lifetime. He notes that SONAs are based in part on a fifteen-year study of 13,500 American men and women, led by Drs. Emanuel Cheraskin and W. M. Ringsdorf, Jr., of the University of Alabama School of Medicine. Their study compared nutrient consumption with subjects' health and found that those people with the highest nutrient intakes from diet and supplements were the healthiest individuals.

Research on optimal levels is in its infancy. No universal level exists such that scientists can say, for instance, everybody should take 500 mg (milligrams) of vitamin C daily. Some people require higher or lower nutrient levels than others. Those who generally need higher than average nutrient levels include people who

➤ drink alcohol to excess or smoke
➤ live in polluted areas or in areas where food is grown in nutrient-depleted soil
➤ are ill, inactive, or have a small appetite
➤ are overweight or trying to lose weight (one study of eleven diets found that they all fell short of at least one RDA)
➤ are pregnant or breast-feeding
➤ are elderly
➤ have poor intestinal absorption

The point is not to eat lots of junk food and try to get your nutrients from supplements. Nutritional supplements are not a magic bullet. Rather, eat a healthful diet *and* take additional nutrients in supplement form for optimal health.

Everyday Steps to Natural Health

To obtain the optimal nutrient levels listed below we considered the suggestions of Schauss as well as the late Linus Pauling, Ph.D., a Nobel Prize–winning scientist and the foremost proponent of vitamin C therapy, and clinical nutritionist Shari Lieberman, R.D., coauthor of *The Real Vitamin and Mineral Book*. All optimal levels are well below any known toxicity levels.

Optimal levels are compared to either RDAs or U.S. recommended daily allowances (US RDAs). The latter were developed by the Food and Drug Administration from the RDAs for use on food and supplement labels. US RDA levels are similar to though generally higher than the RDAs. US RDAs are simpler than RDAs since US RDAs give a single figure per nutrient rather than a range. US RDAs also use well-known measurements (for example, vitamin A is measured in international units, or IUs, rather than the obscure "retinol equivalents" used for RDAs).

Multinutrient tablets, capsules, powders, and liquids are the best way to take the following vitamins, minerals, trace elements, and other substances. Most "one-a-day" supplements offer 100 percent or higher of the RDA for only a select number of nutrients. Some minerals in particular have large molecular structures. A one-a-day supplement with all the vitamins and minerals would have to be the size of a golf ball just to meet the RDA. Since an optimal supplement program goes beyond the RDAs, it requires you to take four or more tablets or capsules daily.

Take nutritional supplements in divided doses a number of times throughout the day. In general it is preferable to consume vitamins and minerals with meals, though it is not harmful to take them at any point during the day. You can safely and effectively take the following optimal levels of nutrients for short periods or indefinitely. Supplements are widely available not only in natural foods stores but in supermarkets, pharmacies, and by mail order. Prices vary considerably but you can take even a wide variety of high-quality supplements at a cost of only a few dollars per day.

Take a multivitamin supplement that can provide you with optimal levels of the most important vitamins. The ten principal vitamins include six B-complex vitamins and C, which are water soluble and easily eliminated from the body, and the fat soluble A, D, and E, which can (rarely) accumulate in the body and cause toxic reactions. In the body, vitamins work with enzymes and other bodily compounds to help produce energy, build tissues, and remove waste products. Let's look at each and suggest an optimal supplement level.

❏ Vitamin A and beta carotene refer to the same vitamin. Vitamin A is the preformed vitamin found in highest concentration in meats; beta carotene is a plant-based precursor that is as effective and much less toxic. Vitamin A/beta carotene is essential for healthy vision, cell reproduction, wound healing, immunity, and other crucial bodily functions. It is also a potent antioxidant that prevents free radicals from harming the body. Studies have confirmed that vitamin A/beta carotene can help treat or prevent cancer, and it improves resistance to infection. Vitamin A derivatives are used to renew aged skin and treat acne. A study at the Memorial University of Newfoundland in Canada found that subjects who took multiple vitamin and mineral supplements that contained four to five times the RDA for beta carotene (and vitamin E) suffered half the rate of infectious diseases, including colds and flu, compared with those who took a placebo. Another recent study found that taking beta carotene can significantly reduce the incidence of strokes and heart disease.

The US RDA for vitamin A is 5,000 IU. An optimal supplement level is 10,000–20,000 IU of vitamin A/beta carotene or 15–30 mg of beta carotene daily.

❏ Thiamine (B₁) is crucial for the metabolism of carbohydrates and the normal functioning of the nervous system. Since alcohol destroys thiamine, it is important for drinkers to consume optimal levels.

The US RDA for thiamine is 1.5 mg. An optimal supplement level is 25–100 mg daily.

❏ Riboflavin (B₂) is necessary for production of energy, formation of red blood cells, metabolism of nutrients, and maintenance of the body's mucous membranes. It may also play a role in preventing cataracts and visual problems.

The US RDA for riboflavin is 1.7 mg. An optimal supplement level is 25–100 mg daily.

❏ Niacin (B₃) helps the body produce energy, metabolize fats and carbohydrates, and manufacture fatty acids as well as sex and adrenal hormones. Therapeutically it is used in the treatment of schizophrenia, high blood pressure and blood cholesterol, arthritis, and lack of blood circulation to the extremities. It comes in two forms, nicotinic acid and niacinamide. Unlike nicotinic acid, taking in excess of 50–100 mg of niacinamide at one time won't cause a temporary flushing of the skin.

The US RDA for niacin is 20 mg. An optimal supplement level is 25–300 mg daily.

❏ Pyridoxine (B_6) boosts immunity, protects against nervous disorders, produces red blood cells, and plays an important role in hormone balance. It may help regulate eye pressure, alleviate fatigue, and cure carpal tunnel syndrome. Pyridoxine is an important vitamin for healthy bioelectric functioning of the central nervous system and may inhibit certain types of seizures. It also helps maintain a proper balance of sodium, potassium, and magnesium.

The US RDA for vitamin B_6 is 2 mg. An optimal supplement level is 25–100 mg daily.

❏ Folic Acid (folate, folacin) is a B-complex nutrient that helps produce red blood cells, synthesize DNA, and metabolize protein. Pregnant women need to be sure to take sufficient quantities since folic acid is necessary for the fetus to develop proper nerve cells. It is used therapeutically to treat cervical dysplasia (a precancerous condition in women), depression and anxiety, and fatigue. Numerous studies indicate that 95 percent of American women get less than 70 percent of their RDA for folic acid from their diets.

The US RDA for folic acid is 400 mcg (micrograms). An optimal supplement level is 400–1,000 mcg daily.

❏ Vitamin B_{12} (cobalamin) aids in energy production from fats and carbohydrates and in the production of amino acids. It also plays a role in nerve building—a deficiency causes neurological problems and confusion, depression, and memory loss. B_{12} supplementation helps treat fatigue (even with no evidence of a deficiency), depression, and infertility.

The US RDA for B_{12} is 6 mcg. An optimal supplement level is 25–100 mcg.

❏ Vitamin C (ascorbic, from "antiscurvy," acid) is the most popular vitamin in supplement form, widely taken to boost the nervous system and reduce the symptoms of colds, asthma, and allergy. It also strengthens blood vessels, helps the body resist infection, and plays a crucial role in the healing of wounds, broken bones, and surgical operations. In a recent study of over 11,000 adults over a ten-year period, UCLA researchers found that men who took supplements containing 300–500 mg of vitamin C had a 42 percent lower death rate from heart disease and stroke. The C users also "had an increased life span—up to six years for men and one year for women," according to study coauthor Morton A. Klein.

The US RDA for vitamin C is 65 mg. An optimal supplement level is 500–1,500 mg daily.

❏ Vitamin D is a hormonelike substance that promotes the absorption of calcium and helps form bones and teeth. Studies have linked adequate levels of vitamin D with a reduced risk of skin cancer and (when combined with calcium) colorectal cancer. The body manufactures plenty of its own vitamin D if the skin is exposed to twenty to thirty minutes of sunlight every other day or so (see Step 20). People who live in cold climates or get little regular sun exposure are most in need of vitamin D supplementation.

The US RDA for vitamin D is 400 IU. An optimal supplement level is 400–800 IU daily.

❏ Vitamin E, like vitamin C, is a powerful antioxidant that protects the body against problems ranging from cancer to the effects of aging. Vitamin E may also promote virility and protect against heart disease. Eight out of ten doctors who responded to a survey done by the CRN said that on the basis of studies linking vitamin E to reduced heart disease, they take vitamin E in amounts above the RDA and recommend that their patients do the same.

The US RDA for vitamin E is 30 IU. An optimal supplement level is 400–800 IU daily.

Take a multimineral supplement that can provide you with optimal levels. Minerals are metals and other inorganic compounds. They include the major minerals (calcium, phosphorus, potassium, sodium, chlorine, magnesium, and sulfur), which are needed by the body in quantities of over 100 mg per day, and the minor minerals or trace elements (boron, chromium, copper, iron, manganese, selenium, zinc, and a few others), needed in quantities of less than 100 mg per day. Minerals function much as vitamins do to promote and regulate various bodily processes. Minerals also provide much of the structure for teeth and bones. "Mineral insufficiency and trace-element insufficiency are actually more likely to occur than are vitamin-insufficiency states," says Sheldon Saul Hendler, M.D., Ph.D., author of *The Doctors' Vitamin and Mineral Encyclopedia*.

Few Americans need to take supplements containing sodium and chlorine, the minerals found in table salt. Phosphorus is also readily available in widely eaten foods such as red meat, poultry, and soft drinks. The US RDA for phosphorous is 1,000 mg, and you get 500 mg of the mineral in twelve ounces of most soft drinks. Consuming too much phosphorous and too little calcium is a common nutritional problem that has been linked to osteoporosis. Potassium is also found in high amounts in fresh fruits, vegetables, milk, meat, and other common foods. Sodium, phosphorous, and potassium can be readily lost through heavy sweating, in which case supplementation may be necessary.

There is currently no RDA for sulfur, and it is unknown whether daily sulfur supplementation is necessary for optimal health. Garlic and garlic supplements (see page 27) are excellent sources of sulfur-containing compounds that are definitely beneficial to overall health.

That leaves two major minerals to include in your optimal supplement program:

❑ Calcium plays an important role in a variety of essential bodily functions, including building of bones and teeth, transmitting nerve messages, regulating heartbeat, and coagulating blood. Natural healers recommend it to treat or prevent osteoporosis, heart disease, problems of menopause, and certain cancers. Manufacturers produce supplements from a variety of sources, including dolomite, oyster shells, and bone meal. They also produce calcium supplements in different chemical forms, with calcium citrate and calcium carbonate noted for being highly absorbable.

The US RDA for calcium is 1,000 mg. An optimal supplement level is 800–1,500 mg.

❑ Magnesium, like calcium, is required for strong, healthy bones and is concentrated in the body in the bones and teeth. It is important to a variety of other bodily processes: it helps keep cells electrically stable and, with calcium, regulates the body's energy levels and maintains normal heart function and nerve transmission. Some people use supplements to treat premenstrual syndrome, high blood pressure, anxiety, osteoporosis, fatigue, and diabetes.

The US RDA for magnesium is 400 mg. An optimal supplement level is 450–650 mg daily.

Track down those trace elements. Many supplement manufacturers don't include a number of trace elements, such as iodine, iron, and fluoride, in combination trace-element products, even though in minute amounts they have important effects on health. For instance, iodine is needed to produce thyroid hormones and metabolize excess fat. Consuming too little can cause goiter, an enlarged thyroid gland, and possibly increase the risk of breast cancer. Iron helps the body produce energy and maintain proper immune function. It is part of the hemoglobin that carries oxygen in the bloodstream to tissues throughout the body. Fluoride helps build strong teeth.

Consuming too much of these trace elements, however, poses health hazards. In the U.S., salt makers add iodine to sodium chloride to make iodized salt. The average American consumes an estimated 600 mcg of iodine, mostly from salt, while the US RDA and an optimal level for iodine is 150 mcg daily. The body readily stores iron, and too much iron can be toxic or cause cardiovascular disease. Most nutritionists now recommend that people take iron-containing supplements only if an iron deficiency has been clinically demonstrated. The US RDA and an optimal level for iron is 18 mg daily. Many communities add fluoride to the public water supply.

The following trace elements are those with more dramatic differences between the average and the optimal level of consumption.

❑ Boron is necessary to help prevent bone loss and osteoporosis, possibly by working in conjunction with other bone builders such as calcium and magnesium. There's also some evidence that it may help prevent arthritis and tooth decay.

There is no established US RDA or RDA for boron. An optimal supplement level for adults is 2.5–3.0 mg daily.

❑ Chromium affects the hormone insulin's ability to regulate blood levels of glucose, or blood sugar. Studies have shown that chromium supplementation can benefit some adult-onset diabetes and people suffering from hypoglycemia. Chromium's effects on blood sugar can also spill over to affect fat metabolism and blood cholesterol levels. It thus may help prevent heart disease.

There is no established US RDA or RDA for chromium. An optimal supplement level for adults is 150–300 mcg daily.

❑ Copper helps cells produce energy and form bones and collagen (a fibrous protein found in connective tissue). Copper also plays a role in metabolizing vitamin C. Consuming insufficient (or excessive) amounts of copper can cause bone and joint conditions, and problems of the cardiovascular, nervous, and immune systems.

The US RDA for copper is 2 mg. An optimal supplement level is 2–4 mg daily.

❑ Manganese plays a role in the metabolism of fat and protein, helps bones to grow and develop, and aids in reproduction. It is also necessary for central nervous system and brain function—some epileptics take manganese supplements to decrease the frequency of seizures.

There is no established US RDA or RDA for manganese. An optimal supplement level for adults is 5–10 mg daily.

❏ Selenium is a potent antioxidant. High soil levels of selenium have been linked to low cancer rates of local people, and vice versa. Selenium may also be beneficial in the prevention of heart disease and immune-deficient conditions. It helps protect the body against harm from heavy metals and environmental toxins and inhibits aging-related processes.

The adult RDA for selenium is 55–70 mcg. An optimal supplement level for adults is 100–150 mcg daily.

❏ Zinc is a trace mineral essential for proper wound healing, male sexual potency, immunity, liver detoxification, skin health, and numerous other bodily functions. Practitioners use zinc to treat acne and other skin diseases and injuries, colds, infertility, eye disorders, ulcers, and alcoholism. It is often taken before and after surgical operations to speed recovery.

The US RDA for zinc is 15 mg. An optimal supplement level for adults is 17–25 mg daily.

Take three other supplements to round out your optimal program. There are no RDAs for the following, but they can play important roles in preventing chronic diseases.

❏ Coenzyme Q10 is a vitaminlike compound, also known as ubiquinone, that occurs naturally in the body and is taken as a supplement to help the body's cells use oxygen and generate energy. It may help prevent or treat heart disease, hypertension, diabetes, Alzheimer's disease, and obesity. CoQ10 is an antioxidant and may strengthen muscles and improve physical performance and endurance.

An optimal supplement level of coenzyme Q10 for adults is 15–30 mg daily.

❏ Essential fatty acids (EFAs) are fats that are needed by the body but not manufactured by it and must thus be consumed. Sometimes collectively referred to as vitamin F, EFAs strengthen cell membranes and promote the growth of muscles and nerves. Used therapeutically they can thin the blood, inhibit clotting, and improve cholesterol profiles, thus preventing heart disease. EFAs also have natural anti-inflammatory effects potentially useful in the treatment of arthritis, allergies, and asthma. Manufacturers produce supplements from the oil of cold-water fish such as herring and bluefish, or from the seed oil of certain plants including borage, evening primrose, and black currant. Important EFAs include the omega-3s, such as eicosapentaenoic acid (EPA) and docosahexaenoic acid (DHA), and omega-6s, such as gamma linolenic acid (GLA).

An optimal supplement level of EFAs for adults is 250–500 mg daily.

❏ Garlic is the familiar food and medicinal herb. It is a rich source of vitamins A, B complex, and C, various trace minerals, and some two hundred other compounds. Nutritionists recommend it to both treat and prevent heart disease, since it can lower cholesterol levels and blood pressure. It is also an effective antioxidant that studies show may reduce the risk of stomach cancer. It is widely used in cooking, though heat inactivates its enzymes and significantly reduces its medicinal effects. Most supplements are enteric coated to prevent garlic breath.

An optimal supplement level of garlic is 1,250–2,500 mg of fresh garlic equivalent daily.

Short Tips for Supplementation

❏ Store your supplements in a cool, dark place but not in the refrigerator. Once opened, supplements keep for about twelve months.

❏ Take supplements after a meal two or three times each day, rather than just once a day. This increases absorption and helps prevent indigestion.

❏ Compared to tablets, capsules are easier to swallow and digest and can more easily be opened and dissolved in liquids. Tablets have the advantages of being better protected from oxidation, released more slowly into the body, and less expensive.

❏ If your family has a history of heart disease and you are worried about developing it later in life, be sure to take optimal levels of selenium, boron, and vitamins E and C.

❏ If you are worried about cancer, take optimal levels of vitamins A, B complex, C, D, and E, and selenium and zinc.

❏ Avoid taking high levels of just one nutrient. High levels of some individual B vitamins, for instance, can interfere with the absorption of other B vitamins.

For More Information

Books with informative summaries of nutrients' effects include:

The Doctors' Vitamin and Mineral Encyclopedia by Sheldon Saul Hendler, M.D., Ph.D. (New York: Fireside, 1990)

The Real Vitamin and Mineral Book by Shari Lieberman and Nancy Bruning (Garden City Park, N.Y.: Avery Publishing Group, 1990)

Staying Healthy with Nutrition by Elson M. Haas, M.D. (Berkeley, Calif.: Celestial Arts, 1992)

┌─────────┐
│   │
│   4   │
│   │
└─────────┘

CUT BACK ON
JUNK FOODS

Sugar and fat are the Sodom and Gomorrah of many people's diets, the areas of temptation and sinfulness that when overindulged cause the most damaging diet-related health problems. Like the biblical cities, sugar and fat are close neighbors: foods that are high in refined sugars are also often high in fat. Packaged junk foods may contain as well other undesirable ingredients, such as artificial colors, flavors, and preservatives and high levels of salt. Meanwhile, healthful ingredients such as fiber, vitamins, and minerals have been refined out.

Eating large amounts of nutritionally empty junk foods packs a triple whammy. One, you fill up without consuming valuable nutrients. Unless you take a complete set of nutritional supplements, you increase your risk of suffering from various nutritional deficiencies. Two, sugar and fat both have a tendency to increase appetite, unlike foods high in complex carbohydrates and fiber, which satisfy your appetite with fewer calories. So it is difficult to limit your indulgence to just a taste of sugary, fatty foods. Three, and more importantly, the unhealthful macronutrients in junk foods, especially sugar and fat, increase your risk of developing chronic diseases. Excessive sugar consumption has been tied to tooth decay, mood swings, hyperactivity in children, and diseases such as diabetes and obesity. Overindulging in sugary foods may also weaken the immune system, accelerate aging, and raise blood fat levels (thus increasing the risk of heart disease). Fat's adverse health effects are more pronounced and even more solidly documented than sugar's, including obesity, heart disease, and cancer.

How much is too much? People in the industrialized world eat extremely large amounts of refined sweeteners. In the U.S. consumption averages over 140 pounds per person per year—almost 25 percent of a person's total caloric intake. Two-thirds of this sugar is from processed foods and beverages. Refined sweeteners are not needed in any amount by the body, but even if zero consumption is unrealistic, certainly cutting average consumption in half would provide numerous health benefits.

Average fat consumption in the U.S. is also high. Most Americans obtain 35–40 percent of their calories from fat, amounting to 80–100 grams daily. Nutritionists now agree that you should get no more than 30 percent of your calories from fat, and many in the field say 20–25 percent is an even better target. In other words, if you take in about 2,000 calories per day, your total fat consumption should be less than 65 grams; for 2,500 calories, less than 80 grams.

Everyday Steps to Natural Health

Controlling your consumption of junk foods and other nutritional nightmares is an important step toward dietary responsibility.

Substitute more healthful snack foods for sugary, fatty ones. Popular snack foods that add little nutrition to a diet and are often full of fat and sugar include cookies, candy, doughnuts, cakes and pastries, potato and corn chips, soft drinks (does the "soft" refer to what they do to your teeth?), and ice cream. Rather than vowing never to eat these foods, try to minimize their place in your diet. If you typically consume a number of these foods on a daily basis, your diet is probably increasing your risk of health problems.

Fresh fruit is at the top of the list for more healthful snack foods. Its natural sweetness and juiciness is satisfying to the taste and it contains various bodybuilding nutrients. Fruit is naturally rich in fiber and complex carbohydrates, which help to reduce hunger sensations. The natural sugar fructose may also play a role in limiting appetite. Researchers have found that people who consume fructose not only eat less food but they eat less fat in particular.

Here are some other suggestions for more healthful snack foods:

➤ raw vegetables such as sticks of carrot, celery, cucumber, and green peppers
➤ raisins and other dried fruit, such as apricots, dates, figs, pineapples, and bananas
➤ natural, whole-grain crackers, graham crackers, ginger snaps, and other low-fat treats
➤ low-fat granola bars (read labels carefully: many granola bars, "natural" or not, have more sugar and fat than some candy bars)
➤ popcorn (again, read labels carefully: many brands of microwave popcorn have high levels of fat)
➤ homemade pretzels, breads, muffins, and cakes
➤ trail mix or gorp mixes, containing raisins, unroasted nuts and seeds, and dried fruits

Cook your own cakes, pies, cookies, puddings, sweet breads, and pastries. There are a number of advantages to this strategy. One is that cooking takes more time and planning than running down to the convenience market, so you are likely to have less of a ready supply of these foods. More importantly, as the cook you can control the ingredients and thus the overall healthfulness of the finished products. You can substitute whole or partially milled flours (such as whole-wheat pastry flour) for refined white flours, natural sweeteners (such as honey, maple syrup, and barley malt) that are marginally (or dramatically, in the case of molasses) more nutritious than white sugar, high-quality oils for lard and hydrogenated fats, and fresh fruits and spices for artificial flavors.

Watch out for hidden fat. There are three simple steps to determine the fat content of a food: multiply the grams of fat by nine to get calories from fat, divide the result by the total calories, and multiply the resulting fraction by 100 to get a percentage. For instance, for a food that has 10 grams of fat and 120 calories, multiply 10 by 9 to get 90 calories from fat, divide 90 by 120 to get .75, and multiply .75 by 100 to get 75 percent of calories from fat. New food-labeling regulations for packaged foods that went into effect in mid-1994 make this calculation simpler. They require that nutritional labels provide the figure for total calories from fat, thus eliminating the first of the three calculations.

To stay healthy, eat foods that are far in excess of 30 percent of calories from fat only occasionally and in small amounts. If you take the time to read labels, you'll find that many junk and fast foods are quite fatty. Some nutritionists say that the term *sweet tooth* is more accurately phrased as *fat tooth,* since many people seem to crave the pleasant taste and texture of rich, fatty foods as much as sweetness per se. A recent study of almost five hundred obese men and women xnsupports this thesis. Researchers at the University of Michigan School of Public Health asked obese people what foods tempted them the most. The response was a mixture of sweet and nonsweet foods—candies, cakes, doughnuts, meats—that were all fatty. Indeed, most of the calories in foods such as ice cream and chocolate bars comes from the fat, not the sugar.

"See if you can satisfy your sweet tooth with sugar alone," suggests Andrew Weil, M.D., author of *Natural Health, Natural Medicine.* He notes that dried fruit, hard candy, and fruit ices are healthier treats because they are fat free. "Try to use them consciously—as a way of rewarding yourself, for example, instead of just eating them for no reason," he says.

Uncouple your dietary bad habits from the everyday actions that promote them. Even people who are eating healthful foods at mealtimes may slip into poor eating habits at other times. For instance, people who work at home must avoid the temptation to constantly snack on sugary treats while working, since the kitchen is often only a few steps away. Those who travel may yield to the temptation to eat at fast-food restaurants as a matter of course.

Perhaps the most common unhealthful association of diet and activity is eating junk food while watching television. A recent study of almost twelve thousand people found that those who watch television three to four hours per day had about twice the risk for developing high cholesterol, compared to people who watched TV less than one hour daily. Researcher Larry A. Tucker, Ph.D., of Brigham Young University in Provo, Utah, surmised that the increased risk was due partly from lost opportunity to be physically active and partly from the usual dietary habits people have while watching television. "A person who watches too much TV tends to eat while watching—and it's usually fattening stuff," he commented.

Television can also have a negative effect on children's eating habits, since programs they watch are targeted by advertisers who spend hundreds of millions of dollars annually to promote candy, soft drinks, cereals that are more than half sugar, and other nutritionally suspect foods.

Eating while working, watching television, or doing other activities is often addictive in nature. The person may not even fully experience the taste, smell, and texture of the food as it's eaten. When you are eating to satisfy your soul rather than your stomach, you often end up eating too much of the wrong foods. See Step 2 for suggestions on eating with more consciousness and Step 35 for how to break addictive habits.

Short Tips for Junking Junk Foods

❏ Practice defensive shopping. That is, resist buying sugary snack foods as a first step toward cutting your consumption. Once those cookies, cupcakes, and candies are sitting in your cupboards, they are much harder to say no to. Many people succumb to the rationalization, "Well, I'll just finish the package and then I won't buy any more." Cut junk foods off at the source, taking the opportunity instead to load up at the supermarket on the fresh fruits, popcorn, and other foods you'll be substituting for them.

❏ Keeping your kitchen stocked with pizza dough, tortillas, grated cheese, salad greens, fresh vegetables, and assorted leftovers will help you fight the urge to go out for fast food, notes Mollie Katzen, natural-foods cook and author of *Still Life With Menu*. "Pizzas, polentas, burritos, quesadillas, nachos, enhanced ramens, sautéed or broiled breads, and giant cheese-filled biscuits are all very easy dishes that can readily be expanded into full-blown meals," she says.

❏ Cut back on your fast-food intake by planning your shopping trips and other excursions so that you can eat at home before you go.

❏ Rinse your mouth, brush your teeth, or eat a hard vegetable such as a carrot after eating a sticky, sugary food to prevent tooth decay.

❏ Drink some water before you eat any junk food. You'll be less hungry and the water itself is healthful (see Step 6).

❏ Eat breakfast, lunch, and dinner. Skipping meals can cause wide swings in your blood sugar levels that make you more subject to cravings, binges, and high-fat snacking. Plus, if you eat breakfast, your body responds by burning more calories than if you skip it.

For More Information

Natural foods cookbooks with valuable recipe ideas include:

Still Life With Menu by Mollie Katzen (Berkeley, Calif.: Ten Speed Press, 1988)

Sweet & Natural Desserts from the Editors of *Natural Health* (Brookline, Mass.: East West Health Books, 1986)

5

THINK FASTS

Fasting—the practice of abstaining from all or certain foods and liquids—has long attracted spiritual seekers and health devotees. Biblical characters, the Greek "father of medicine" Hippocrates, and medical pioneers such as Galen and Paracelsus practiced fasting either to attain spiritual purification or to reinvigorate the body. Today, many naturopaths, chiropractors, herbalists, and other practitioners of natural medicine recommend fasting to speed elimination of toxins, allow the digestive system to rest, and even promote healing of some illnesses. Fasting for even a day may also help

- ➤ clean your liver, kidneys, and colon
- ➤ remove toxins and impurities from your blood
- ➤ clear your eyes and freshen your breath
- ➤ calm your mind, sharpen your senses, and provide you with a feeling of greater energy
- ➤ increase your appreciation of food

Fasting is "one of the quickest ways to increase elimination of wastes and enhance the healing processes of the body," conclude naturopathic doctors Michael Murray and Joseph Pizzorno, authors of the *Encyclopedia of Natural Medicine*. When the body is deprived of energy from food, it begins to eliminate fat-soluble toxins, such as pesticides and food additives that you've consumed, by increasing metabolism of body fat. The toxins are released into the bloodstream and then processed for excretion through the urine (which may initially turn dark during a fast), sweat, and even the breath (strong body and breath odors are not uncommon during the first days of a fast).

A short fast can be a useful home remedy for colds, the flu, constipation, indigestion, skin problems, and some types of toxic conditions. Practitioners of natural medicine may use it most frequently to help relieve a fever, a therapeutic action for which there is both anecdotal evidence (animals and children will often naturally fast when they get a fever) and a physiological explanation (during a fever hormonelike peptides in the body boost the immune system and affect the body's internal thermostat, which in turn decreases appetite).

Fasting has even become an area of study among practitioners of conventional Western medicine, who have focused on its use primarily as a weight-loss program but also as a treatment for chemical poisoning, arthritis, and other medical conditions. In the industrialized world, where problems of overnutrition are more of a health threat than undernutrition, fasting offers unrealized promise, says Elson M. Haas, M.D., author of *Staying Healthy with Nutrition.*

Haas also discusses an often-overlooked psychological benefit from occasional fasting. He notes, "We go on vacations from work to relax, recharge, and to gain new perspectives on our life; why not take occasional breaks from food? Most people cannot break out of the conditioned pattern of eating three meals daily. Eating is a habit, an addiction. Most of us do not need nearly the amounts (and types) of food we consume."

Everyday Steps to Natural Health

There are many ways short of starving yourself for forty days and forty nights in the desert to take advantage of the benefits of fasting. In its strictest sense fasting is total abstinence from all solid food and any liquid except water. Thus, some would say that a "juice fast" or "fruit fast" is an oxymoron, and that such fasts should more appropriately be called special diets. But in popular usage *fasting* refers to various ways of restricting your food and beverage intake for internal cleansing or spiritual insight.

Do a twelve-hour water fast every day. This is a total fast from food and all liquid except water (some people follow a modified water fast that allows herbal teas). Since you consume no calories or nutrients, water fasts provide a more complete rest for the digestive system and help eliminate toxins more quickly than do other types of fasts.

Fasting for what amounts to half your life may sound difficult at first, but all that's really required is not snacking after dinner. If you finish dinner at seven P.M. and don't eat again until you have breakfast the next morning at seven A.M., you've successfully fasted for twelve hours. By not eating late at night you allow your body's digestive system to rest while you sleep. Since most people's late-night eating habits tend toward junk foods and TV snacks anyway, establishing a regular habit of twelve-hour daily fasts can be doubly beneficial to your overall health.

If you need to break yourself in to a daily water fast, start by drinking only fresh juices after dinner, or eating small portions of fresh fruits or other healthful snacks such as carrots.

Do a twenty-four-to-thirty-six-hour water or juice fast once a month or so. Juice fasts are probably the most popular types of fasts, providing excellent results but being simple and easy to stick to for beginners. You can use a centrifugal or triturating (pulverizing) type of juicing machine to obtain the juice of fresh raw

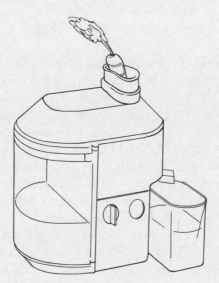

fruits or vegetables. Vegetables can also be gently boiled to obtain a broth. Fresh juices are readily digested and offer some simple carbohydrates and easily absorbed nutrients.

Most people prefer to juice such fruit as lemons, oranges, grapes, grapefruits, watermelons, pineapples, and apples, and vegetables such as carrots, celery, cucumbers, and spinach. Dark green leafy vegetables are especially high in nutrients, but most people prefer them blended with other fruits and vegetables to make a sweeter, more tasty juice. A popular juicing recipe is carrot, apple, and any green leafy vegetable in a 3:2:1 ratio. It is important to start with fresh, high-quality, preferably organic produce to obtain the most nutrients and avoid pesticides and wax. You should thoroughly wash the fruit or vegetable before juicing and remove tough skins, seeds, and cores.

Concentrated green drinks such as those made from the edible microalgae spirulina or chlorella, or the tender young shoots of barley or wheat-grass plants, can also make excellent fasting fare. Like the dark green leafy vegetables they are rich in nutrients that can promote detoxification.

You can do a twenty-four-hour water or juice fast by eating a healthful breakfast and then skipping lunch and dinner that day. A simple way to do a thirty-six-hour water or juice fast is to eat a healthful dinner and then skip the next day's meals, breaking your fast with breakfast on the day after that.

The weekend often works well for either type of fast. You can more easily make fresh juices at home than at work, and you can pace and control your activities and schedule.

Try an annual or semiannual two-to-three-day fruit fast. You do a spring cleaning of your living space every spring; why not a spring cleaning for your body as well? Even an occasional, short-term fast of a few days can help renew your physical and emotional strength and revitalize your internal organs.

A fruit fast obviously stretches the meaning of the word *fast,* since to follow it you eat fresh fruit and drink juice. Still, fruit is among the lightest and more easily digested foods, so restricting your intake of solid foods to fruit can give you some of the health benefits of a more strict water or juice fast.

On a fruit fast you may prefer to first process your fruit with a blender or liquefier. Unlike juicers, these food machines leave the skin, pulp, and other solid parts of the fruit in the finished product.

The mashed-up fruit is assimilated more easily than solid foods, but you are continuing to consume fiber and complex carbohydrates.

The second day is the Heartbreak Hill of fasting: if you can make it past it, the rest of the way is downhill. That's because some people get a headache, skin rash, or other symptom of a healing crisis (which is an acute but short-lived symptom brought on during the early stages of a therapy), and hunger pangs may be bothersome during the first day or two of a fast. Both healing crises and hunger pangs are often short-lived, though hunger usually reappears after three or four more days. So if you can get past the first two days of a fast, the last day may be easier than you suspect. You may well feel so clearheaded and light on your feet that you'll be tempted to extend your fast. (Resist the temptation to continue, at least the first time, till you're more experienced with fasting.)

Follow some general guidelines for safe and effective fasting, no matter for what type or length of fast you try. What works best for you and your body will depend on individual factors, but practitioners of fasting have discovered that the following guidelines apply to most people.

❑ Don't overdo your fast. Fasting is not a panacea for all diseases, nor is it without some risks. If you're inexperienced and you undertake an extended water fast, you risk starving yourself of vital nutrients. Fasting that goes on too long can cause nutrient deficiencies, wasting of internal organs, and loss of muscle mass.

Juice fasting is safer than water fasting, notes Haas, "because it supports the body nutritionally while cleansing and probably even produces a better detoxification or quicker recovery."

Though individual safety varies considerably, a general rule is not to attempt a long-term fast without first discussing your plans with an M.D. or qualified medical practitioner. For beginners, that means seek counsel before attempting a juice fast for more than three days or a water fast for more than thirty-six hours. Long-term fasts are best done in a facility with trained professionals or with some other form of medical supervision.

❑ Postpone your fast if your overall health is poor. Even a short-term fast can deplete the body of certain minerals, including calcium and iron, or cause toxins stored in fat to enter your bloodstream at too high a rate. Certain people generally should not fast because their state of health increases the risks. Anyone who is extremely underweight or already deficient in nutrients, for instance, should not fast. Even people who have been eating a standard American diet should prepare for a fast by consuming a broad spectrum of healthful foods and nutrients. You may need to take special steps preparing for a fast if you're on medication or have chronic degenerative diseases or conditions. The elderly, those with cancer, heart disease, or diabetes, and pregnant women are not candidates for fasting.

❑ Consult with a medical practitioner if symptoms such as dizziness, headache, or muscle cramps that come on during a fast have not cleared up within one or two days after ending the fast.

❑ Prepare for a fast. You'll get more out of a fast by taking a day or two before it to ready your body. Before a fast of two to three days it is a good idea to reduce fatty animal and dairy foods, drugs such as alcohol and caffeine, and highly processed foods. Make your last meal before starting a fast mainly fresh fruits and vegetables.

❑ Always continue to drink plenty of water. Depending upon your health, your body has enough energy reserves to survive for weeks or months without food, but only enough liquid reserves to survive a matter of days without water. There is no known health advantage and plenty of health dangers associated with dehydration. When you become dehydrated during a fast, you're likely to become constipated and unable to urinate, thus preventing these excretory systems from eliminating toxins.

Keep in mind that the body's mechanism for telling you that you need to drink is not very sensitive. Typically it kicks in only well after you've needed liquids for some time and are already partly dehydrated.

❑ Don't fast for the purpose of losing weight, unless it is to use the fast to kick off a new commitment to eating better and more healthfully. Fasting is sometimes recommended by doctors as part of a weight-loss program for extremely obese people, but it's not likely to be an effective method for the average person who wants to quickly take off some extra pounds. Most of the initial pounds that come off will be from water loss through urination or decreases in muscle mass, not fat loss. And if you fast just to lose weight, the chances are you'll put it right back on, a process that may be more damaging to your long-term health than just staying overweight.

Overweight people may also be poor fasting candidates because it is likely they are undernourished. That is, they have gained unwanted pounds by eating too many snacks and other sources of empty calories. Though such people are routinely consuming excessive amounts of protein and calories, they may have significant deficiencies of vitamins and minerals, deficiencies that can worsen during an unsupervised fast, depriving vital organs like the heart and brain of what they need to function.

Like dieting in general, fasting is the wrong way to lose weight. The only right way is that which allows lost pounds to stay off: becoming more physically active and establishing a pattern of eating for a lifetime of health.

Short Tips for Better Fasting

❑ Be flexible in your fasting. Types and lengths of fasts can be combined, for instance, so that you can do a one-day fruit fast followed by a one-day fruit-juice fast and then a one-day water fast.

❑ Conserve your energy. During a fast you should try to relax. Avoid rigorous, competitive exercise, instead opting for light physical activities like walking and stretching. Many people say that breathing exercises work well to increase energy during a fast. Others recommend napping and meditation.

❑ Stay warm during your fast. Fasting causes your body's metabolic rate and core temperature to fall slightly, so wear adequate clothes, drink hot herbal teas, and take other steps to avoid becoming chilled.

❑ Don't become obsessed with food and eating. So that you're not tempted during a fast, you may find it helpful to avoid restaurants and other places where people are eating. Also, the day before a juice fast, buy the fruit you need so you don't have to go into a food store during your fast, thus unnecessarily challenging your will.

❑ Break your fast sensibly. You may be tempted to make up for lost eating time by gorging at your first meal after a fast, but that will only overload your dormant digestive system and reverse any benefits you realized from the fast. You'll feel much better if you break your fast by eating a light, easily digested meal of fresh fruit or vegetables, small amounts of plain food such as brown rice chewed well, a salad, or soup. After the first postfast meal gradually reintroduce healthful foods such as grains, legumes, and beans before incorporating seeds and nuts, tofu, meat, and other protein foods.

❑ Don't chew gum while fasting. Chewing tends to increase hunger pangs by secreting enzymes into your stomach and intestines and kick-starting digestion.

❏ Avoid taking drugs while fasting, including alcohol, nicotine, and caffeine. Of course, certain types of medication should be stopped only after checking with your doctor.

❏ Seek the company of like-minded friends during a fast. They can support your plans and help you to reach your goal. Before or after a fast is a better time to deal with naysayers and skeptics who criticize your actions and question your motivations for fasting.

For More Information

See the following books for more on the benefits of fasting:

Encyclopedia of Natural Medicine by Michael Murray, N.D., and Joseph Piz-
    zorno, N.D. (Rocklin, Calif.: Prima Publishing, 1991)

Juice Fasting and Detoxification by Steve Meyerowitz (Great Barrington,
    Mass.: The Sprout House, 1984)

Staying Healthy with Nutrition by Elson M. Haas, M.D. (Berkeley, Calif.:
    Celestial Arts, 1992)

DRINK RIGHT

If you were stranded on a desert island and offered the choice of only one book, what would you want? Even before considering titles like *Principles of Food Foraging, Practical Shipbuilding, Living With Loneliness,* or *The Complete Works of William Shakespeare,* you might request one with a title such as *Finding and Purifying Water.* Without water, you'd barely have time to strap together a raft or finish *King Lear* before experiencing adverse effects. You'd have weeks or months to learn how to forage for food before dying of hunger, but you'd die of thirst in a mere three to five days unless you found water.

Water serves a number of crucial roles in the body. An adult's body weight is approximately 55–65 percent water and an infant's as much as 70 percent. Body cells need regular replenishment of their fluid stores to function properly. Water is a major component of not only blood and other bodily fluids but seemingly solid body parts such as bones, which are 20 percent water.

Among water's most important functions is its role in helping the kidneys to filter blood and remove both ingested poisons and the toxic wastes of metabolism. According to Andrew Weil, M.D., author of *Natural Health, Natural Medicine,* "This purification system can operate efficiently only if the volume of water flowing through it is sufficient to carry away the wastes. Dehydration is the greatest threat to the process of blood purification and the commonest stress on the kidneys. Many people go around in a state of mild to moderate dehydration just because they forget to drink fluids or because they drink beverages that stress rather than help the filters."

Water is necessary for digestion, circulation, and elimination. When deprived of water, your brain can shrink slightly, leading to such problems as fatigue and loss of coordination. Water is also your body's coolant, required in sufficient quantities to prevent overheating. This is particularly true when you exert yourself on hot, humid days. Generous consumption of water

➤ prevents kidney stones and gallstones from forming
➤ promotes immune function
➤ relieves constipation
➤ maintains supple skin
➤ provides minerals such as calcium and magnesium
➤ helps you to lose weight and maintain your ideal body weight

How much liquid do you need to drink every day? An average-sized person loses about two and a half quarts of fluid a day from normal activities, mostly in the form of urine but also through stools, sweat, and vaporized water that escapes from the lungs with each breath. (Exercise- or heat-induced perspiration may dramatically increase the loss.) Since foods such as fruits and vegetables, which are 70–90 percent water, supply about one quart of liquid each day, the average person still needs to drink at least one and a half quarts of water or other liquids just to replenish lost fluids. Drinking less than this may cause your body to exhibit subtle signs of a liquid deficiency, such as constipation or a difficulty with sweating. Many health authorities say that an optimum water intake necessary to actively promote better health is at least a quart a day in addition to this average fluid replacement level of two and a half quarts.

Everyday Steps to Natural Health

Water is a simple compound and the guidelines for taking advantage of its remarkable health advantages are also simple.

Be aware of signs of drinking too little fluid. You should immediately increase your intake of water if you have any of the following symptoms:

➤ urine that is scanty, dark, and concentrated looking
➤ dry lips and mouth
➤ skin that is dry, easily wrinkled, or old looking
➤ small, rocklike feces
➤ a drop in performance and endurance levels while exercising

An extreme lack of fluid intake, especially when combined with excessive fluid loss (as from heavy sweating), can cause life-threatening dehydration. The volume of blood circulating in the body falls, the blood itself thickens, and electrolytes (minerals such as potassium, sodium, calcium, and magnesium dissolved in the blood and other bodily fluids) are lost through the sweat. Without sufficient electrolytes, muscles get weak and lose coordination, the heart beats abnormally, and the body's heat regulator falters.

Team coaches who prevent athletes from drinking water during summer practice sessions endanger players' lives. Under certain conditions you can sweat a quart of fluid or more every hour—one study found that top swimmers can sweat a quart in forty minutes of swimming. An illness or activity that results in as little as a 10 percent loss of body water may pose a significant health hazard, while a 20 percent loss can be fatal.

Before exercising or exerting yourself, you should drink a cup or more of water. "Lack of water is the single most frequent fatal flaw in the diet of almost every athlete I've studied or advised," says nutrition expert Robert Haas, author of *Eat to Win*.

In addition to hot-weather exertion, it is also possible to become dehydrated from prolonged bouts of constipation, diarrhea, vomiting, or fever. Because of infants' faster metabolism and elderly people's less sensitive thirst mechanism, these groups face a greater risk of dehydration than do most adults. You can also become dehydrated during cold weather, when you can lose larger than normal amounts of moisture in the form of vaporized water particles lost through each breath.

Become reacquainted with plain old water. Most people would benefit by drinking more water—at least four to six glasses every day and preferably six to eight. It's difficult to drink that much water by merely sipping from the office cooler every once in a while. Try to establish a personal water supply. For instance, keep a bottle of water nearby while you're working at your desk, doing yard-work, playing tennis, or commuting to work.

Many people find it easier to drink a little water on a frequent basis than to down a full ten- or twelve-ounce glass and feel bloated. A computer professional who works at home says, "I keep a small, six-ounce glass of water on my desk. Whenever I finish it, I go fill it up immediately so it's never empty." Another technique is to fill a half-gallon container in the morning. Keep it at hand and drink from it regularly enough during the day to empty it by bedtime.

A new product available through mail-order catalogs (see "For More Information") is a miniature water dispenser and filter. It looks just like a regular-sized office watercooler but is about two feet tall and holds exactly eight glasses of water. Drink it empty every day and you'll keep dehydration at bay.

Drink water all day. If you prefer, drink during meals as well—the water will pass through the stomach without diluting digestive enzymes.

Drink water that is pure and clean. Quality is an important consideration. The cheapest, most easily available water comes from the tap, but tap water may or may not be fit to drink. In the U.S. it is generally safer to drink tap water than in most places in the world, but problems are not uncommon. In 1992, Arizona and three other states served more than 20 percent of their citizens with water systems that had been cited for violating the Safe Drinking Water Act. Even pure, high-quality water from your local reservoir or your own well may be polluted by the time it reaches your tap. The heavy-metal lead in plumbing systems, for instance, is a common problem. (Drinking water should contain fewer than ten parts per billion of lead.) Other common water contaminants include

> ➤ microbes (bacterial and viral contamination led to over four thousand cases of illness and four deaths in 1989–90, according to the Centers for Disease Control)
> ➤ toxic heavy metals such as cadmium and mercury
> ➤ synthetic organic chemicals from industrial and agricultural pollution, including benzene, pesticides, and PCB
> ➤ chlorine and carcinogenic byproducts of chlorination, such as trihalomethanes (THMs)

A number of labs will check your tap water for these and other pollutants (see "For More Information" for the names and phone numbers of two). Prices range from about $25–200, depending upon the number of contaminants tested for. Test water taken from the tap, since your home's plumbing system may be a source of pollutants, particularly lead.

If your tap water contains impurities, you may decide to buy bottled water on a regular basis or to purchase a water filter for your home. Each option has advantages and disadvantages.

Most bottled-water companies are reputable and do extensive testing and quality control. Even those that do, however, may experience contamination problems, as did the water giant Perrier. In 1990 the FDA found unacceptably high levels of benzene in Perrier, prompting the company to make a global recall of 160 million bottles. Bottled water that is marketed across state lines has to meet extensive federal regulations, although enforcement is sporadic. Quality varies tremendously. Some bottled water is tap water that has been filtered; some comes from springs that may or may not be pure and clean. If you'll be drinking a quart or more a day of bottled water, it is worth the effort to check into the company's source, quality-control procedures, and filtration methods. Reputable companies test their product more frequently than the FDA requires and provide test results to consumers to prove that the water meets or exceeds federal standards for microbes, heavy metals, and other pollutants. Home delivery of five- or six-gallon containers can cut the cost and lessen the inconvenience somewhat.

Your other alternative to drinking tap water is buying a water filter, an option taken by 2 million Americans annually. If you're considering a filter, a tap-water test is useful because some types of filters are better than others at removing certain contaminants. The three most common types of water filters are

> ➤ activated carbon, which uses a granulated or solid block of carbon to absorb toxins as they pass
> ➤ steam distilling, which boils the water and then collects and delivers the condensed steam
> ➤ reverse osmosis, which filters water through a semipermeable membrane that prevents the passing of toxic compounds larger than water molecules

All three types of filters generally remove microbes, synthetic organic chemicals, and chlorine and THMs. Activated-carbon filters alone leave in toxic heavy metals; on the plus side, carbon filters also leave in beneficial minerals including calcium. Other advantages to carbon filters are that they are compact and mechanically simple, don't require energy to operate, and are usually the least expensive option. A disadvantage is that the carbon in these filters usually must be changed twice a year or so. If you neglect to do this, the unit will begin to dump accumulated toxins back into your water at even higher levels than if you were using no filter at all. Some home water-filtration systems include more than one type of filter. Water might pass, for instance, through a reverse osmosis unit and then a carbon filter.

A less frequently used filtration option for drinking water is water softening, which uses an ion-exchange process to remove dissolved minerals and heavy metals. Some water softeners, however, add sodium. Since the calcium and magnesium that they remove are beneficial to health, and water softeners can leach lead from lead pipes, water softeners are not the best choice for filtering your drinking water. Water softeners may be installed so that they soften the water you use for washing (allowing soap to work better and preventing a sediment from depositing on surfaces) but not drinking.

Water filters range in price from $25 to over $1,000.

Go easy on the fluids that pose the most risk of causing health problems. These include beverages that contain drugs, such as the alcohol found in beer, wine, and spirits, and the caffeine found in coffee, tea, and cola drinks. Both alcohol and caffeine are diuretics, which means they cause the body to lose fluids rather than gain them. Alcohol and caffeine can also irritate the urinary system.

Herbal teas that should not be overconsumed because they are potent diuretics include dandelion, horsetail, yarrow, and nettle.

Milk is rich in certain nutrients, including calcium, but it is also high in protein, which most Americans get too much of rather than too little. Milk may also be high in fat.

The average American drinks more soft drinks than any other beverage. Unfortunately, soft drinks are often high in sugar (as many as ten tablespoons per twelve ounces), artificial flavors and colors, and phosphates (which have an adverse effect on bodily calcium levels). Soft drinks may also be caffeinated.

If you drink only a little water, better choices than the above include

➤ the juice obtained from fresh fruits and vegetables (see Step 5 for tips on making your own fresh juice)

➤ mineral water, straight or flavored with small amounts of fruit juice

➤ diluted fruit juice (mix natural, 100 percent fruit juice with sparkling water to make a more healthy soft drink)

➤ herbal teas that don't contain either caffeine or ephedrine (a caffeinelike powerful central-nervous-system stimulant; it is found in species of ephedra, including the Chinese plant ma huang)

If you are doing heavy exercise on a hot, humid day, you may want to drink a natural, electrolyte-added sports drink. The vast majority of people who exercise or otherwise exert themselves can meet their fluid needs with water or juice. A potential benefit of electrolyte-added sports drinks, according to one study, is that people tend to drink slightly more of them than water.

Short Tips on Drinking Right

❑ If your tap water is pure except for too much chlorine, air filter it. Simply leave drinking water in a pitcher or other uncovered, wide-mouth container for a number of hours. This dissipates the chlorine into the air.

❑ If your house is an old one that contains lead pipes or pipes that are lead soldered (lead soldering was used in plumbing pipes until 1986), run your faucet for two to four minutes in the morning—or whenever water has sat in the pipes for a number of hours—before drinking water from it. This drains the water that sat in the pipes and collected lead. (If you live in an apartment building this won't work since the plumbing system is much larger.)

❑ During heavy exertion in hot weather, drink water every twenty to thirty minutes even if you're not thirsty. The special cells in your brain that stimulate the sensation of thirst are unreliable for preventing dehydration. They don't kick into action until after you've lost a lot of fluid from sweating. By then your electrolytes could be falling and your body temperature rising, a dangerous combination.

❑ Use only your cold water tap for drinking and cooking. Hot water more readily leaches lead from pipes and joints than does cold water. Your hot-water tank is also likely to be a less-than-sterile environment.

For More Information

For the names of water-testing labs in individual states or the pamphlet "Lead in Your Drinking Water" call:

The EPA Safe Drinking-Water Hotline
(800) 426-4791

Some private water-testing labs include:

National Testing Laboratories
(800) 458-3330
Suburban Water Testing Laboratories
(800) 433-6595

The magazine Consumer Reports *periodically tests and evaluates dozens of brands of water filters, most recently in the Feb. 1993 issue. For a copy of the issue send $4 to:*

Consumer Reports
Back Issues
P.O. Box 53016
Boulder, CO 80322

The Mini Water Dispenser Filter System is available by mail order from the following source:

SelfCare Catalog
5850 Shellmound St.
Emeryville, CA 94662
(800) 345-3371

PRESERVE YOUR TEETH

Humanity's dental report card has exhibited some high marks in recent years. For reasons that are not entirely understood, the incidence of cavities among children in the U.S. and Northern Europe has declined by about 50 percent in the past two decades. Dentists speculate that the reasons include a greater awareness of the harmful effects of sugar, more regular brushing and flossing, an increase in the fluoridation of water, and the advent of sealants placed on tooth surfaces.

Unfortunately, the report card also carries marks that would shame the average schoolboy. By the time most Americans reach middle age, they have had ten cavities filled and lost four to eight of their thirty-two permanent teeth. Another ten teeth have disappeared to the forces of decay, gum disease, and injury by age sixty-five. On average one in ten Americans have lost all of their teeth.

Most dental problems can be traced to the person allowing a film of bacteria and food, called dental plaque, to build up on the teeth. Plaque that is not removed can accumulate calcium and harden into the tough coating known as tartar. Bacteria in plaque or tartar feed on simple carbohydrates such as sugar and produce acids that attack the minerals of the teeth, removing calcium and softening teeth.

These acids first start to form cavities, or caries, in the enamel, the thin layer covering the part of the tooth above the gum line.

When enamel is healthy, it is hard and white and tapers to a knife edge at the gum line. Once acid works its way through the enamel, it reaches the softer, yellowish dentin. If the cavity is not detected by a dentist and filled, it will continue into the pulp, the soft tissue at the center of the tooth that contains blood vessels and nerves. At this point the tooth will ache or become extremely sensitive to heat and cold. Decay is so advanced that the whole tooth is endangered.

Tooth decay cannot be reversed, so it's important to prevent cavities. Diet is a major factor. Cavities are largely a byproduct of the industrial revolution and the development of modern food manufacturing and refining techniques. Primitive people rarely developed tooth decay.

Forces similar to those that injure teeth can also cause harm to the surrounding gums, particularly among adults. This is because adults' oral fluids are less acidic than are children's, making adult teeth more susceptible to decay. An estimated nine out of ten adults in the U.S. suffer some degree of gum disease. Healthy gums are pink and tough; early stages of gum disease are characterized by gums that bleed and are puffy and swollen. Advanced cases can recede gums, loosen teeth, and cause infection of the jawbone.

Preserving your teeth and gums is more important than just for chewing, digestion, and cosmetic appearances. Dental health can have ripple effects that reach the jaw joint and the upper part of the spine. "The relationship between teeth, cranial bones, and muscle movements remains dynamic throughout life. Any adverse change in this complex relationship can be directly related to the appearance of aging," says L. Larry McKinley, D.D.S., a holistic dentist practicing in Houston.

Everyday Steps to Natural Health

Some of the steps for preserving your teeth and gums are common sense ones that are worth reemphasizing. Other steps are less frequently mentioned but also important.

Make brushing and flossing regular habits. These self-care steps are the best way to make sure that harmful plaque and bacteria are swept from tooth surfaces. Dentists recommend brushing first and flossing afterward.

Most dentists say that you should brush thoroughly at least twice a day and preferably three times, after each meal. Use a proper, up-

and-down technique and a toothbrush with nylon bristles (natural bristles are overly hard and inflexible). Electric and battery-powered toothbrushes with rotating bristles can help to remove plaque along the gum line. Toothpaste brand is a minor factor in oral health. Natural toothpastes such as those made by Tom's of Maine, Weleda, and Nature's Gate have the advantage over conventional products of containing no potential carcinogens (including synthetic colors and sodium saccharin). Fluoride is mostly irrelevant in toothpastes, since it needs to stay in contact with tooth surfaces for at least two minutes to be moderately effective, and most people brush for less time. Another safe and effective substance to brush the teeth with is baking soda (many people use equal parts baking soda and sea salt).

Floss only those teeth you want to keep, goes the saying. Flossing is crucial to prevent periodontal (gum) disease. Dentists recommend starting during childhood, though flossing is even more essential for adults, who are more likely to lose teeth from gum disease than from cavities. Use unwaxed floss to more effectively grab on to and remove plaque.

As your old fillings wear out or new cavities develop, request that your dentist use nontoxic filling materials. Some conventional dentists like to refer to the standard dental filling as *silver,* presumably referring to the color but also misleading people into thinking silver is the primary ingredient. *Mercury filling* is more accurate, as is the technical term *amalgam,* which means a mixture of mercury with another metal. Most amalgam fillings are approximately 50 percent mercury, 33 percent silver, and the rest copper and other metals.

Perhaps dentists would be more straightforward if mercury were not such a toxic material. Unfortunately, it is among the most toxic natural substances known, more poisonous than lead or arsenic. One of mercury's principal industrial uses outside of dentistry is to kill living things, such as weeds (in herbicides) and insects (in pesticides). Nobody denies mercury's extreme toxicity, though most conventional dentists and the American Dental Association contend that its toxicity is irrelevant since mercury emissions from fillings are small and harmless.

Claims that amalgam fillings are harmless have increasingly been challenged by a growing minority of dentists as well as a growing body of clinical evidence. Studies have confirmed that elemental mercury particles liberated from fillings as they wear down in the mouth are inhaled into the lungs or swallowed. Studies have also repeatedly found that mercury levels found in the brain or kidneys are directly related to the amount of mercury fillings used in teeth. The final link in the cause-and-effect chain is the most elusive, since mercury in the body embeds itself in tissue and fat and doesn't reliably show up in the blood or urine. This makes assessment of total mercury exposure and diagnosis of chronic mercury poisoning difficult. Researchers at the World Health Organization have established that mercury fillings are by far the greatest single source of mercury exposure for humans. Health authorities also know that even the lowest levels of exposure to mercury can adversely affect the nervous system (causing behavioral disorders and emotional problems), the immune system, and various internal organs.

Many people are siding with Dr. David Kennedy, a San Diego–based dentist and a proponent of nontoxic filling materials, who says, "If I have a choice between putting a highly toxic substance in my mouth, a substance that will do damage to my brain, kidneys, and immune system, versus placing a relatively harmless substance in my teeth that may have to be replaced sooner than the poisonous substance, I'm going to choose the safer filling every time."

Alternatives to mercury fillings include gold (though it is too soft except for small fillings) and gold alloys, or mixtures. Metals that are mixed with gold include precious ones such as platinum and base metals such as tin. Gold is a nontoxic and durable material. Its only drawback as a filling material is expense, due to the material itself and to more time-consuming placement procedures. Another alternative is composites, which are mixtures of various plastic resins as binding materials and hard crystalline substances such as quartz crystals or zirconium silicate. A number of competing brands of composites are approved by the FDA. Composites are nontoxic and are relatively durable, lasting an average of 6.5 years compared to 7.6 years for amalgam fillings (many people find that both types last much longer). Composites are colored to match the surrounding teeth and cost more than mercury but less than gold fillings.

Most dentists prefer using amalgam to composites. Almost every American beyond the age of five has at least one amalgam filling. Both types of fillings can be placed in a single sitting. Amalgam fillings, however, are easier to install, partly because of mercury's ability to exist in a liquid form at room temperature. If you do decide to no longer put mercury in your mouth, it is worthwhile to find a dentist who practices mercury-free dentistry (see "For More Information"). It is true that any dentist can put in a composite filling, but the procedure is "technique sensitive," meaning that it takes special skill and practice to place a composite correctly. There are some fundamental differences between working with composites and working with amalgam. A mercury-free dentist will be more practiced at placing composites and have the necessary equipment (such as a wet dam and high-speed suction to keep the tooth dry while the composite is being placed).

Tom Monte, author of *World Medicine* and a twenty-year veteran of natural health, says that he found out about the importance of using a mercury-free dentist the hard way. "I went to an orthodox dentist and asked for an alternative to an amalgam filling. My dentist obliged, but with some reluctance, telling me that the composite would not last long. She was right. The filling fell out five months later. Composites require special methods that my former dentist apparently overlooked."

Eat for strong teeth. A healthful diet is probably the single most important influence on teeth, especially for young people. Whole, natural, and fresh foods high in nutrients can build strong teeth and bones, while overprocessed and highly sweetened and re- fined foods increase the likelihood of cavities and gum disease.

Eat more of the foods that promote strong teeth and gums and fewer of the foods that weaken teeth and gums. Foods that promote healthy teeth include leafy green vegetables and others high in fiber and calcium. Crunchy fruits and vegetables such as apples, carrots, and celery that need to be chewed well not only exercise the jaw muscles and increase circulation to the teeth and gums, they help to clean tooth surfaces at the end of a meal. Dental researchers have also identified a number of foods that, eaten after a meal, may help prevent tooth decay by preventing tooth-eroding acids from forming in the mouth. These tooth-saving foods include peanuts, cashews, and other nuts; tea, which is rich in decay-preventing fluoride; and sunflower and other seeds.

Foods to avoid include any that are sugary, fatty, and sticky. Such foods can affect your mouth and saliva in a way that increases the risk of tooth decay. Highly refined carbohydrates such as table sugar (sucrose) and white bread promote plaque and the production of tooth-dissolving acids. Fatty foods can promote cavities by in- creasing lipid levels in the saliva. Raisins and dried fruits are more healthful snacks than candy or potato chips, but since dried fruits easily stick to the teeth, it's a good idea to brush your teeth soon after eating them.

Also avoid overconsumption of foods high in phosphorous and low in calcium, such as soft drinks, refined sweets, and red meat. These foods can produce phosphoric acid, which eats away tooth enamel. McKinley notes that acidic foods affect your teeth twice: when eaten and then later when bodily fluids, particularly saliva, become more acidic. Other acid-increasing foods include citrus fruits and juices, aspirin, and some chewable forms of vitamin C tablets. It's not necessary to give these things up, but you probably don't want to constantly expose your teeth to them either.

Women who are pregnant need to be especially careful of their diet to help their unborn baby develop a body that will grow strong teeth. Studies show that pregnant women with nutritional deficiencies give birth to babies who develop poor teeth.

If you have gum disease, consider anti-infective therapy before opting for surgery. Anti-infective therapy is a new practice begun in the 1970s and now used by some five thousand dentists and periodontists. It can often reverse periodontal disease without resorting to expensive gum surgery or requiring teeth to be pulled. Both the dental practitioner and the patient play a role in anti-infective therapy, whose goal is to eliminate harmful bacteria from areas of the gums that are infected.

Anti-infective dentists use a special microscope to look at the bacteria that gather in the pockets between the teeth and gums. Rather than as a first step surgically cutting away small parts of the diseased gums, these dentists turn to anti-infective agents. For a mild case of gum disease, you can simply brush the teeth using a baking-soda and hydrogen-peroxide paste (or a baking-soda toothpaste that is at least 60 percent baking soda), available at drugstores. For more advanced cases the patient may also need to use an irrigator or a specially designed tube to clean under the gum line using various-strength antiseptic solutions. Anti-infective dentists may also prescribe oral antibiotics for advanced cases. If the patient conscientiously plays a role in the treatment, gum tissue can reattach, bone can regenerate, and teeth can become more firmly implanted in the jawbone. Surgery is a last resort rather than a first step.

Take nutritional supplements to prevent and treat bleeding gums and loose teeth. In addition to improving your eating habits, start a program of nutritional supplements. All of the nutrients critical to bone health are also essential for teeth. Most people think only of calcium for teeth and bones, but other nutrients are also important. See Step 11 on bone health for other herbs, foods, and supplements that are especially high in the bone-building vitamins and minerals.

Among the tooth-supporting supplements to consider taking every day are

➤ vitamin A, 10,000–20,000 IU in the form of beta carotene
➤ vitamin C, 500–1,500 mg, to improve gum health and speed the formation of bone matrix
➤ vitamin D, 400–800 IU
➤ the minerals calcium and magnesium in a 2:1 ratio (such as 1,000 mg calcium and 500 mg magnesium)
➤ the trace elements manganese, 5–10 mg, zinc, 17–25 mg, and boron, 2.5–3.0 mg, in a balanced mineral formulation
➤ coenzyme Q10, 15–30 mg, since studies have shown that this vitaminlike nutrient reduces pockets and speeds up the healing time of gum disease

Short Tips for Dental Health

❑ See your dentist for a checkup every six months. Dentists can often spot tooth and gum problems before they become critical. Dentists may also be able to identify nutritional deficiencies in a patient. Loose teeth or gum disease, for instance, may be an indication of bone loss and thus an early sign of osteoporosis.

❑ Massage your gums periodically to increase local circulation and prevent gum disease. Use water or break open a liquid-filled capsule of vitamin E and rub in the oil.

❑ Protect yourself from the main sources of mouth trauma. These include sports injuries (when necessary always use a helmet, face mask, or mouthpiece), automobile accidents (wearing a seat belt could prevent 25 percent of the fifty thousand facial injuries, many to the teeth and jaw, sustained in auto accidents each year), and using teeth to open or pull things (don't).

For More Information

To find a mercury-free dentist in your area send a self-addressed, stamped #10 envelope to:

Foundation For Toxic Free Dentistry
P.O. Box 608010
Orlando, FL 32860

At the same address as the FTFD is the following organization, which provides newsletters, information packets, and books on natural dentistry:

Bio-Probe, Inc.
P.O. Box 608010
Orlando, FL 32860
(800) 282-9670

For referrals and more information on anti-infective therapy contact:

International Dental Health Foundation
11484 Washington Plaza West
Reston, VA 22090
(703) 471-8349

SIMPLE STEPS
TO
NATURAL HEALTH

ACTIVITY
AND EXERCISE

MAINTAIN YOUR
IDEAL WEIGHT

Maintaining an ideal body weight is a key to overall health, lowering your risk of heart disease, diabetes, breast cancer, and other killer diseases. It eases physical activity, improves your appearance, makes you feel better, and gives you more energy. It also reinforces a positive self-image—a recent poll of eighteen- to twenty-five-year-old women done by *Esquire* found that over half of the respondents said that they would rather be run over by a truck than gain 150 pounds! Yet optimum body weight is a goal that many people seem never able to reach: at any one time in the U.S., an estimated one in three women and one in four men are dieting. Every year dieters spend upwards of $30 billion on weight-loss programs, low-calorie foods, books, supplements, and other dieting-related products.

Unfortunately, most of this money is wasted, according to health authorities and numerous surveys of dieters. A recent National Institutes of Health panel that reviewed the effectiveness of various commercial diet programs determined that none could prove long-term success. This lack of success actually boosts the diet industry, since it ensures that they have a virtually endless recycling of customers for their pitches and products. But it is bad news for anyone expecting to slim down by dieting.

Everyday Steps to Natural Health

Library shelves are overflowing with books related to dieting and weight. Let's simplify things here and cover the essentials of a workable alternative to dieting.

Consider your body-fat percentage as well as your weight. Hopping onto the scales every three hours is unnecessary for everyone except boxers trying to make the weight limit for tonight's fight. First, if you're losing more than about a pound a day, you are probably dieting rather than eating. You are probably losing fluid and muscle, making you less healthy, not more, and almost assuring yourself that you'll gain back all the lost pounds plus a few more in the near future. Second, if you are eating mostly complex carbohydrates and you are exercising, you may be adding healthy muscle to your body as fast as you are losing fat, showing no net weight loss but nevertheless gradually gaining in overall healthfulness.

For most people, a scale should be a handy tool to turn to only occasionally. Forget about how much you weigh and concentrate on how you feel, whether you can do the things you want to do, how you look to yourself and others, and how frequently and acutely you become ill.

A scale can be useful to help you set and meet your goals. The numbers are right there in black and white, and unless you are dieting, they may be indicating real progress. A better set of numbers, however, represent the percentage of your weight that is represented by fat. The lower this number, the more lean muscle you have. Unless you take it to extremes (young women with less than 10 percent body fat can stop menstruating, possibly increasing their risk of bone loss), lower body fat percentages are generally associated with health, increased athletic performance, and longevity.

There are a number of ways to determine your body-fat level, though the most accurate is hardly a self-care technique: weighing yourself underwater. Since muscle is denser and less buoyant than fat, a two-hundred-pound musclebuilder will weigh more underwater than a two-hundred-pound couch potato. You also need to exhale as much air from your lungs as you can while you're underwater being weighed and have the technician take into consideration residual air in your lungs that you can't exhale. University health clinics and other large facilities may have the necessary technology.

A much simpler and cheaper method for determining body fat

is to measure the fat in skin folds under the upper arms and at a half dozen other places on the body. You need calipers and some practice to do it accurately. The easiest test yields only a ballpark estimate, but anyone can do it: jump into a fresh-water pool, fill your lungs, and see if you float (body fat over 20 percent) or slowly sink (under 20 percent).

From there you need to find out whether your body-fat level is within the ideal range for your age and sex. For instance, world-class marathoners have body-fat percentages in the 4–8 range, a top athlete in his twenties may have a body-fat level of 8–12 percent, and an average fifty-five-year-old American man may have 30–35 percent body fat. Most men may want to shoot for a body-fat level in the 10–20 percent range and women in the 15–25 percent range. Women naturally have higher body-fat levels because of fat in the breasts and in tissues related to childbearing.

Set goals based on what works for you and your body. Every person is unique. Your ideal weight and body-fat level depend on such factors as gender, frame size, metabolism, and favorite activities. Body fat can even change routinely with the seasons. Researchers have found that postmenopausal women experience increases in muscle and bone mass in the summer and fall and decreases in the winter and spring, regardless of body weight and the level of activity. Hormones affected by light may be a factor.

What exactly is an ideal weight? Popular tables include those put out by the Metropolitan Life Insurance Company and the U.S. Department of Agriculture. Most "recommended desirable weights" (RDWs) have been going up since the 1950s. For instance, in 1959 a man who was thirty-five years old and five feet ten inches tall had an RDW of 137–172, according to Metropolitan tables. By 1990 the USDA said that the same age and size man had a desirable range of 146–188 pounds. This weight inflation has occurred in spite of the fact that studies indicate that people with lower body weights have lower death rates, when controlled for factors such as smoking, which can make people unhealthfully thin. (See Step 43 for information about the positive effects of a low-calorie, nutrient-dense diet on longevity.) According to the authors of a recent study comparing body weight and death rates, "The upward trend in recommended desirable weights appears unjustified by these data."

Ranges are helpful, but people still need to know that there is no magic number that all thirty-year-old women who are five feet four inches tall, for example, should aspire to. Women in particular confront the effects of cultural influences, the fashion industry, and peer pressure as they make choices about their bodies. "The really insidious thing," says Susie Orbach, author of *Fat Is a Feminist Issue,* "is that women who look very much within the normal range and perfectly gorgeous are walking around with body-image problems. It's not just anorexics or women who are obese. It's women of the most ordinary sizes who are entirely obsessed with their bodies and what they're eating and not eating."

You don't have to look like a *Vogue* model or have the body-fat percentage of a dedicated triathlete to be healthy. Set goals appropriate for your body and lifestyle and constantly reevaluate them in light of experience. If you put into practice the steps that follow and still can't reach your ideals for weight and body fat, question the motives and influences behind those ideals and possibly revise them.

Eat, don't diet. Various studies have shown that two-thirds of people who diet to lose weight gain it back within a year. Neal Barnard, M.D., author of *Food for Life: How the New Four Food Groups Can Save Your Life,* agrees that dieting almost never results in a permanent weight loss. "For the vast majority of people, being overweight is caused not by *how much* they eat but by *what* they eat," Barnard says. Along with a growing number of doctors and nutritionists, including Dean Ornish, M.D., author of *Eat More, Weigh Less* and the first doctor to convincingly demonstrate that diet and lifestyle changes could actually reverse heart disease, Barnard says that the primary consideration is not total calories but the fat content of your diet.

Barnard observes that researchers who compare fat and thin people don't find great disparities in total calorie consumption. What researchers do notice is that overweight people eat more fat, thin people more complex carbohydrates. Cutting back on total calories doesn't cause you to lose weight because your body refuses to cooperate. Your mind decides you want to look thin but your body has another agenda: survival. What the human body has learned through eons of time is that when food is withheld, it needs to slow overall metabolism to prevent starvation. It also programs the person, Barnard says, to get ready to binge on the first available food. (A recent survey of *Natural Health* readers found that bingeing was the main reason for falling off a diet.)

Thus, eating less makes it more difficult to lose weight. "Indeed, eating ample portions—of the right foods—is essential to long-term weight control," claims Barnard. Studies have confirmed that when dieting is over, the slowed metabolism takes five weeks or more to return to full speed. Meanwhile, people go back to eating how they did before the diet. They get an unwelcome surprise: they gain pounds faster than before they went on a diet and often fly right past their old weight. This infamous yo-yoing of weight loss, bingeing, and weight gain becomes a vicious cycle.

Ornish, who uses a low-fat vegetarian diet to help his patients lose weight, along with exercise and lifestyle modifications, says that people on his program eat anytime they want and as much as they want. "In most diets, you still eat the same types of food, but you restrict the amount. So you're eating maybe a 30 percent or 40 percent fat diet, but you restrict the portion sizes, and people generally go around feeling pretty hungry. Sooner or later people get tired of feeling hungry. They go off the diet, they often gain most of the weight back, and then they feel even worse."

The best way to cut the string on your weight's downward yo-yo circuit is to limit your intake of high-fat foods and eat more high-fiber complex carbohydrates. Foods to emphasize include fresh vegetables and fruits, lentils and other legumes, and whole-grain cereals, breads, and pastas. "Besides being low in calories, complex carbohydrates have another advantage for dieters. Their consumption can actually boost your metabolism and speed the burning of calories," Barnard says. Fats have no metabolism-boosting effect. Complex carbohydrates will prevent dramatic swings in your blood sugar and thus feelings of starvation and cravings. Even though they have less than half the calories per gram than fat (four calories per gram of carbohydrates compared to nine calories per gram of fat), complex carbohydrates keep you feeling full longer and cue the body to stop eating. Finally, fat calories are easily stored by the body as fat, while complex carbohydrates are more likely to be burned as fuel.

"The answer for permanent weight loss," Barnard concludes, "is to base your diet on grains, beans, vegetables, and fruits. These foods are more powerful in controlling weight than any weight-loss scheme. Most people can eat all they want, anytime they want, and stay slim."

Stay active. Trying to lose weight or maintain your ideal weight while leading a sedentary life is like trying to educate yourself without reading—it may be possible but you'll always be missing something. Studies have shown that if you want to reduce your body fat, it is more effective to increase the amount of exercise you get than to decrease your food intake. Studies have also shown that people who combine an exercise program with a low-fat diet lose weight the quickest. Staying active has three major effects on weight and body fat:

1. It burns calories. Without exercise or physical activity to burn off some of the calories you consume, your daily requirements for food may drop to 1,500 calories or less. It is exceedingly difficult for most people to restrict their food intake to such a drastic degree.

2. It raises your metabolism. Physical activity has a number of positive effects on metabolism. It increases your body's overall metabolic rate by raising your set point, the number of calories you burn all the time. Exercise does this by building muscle, and even when it is inactive, muscle tissue has a higher resting metabolic rate than fat tissue. Movement also has an effect on your postexercise metabolic rate. That is, after exercising you maintain a higher-than-set-point metabolism for a short time. This afterburner effect is most pronounced when the exercise has been moderately vigorous.

3. It helps you keep your appetite under control. "After a tennis game or an hour on the dance floor, people are actually less likely to overeat, even though they have just burned off a lot of calories," says Barnard. He does note that overweight people are less likely to notice this effect.

Any kind of exercise helps, no matter the intensity or duration. Of course, rigorous aerobic exercises (see Step 14) such as cross-country skiing that work all of your limbs burn fat quicker than exercises such as walking that use only the legs. The key is to stick with it, says Joanne Maglione, an aerobics instructor in Hudson, Massachusetts. "Unwillingness to remain constant about their exercise habits is the main problem for many people. People have to be patient and persistent. You may not see the change in weight or body fat initially. That comes later."

Exercise is not the only way to move your body and burn calories. You can also stay active in your daily life. Climbing stairs, raking leaves, vacuuming, walking to the corner store, and even washing the dishes can add up in their effects. Eating the same foods over the course of a year, every fifteen calories of fat-burning activity per day will keep you from gaining a pound. Thus, doing an extra three hundred calories worth of activity per day can keep twenty pounds of fat off your body in a year. (See Step 9 for more suggestions on how to increase your routine activity levels.)

Short Tips for Weight Control

❑ Cut back on sugary, fatty between-meal snacks (see Step 4). On the other hand, you can eat low-fat snacks (or drink some water) whenever you're hungry. This helps you to avoid binges and keeps your energy up throughout the day.

❑ Your thyroid gland must function properly to maintain an optimal metabolic rate. If your thyroid is producing insufficient amounts of the hormone thyroxine, you'll gain weight easily and have difficulty taking it off (you'll also be cold and tired). A blood test or a regular morning body temperature (measured for ten minutes in the armpit) of lower than 97.8° F can confirm an inactive thyroid. If this is the case, have your health practitioner check for a deficiency of the trace element iodine. To support your thyroid take optimal daily dosages of beta carotene (10,000–20,000 IU), B complex (50–100 mg), vitamin E (400–800 IU), and zinc (17–25 mg).

For More Information

Two excellent books on diet and weight loss are:

Eat More, Weigh Less by Dean Ornish, M.D. (New York: HarperCollins, 1993)

Food for Life by Neal Barnard, M.D. (New York: Harmony Books, 1993)

MOVE IT OR LOSE IT

There's a certain irony in a person's driving five miles to the health club to ride the exercise cycle for twenty minutes instead of just riding a bicycle to the club, turning around, and riding home again. Granted, exercise is a sometimes incidental factor in the health-club social scene, but many people give little thought to how they might increase their fitness in ways that don't involve sports, aerobics classes, exercise machines, or spending money.

The distinction between exercise and physical activity has grown in recent years. For most Americans today, exercise is something that, if done at all, gets scheduled into the weekly calendar and occurs at a health club. When not exercising, most people take every opportunity available to use labor-saving—physical-activity-saving—devices. They'll think nothing of hopping into the car to drive two blocks to rent a video, or buying a snowblower for use on a thirty-foot driveway. It wasn't always so, as anyone who grew up on a working farm can confirm. Until fairly recently, the everyday activities of living—growing and gathering food, getting from one place to another, heating the home—required a fair amount of physical activity. "Exercising" was built into life.

Today an estimated three out of five Americans are sedentary. Not only have they lost the need—and the urge—to use their bodies in any appreciable way for the routine chores of living, they also don't exercise or participate in any sports. The nation's high rate of heart disease is one of the results.

Yet in recent years a number of large, long-term studies have found that there's no threshold level of fitness for reducing the health risks of inactivity. In other words, it is not necessary for you to attend aerobics classes three times weekly or to get your heart racing to 70 percent of its capacity to benefit from activity or exercise. Researchers have proven that people who engage in mild physical activity—brisk walking, climbing stairs, sweeping the sidewalk—have lower mortality rates than those who are sedentary. For instance, a 1977 Stanford Medical School study of seventeen thousand men found that just two thousand calories a week of additional physical activity can reduce the risk of heart attack by almost two-thirds. When it comes to your body, any movement is better than no movement.

Among the potential benefits of even moderate physical activity are

➤ enhanced metabolism of fats
➤ suppression of appetite
➤ relief from stress
➤ elevation of mood
➤ increased resting metabolic rate for some time afterward
➤ loss of weight (a thirty-minute walk three to four times per week burns enough calories to allow you to lose nine pounds in a year)

Everyday Steps to Natural Health

Here are some ways you can stay fit by doing dozens of little things that increase your routine activity and exercise levels.

Integrate physical activity more naturally into your daily life. It's great to schedule regular exercise time into your weekly calendar. But even if you can keep to your exercise schedule, increasing your everyday level of activity will provide healthy dividends. Studies have shown that the average person expends much more energy going about the everyday activities of his or her daily life than from exercising for an isolated period of time during the day. Grab those opportunities to do anything that will get your body moving:

❑ If you work in an office, take a brisk walk at lunchtime. Even a fifteen-to-twenty-minute walk can invigorate mind and body.

❑ Walk or bike to local shops or to a friend's house instead of driving.

❑ Ride a bike to work, or even from your home to the train station. There are many reasons why this is not convenient, from the lack of safe bike paths to the perceived need to shower once you arrive, but the fact is that more than half the working people in the U.S. live within biking range (five miles) of work and fewer than 1 percent of people actually do ride. With the right equipment and a little planning, it is a viable option that you may consider trying.

❑ Search out the stairs and use them rather than the elevator or escalator.

Identify your most sedentary and passive activities and see what you can do to make them more active. Sedentary time for many people is the time spent at a desk, working or studying or talking on the phone, or in front of the television (where the average American spends a whopping five hours per day). It's best to reduce sedentary time to a minimum, but turning stationary activities into even mildly active ones can be fun and rewarding.

❑ Get a long extension cord or a cordless phone that allows you to pace back and forth when talking on the phone.

❑ Intersperse the time you spend watching TV with stretches (see Step 12) or light exercises. At the very least you can get up and move around during commercials. You might also keep dumbbells in the TV room to do some strengthening exercises every once in a while, or do push-ups, leg lifts, and the like (see Step 13). Another option favored by many is to work out on a cross-country skiing or bicycle machine while watching television.

❑ Keep a tennis ball or hand-exerciser at your desk and pick it up and squeeze it when you're talking on the phone, thinking, or listening.

❑ Schedule a meeting with an office mate to be held during a walk outside instead of at the conference-room table.

❑ Perform simple isometric exercises, in which you push or pull on an immovable object, while sitting at your desk or while stuck in a traffic jam in your car. An easy one is to hold your hands in front of your chest, one palm facing out and the other in, with the forearms in a line and parallel to the ground, such that you can grab the fingers and try to pull the hands apart. In effect, opposite sets of muscles provide the resistance that builds each other. Hold the pull for five to fifteen seconds and then relax.

Use your labor-saving devices selectively instead of routinely. If you are constantly in such a hurry that you always need to use machines to do what your body and a simple tool can do as well (if somewhat slower), you would probably benefit from some priority setting. For many people, machines are also status symbols. "As we become more affluent," notes Svevo Brooks, author of *Common Sense Diet and Health,* "we are encouraged to use electric washing machines, can openers, knives, lawn mowers, clothes dryers, and elevators as proof of our economic health. Being a success is often economically defined; even though our health has deteriorated, we are considered successful because our financial health is so vibrant."

If you do choose to buy a leaf-blower, at least don't throw away your rake. When you need to move leaves, consider whether a somewhat longer time spent with the quiet rustle of rake against ground, the sun and wind caressing your skin, your body slowly heating up from the movement, may be more satisfying than the quick and noisy leaf-blowing. You'll be doing not only your body but the earth a favor, adds Bill McKibben in *The End of Nature,* pointing to leaf-blowers' oil consumption. "Never mind," he says, "that they make a horrible racket, or that when you use one, the chance of daydreaming disappears—and certainly never mind the thought that they give off greenhouse gases."

Using quality human-powered tools helps. If you're willing to spend $300 for a food processor, consider as an option spending half of that for a set of high quality, well-balanced kitchen knives. If you need a new lawn mover, the new generation of human-powered pushmowers is lighter and easier to use than its ancestors.

Common activities that do not always need to be done with the aid of a machine include

➤ mowing and raking the lawn
➤ mulching the garden
➤ kneading bread
➤ cutting food
➤ shoveling snow

➤ chopping wood
➤ clipping the hedges
➤ washing the car

Even routine housework provides an opportunity to keep the body active without paying any club dues. Simple activities such as mopping floors, vacuuming, and cleaning windows will burn 250–300 calories per hour. More importantly they stretch and strengthen muscles and build endurance and stamina in persons whose main source of activity may otherwise be moving the steering wheel of an auto.

Speaking of which, moving the steering wheel is nevertheless an activity that burns calories. Even seemingly minor technological advances, such as power steering, make you a bit more sedentary. Consider all of the tiny innovations in recent years that save you from having to move any muscles: power windows/antennas/locks/ etc., in cars, TV and stereo remotes, cellular phones, bread machines, home shopping networks, and so forth. For a 150-pound person, using any of these labor-saving devices may cause you to miss out on burning a paltry fifteen calories over the course of a day. Yet even that tiny amount of lost activity will eventually cause you to add about a pound of fat to your body. Missing out on burning hundreds of calories a day can make you gain dozens of pounds.

The American home should be designated "exercise device of the year," according to Bryant A. Stamford, Ph.D., and Porter Shimer, the authors of *Fitness Without Exercise*. "Between the sweeping, dusting, scrubbing, scraping, painting, polishing, shoveling, raking, pruning, sawing, hammering, watering, and weeding, there's not a muscle of the body that could go untouched. . . . We've got to start looking at our homes less as fitness enemies than as fitness allies."

Short Tips for Increasing Your Activity Levels

❑ Leave a little earlier in the morning for your commute to work. Get off the train or subway a stop or two before your exit and walk the rest of the way to work. If you drive, park some blocks away and walk.
❑ Rediscover your sense of play. Dancing or just horsing around

with children is a great way to do this. Andrew Weil, M.D., author of *Natural Health, Natural Medicine,* emphasizes to his patients the importance of play and has even taught workshops "in noncompetitive (that is, fun) wrestling." He says, "Young children will wrestle playfully for hours, developing strength, coordination, and agility while getting a terrific aerobic workout and having the time of their lives. It is a pity that more grown-ups don't do the same. . . . Use [health club] facilities if they help you develop good exercise habits, but also find ways to increase your activity that are creative and playful, using the resources of your own environment."

For More Information

Two excellent books on rediscovering the joys of everyday physical activities are:

Common Sense Diet and Health by Svevo Brooks (Capitola, Calif.: Botanica Press, 1986)

Fitness Without Exercise by Bryant A. Stamford, Ph.D., and Porter Shimer (New York: Warner Books, 1990)

TAILOR YOUR EXERCISE

The most popular forms of exercise in the 1990s include walking, bicycling, doing aerobics, lifting weights and using resistance machines, operating exercise machines such as treadmills, stair-climbers, cross-country skiers, rowers, and stationary cycles, and running, according to the Sporting Goods Manufacturers' Association. Yet your fitness options are hardly limited to these popular activities. There are dozens if not hundreds of other activities, sports, and exercises that you can choose from, including swimming, playing racket sports such as tennis and racquetball, doing martial arts, ice-skating, square dancing, skiing, hiking, roller-skating, jazz dancing, canoeing, bowling, and playing golf. How should you choose from among the many possibilities?

A major factor to consider is whether your choices provide a balance of the chief attributes of fitness:

❑ Endurance. Your endurance is enhanced by activities that boost your heart rate and breathing for twenty minutes or more, such as jogging, aerobics, bicycling, and using exercise machines.

❑ Strength. Strengthening activities are those that tone or build the major skeletal muscles, including weight lifting, using resistance machines, and operating rowing and cross-country-skiing machines.

❑ Flexibility. Flexibility is enhanced by exercises and activities that stretch muscles, such as gymnastics, tai chi, yoga, some forms of dance, and swimming.

❏ Balance and coordination. These are improved by racket sports that require quick movements and hand-eye coordination, martial arts like aikido, rock climbing, and other activities.

A well-rounded approach to fitness provides some elements of all of these. Most people are more attracted to one or two of these aspects of fitness than the others. Typically, a stocky, well-built person will gravitate toward the weight room, and the light, small-boned person will take up jogging. A better approach is to maintain your strengths while addressing your weaknesses. If all you do is lift weights, you may end up strong as a pillar and about as mobile as one, too. If all you do is jog, you'll never get tired on a hike but you may have trouble carrying the firewood to camp.

Here is a list of common activities rated by the degree to which they promote the main attributes of fitness.

Activity	Strength	Endurance	Flexibility	Balance Coordination
Basketball	med	med	med	high
Bicycling	low	high	low	med
Gymnastics	high	low	high	high
Hiking	high	med	low	low
Jazz dancing	low	med	high	high
Martial arts	med	med	med	high
Rowing	high	high	low	med
Running	low	high	low	low
Ski machine	high	high	low	med
StairMaster	low	high	low	low
Swimming	med	med	med	low
Tennis	med	med	low	high
Walking	low	med	low	low
Weight lifting	high	low	low	low
Yoga	med	low	high	med

Everyday Steps to Natural Health

Find the right exercise program for your lifestyle, body type, and personality. A fitness program that is ill-suited for you will be more work than fun. You'll likely end up discouraged, injured, and sedentary. Here are some important additional factors to consider as you develop a program that is challenging, rewarding, and fun.

Determine what types of activities and exercises best fit your lifestyle. A fitness program that is best for a rural tree-worker whose work is seasonal needs to differ from that of an urban banking executive working nine to five. Consider your personal preferences in the following lifestyle factors:

❑ Time available for fitness. How flexible is your schedule? Can you take time off during the day to work out? (If you say you have no time, you need to reexamine your priorities.) If you can fit exercise in only on the spur of the moment, you'll need to concentrate on activities like walking that require no scheduling, preparation, or equipment.

❑ Morning vs. evening. Are you a morning person or a night owl? Schedule most of your fitness work accordingly. Night owls need to keep in mind that studies have shown that people who exercise in the morning tend to stick with their fitness program more reliably than do those who exercise at night.

❑ Indoors vs. outdoors. Which do you prefer? Many activities can be done in either location, though you may have to search (and pay) if you love to run but are not keen on the outdoors. Keep in mind that if you're the indoor intellectual type with a slight but well-coordinated body, you may be best off by trying to address your weaknesses, such as lack of strength.

Look objectively at your body and determine how your body type is affecting your fitness choices. An important factor for any body type is current level of fitness. If you're over forty-five and have been leading a sedentary life, or are younger with a history of heart problems or major illnesses, you should have a physical before doing any vigorous aerobic exercising. Health practitioners can administer an exercise stress test during which they monitor your heart while you're walking on a treadmill. The vast majority of people who are healthy, however, don't need to do anything to start a moderate exercise program.

Also, if you're out of shape, don't join an advanced high-step aerobics class. Rather, tailor your program so that you don't quickly get worn-out or discouraged. You might start with brisk walking, light running or beginning aerobics and work your way up to more demanding exercises.

In addition to level of fitness, what is your basic build and body type? The type and shape of your body affects not only what you do well, but where you are potentially strong and weak. Many people are one of the following three types. Others share a number of characteristics of each type or don't fit the mold at all.

❑ Reed. The typical reed is tall and thin with narrow shoulders, chest, and hips. The arms and legs are long while the ankles and wrists are small. Reeds usually have low amounts of body fat, and this lack of padding is more likely to reveal underlying bones than underlying muscles. Famous reeds include distance runner Bill Rodgers and comedian Stan Laurel. Reeds naturally excel at running, basketball, and racket sports rather than at weight lifting, swimming, and football. In most cases they need to emphasize strengthening exercises, while they can sometimes downplay their natural physical skills, which are endurance and balance and coordination.

❑ Acorn. The typical acorn is chubby and wider at the hips than the shoulders. Like reeds they're often small-boned and not very muscular looking, though some acorns may be powerful. Their bodies contain higher than average amounts of body fat. Famous acorns include John Candy, Babe Ruth, and Oprah Winfrey. With their high fat levels providing extra buoyancy, acorns find it easy to do swimming and water exercising. Activities that require acorns to pound their weight into the ground, such as running and high-impact aerobics, are hard on their bodies, while activities such as walking, biking, and cross-country skiing that don't take such a toll on joints are more easily tolerated. Acorns usually need to emphasize cardiovascular activities and can sometimes downplay flexibility.

❑ Wedge. Typical wedges are large-boned and well-built, with wide shoulders and a narrow waist. Famous wedges include Evander Holyfield, Bo Jackson, Sylvester Stallone, and Martina Navratilova. Wedges are perfect for sports that require power and speed, like rowing. Their bodies are less appropriate for long-distance running.

In most cases they need to emphasize flexibility, endurance, and balance/coordination while they can usually downplay strengthening exercises. For instance, racket sports, basketball, and yoga can help these people develop their weaknesses. Wedges may be naturally drawn to lifting weights and working on resistance machines, but they should resist the impulse to make these activities their only exercise.

Balance between upper body and lower body can be as important as body type. If your chest and arms are strongly developed but your legs are wimpy looking (the case with some people who over-emphasize weight lifting), you should consider jogging, stair climbing, and other activities that build lower-body strength.

Determine your fitness personality and choose an exercise accordingly. Your fitness personality usually matches your overall personality—if you're a hard-charging, aggressive, type A person, your approach to exercise may likely be that of "the zealot" described below. As with body type, fitness personalities cut both ways. Your personality may indicate activities that you'll naturally excel at and that will come easiest to you. If you're not exercising at all, these activities will be good starting points. Over the long run, however, you may develop a more balanced body and well-rounded personality by going against type.

❑ The life of the party. If you're outgoing and sociable, you probably like exercise classes, tennis groups, and team sports. You're not the type to stay at home and spend hours riding the stationary bicycle. You're also unlikely to spend a lot of time jogging by yourself. If running appeals to you, you need a partner—or three. Your weakness is allowing the social aspects of your physical activity to overtake any effort to actually exercise—you're happy to play one set of tennis and then schmooze. You also need to guard against becoming inactive when the group breaks up or can't get together.

❑ The loner. You prefer to spend your free time by yourself. You tend to feel distracted and overwhelmed in a group of people. Long-distance running suits your temperament, though it may or may not suit your body. Joining classes and playing on teams aren't your first choices, though these are often exactly what you need to overcome your limitations.

❑ The dilettante. You dabble in one thing after another, often starting more than you finish. You get tremendously enthused about new exercises and activities. You sometimes impulsively run out and buy expensive equipment only to have it shortly pile up unused in the closet. You need to set clear goals and decide upon a couple of activities or exercises that you like most of all. Then make a commitment to stick with these even as you experiment with new exercises.

❏ The high-techie. You feel more at home with mechanical devices and gadgets than with other people. Not surprisingly, you're a natural for exercise machines—the more controls, monitors, buzzers, and timers the better. You have a tendency to stop when you're no longer fascinated by the machine; also to spend more time reading the latest Hammacher Schlemmer catalog than actually exercising. One good antidote for your preoccupation with machines and gadgets is to take up any sport that uses a ball.

❏ The zealot. You get into everything full tilt. If you take up jogging, you're soon training for marathons. If it's tennis, you go on vacation to a tennis camp. You believe that if some exercise is good, more is better. You tend to get restless and depressed if you miss a workout. You also have a tendency to ignore pain or other signs that you need to stop. Combined with your hard-charging attitude, this causes you to suffer frequent injuries. You are also a candidate for frequent burnout, after which you may do little exercise at all for some time. You need to frequently examine your priorities and determine whether exercise is taking over your life. Your perspective on health must broaden to include emotions, attitudes, creativity, and relationships. Playing a team sport is a good first step. You're also likely to benefit from creative, noncompetitive activities, such as any type of dance or martial art.

Few people are a perfect fit for any one category, whether it is lifestyle, body type, or personality. Rather, recognize your tendencies and develop a program that works for you.

Short Tips for Tailoring Your Exercise

❏ If your basic orientation is toward competition, individual sports will provide a satisfying fitness outlet. Team sports combine elements of both competition and cooperation. If cooperation attracts you, consider dance, aerobics classes, skiing, and other such activities.

For More Information

Some books with useful information on designing an individual exercise program are:

Dr. Abravanel's Body Type Program for Health, Fitness, and Nutrition by Elliot D. Abravanel, M.D. (New York: Bantam Books, 1985)

The Exercise Exchange Program by Dr. James M. Rippe (New York: Simon & Schuster, 1992)

BUILD BETTER BONES

Bones and teeth seem hard and rocklike, so it is natural to assume that they actually are rocks: lifeless mineral compounds that change little over eons of time. Of course, skeletal structures such as bones and teeth are not rocks at all. They are more like muscles, constantly being replenished by the blood and growing stronger or weaker depending on five basic factors: heredity, sex hormones, lifestyle, exercise, and diet.

Of these five factors, heredity is a given and bodily levels of sex hormones are primarily determined by age. Men continue to produce sex hormones, which are involved in bone metabolism and other body functions, until age seventy-five or so. Women experience a dramatic drop in the production of the female sex hormone estrogen at menopause, which usually comes during the mid to late forties. Estrogen-replacement therapy is a common postmenopausal treatment recommended by doctors to help prevent bone loss and the brittle-bone disease, osteoporosis. Unfortunately, while estrogen-replacement therapy definitely helps prevent osteoporosis, it also seems to increase the risk of uterine cancer and heart attacks.

Luckily, the other three factors that affect skeletal health—lifestyle, exercise, and diet—are readily influenced by the personal choices you make every day. Developing sturdy bones that resist breaking and hard teeth that resist cavities should not be postponed until the threats of osteoporosis and tooth loss loom in later years. Bone mass is usually gained up to the age of thirty-five or so and slowly lost thereafter. By developing early in life the health habits that strengthen teeth and bones, you dramatically reduce your risk of skeletal problems later in life.

Everyday Steps to Natural Health

Here's how to make the choices that will keep your teeth firm and your bones strong well into your sunset years.

Avoid the habits that are harmful to teeth and bones. Little controversy surrounds the question of the best and worst lifestyle choices that can be made when it comes to bone health. Medical experts across the spectrum agree that the following factors increase your risk of breaking bones or developing osteoporosis as you grow older:

➤ excessive consumption of alcohol, caffeine, or soft drinks
➤ regular, long-term use of cortisonelike steroid drugs, such as prednisone
➤ smoking
➤ prolonged emotional stress and nervous tension
➤ excess aluminum consumption, such as from regular use of aluminum-containing antacids (Mylanta, Maalox), baking powders, and antiperspirants; buffered aspirin; and aluminum cookware
➤ lack of exercise, or excess intense exercise among young women (to the point that menstrual periods stop from lack of estrogen)
➤ high-protein diet

Most of the above factors affect bone health by either decreasing the body's absorption of calcium, pulling calcium from the bones, suppressing the growth of new bone, or increasing the excretion of calcium in the urine. Smoking inhibits the conversion of vitamin D into its active form, increases the solubility of bone minerals, and, in women, reduces estrogen levels.

Get plenty of weight-bearing exercise. One of the best ways to prevent weak bones is to engage in plenty of weight-bearing activity or exercise, such as walking, running, and playing tennis. Almost all sports with the exception of swimming promote bone health. Swimming does not harm bones but does not directly build them either since the water's buoyancy prevents them from being stressed. It is the active pushing of the bones against the floor or an object, like dumbbells or a ball, that benefits bones. The saying "use them or lose them" applies to bones—people who are so inactive that they never put any stress on their bones risk becoming wormlike.

The mechanism responsible for stress-related bone growth may be partly electrical. "Stress-related bone growth is actually remodeling of the shape of a bone so that it can better resist mechanical stress," says Robert O. Becker, M.D., author of *The Body Electric*. In *Cross Currents,* Becker says that a "piezoelectric effect 'tells' the bone how much stress is being applied and in what direction. . . . The piezoelectric effect is the generation of an electrical charge in some crystalline materials, produced by bending or pressing on these materials . . . bone is somehow able to 'sense' mechanical stress and grow, so as to produce an anatomical structure best able to resist the stress."

Proof of the importance of weight-bearing activity on bone health comes from space travel. Scientists have found that astronauts subjected to long periods of weightlessness experience small but significant losses of bone density. Space capsules now routinely carry exercise equipment that allows astronauts to stress their bones.

Gravity on earth supplies some resistance but needs to be supplemented with exercise. People who are bedridden by illness, for instance, excrete higher amounts of calcium and eventually suffer significant bone loss. Studies have found that one hour of moderate activity three times a week prevents bone loss and may even increase bone mass in postmenopausal women. How long you exercise is more important than how fast or hard you do it. Try for forty-five to sixty minutes of activity three or more times per week.

Weight lifting is a good weight-bearing exercise, by definition, but it is hardly necessary to pump iron to build or retain bone mass. Brisk walking is one of the best exercises for those who are mostly sedentary. Jumping rope is not for everyone but does pound those bones. Like dancing and using aerobic machines, it offers the added benefit of improving cardiovascular health while also building stronger bones.

Eat a mostly vegetarian diet. Eating the right foods can make or break bones, to use an appropriate cliché. A diet for healthy bones should include lots of dark green vegetables such as collards and broccoli (though avoid excessive amounts of chard and spinach because they are high in oxalic acids, which can hinder calcium absorption), whole grains, legumes, fruits and nuts, sesame seeds, and tofu. Sea vegetables such as kelp, nori, and wakame are good for bones. If you're new to sea vegetables, one of the easiest ways to incorporate them into your diet is as a condiment. For instance, nori comes in thin sheets that can be toasted by briefly holding them over a gas flame, then crushed up and sprinkled in soups and salads.

These foods are rich in the bone-building mineral calcium as well as vitamins, trace minerals, and nutrients that strengthen bones. The level of calcium in foods is an important dietary factor, but it is not the only factor. Foods that, when consumed to an excess, have a negative impact on bone health include those that are high in

- ➤ phosphorus and low in calcium
- ➤ protein
- ➤ fat

Too much phosphorus has a negative effect on bones by causing calcium to leach into the blood. Foods high in phosphorus and low in calcium include most soft drinks and some highly processed foods. Many soft drinks have 500 mg or more of phosphoric acid along with only a few mg of calcium. Naturopaths Joseph Pizzorno and Michael Murray, authors of the *Encyclopedia of Natural Medicine,* recommend eliminating from your diet carbonated beverages loaded with phosphates.

When the body metabolizes protein, acid levels in the bloodstream increase, causing the bones to secrete more calcium, an alkalizing substance, to neutralize the acid. The calcium is eventually excreted in the urine. Excessive fat intake interferes with calcium absorption.

You don't have to give up meat but it shouldn't be a major part of your diet. Studies have found that vegetarians suffer from lower rates of osteoporosis than do meat eaters. While vegetarians and meat eaters have similar levels of bone mass into middle age, elderly vegetarians lose bone mass less quickly than do elderly meat eaters. Researchers suggest that, compared to average American meat eaters, vegetarians tend to consume more calcium, fewer processed foods, and less protein and fat.

Dairy foods are widely promoted for their rich supplies of calcium. Consumed in excess, however, the high levels of fat and protein in some dairy foods negate the positive effects of the high calcium levels.

Take nutritional supplements that build strong teeth and bones. The principal bone-building nutrients include

➤ the major minerals calcium and magnesium
➤ vitamin D
➤ trace minerals such as silicon and boron

Calcium is the most widely recognized bone-building nutrient. It also plays an important role in other essential bodily functions, including transmitting nerve messages and regulating heartbeat. It is the most abundant mineral in the human body, accounting for almost 2 percent of your body weight. Virtually all of the three pounds of calcium in a 150-pound person is stored in the teeth and bones.

Up to 50 percent or more of the calcium people consume does not make it into the blood. Thus, some nutritionists estimate that 30 percent of Americans don't consume enough calcium. An optimal supplement level is 800–1,500 mg daily. Too much calcium, on the other hand, can promote kidney stones or have other adverse effects, so don't overdo it.

Calcium comes in different chemical forms, with calcium citrate and calcium carbonate noted for being highly absorbable. Calcium supplements derived from dolomite and bonemeal may contain high levels of toxic metals. Other sources include oyster and egg shells. Calcium is often combined with magnesium and other minerals. It is available as tablets, capsules, and liquids. Take it in a 2:1 ratio with magnesium, such as 1,000 mg calcium and 500 mg magnesium.

Like calcium, magnesium is concentrated in the bones. Magnesium is intimately connected with calcium and phosphorus. Taking too much of one of these minerals can play havoc with not only the bones but nerves, muscles, and the heart. An optimal supplement level for magnesium is 450–650 mg daily. Foods rich in magnesium include fish, leafy green vegetables, whole grains, nuts, and beans.

Vitamin D is a hormonelike substance that helps regulate blood levels of calcium and is crucial for proper calcium absorption. Dietary sources of D are limited to fatty fish, liver, and egg yolks, foods that have drawbacks of high levels of fat and cholesterol. You can get plenty of D, however, by regularly exposing your skin to full-spectrum light, as from natural sunlight. Sunlight reacts with certain chemicals in the skin to form vitamin D.

A lack of vitamin D can lead to bone problems, including rickets. On the other hand, D is a fat-soluble vitamin that can build up in the body. Too much D, whether from dietary sources or exposure to sun, is toxic. Fifteen minutes of sun per day on the head, neck, and arms is usually enough to manufacture sufficient vitamin D (see Step 20). The US RDA is 400 IU. If you can't get any sunlight, consider supplementing the diet with an optimal level of 400–800 IU daily.

Silicon has only recently begun to gain scientific recognition for its role in the formation of bones, cartilage, and connective tissue. Studies have shown that animals fed a silicon-deficient diet develop bone and skeletal abnormalities that are corrected by silicon supplementation. The highest levels of silicon in the body are found in connective tissue, bones, teeth, and nails. The most common dietary sources include whole-grain breads and cereals, vegetables, cooked dried beans and peas, and seafoods. Some researchers believe that the overprocessing of industrialized nations' food supplies has led to a general deficiency of the trace mineral. The federal government says that although "there is substantial evidence" to establish that a number of trace elements including silicon are essential, "there are no data from which a human requirement could be established and thus no provisional (dietary) allowance can be set."

Though toxic if inhaled (as silica dust, a byproduct of semiconductor production), no adverse effects have been reported from consuming silicon supplements. An average daily dose is 20–30 mg.

Boron is a trace mineral found naturally in legumes and some fruit. There is no established RDA, though it may be necessary to help prevent bone loss and osteoporosis, possibly by working in conjunction with other bone-builders such as calcium and magnesium. There's also some evidence that it may help prevent arthritis. It is often combined with other minerals. It comes in tablets and capsules and an optimal supplement level is 2.5–3.0 mg daily.

Supplements should supplement rather than substitute for a healthful bone-building diet. According to physiologist Henry Lukaski, "You can't expect to maintain bone mass just by taking supplements. . . . In fact, I don't recommend reliance on supplements. Supplements create an illusion of protection and allow people to think they can eat anything as long as they're taking pills. It's much healthier to eat a wide variety of foods."

Short Tips for Better Bones

❑ Lower your likelihood of suffering from serious bone injuries. Many are due to sports injuries and may not be easily prevented. You can, however, limit the possibilities for falls and accidents around the home and workplace by identifying and removing unsafe conditions, such as inadequate lighting, slippery floors, and objects left lying about.

❑ Don't diet. According to a recent study at the Human Nutrition Research Center in Grand Forks, North Dakota, women who diet to lose weight probably also lose bone mass. Researchers studied fourteen obese women under forty years old who lost an average of eighteen pounds over five months. Bone-mass loss averaged 2–3 percent. The bone loss occurred even though the women ate a carefully monitored diet that furnished ample amounts of all nutrients, including 850–1,000 mg of calcium daily, and engaged in two hours of weight-bearing aerobic exercise daily.

❑ Take field horsetail *(Equisetum arvense)* or stinging nettle *(Urtica dioica)*. Both of these herbs are rich sources of bone-building minerals such as calcium, silicon, and magnesium. Field horsetail is a traditional European remedy for helping to repair broken bones. Herbalists also recommend stinging nettle as an excellent nutritional boost for healing injuries to bones and tendons. Horsetail extracts, powders, and tinctures are available from a number of herb companies. An average dose is one to three 500 mg tablets daily with meals. An average dose of stinging nettle is 300 mg in capsules daily.

For More Information

For further information on natural remedies to treat or prevent bone loss consult:

Encyclopedia of Natural Medicine by Michael Murray, N.D., and Joseph Pizzorno, N.D. (Rocklin, Calif.: Prima Publishing, 1991)

STAY FLEXIBLE

Most people recognize the benefits to their hearts and lungs from aerobic exercise, and to their bones and muscles from strength conditioning. But some of the same people too often ignore the positive effects of keeping the body supple and flexible. Following a regular program or activity that increases flexibility can offer you important health advantages. Stretching the body

> ➤ reduces lactic-acid levels in muscles, helping you to avoid cramps and sore, tired muscles
> ➤ flushes muscles with freshly oxygenated blood and raises the muscles' internal temperature, preventing sprains, strains, and other injuries
> ➤ removes unwanted wastes from the body by boosting the flow of lymph fluid in cells and vessels throughout the body (when muscles are stiff and overly contracted, they can't expand in a way that helps to pump lymph throughout the body)
> ➤ encourages a full range of motion around joints, reducing the risk of developing poor posture, improper body-use habits, and awkward movements
> ➤ returns muscles to a relaxed, more extended state after use (muscles don't stretch on their own but rather tend to stay in a slightly contracted position after exercise)

If your main exercise program focuses almost exclusively on muscle development—through weight lifting or working on machines that simulate cross-country skiing, rowing, or bicycling, for instance—it is especially important that you take some steps to keep your body supple and limber. When strength programs are followed to an extreme, you can become muscle-bound, literally so tightly wrapped in hardened, shortened muscles that you can no longer move easily and fluidly.

Everyday Steps to Natural Health

Even if you're not doing regular strength exercises, you should take steps to maintain or increase your body's flexibility. Some muscles can become overly tight from not using them at all, or habitually using them incorrectly. Popular sports such as tennis and jogging not only don't do much to increase participants' flexibility, they can cause muscles to shorten. You can increase your flexibility somewhat by regularly engaging in a few activities, including swimming and martial arts like aikido. For optimum results, however, you should consider either a stretching program or yoga, the set of movements and postures developed in ancient India.

Stretch the major muscle groups on a regular basis. The safest and easiest way to increase your flexibility is to perform simple stretches, ideally on a regular basis or at the least before and after you exercise. Stretches should be performed slowly and carefully to avoid pulling muscles or damaging connective tissues in joints. Don't stretch in a way that causes pain. Stretch a muscle or muscle group to the point where it feels as if it is being stretched and try to hold the position for thirty to sixty seconds. You can work with a partner if want, having the other person pull or push gently on the body part being stretched. Provide a partner with constant feedback to prevent injury.

The following are some of the most popular stretches for each of ten major parts of the body. These can be done by beginners or more advanced practitioners, either individually or as part of a regular program. See "For More Information" for books that can provide more detailed descriptions and further stretches.

❑ Neck semicircles. You can do this neck stretch whenever you have a few minutes while sitting at your desk or parked in your car.

With your back straight and your head balanced on top of your spine, slowly lower your head toward your chest, tucking your chin though not actually touching it to your chest. Return your head to an upright position and then release it downward toward one ear, keeping your head's weight under control at all times and your shoulders down. Bring your head back up and repeat the movement toward the other ear and back. Now slowly tilt your head backward so that you are looking up (but not straight up, which can compress the vertebrae of the upper spine), then bring your head back up. Next bring your ear toward one shoulder and then rotate your head forward in semicircles, from one ear then back down front and to the other ear. Doing these half-circles is much less likely to harm neck muscles and ligaments or to compress vertebrae than is doing full neck circles.

❑ Upper back and shoulders. The following stretch can help improve your posture and relieve tension in your upper body. It requires a rope (a belt or towel will also work). Grasp the rope about three feet apart so that it is taut. Lift it over and behind your head. Move your arms up and down behind you, keeping the rope taut as you rotate its position and stretch your shoulder muscles. Avoid arching your lower back while doing this rope stretch.

❑ Arms. Stretching arm muscles is especially important if you play tennis or any sport that involves a throwing motion. To stretch the triceps in the upper arm, stand sideways about two feet from a wall, lean over, and raise and place the side of your palm and upper arm against the wall. As you lean farther toward the wall and slide your arm up it, your triceps and shoulder muscles get a good stretch. Be sure to stretch both arms.

❑ Wrists and hands. Writers, typists, and others can benefit from keeping their wrists and hands supple. Bring your palms together at your chest in the traditional prayer position. Keeping each of the five fingers pressed up against its counterpart on the other hand, spread the fingers. Begin by keeping the palms flat against each other and then bring the palms and base of the fingers away, keeping the fingers pressing at their tips to allow for maximum stretch.

❑ Chest. Here is a good way to expand and stretch the pectoral muscles of your chest. Stand in a doorway, placing one foot behind the other and resting your forearms on the outside of the door frame. Lean forward, holding on to the doorframe with your hands as you push your chest through the door. Adjust your degree of lean to obtain a greater or lesser stretch.

❑ Lower back. Back problems are almost epidemic in modern society. Frequent stretching, along with better posture and correct use of the back, can help prevent much back pain.

One of the best ways to stretch and relax the muscles of the lower back is to lie down on the floor and bend your legs at the knees to bring your upper legs on or toward your chest. Wrap your forearms over the back of your thighs and pull your knees toward your chin (keep the back of your head on the floor) to help flatten your lower back on the floor. Try to lift the tailbone and release any tension in the hips. You can also do one leg at a time, keeping the other leg extended out straight and flat on the floor.

❑ Abdomen. Gently bending at the waist in all directions while standing is a simple way to stretch the abdomen. Another effective stretch is the triangle, which lengthens and stretches the muscles down the side of your abdomen, as well as muscles from the lower legs to the arms.

Standing, spread your feet about three feet apart with the left foot facing forward and the right foot perpendicular to it. Bring your arms up parallel to the floor, palms down. Slowly lower your upper trunk to the right, bending at the hips and keeping the entire body facing straight ahead. Place your right hand at a point between the knee and the foot, depending upon how limber you are, twist your head to look toward the ceiling, and raise your left arm toward the ceiling, trying to keep it in line with the right arm. Hold for thirty to sixty seconds, return to an upright position, and do the same stretch on the other side of the body.

❑ Groin. Variations on the classic splits, with one leg extended forward and the other backward on the floor, can help stretch the muscles of the groin and inner thigh. You can work up to splits by doing a type of lunge. From a standing position, extend your right leg in front of you so that the bottom of the foot rests on the floor. Extend your left leg behind you so that its shin rests on the floor and the left foot is pointing straight back. Place your hands on each side of the right leg for support and bend at the waist to bring your chest down to your right thigh. Inch the right foot forward or backward to adjust the degree of stretch in your legs and your groin.

❑ Upper leg. The hamstrings are the series of muscles in the back of the thighs that baseball players and sprinters are always pulling. There are a number of simple ways to stretch these muscles. For instance, sit on the floor with one leg extended and the other bent so that the foot is facing the knee of the extended leg. Keeping your back straight, slowly reach forward toward the extended foot to stretch the hamstring.

❑ Lower leg. The most popular calf stretch is accomplished by leaning forward against a wall. Start with the feet facing the wall, one foot about twelve inches from the wall and the other about thirty-six inches. Support your body against the wall with your forearms as you lean forward and stretch the calf muscle on the back leg. Keep your body in a straight line from calf to neck. Move the back leg closer or farther from the wall to decrease or increase the stretch. Reverse leg positions and stretch the other calf muscle.

❑ Ankles and feet. Standing, raise one foot a few inches off the ground (use one of your hands to maintain balance, if necessary). Slowly flex your foot up and down a number of times, keeping the toes relaxed and allowing the ankle muscles to do the work. With the foot pointing down, move the toes in a circle, doing it five times in one direction and then the other.

Do the twelve-step yoga routine known as the sun exercise. When practiced correctly yoga can not only stretch but strengthen and relax the body. The sun exercise is a popular sequence of twelve postures that can be held momentarily or for thirty to sixty seconds for greater effect. It is often used to limber up the body before a yoga routine. In India the sun exercise is traditionally practiced in the early morning, facing the sun (thus its name). It stretches all of the body's main muscle groups.

Some yoga teachers offer slight variations on the twelve steps, but the following is a common way to do it. The sun exercise should be done in sets of two, alternating which legs are brought backward and forward in steps four and nine. The movements should be re-laxed and rhythmical, not forced and jerky. You'll gain greater bene-fit by doing one set slowly and carefully than by bolting through many sloppy repetitions. Yoga practitioners also pay close attention to breathing. By breathing deeply and with awareness, you can in-crease the degree of stretch since proper breathing can help muscles relax and extend. Use your diaphragm rather than your chest to breathe (see Step 26) and try to breathe through your nose rather than your mouth.

Wear loose or stretch clothing and practice barefoot (or with socks on) on a blanket, rug, or rubber mat. As with other forms of stretching, avoid bouncing or overdoing a stretch to the point of pain.

1. Stand erect with your palms together at your chest and your feet together.

2. Inhale while stretching both arms over your head and bending backward from the waist.

3. Exhale while bending over forward at the waist, bringing your forehead toward your the knees (with practice you may be able to touch the knees). Place your hands next to your feet on the floor or dangle them to the side of the feet if that's more comfortable; keep your legs straight or only slightly bent at the knees.

Step 2   Step 3

4. Inhale while taking a long backward step with your right leg, so that you're kneeling with your chest resting on the left leg, your hands on the floor on each side of the left foot. Bend your neck back so that you're looking toward the ceiling.

5. Hold your breath while kicking your left leg back and coming into the classic push-up position, with your body straight from head to feet, supported only at the toes and the hands.

6. Exhale as you lower your body to just off the floor. Bring the knees, chest, and forehead into contact with the floor, allowing the buttocks to stick up in the air.

7. Inhale while bending backward at the waist, raising your chest off the floor, and straightening your arms. Leave your hands firmly planted on the ground. Flatten the tops of your feet on the floor, getting your upper thighs off the floor if you can. Arch your head back to look up at the ceiling.

8. Exhale while lifting your trunk into an inverted V shape. Keep your palms and the bottoms of your feet flat on the floor if you can (beginners have a tendency to pull their heels off the floor). Your head and neck should be in line with your spine.

Step 8

Step 9

9. Inhale while kicking your left leg back and bringing your right leg to under your chest in a kneeling position, hands on the floor next to the right foot. This is the same position as position four but with the opposite leg brought forward.

10. Exhale while bringing your left foot forward and straightening your legs. Assume position five, with your forehead on or near your knees and your hands beside your feet on or toward the floor.

11. Inhale while straightening up and raising your arms over your head, as in position two.

12. Exhale, return to position one, standing erect with your palms together at your chest and your feet together. Focus on your breath while you relax all the muscles in your body.

If you like the sun exercise and want to learn more, there are some good books, though it is best to learn yoga from an experienced teacher. Many of the postures have nuances that are best pointed out during practice. See "For More Information" for books and how to find a yoga teacher.

Learn how to properly align and use your body to get the most out of any stretching program. Regular stretching will benefit almost anyone. Some people, however, may need some help just to get started, including those who haven't stretched in a long time and those who have experienced years of poor posture or awkward movement patterns. Such people may have muscles that are abnormally shortened and joints or spines that are out of alignment. In some cases years of improper posture or body use can make the fasciæ, the protective connective sheaths surrounding each muscle, become short and rigid. This is often the case with people who have pronounced sloped shoulders, tilted head, pigeon toes, or arched back. When people with such intractable problems try to stretch, they may attain some additional suppleness but never fully address the root of their problem.

In such instances, some form of deep bodywork and "movement retraining or reeducation" can nicely complement a flexibility program. A number of holistic health practices have flourished in recent years that focus on proper body structure and the mechanics of movement. These include

❑ Chiropractic. Chiropractors manipulate the spine and adjust the body's joints to align its parts and allow the free flow of vital energy.

❏ Osteopathy. Osteopaths manipulate the muscles, bones, and joints (craniosacral osteopaths focus on the head and neck) to restore the body's natural ability to heal itself.

❏ Rolfing. Rolfers practice a form of deep-massage therapy that attempts to reorganize the body's structure by manipulating the fasciæ around muscles and joints.

❏ Feldenkrais reeducation. Feldenkrais practitioners use body-work and exercise to reprogram the brain to allow more fluid and effective patterns of action, movement, and awareness.

❏ Alexander technique. Alexander practitioners help clients become more aware of ways they can improve how they use their bodies to make routine movements.

Most of these practices recommend a series of sessions over weeks or months; costs vary, but full treatments usually run into the thousands of dollars. Still, such practices can tremendously speed up flexibility programs and ensure that the results from stretching are permanent and far-reaching. See "For More Information" after Step 22 for addresses of membership associations.

Short Tips for Flexibility

❏ Take a few minutes to relax your body after a stretching routine. If you can lie down after doing a series of stretches, the yoga pose aptly labeled "the corpse" is easy and effective. Lie on your back with your arms at your side, palms up. Stretch the legs out and allow your feet to fall open. Maintain a deep and even breathing pattern, inhaling and exhaling through the nose. Consciously tell each part of the body to relax, starting at the top of the head and proceeding to the scalp, eyes, face, neck, and so on down the body. After you've relaxed all of the major muscle groups, maintain the position for five to ten minutes. The corpse pose can be so relaxing that it will cause some people to fall into a light sleep, though your goal is a calm, meditative, but awake state.

For More Information

Books with valuable stretching exercises include:

The Acupressure Warm-Up by Marc Coseo (Brookline, Mass.: Paradigm Publications, 1992)

Relaxercise by David Zemach-Bersin, Kaethe Zemach-Bersin, and Mark Reese (San Francisco: Harper & Row, 1990)

Stretch & Strengthen by Judy Alter (Boston: Houghton Mifflin, 1986)

The Complete Illustrated Book of Yoga by Swami Vishnu-devananda (New York: Harmony Books, 1988)

The bimonthly Yoga Journal *publishes an extensive annual Yoga Teachers Directory, most recently in the July/August 1994 issue, listing yoga instructors in the U.S., Canada, and abroad. Send $5.00 for a copy of the issue to:*

Yoga Journal
2054 University Ave.
Berkeley, CA 94704
(800) 359-YOGA

TONE YOUR MUSCLES

The extremes of modern bodybuilding and the monotony of weight-lifting routines have made muscle-strengthening exercises off-putting to some people. You don't have to be a bodybuilder, however, to benefit from trim, firm muscles. It's also important to keep in mind that cultural perceptions of "the ideal body" have varied much throughout history. In future years today's standard as epitomized by the monstrous muscles of professional bodybuilders may well be seen as a strange aberration. In previous times the ideal male body was closer to the classical statues of the Greeks—not hugely muscled but well sculpted for power and grace.

The human body contains over six hundred muscles. Along with bones and nerves, the muscles shape your body and allow it to move. Well-toned muscles provide the strength and endurance necessary to work and play. Muscles are remarkable engines of movement. Over the course of a single day the average person's muscles perform millions of foot-pounds of work.

Some of your muscles are not normally controlled by voluntary movements nor do they need to be exercised. These include the "smooth" muscles that are found, for instance, in the intestinal tract. Smooth muscles may be inactive for years (as are the muscles that push a fetus from the uterus) but still work when called upon.

Unfortunately for couch potatoes, the more common skeletal

muscles—those that control the arms, legs, torso, and head—do need to be worked lest they waste away. Skeletal muscles are attached to adjacent bones. These muscles work by shortening and thus pulling the bones closer together. At the same time nearby muscles must stretch and relax. Since skeletal muscles are elastic, they can regain their shape after stretching.

Cardiovascular muscles share some of the characteristics of both smooth and skeletal muscles. Even when your body is at rest, the muscles of the heart and rib cage keep the body alive by helping to circulate blood and breathe in air. (See Step 14 for how to keep these muscles fit.)

Muscles are collections of long, slender cells organized as bundles of fibers laid side by side. The number of muscle fibers in one person's biceps is similar to anyone else's, but some people have considerably increased the size and strength of these fibers. When nerves give the signal, muscle cells can contract their length, thus converting the chemical energy of oxygen and glycogen into mechanical energy and motion. As muscles are exercised, blood flow through them increases, helping to build new cells and allowing the muscle to grow in strength and bulk.

Some of the body changes that result from strengthening exercises are cosmetic, but many more relate to better health. The health advantages of strengthening exercises and keeping your muscles in proper tone include

➤ working muscles against resistance increases bone density
➤ strengthening the body raises its resting metabolic rate, since you can expect to burn approximately seventy-five calories per day for each added pound of muscle
➤ fit muscles are like auxiliary hearts, pumping blood more efficiently throughout the body and taking stress off the heart
➤ muscles that are out of shape are less efficient and are more subject to cramping
➤ muscles act as the body's shock absorbers, enhancing the integrity of joints and protecting connective tissue in the back and elsewhere from injuries
➤ building muscle displaces fat, thus reducing your risk of chronic diseases
➤ having firm muscles can improve your self-image by helping you to feel good about yourself and your body

➤ fit muscles improve the body's ability to use insulin, thus decreasing your risk of diabetes

➤ strengthening exercises can decrease the time it takes food to pass through your intestines, thus reducing the risk of constipation and other intestinal disorders

According to Dr. William Evans of the Human Nutrition Research Center on Aging at Tufts University, "Much of what we call aging is nothing more than the accumulation of a lifetime of inactivity. Muscles shrink. Body fat increases. The results are an increased risk of diabetes, hypertension, and osteoporosis. By preserving muscle mass we can prevent these problems from occurring."

Everyday Steps to Natural Health

You use many of your muscles in everyday activities, whether walking, climbing stairs, or carrying groceries. If you get regular aerobic exercise or play a sport, you work muscles even more. Yet many people today are relatively sedentary. Also, sports like tennis work some muscles much more than others. Strengthening exercises can help balance the body by working on those muscles you use the least. Other advantages to a properly performed muscle-fitness program, compared to aerobics and playing a sport, include:

➤ it allows you to build muscle at little risk of injury
➤ it strengthens the muscles through a full range of motion
➤ it builds muscle and causes you to lose fat much faster and more efficiently

Even if you have an exercise machine like a Nautilus at home or have access to one at a health club, the following steps can help keep your muscles firm.

Do simple resistance exercises using handheld weights. These are easy to do at home or in the office, since they require only a set of two small weights. Most people do fine with five- or ten-pound dumbbells.

When working with weights (or on a resistance machine) it is important to stress the quality of each movement rather than either the quantity of weight lifted or the number of repetitions. By moving the weights slowly and precisely, you build muscle more quickly and efficiently since you're not taking advantage of the weight's momentum to move it. Slow movements also allow you to isolate the muscles responsible for each movement and you are less likely to injure joints and tendons.

Injuries that occur from using weights are usually due to lifting too much weight. It is better to use lower amounts of weight and do more repetitions. When you use a weight that is too heavy, it is easy to succumb to the temptation to jerk the weight, use muscles other than the ones you're targeting, or sway the body to move the weight. All of these bad habits lessen the usefulness of the exercise and increase the risk of strain or injury. Begin with a weight that is easy to lift and add weight slowly. It is also a good idea to check your form in a mirror. You should also stretch before and after strengthening exercises to prevent becoming too tight or restricted in the joints (see Step 12).

Make the two sequences of weight lifting—lifting and lowering—equal in duration and emphasis. For example, as you do an overhead shoulder press, bring the dumbbell or weight up from your shoulder to above your head using a count of four, pause, then lower the dumbbell back to your shoulder on another count of four. The two actions of slow lifting and lowering complement each other and are more effective at strengthening muscles than if you jerk the weight up or allow gravity to pull it quickly down.

Don't hold your breath—exhale as you lift and inhale as you lower. In addition, alternate strengthening exercises that target the upper body with those that target the lower body.

For each of the following exercises, try to do eight to ten slow repetitions over the course of a minute or so. Use enough weight that eight to ten repetitions presents a challenge—this should be about 60–75 percent of your onetime lift capacity. That is, if you can curl fifty pounds once, do eight to ten repetitions using 30–37.5 pounds.

The quickest way to build new muscle is to work the muscle to the point of momentary fatigue. Strengthening exercises are helpful, especially for beginners, even if you don't exercise a muscle to that point. Do one or two sets of each exercise per workout. Don't do more than three weight workouts per week, since muscles need time to recover.

❑ Shoulders and arms. A simple overhead press works these muscles. Sitting or standing, hold the weights at your shoulders, palms facing each other. Slowly raise the weights overhead by straightening the arms. Lower to the starting position.

❑ Deltoids. These are the triangular muscles of the shoulder that raise the arms away from the sides. Two useful strengthening exercises are the lateral and front raises. To do the lateral, stand with your arms at your thighs, palms facing each other. With elbows locked and without twisting the arms, slowly raise the weights to your sides in an arc to shoulder height, then return to the starting position. For the front raise, hold the weights at your thighs with your palms facing back and raise the weights to shoulder height in front of you.

❑ Biceps. The biceps are the larger muscles on the front of the upper arm. The classic strengthening exercise for them is the curl. Put your arms down and hold the weights in front of your thighs, palms forward. Bring the weights up to your shoulders by bending at the elbows, keeping your elbows and upper arms stationary. Lift, don't swing. Also, don't arch your back or lean backward. Slowly return to the starting position.

❑ Triceps. These are the larger muscles at the back of the upper arms that extend the forearms when contracted. Use one weight to do a triceps curl. Hold the weight with both hands, arms extended straight over the head. Bending the arms at the elbows, slowly bring the weight down behind the head to neck level (be careful not to hit your head), then return to the starting position.

❑ Forearms, wrists, and hands. Do wrist curls one arm at a time in a sitting position. Rest your forearm on your thighs with the wrist and hand hanging unsupported over the knee. Holding the weight palm up and keeping the fingers curled, slowly lower the weight and let it roll slightly down the hand onto the fingers—don't drop it. Pull your wrist back up, letting the weight roll back onto the palm.

❑ Back and arms. Do the upper-back row by holding the weights with your arms straight out in front of you, elbows locked and palms down. Keeping the arms and weights at shoulder level, slowly bend the elbows to bring the weights back toward your shoulders. Push the weights away from you to return to the starting position.

❑ Chest. The fly lift strengthens the pectoral muscles and expands the rib cage. Lie on your back. Hold a weight in each hand, palms up, with the arms extended to the sides. Keeping the arms straight, slowly bring the weights up over your head. Lower them to just

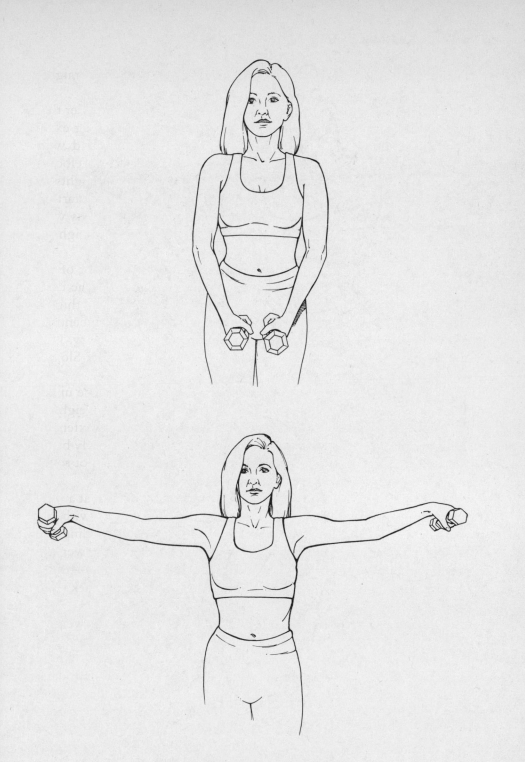

Lateral raise to strengthen deltoids.

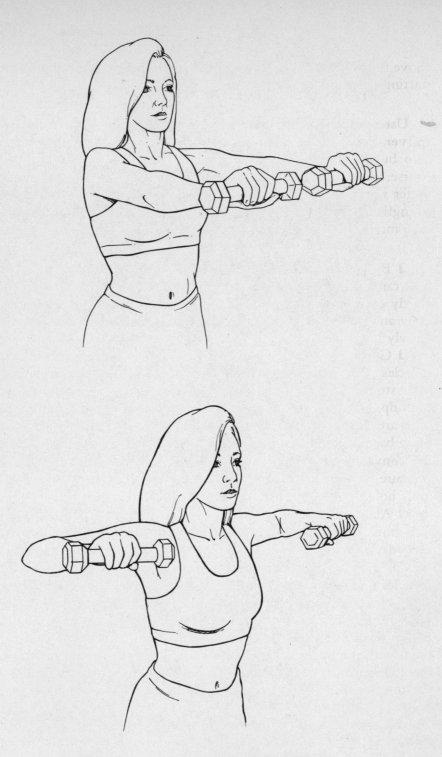

Upper-back row to strengthen back and arms.

above the floor and then pull them up again before returning to the starting position.

Use the weight of your own body to resist your muscles' movements. The previous resistance exercises with dumbbells can help build strength in the upper body, back, and abdomen. Of course, lower-body strength is also important. Plus, some people prefer not to use weights at all. You can combine the following strengthening exercises with hand-weight work, exercises on resistance machines, and muscle-strengthening sports.

❏ Back and shoulders. Pull-ups efficiently work these muscles. You can use a special bar hung in a doorframe, a tree branch, or sturdy (and cool) basement pipe. Grab it with your palms facing away and pull your body up to the bar without kicking your legs. Slowly lower yourself.

❏ Chest. Push-ups are good chest builders. They also exercise the muscles of the shoulders and the back of the upper arms. Lying on your stomach on the floor with your hands under your shoulders, push up, either onto your toes or your knees if you can't, until your arms are almost straight. Don't lock the elbows. Slowly lower your body back to within an inch of the floor before pushing back up. If the conventional straight body positions seems to put too much pressure on your pelvis, *Stretch & Strengthen* author Judy Alter suggests holding the buttocks up and out of line with the body.

❏ Abdominals. Along with the muscles at the back of your shoulders, muscles of the abdomen don't normally get strengthened by everyday activities or sports. Keeping the abdominal muscles fit may help prevent lower-back trouble by strengthening and balancing the muscles that support the spine. A simple exercise for the abdomen is the bicycle. Lie on your back with your hands behind your head, put your feet up, and move your legs as if pedaling a bicycle. If you prefer sit-ups, prevent injuries to the lower back by performing them with the knees bent. Or do "crunches" by rising only two to three inches until your shoulder blades are just off the floor, holding the position for a few seconds, and then slowly returning to the floor.

❏ Upper leg and thighs. To do leg raises to the side, lie on your right side with your right arm stretched out and your head resting on the biceps. Put the left hand on the floor in front of your chest and slowly raise the left leg, keeping it straight. Wear ankle weights for added resistance.

❑ Lower leg and feet. The following heel raises suggested by Alter can strengthen the muscles of the calves and toes. Holding on to the side of a desk or a rail at waist height with one hand, align the knees and feet. Bend the knees slightly and raise heels off the floor, straightening but not locking the knees. Bend the knees again slightly as you return your heels to the floor.

Short Tips for Firmer Muscles

❑ You can compress the time needed to do any strengthening exercise by working the muscles extremely slowly. For instance, when doing a curl, raise the weight to a count of 15 and lower it to another count of 15.

❑ Keep a light handweight in your office and another in one or more rooms of your home. Even if you're not going to do a full workout, do a few repetitions of various strengthening exercises as time allows.

❑ Don't mistake a hulking, bulked-up body for a healthy body. There is no particular health benefit to huge muscles. "At its worst, bodybuilding actually sacrifices health for superficial appearance by encouraging unsound dietary practices (consumption of high-protein foods and protein and amino-acid supplements), the use of dangerous drugs (anabolic steroids), and neglect of the real work of preventive health maintenance," says Andrew Weil, M.D., author of *Natural Health, Natural Medicine.* "The bodybuilders I have known are not as a group any healthier than other people, and some of them are less healthy because of the ways they think about and treat their bodies."

❑ Don't worry about getting too huge anyway. As one bodybuilder has put it, the chances of a person taking up strengthening exercises and ending up looking like Mr. Olympia are about the same as a beginning piano student becoming the next Mozart. Women in particular don't have to worry about developing large and unsightly muscles, since they have lower levels than men of the sex hormones that are needed for quick bulking up.

For More Information

Safe and precise strengthening exercises using your body weight for resistance can be found in the following book:

Stretch & Strengthen by Judy Alter (Boston: Houghton Mifflin, 1986)

INCREASE YOUR
ENDURANCE

Only one in five Americans get regular endurance exercise, a statistic that is closely related to certain other vital statistics: 60 million Americans suffer from high blood pressure, surgeons perform a thousand heart-bypass surgeries every day in the U.S., there is a heart attack every twenty seconds somewhere in the U.S., and cardiovascular disease is the nation's number one killer, accounting for nearly six-hundred thousand deaths annually.

Regular endurance exercise is crucial for maintaining the overall fitness of your heart, circulatory system, and respiratory system. Also known as aerobic ("oxygen-consuming") and cardiovascular exercise, endurance exercises such as jogging and swimming improve the body's ability to transport and burn oxygen efficiently. By increasing the speed of your heartbeat, aerobic exercise trains the heart muscle to grow larger and stronger. Each beat of the heart pumps an increased volume of blood, so the heart can beat fewer times to accomplish the same amount of work. The body responds to the increased demands for oxygen by producing more red blood cells to carry the oxygen. Muscles also respond by actually developing new capillaries, tiny blood vessels that can carry more efficiently the oxygen-rich blood to all parts of the muscle.

Over time, regular endurance exercise thus increases your stamina and overall fitness. It allows you to feel more vigorous and alert and look slimmer and more muscular. Among its other potential benefits, endurance exercise can

> ➤ decrease your risk of all sorts of chronic diseases, including diabetes and heart disease. According to most cardiologists, regular moderate exercise has more of a preventive effect against heart disease than any dietary steps you could take.
> ➤ boost your brainpower and improve your short-term memory. One study of thirty people over nine weeks found that those who did three sessions weekly of water aerobics (along with some strength training) performed better on memory tests than those who didn't work out, possibly because the exercise delivered more oxygen to the brain.
> ➤ maintain your ideal weight and body-fat percentage. One study that looked at people who did twenty minutes of strength training and twenty minutes of aerobic exercise three times weekly found that they lost six pounds of fat while gaining three pounds of muscle.
> ➤ give a sense of emotional and psychological well-being. Exercise stimulates the release of endorphins, potent brain hormones that act as pain relievers and pleasure inducers in your bloodstream.
> ➤ strengthen your immune system
> ➤ reduce the adverse effects of too much stress

Aerobic exercise can also have positive spillover effects. For example, it often provides the incentive for you to make positive changes in other aspects of your life, particularly diet—most people are less likely to overindulge in fatty snacks if they are getting regular aerobic exercise.

Everyday Steps to Natural Health

While it is possible to gain some cardiac benefits from everyday activities pursued with some vigor, such as raking leaves and shoveling snow, the chief way to boost your endurance is to do regular aerobic exercise. Here are some suggestions for making that possible.

Schedule exercise into your life, set goals, and make a commitment to a program that works for you. The lament that "I'm too busy to exercise" is an oft-heard one. Few people, however, spend every waking minute rushing from one vital activity to another. Even the president of the nation finds time to jog—are your responsibilities more demanding? In any case, exercise doesn't *take* time, it *creates* time, by allowing you to be more productive, alert, and energetic when you are not exercising. Schedule it into your life and make it a priority that is at least as important as eating well and developing loving relationships.

Many people find that exercising at the same time every day (or every other day) works well, whether that time is upon rising in the morning, at lunchtime, or after dinner. Planning exercise as a natural sequence to another activity (exercising as soon as you get home from work, for instance) is another effective strategy.

AnneMarie Calhoun, director of Harvard University's Health and Fitness Department, says that goals are especially important for the beginner. "Making a calendar commitment effects a behavior change," she says. Setting goals, however, that are too high can be counterproductive. "Set a realistic goal," Calhoun says.

At the same time keep in mind that your intention is not to stop exercising when you reach your goal, but to have made cardiovascular exercise an integral part of your life, something you accept as necessary for life's full enjoyment. "The reward is in the process, not in meeting the goal," reminds Zoe Stewart, a yoga teacher in Cambridge, Massachusetts.

Sports clinics and medical facilities can help you assess your current status and set up some goals. Machines that can measure your maximum oxygen intake are a high-tech option for determining your fitness level, but there are also a number of ways you can personally monitor your cardiovascular progress. Once you've become more fit, your resting heart rate will drop. Take your pulse upon awakening in the morning. (Use your fingertips pressed into the inside of your wrist to count beats for ten seconds, then multiply that number by six to get heartbeats per minute.) Do this over a period of weeks and watch how your resting heart rate falls as you build cardiovascular strength. A top athlete has a resting heartbeat of thirty-five to forty per minute while the average (and sedentary) American's is seventy to ninety. You can also set goals in terms of the time it takes you to walk or run a certain distance, or how long you can do an exercise before feeling really winded. Recovery time after stopping exercise and body-fat percentage (see Step 8) are also prime indicators of aerobic health.

The safety of endurance exercise is a concern. Especially if you have been inactive, start slowly. If you begin with a nonstressful form of exercise, such as walking, you are less likely to be injured. Injuries are commonplace with some types of exercise, particularly running and high-impact aerobics. For a limited number of people, heart attacks are also a concern. Those at highest risk are men older than forty-five who are overweight, hypertensive, and have been inactive for a number of years. A number of recent studies have shown that people who are sedentary and then begin suddenly to exert themselves experience a risk of nonfatal heart attack that is as much as one hundred times greater than the risk during lighter activity. Also at risk are those with a personal or family history of heart disease. If you are middle-aged and sedentary, talk to your health practitioner about a cardiac stress test or at the least begin slowly. When doing aerobic exercise, always stop if you get dizzy or have chest pains.

Vary your exercises. Most people think only of running, aerobics classes, and cycling machines for cardiovascular exercise. Yet you can also choose from among outdoor activities such as bicycling, rowing, and cross-country skiing. A wide array of exercise machines now lets you, in the comfort of your home, mimic the movements of these activities as well as a half dozen others, including climbing stairs, rowing, ice-skating, and rock climbing. You can also swim, jump rope, hike, and bounce on a minitrampoline. Aerobics comes in a variety of forms, including dance, step, and low impact.

"Routines are helpful in the beginning, but it's also important to build a repertoire of activities over time," says Calhoun. Many people find that doing only one type of exercise quickly becomes boring. Switching back and forth among a number of different exercises helps to move different muscles and balance your body development. It also helps prevent injuries from overuse of certain muscles and joints.

Emphasize frequency of exercise rather than how long or vigorously you do it. Up until just a few years ago, exercise physiologists thought that you needed to boost your heart rate up to 60–80 percent of its capacity (220 minus your age) for twenty to thirty minutes to gain any heart benefits. A number of recent studies have cast doubts on this assumption by demonstrating that less vigorous aerobic exercise also benefits the heart. For example, one study found that women who walked for three miles a day three to four times per week realized some of the same benefits (such as an increase in "good cholesterol" levels and thus an almost 20 percent drop in heart-attack risk) whether they walked as fast as they could or strolled at a normal twenty-minutes-per-mile pace.

Even if you devote only an hour a week to aerobic exercise, you can still improve your health by doing it. You are probably more likely to make a habit of aerobic exercise and less likely to injure yourself if you can spread your exercise out over a number of days each week and make your workouts moderate in intensity. If the exercise is enough to make you breathe a little faster and feel a little warm from the exertion, then you're gaining in endurance and fitness.

How frequently should you do aerobic exercise? Most health authorities agree that four days a week for about half an hour each day is all that it takes to keep your circulatory and respiratory systems fit.

Make it fun (but do it anyway even if it is not!). It's important to find ways to make your endurance program attractive to your mind as well as your body. Any fitness program that becomes a drudgery is likely to be short-lived. If it is not fun and obviously rewarding, continuing to force yourself to do it while harboring a negative attitude toward the whole enterprise will tend to negate its benefits in any case.

What can you do to spice up your endurance exercising? Here are a few suggestions:

❑ Work out with a friend or family member. An exercise companion to share your trials and triumphs can help you stay motivated. Plus, when you jog or exercise with another person, you are less likely to skip a workout because of a minor inconvenience.

❑ Take a class. Classes can provide instant camaraderie and an enjoyable environment for exercise. (Music seems to play an important part; try it at home, too.) A savvy instructor can keep you going when you might otherwise have decided to quit.

❑ Get outdoors. Exercising outdoors can be daunting when winter temperatures dip into single digits, unless you love skiing or skating. When weather permits, taking your workout into nature relieves boredom by providing fresh sensory stimulation in the form of new sights, sounds, and smells.

   Supplement your diet to get the most out of your aerobic exercise. Intense aerobic exercise offers a bundle of long-term benefits. There are, however, some short-term harmful effects. That's because exercise increases your oxygen intake, and oxygen in the body can produce free radicals, unstable molecules that can damage tissue. The antioxidant nutrients can help to neutralize free radicals. A number of other nutrients can also help to rebuild muscle tissue. Especially if your aerobic workouts are vigorous, consider taking the following supplements on a daily basis:

➤ beta carotene (10,000–20,000 IU), for its antioxidant properties
➤ vitamin B complex (50–100 mg), to encourage a healthy supply of red blood cells. Deficiencies of some B vitamins (especially folic acid and B_{12}), along with a lack of iron, can cause the body to produce fewer red blood cells. Supplementation can produce an effect similar to blood doping, in which athletes inject themselves with blood before a competition. Unlike blood doping, B vitamins are safe and legal.
➤ vitamin C (500–1,500 mg), an antioxidant. In 1991 researchers at Auburn University found that taking vitamin C supplements may also improve cardiac efficiency. Apparently C reduces the working heart rate during workouts and keeps blood pressure lower. It also limits secretions of stress hormones that commonly increase during exertion.
➤ vitamin E (400–800 IU), an antioxidant. Along with C, researchers have found that vitamin E reduces tissue damage and prevents muscle breakdown during and after intense aerobic workouts.
➤ magnesium (450–650 mg), which may improve endurance
➤ chromium (150–300 mcg), to help build muscles and reduce fat
➤ selenium (100–150 mcg), an antioxidant

Many supplement producers now sell combination antioxidants such as the popular ACES formula, which combines the vitamins A, C, and E and the mineral selenium.

Short Tips for Increasing Your Endurance

❏ Dancing can be aerobic if it is done vigorously enough, and it is a favorite for meeting people and having fun. Try to find a smoke-free environment if you go out dancing since even secondhand smoke has an adverse effect on heart health, and when you dance vigorously, you increase your intake of any toxins in the surrounding air.

❏ Don't overdo it. Exercise causes some stress and wear and tear on the body, and it is possible to get too much of a good thing. If your exercise program is causing your joints to ache or you become fatigued easily, lose your appetite, or have trouble sleeping, you may be taxing your body beyond its healthy limits.

❏ Talk or sing while you do endurance exercise. If you can just barely carry on a conversation with an exercise partner, or sing out loud to yourself, you are within your target heart rate of 60–80 percent of maximum. If your breathing is so fast that talking or singing is impossible, slow down.

For More Information

A well-rounded book on endurance exercises is:

The Aerobics Program for Total Well-Being by Kenneth Cooper (New York: M. Evans, 1982)

15

IMPROVE YOUR BALANCE, AGILITY, AND COORDINATION

Considered as a whole, balance, agility, and coordination is one of the four crucial elements of a well-rounded fitness program, along with flexibility (see Step 12), strength (see Step 13), and endurance or cardiovascular health (see Step 14). The abilities to quickly reestablish a state of equilibrium or stability (balance), to change direction easily and deftly (agility), and to move the hands, eyes, and other body parts in harmony and unity (coordination) are valued in sports as well as life. Balance, agility, and coordination allow the body to move with grace and ease through space, whether to hit a tennis ball or to have fun on the dance floor. They let the body function to its best ability and adapt to new conditions and stimuli.

In some ways activities and exercises that develop these three physical assets have more everyday applications than do those that develop endurance, strength, and flexibility. For the mother who is putting together dinner, talking on the phone, and dealing with the demands of three young children, balance, agility, and coordination are prerequisites for mental and emotional health, to say nothing of an unburned entrée.

Balance, agility, and coordination are functions of various bodily organs and systems, including the muscles, nerves, and senses. Even when you are still, hundreds of muscles in the body are constantly making many minor adjustments. Muscles stretch and tighten by reflex to compensate for the tiny swaying movements caused by breathing, the body's top-heavy weight distribution, the flow of blood, and even the working of the organs. A finely tuned feedback system between muscles, the eyes, touch receptors, and the brain allows you to stay upright and light on your feet.

Balance is also partly determined by the ear. Each ear contains three semicircular canals, small tubular structures that have retained their ancient, equilibrium-maintaining function even as the ear evolved into a hearing organ. The canals are set at right angles to each other to detect motion in the three dimensions. Each canal contains a fluid that is pressed back into the end of the canal by movement, where tiny hairlike nerve cells sense the fluid and send messages to the brain about the body's orientation in space.

Everyday Steps to Natural Health

What can the average person do to retain poise, quickness, ease, and harmony of movement? Here are some suggestions.

Do more of the activities and sports that increase balance, agility, and coordination. For many people, ball and racket sports are probably the easiest, most interesting, and most accessible ways to help develop these physical qualities. Sports such as basketball, baseball, squash, racquetball, tennis, and table tennis help develop better hand-eye coordination. The acts of catching, shooting, and hitting a ball demand quick and precise movements of the hands, arms, trunk, and legs. Agile footwork is also important. The sheer fun of playing ball and racket sports accounts for much of their immense popularity. They do have a few disadvantages, including a relatively high rate of injury and the expense necessary to play year-round in colder areas of the country. In addition, when used exclusively as an exercise, racket sports can overdevelop one side of the body. Ball and racket sports are moderately good at developing flexibility and strength and can enhance endurance if played strenuously.

Other activities and sports to increase balance, agility, and coordination include

❏ Dance. Dance has the advantages of coming in many forms (jazz, ballroom, rock, square, country, contra, line), being easy and inexpensive, and needing only some music and floor (or grass) space. It is an excellent social activity, though it can also be done solo. A number of progressive communities have organized regular alternative dance happenings that are alcohol and smoke free. Depending upon how vigorously you dance, it can be a good activity for endurance and flexibility as well as balance, agility, and coordination.

❑ Skiing, skating, and surfing. Whether on land, in snow, or on water, these sports are fun and physically challenging. The body's many constant adjustments as it glides over a rough and quickly changing surface must be well honed or you'll spend more time sitting than standing. Skiing, skating, and surfing also emphasize to some extent flexibility and strength. Cross-country skiing can be quite aerobic. Some disadvantages include the seasonal nature of skiing and surfing, high equipment and use fees (especially for snow skiing), and a potential for injury (especially with in-line roller-skating and skateboarding).

❑ Rock climbing. Rock climbing and its younger cousin bouldering (using gymnasticlike moves to climb difficult but close-to-the-ground objects) are physically demanding. They also require more forethought and problem-solving effort than, for instance, most ball sports. You need the right equipment, good judgment, and a fair amount of instruction to rock climb safely and avoid serious injuries from falls. Rock climbing and bouldering also build strength and flexibility.

❑ Jumping rope. This exercise also provides an excellent cardio-vascular workout. The equipment is inexpensive and portable, and the activity can be done anywhere there is sufficient headroom.

Learn a new skill that requires balance, agility, and coordination. If you're already fairly proficient at sports and activities that emphasize these physical attributes, you may be open to somewhat more difficult physical challenges.

❑ Gymnastics. This is an excellent fitness activity for balance, agility, and coordination, as anyone who has seen a graceful and athletic floor exercise or high-bar performance can attest. Most cities have facilities featuring gymnastics programs for adults and children. Prior gymnastic experience is not necessary, though you should be in relatively good overall shape and be at least average in strength to benefit from gymnastics. The need for instruction, supervision, and an indoor facility makes this an expensive sport. It is excellent for developing flexibility and strength. A significant disadvantage is that gymnasts have a higher injury rate than football players and any other athletes as well.

❏ Juggling. "By learning to juggle material things, physical, emotional, and intellectual abilities and sensitivities are enhanced," says juggler Steve Cohen. "Balanced coordination can be learned; juggling teaches it through training and exercise." Keeping objects in motion through the air by alternately tossing and catching them requires skill, agility, and dexterity. It is also an interesting way to develop better balance and coordination. Juggling takes practice to learn but almost anyone can do it. It is inexpensive, can be done indoors or out, and develops both hands plus visual dexterity.

Cohen suggests that you begin by practicing indoors, in a corner, over a bed so that you don't have to chase your drops far. Start by getting proficient at tossing two balls between hands, crossing them over in a butterfly or X pattern. Then try the simplest real juggle, the three-ball cascade, in which you start with two balls in your dominant hand, one in the other, and toss the balls from hand to hand so that two are in the air at any one time. Don't pass a ball horizontally from one hand to the other—that's a more difficult juggling routine called a shower that you should learn only after you master easier routines like a cascade.

❏ Unicycling. Most children learn to balance on one foot for three to four seconds at age three and for ten seconds at age four. At age five to six, they learn how to ride a bicycle. After that, few people face any further learning tests involving balance that are genuinely challenging. Once you learn how to ride a bicycle, the many tiny and constant adjustments necessary to keep from falling become second nature. For a further adventure in balance, try learning how to ride a unicycle. It is a valuable activity not only for balance but for agility and for strengthening the leg muscles.

A self-taught unicyclist says, "Find a set of sturdy poles sunk into level ground about three feet apart and at least five feet tall. A basketball backboard mounted on two four-by-four posts works well. Holding on to the posts, sit on the unicycle, put your feet on the pedals, and start pedaling. Do this a couple hundred times and you'll soon be riding a unicycle."

Take up a discipline that combines an element of meditation with balance, agility, and coordination. Chief among these are yoga and martial arts like tai chi.

Yoga is a system of precise movements and postures that has been practiced and refined in India since ancient times. Yoga practitioners pay close attention to breathing and coordinate it with stretching movements. Yoga is most widely known for its positive effects on flexibility, but it is also an effective discipline for improving balance and agility. (See Step 12 for a popular yoga stretching series called the sun exercise.)

An ancient Chinese movement and martial art, tai chi features a series of choreographed, dancelike steps that harmonize the flow of vital energy (or chi, as the Chinese call it) within the body. Tai chi is less aggressive and less likely to cause injury than more well-known martial arts such as karate and aikido. Practitioners usually move in slow motion, though tai chi can be speeded up for a more energetic (if not aerobic) workout. Practitioners emphasize deftly shifting the body's center of gravity from one foot to another. Done correctly it quickly develops better balance, poise, and concentration. The thigh and other muscles are strengthened, but joints and limbs are not overtaxed.

"A master's steps are light, balance flawless," says writer and tai chi practitioner Paul Dunphy. "In one challenging series of moves, you must stand on your right leg and raise your left in an unbroken motion and slowly deliver a kick to an imaginary foe. Then, lowering your left leg slightly, bending it at the knee and hip and drawing it close to your body, you collect yourself, spin one hundred and eighty degrees on your right heel, and slowly kick again. To move with such grace requires strength as well as concentration and coordination, but strength without rigidity."

Like yoga, tai chi can be approximated by reading about it and practicing it on one's own. The most popular form comprises 108 moves that can be learned in a few months of daily practice. To really master tai chi, however, it should be studied and practiced with a teacher, either one-on-one or in a class.

Short Tips for Developing Better Balance, Agility, and Coordination

❏ "One of the best ways to improve coordination, agility, and balance is to walk, run, or even dance over rough and uneven terrain," says Andrew Weil, M.D., author of *Natural Health, Natural Medicine.* "If you have never walked over rocks or up streambeds, try this cautiously at first and then be more daring."

❏ Limit the time you spend playing video or computer games. These games are good for developing hand–eye coordination but not balance or agility. Most games also have the disadvantage of not requiring any movement from body parts beyond the hand and wrist. If you don't pay attention to posture and take frequent breaks, the addictive and static nature of these games can result in various aches and pains.

❏ Take the herb ginkgo. Studies have found that ginkgo has a positive effect on the inner ear, where some of the important organs of balance are. You can find ginkgo in tablets, capsules, or liquids at most natural foods stores. An average dose of a common powdered form known as a "standardized extract containing 24 percent ginkgo heterosides" is 40 mg three times per day.

For More Information

Some valuable instruction books include:

Juggling for the Complete Klutz by John Cassidy and B.C. Rimbeaux (Palo Alto, Calif.: Klutz Press, 1989)

Just Juggle by Steve Cohen (New York: McGraw-Hill, 1982)

The Essential Movements of T'ai Chi by John Kotsias (Brookline, Mass.: Paradigm Publications, 1989)

SIMPLE STEPS
TO
NATURAL HEALTH

POSTURE

STAND TALL

Many people give more thought to the alignment of their car's wheels than to the alignment of their own body. Yet the effects of a misalignment are similar. Your car shakes and rattles, gets worse performance and mileage, and your tires wear out unevenly and prematurely. A misalignment in your body, such as from years of poor posture, causes back or neck pain, limits your athletic ability, and possibly even prematurely wears out knee and other joints. Identifying and correcting your body's alignment is somewhat more difficult than checking and correcting your car's, but the effort pays off with long-term health benefits.

Posture is the position or carriage of the body. It is determined by how body parts relate to each other, especially the head, the spine and rib cage, the pelvis, and the legs and feet. When these parts are balanced and working in harmony with each other, you stand tall, sit up straight, and move gracefully. Proper posture allows you to use muscles in front, back, and on both sides of the body evenly and efficiently, burning the fewest possible calories. Correct body alignment requires effort and concentration, especially if you're trying to break bad habits, but ultimately saves energy and adds strength and resiliency.

A misaligned body and poor posture can result in all sorts of unwelcome consequences. When the body's functional units are not lined up, extra strain and wear is put on the muscles and bones. Body parts wear out more quickly, moving fluidly becomes more difficult, and injuries happen more readily. Poor posture can also push abdominal organs out of place and interfere with their proper functioning.

"I strongly believe, along with many other experts who treat back problems, that the great majority of back pains are related to poor posture," says Leon Root, M.D., author of *No More Aching Back*. Along with back pain, poor posture may cause stiff neck, headache, vision problems, breathing difficulties, numbness in arms, wrists, or feet, and temporomandibular joint (TMJ) dysfunction. It can even lead to the loss of an inch or more of height as the spine develops deep curves. Perhaps most alarming to some, poor posture can cause loss of physical beauty. Few people find attractive a pot-belly, sagging bust, double chin, knock-knees or bowlegs, all of which may be posture related.

In some cases the effects of poor posture are immediately notice-able. Hours of uninterrupted slouching on the sofa while watching television may cause a stiff neck, for instance. The results can also be cumulative. Habitual poor posture may weaken the muscles of the back and spine, loosen ligaments, or cause some muscles to be more flexible than others. You bend over to pick up an object that you've picked up dozens of times before in the same way, and this time you tear a ligament or injure a disk. The poor posture was as much of a factor in the injury as the lifting episode.

Poor posture is usually due to habitual ways of holding or carrying the body. After years of slouching while sitting, or shifting weight to one leg while standing, the position feels normal even though it is likely to result in long-term problems. Other factors in poor posture include

➤ fatigue
➤ poor muscle tone (especially of the abdomen)
➤ injury
➤ wearing high heels
➤ pregnancy and obesity (which add extra weight to the abdo-men and shift the body's center of gravity)
➤ vision defects (which cause some people to push their head and neck forward)

Good posture means an erect bearing but not a rodlike straightness to the back. That's because the spine should be a straight shaft only when viewed from the front and back. From the side the spine traces a subtle S shape, bending forward slightly at the neck or cervical spine, back in the area of the ribs (thoracic spine), forward again in the lower back or lumbar area, and back again at the sacrum. In a healthy spine the bends are opposite and of approximately equal degree.

Everyday Steps to Natural Health

Proper posture means staying aligned both in static positions such as standing, sitting, and reclining, and in dynamic movements, such as walking, running, and doing daily activities. Here are some ways to improve your posture in your everyday life.

Learn to recognize the warning signs of poor posture. Physical symptoms such as backache and a stiff neck are frequently the result of postural problems. You needn't wait until these develop, however, to gauge your posture. Use a full-length mirror to judge both your standing and sitting posture.

The noted Australian posture and movement innovator F. M. Alexander, then an actor, used this technique to develop his method in the early 1900s. He noticed after watching himself in the mirror that when speaking he tensed his muscles and pulled his head back and down. This depressed his larynx and impaired his breathing, which caused him to lose his voice. Alexander went on to develop a comprehensive program of movement, posture, and body-use instruction for better alignment of the head, neck, and torso.

Looking in a full-length mirror while shifting positions, see if you exhibit any of the following common postural problems:

❑ Head jutting forward, tilted or twisted to one side, or pressing back and down. Your body follows your head. If your head is off center, the rest of your posture is out of kilter. The head should be sitting on top of the spine so that the ears are over the shoulders. Your head weighs twelve to fifteen pounds, as much as a bowling ball; if you can balance it on top of your neck rather than hold it there using various muscles, you'll be freer and more relaxed in your movements.

❑ Shoulders sloped or hiked up toward the ears. When you round off your shoulders, the spine tends to develop a swayback in the lumbar area, resulting in pain and discomfort. You want the shoulders to release out to the sides. This action differs slightly from holding your shoulders back, an action that may result in muscle tension. Ideally the shoulders are on top of and held to the sides of the rib cage.

❑ Chest and rib cage pulled too far forward, ribs sunken or held up rigidly. Your rib cage should be directly above the pelvis.

❑ Lower back overarched or flattened, or stomach sticking too far out or sucked in. The lower back should have a gentle inward arch.

❑ Pelvis tipped forward or to one side. Tipping the pelvis forward causes overarching of the lower back. If it is tipped to one side, one hip will be higher than the other.

❑ Knees locked or knocked, or feet toed in or out. Locking the knees causes your body weight to shift backward onto your heels, while rocking your entire body forward about an inch moves your pelvis and shifts your center of gravity slightly forward. Your feet should be comfortable while pointing straight forward. You want to center your body's weight over the place just behind the balls of your feet.

Feel proper posture. Demonstrate harmonious alignment while lying on the floor. Lie down on your back. Bend your knees and place your feet together on the floor close to your hips. Spread your knees slightly apart. Put your arms on the floor at your sides with the palms up. Roll your pelvis back so that the small of your back at the waistline touches the floor. Push your ribs up and away from your hipbones but don't lift your spine from the floor. Extend your ears away from your lower body but keep your chin at a right angle to your neck. Keep your shoulders back and down, as flat on the floor as possible.

Stand tall. The conventional recommendation of "chest out, chin up" for standing posture is great for displaying metals but a disaster for your lower back, where it causes overarching. It also requires that you keep muscles contracted and thus leads to unnecessary tension.

Another common postural problem when standing is shifting most of your weight onto one leg. Typically, the leg bearing weight is kept straight and the knee locked. This tilts the pelvis and curves the spine. It also crowds the ribs on one side (thus restricting one lung's function) and pushes one shoulder higher than the other.

To achieve proper posture while standing, keep the head balanced over the spine and pelvis. Alexander-technique teachers recommend that you think of the head as being suspended from above, such that an invisible line of support gently pulls the back top part of the head up and away from the body. This lengthens the spine and torso and aligns the entire body under the head. The line should pass through the earlobe, shoulder joint, hip joint, knee joint, and slightly in front of the ankle bone.

The pelvis also plays an important role in standing posture. Rolling it forward or backward can cause either overarching in the lower back or slouching.

"The secret to aligning your pelvis and your rib cage correctly is to unlock your knees," says Judy Alter, author of *Stretch & Strengthen*. "When you stack your thighbone directly above your lower leg bone in a straight line, your pelvis will naturally hang directly down in its correct vertical position . . . by unlocking your knees and stacking your leg bones one on top of the other, you can align almost all of your body correctly."

Sit right. Since many people spend hours at a desk, sitting properly is an excellent posture builder, notes Ronald Kotzsch, a teacher of the Alexander technique in western Massachusetts. "You can maintain good posture," he says, "whether you sit on a stool, which is what I do, or use an executive chair. The principles are the same." He suggests keeping the following points in mind while sitting.

❑ Sit on your sitting bones. The bottom of the pelvis has two arches of bone, known as the ischial tuberosities, whose lower rims make perfect sitting platforms. "These are like the feet when standing," says Kotzsch. They act like columns to support the body's weight as it is passed on by the spine. Unfortunately, most people tilt these columns while sitting and thus negate their structural strength. For instance, when you roll your back down and your bottom under you, part of the weight gets transferred to the lower spine. When you lean forward or backward, shift to one side, or cross your legs, you also make it more difficult for the sitting bones to perform their job correctly. You also contract muscles so that you don't fall over, thus creating unnecessary tension. The most relaxed sitting position balances the torso's weight directly on the sitting bones.

❏ Keep your thighs parallel to the ground and your feet flat on the floor. This allows the feet to support the weight of your legs.

❏ Stay upright and keep your shoulders back. If you write or draw, use a desk with a slightly inclined surface to maintain an erect posture.

❏ Use the chair's back to guide you rather than support you. Unless the chair is poorly designed (and many are), the back should be long, straight, and upright enough to allow you to relax while gently resting your lower and thoracic spine against it. If your lower back lacks a normal inward curve, a lumbar support may be helpful for a time. Over reliance on lumbar supports, however, can cause excessive arching of the lower back.

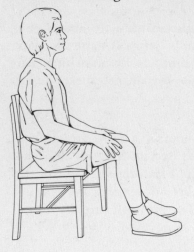

An upright sitting position (top) is a better posture-builder than a cross-legged slouch.

Become more conscious of your posture and unnecessary muscle tension when you move and do physical activities. One of the methods that practitioners of the Alexander technique teach is a type of body-use self-examination. They encourage clients to become more conscious of their bodies during routine activities. For instance, constantly ask yourself whether you feel unnecessary stress or muscle tension while doing something. When you brush your teeth, do you clench your jaw, grip the toothbrush as if it's a murder weapon, and lean over the sink with locked knees? If so, how could you begin to do this activity in a more relaxed manner and with better posture and use of your body?

"I call this 'minimum necessary tension,'" says Kotzsch. "Try picking up a pencil as if it were as light as a feather, which it almost is. Use only those muscles that you need to accomplish the task. Using unnecessary muscles only saps energy from the main task."

Picking up objects considerably heavier than a pencil is a frequent cause of unnecessary tension. Many people clench their teeth, tighten the muscles of the face, or hunch their shoulders up by their ears. You'll find it easier using proper body mechanics (lift with the strong leg muscles, for instance, rather than the much weaker back muscles), contracting the lifting muscles, and trying to relax all other muscles.

Short Tips for Better Posture

❑ Check your auto posture. The driver who is hunched over the steering wheel, his face almost plastered to the windshield, is a menace to himself if not society. Sit back. Keep your legs flexed rather than stretched out straight while driving. Tilt the seat slightly back and use it to support your back in an erect position.

❑ Improve your telephone manner. Tilting your head to the side or cradling the telephone between your head and shoulder often causes neck problems. Lift the receiver to your head (rather than leaning over with head and torso toward the phone) and keep your head aligned with your spine. If your work requires long periods on the phone, consider using a speakerphone or a light, comfortable headset. A cordless phone also allows a greater range of movement.

❑ If you work on a computer, the screen should be about sixteen to twenty-two inches from your head and about twenty degrees below horizontal. Make sure your chair and desk combination allows your hands and lower arms to be relaxed while typing. Use a detachable keyboard for optimum positioning of your hands. Your upper arms should hang straight down and make a ninety-degree angle at the elbow. Your feet should rest flat on the floor.

❏ Do light massage of the back and side of your neck and lower skull. Start by feeling the back of the neck, how the head relates to it and how the muscles often feel tight. Become more aware of what it feels like for your head to go up, lengthening your spine and floating on your body in the natural way that toddlers carry their heads. Learn to relax and stretch those muscles so that your head is more likely to maintain its correct position balanced atop the spine.

❏ While standing, place one foot on a step or footrest. This prevents the pelvis from dropping forward and you'll be able to stand more comfortably. Change feet periodically.

For More Information

Books with useful techniques for improving posture include:

The Alexander Technique by Richard Brennan (Rockport, Mass.: Element, 1991)

The Alexander Technique by Judith Leibowitz and Bill Connington (New York: Harper and Row, 1990)

The Articulate Body by Sidi Hessel (New York: St. Martin's Press, 1978)

To find a practitioner of the Alexander technique in your area, contact:

North American Society of Teachers of the Alexander Technique
P.O. Box 517
Urbana, IL 61801
(800) 473-0620

17

KEEP YOUR BACK
SUPPLE AND STRONG

The bad news is that back problems are epidemic in modern society. An estimated four out of five Americans suffer from backaches at some point in their lives. Backache is second only to the common cold in causing people to stay home from work sick, and second only to childbirth as a reason for hospitalization. The good news is that the overwhelming majority of these problems can be prevented by taking better care of the back. Moreover, some of the same simple activities, exercises, and stretches that can prevent back problems can often also help to treat an existing backache.

Accidents and lifting heavy objects do account for some back problems. For instance, a fall may push vertebrae of the spine out of alignment. Using the muscles of the lower back, instead of the much stronger leg muscles, to lift a bulky object may cause muscles in the back to contract, or spasm. The result may be severe pain or an inability to straighten the back.

Such acute back pain calls for the standard first-aid treatment known as RICE, for rest, ice, compression, and elevation. After the initial pain and swelling has gone down, heat or alternating heat and cold treatments can promote healing.

More frequently, back pain results from long-term habits that have a cumulative, detrimental effect on the back. Because of its central location in the body, the spine is intimately affected by how

131

you hold and move your head, neck, and limbs. The spine is also a major carrier of nerves to and from the brain. Imbalances that affect nerves, muscles, and bones almost anywhere in the body may eventually manifest themselves as back pain.

The role of emotional stress and anxiety in causing back pain is often overlooked, according to Dr. John Sarno, author of *Mind Over Back Pain*. Sarno says that some 80 percent of the backache patients he sees suffer from tension myositis syndrome (TMS), contracted or inflamed muscles of the back that can be traced to an emotional cause. Counseling, relaxation techniques, and suggestions for dealing with stress often lead to permanent cures.

Not all back experts agree that stress is responsible for the majority of back pain. Some of the most commonly cited enemies of the back include

➤ lack of exercise or weak abdominal muscles, which cause added strain on the back muscles

➤ overly tight back muscles, from unbalanced activities or lack of stretching, which limits the back's range of movement and increases the risk of spasm

➤ poor posture, which causes unequal pressures on parts of the spine

➤ high heels, which cause the wearer to lean backward to compensate for the lift in the heels

➤ pregnancy, which causes women to lean backward to compensate for the added weight to the abdomen

➤ heavy loads, such as a large handbag, which when constantly carried on only one side of the body pull body parts out of alignment and cause strain

➤ overly soft mattresses, which when slept on sag in the middle and distort the spine

➤ poorly designed car seats, which when sat in for an extended time cause the sitter to slump into poor posture

If you've addressed and corrected your worst back habits, it is possible that your body or your back has subtle structural problems. A number of natural-health practitioners who do manipulative or movement therapies may be able to help. These include chiropractors, who manipulate the vertebrae of the spine; Feldenkrais practitioners, who use bodywork, exercise, and guided movements to relax and retrain muscles; craniosacral therapists, who work primarily on the membrane sac that envelops the brain and spinal column; Rolfers, who massage and manipulate the fasciae, the web of connective tissue around the muscles and bones, to realign the body; and Alexander-technique practitioners, who teach proper "use" and movement of the body.

Osteopaths, who work on the body's structure by manipulating the muscles, bones, and joints, also frequently have success treating back patients. In a British study, 450 backache sufferers were divided into four groups. One group received conventional painkillers and rest, a second received back braces, a third physiotherapy, and a fourth group was treated by osteopathy. The osteopathy group showed more improvement than the others and yielded more subjects who felt they no longer needed treatment because their condition had improved so much.

Osteopaths hold D. O. (doctor of osteopathy) degrees and are similar to M. D.'s in that they can prescribe drugs and perform minor surgeries. A minority of osteopaths are holistically inclined and use manipulation almost exclusively, while many osteopaths today are almost indistinguishable from conventional medical doctors. Discuss your osteopath's preferred methods of treatment before establishing a relationship. See "For More Information" for organizations that can help you to find osteopaths, chiropractors, Rolfers, and others who treat chronic back problems.

Regardless of whether you work with a back therapist, there is much you can do on your own to both cure and prevent back problems. The relaxation techniques detailed in Step 41 can help you to deal more effectively with emotional stress, thus eliminating a primary cause of back problems. Also see Step 16 for suggestions on how to improve your posture. And choose from among the following effective activities, exercises, and stretches for maintaining a healthy back.

Everyday Steps to Natural Health

Routine back care involves choosing activities that keep your back supple and strong, developing better muscle tone in the back and abdomen, and doing some simple back and leg stretches.

Learn to love the activities that are most likely to be kind to your back. The best activities for the back gently stretch and strengthen the muscles of the abdomen and the spine, while providing the least risk of injury. Your back's muscles are mostly short ones that are not among the body's strongest. It is also easy to injure the muscles of the lower back by doing inappropriate strengthening exercises. For instance, some weight lifters work the back muscles by putting a barbell behind the head and doing deep forward bows, keeping the legs straight. It's possible to strain the back in such a manner even without the added weight.

Sports such as tennis, basketball, baseball, golf, and bowling that require you to twist while bending, arching, jumping, and swinging or lifting an object require a strong back. The pounding associated with jogging and high-impact aerobics can also aggravate a bad back. Rowing machines are rough on the lower back, especially if you have tight hamstring muscles. Bicycling while in a relaxed, upright position is a good exercise for the back. If your bike, however, has handlebars that require you to bend over to reach them, you may find bicycling leads to back problems.

Some of the better sports and activities to strengthen the back and prevent lower back pain include the following:

❑ Swimming and water aerobics. These improve circulation in the back while taking advantage of the water's buoyancy to prevent undue strain. Some people with back problems, however, find that they must swim on their side or back, since doing the crawl or the breaststroke may cause overarching of the back.

❑ Yoga. When done correctly, this time-honored Indian stretching practice safely loosens and strengthens the muscles of the back and abdomen. A good beginning stretch is the twelve-part sun exercise (see Step 12). On the other hand, certain yoga postures, such as those that call for deep forward and backward bends, can strain the lower back. If you have back pain, it is best to have at least a few sessions with a qualified yoga teacher.

❑ Tai chi. This is an ancient oriental movement practice that is part dance and part martial art. The slow, precise movements emphasize balance, agility, and leg strength. While it is possible to learn the basic movements from a book, classes are necessary to refine the subtle aspects of tai chi.

❑ Walking. If you experience back pain from walking, it may be because of a slight difference in the length of your legs. Have them measured and get shoe lifts if necessary.

Other activities that are generally good for the back include skiing and working out on cross-country ski machines.

Exercise to strengthen and balance the muscles that support the lower back and the spine. Sit-ups are the classical abdominal exercise, but not the best one. Exercise physiologists have determined that sit-ups, whether done in the straight-leg or knees-up position, put undue strain on the back. The first few inches of sitting up exercise the abdominal muscles; after that you're using muscles in the lower back that can easily be strained. Here are some safer and more effective abdominal exercises.

❑ Buttock lifts, during the acute stage of back pain (you are experiencing moderate to severe pain or muscle spasms). This is a good exercise for relieving tension and increasing mobility in the lower, or lumbar, region of the back. Lie on your back with your knees bent and your feet flat on the floor about a foot apart. Place your hands next to your thighs, palms down. Tightening your stomach and buttock muscles, slowly lift your buttocks off the floor as high as you can without arching your back. Hold for five seconds and then lower yourself back down. Repeat five times.

❑ Abdominal crunches, during the strengthening stage (pain has subsided and you have normal mobility). Lie on your back with your knees bent and your feet flat on the floor about a foot apart. Place your hands on opposite shoulders. Slowly curl your head and shoulders off the floor a few inches, leaving your lower back flat on the floor. Hold for five seconds and then lower yourself back down. Repeat ten times.

Stretch to relieve back pain. The following stretches can be done both to relieve minor pain of the lower spine and to help prevent back muscles from becoming overly tight and injury prone.

❑ Reclining back stretch, during acute stage. Lie on your back either in bed (if your mattress is firm) or on a carpeted floor. Keeping your legs and hips relaxed, draw your right knee up toward your chest and clasp your hands around the knee. Hold for five seconds while straightening the left leg, then slowly relax and let your leg down. Repeat, switching legs. Unless it causes you pain, try bringing both knees toward the chest and clasping your hands around them.

If this latter position provides dramatic relief from your back pain, you can approximate it for extended periods of time. Lie on your back in front of a chair whose seat is your thigh-length high. You can also use a stack of sofa cushions. Put your arms out to the sides and place your feet and lower legs on the seat. Your lower legs and thighs should form a ninety-degree angle, and your lower back should be resting on the floor. Relax for as long as you need.

Here is a useful variation on the reclining back stretch. Pull your knees up toward your chest. Keeping your legs together, slowly rotate your legs to one side and then the other to stretch and loosen the base of the spine. Stop if you feel pain.

❏ Sitting back stretch, during strengthening stage. Sit on the edge of an upright chair with your feet on the floor. Spread your knees wide enough apart to allow your head and arms to fall between them. Slowly bend forward (stop if you feel pain) and let your shoulders and arms hang loosely between your knees. Remain in this position, which provides a gentle stretch for the lower back, for about ten seconds and then slowly return to an upright position.

To promote better posture and back health, you also need to keep your leg muscles limber, especially the hamstrings in the back of the thigh. "People with tight hamstrings are very prone to have back problems," says Leon Root, M.D., author of *No More Aching Back*. "The tight hamstrings limit normal pelvic motions, which in turn cause a great deal of additional strain on the lower back. Incidentally, until those hamstrings are properly stretched and lengthened, your back problems are likely to recur." (See Step 12 for a simple hamstring stretch.)

Short Tips to a Better Back

❏ Over time, slouching will strain the ligaments in your spine. When sitting, keep your shoulders back and your lower back against the back of the chair. Use a small pillow or lower-back support just above waist height in the back to emphasize the natural curvature of the lower spine.

❏ If your bed is overly soft, firm it up by putting a sheet of three-quarter-inch plywood between the box spring and mattress.

❏ Bend your knees before bending over, whether to lift an object or just to look at something. Your back will thank you.

❏ Stay mobile. Maintaining the same position for long periods of time increases the risk of back strain. If you work at a desk, take a minute or two every hour to get up, stretch, or walk around.

❏ Try the herb valerian *(Valeriana officinalis)* for symptomatic relief of backache. Valerian is primarily used to calm the nerves, but it also reduces muscle tension. An average dose is one to two dropperfuls of the tincture or concentrated drops, taken directly onto the tongue or added to a few ounces of drinking water.

❑ Treat your back to an occasional massage to help reduce muscle tension and improve circulation. Concentrate on the back, neck, and shoulders. For increased soothing effect, add three to five drops of essential oil of lavender per tablespoon of massage oil.

❑ Take extra levels of the following nutrients every day to help promote healing of tissues and relieve stress in the back muscles: bioflavonoids (250–500 mg), calcium (800–1,500 mg) and magnesium (450–650 mg) or a multimineral supplement, and vitamin B complex (50 mg).

❑ If you have a desk job, sit right. Your chair should be high enough for your thighs to be parallel to the ground, your feet to rest flat on the floor, and your elbows to fall at roughly desk height.

For More Information

A simple program for maintaining a healthy back is found in:

No More Aching Back by Leon Root, M.D. (New York: Villard Books, 1990)

To locate a natural-health practitioner who can help you treat or prevent back pain, see "For More Information" after Step 22 for addresses and phone numbers of the following organizations:

American Osteopathic Association
American Chiropractic Association
Feldenkrais Guild
The Upledger Institute (for craniosacral therapy)
North American Society of Teachers of the Alexander Technique
Rolf Institute of Structural Integration

SIMPLE STEPS
TO
NATURAL HEALTH

ENVIRONMENT

CREATE A NONTOXIC
BEDROOM

Unless you lead wilderness expeditions for a living, you're likely to spend one-third of your life in your bedroom. Most of that time you'll be asleep, ideally gaining the rest you need to awaken refreshed and energized. Many factors prevent healthful sleep, including the presence of stimulants or other drugs in the body, medical disorders, and the state of your emotional health (see Step 31 for how to improve your sleep). An often overlooked factor is the indoor environment. Do you have a health-inducing bed and bedroom? Is the air clean and fresh or full of pollutants from toxic materials in the room? Is the room harmoniously arranged and quiet and appropriately lit? The answers to these questions will affect not only the quality of your sleep but also the state of your long-term health. The bedroom is well worth the small amount of effort it takes to make it more safe, healthful, and relaxing.

A number of potential pollutants are often found in the bedroom, ranging from formaldehyde (emitted by carpets, pressed-wood products, and other substances) to trichloroethylene (released from dry-cleaned clothes) to electromagnetic fields (emanating from electric clocks and other electrical appliances). Studies have linked various adverse health effects to such pollutants, including sinusitis and respiratory conditions, itching or burning eyes, headaches, memory problems, light-headedness, nervousness, depression, and even cancer. Removing the source of these pollutants can improve your health, especially if you're one of the increasing numbers of people who are sensitive to small amounts of chemical substances. (Researchers estimate that 10–30 percent of the population may be sensitive to formaldehyde.)

Everyday Steps to Natural Health

Here are some ways to boost the overall healthfulness of your bedroom.

Remove toxic carpeting. One of the most common sources of the harmful chemicals that get into the air of your bedroom is wall-to-wall carpeting. Adults who are experiencing subtle, ongoing health problems should seriously consider removing any wall-to-wall carpeting in the bedroom, according to John Bower, a nontoxic-house builder and consultant, and the author of *The Healthy House*. He says flatly, "When a house or apartment is renovated to reduce indoor pollution, carpeting should be one of the first things removed."

A likely culprit is 4-phenylcyclohexene (4-PC), the distinctive new-carpet-smelling chemical widely used over the past four decades to make the backing on carpets. The carpet industry says that 4-PC is harmless, but an Environmental Protection Agency risk-assessment group predicted that the chemical could create nervous-system and genetic problems. New carpeting can also release formaldehyde and other toxic fumes from chemicals such as ethylbenzene (an eye irritant), toluene, xylene, and styrene. These chemicals are used either to make the synthetically acrylic or polyester fibers of the rug, to produce the carpet's backing, to provide padding, or to treat the carpet so that it resists burning, wrinkling, or staining and repels water and moths.

Adverse health effects are most common among people who sleep in a bedroom with new wall-to-wall carpeting, when chemical outgassing—the evaporation of tiny amounts of carpet compounds in the form of toxic gases—is at its highest levels. After six months to a year the chemical outgassing is usually low enough to affect only those people who are chemically sensitive. As the carpet ages and gets exposed to sunlight, however, it can continue to pollute household air. Its fibers disintegrate into tiny particles that then get kicked up off the floor into the room's air, where they're inhaled.

The potentially toxic particles may also get pulled into the home's hot-air heating system where they're burned. The resulting fumes, which may include toxic gases such as cyanide, then get circulated throughout the house's air supply.

Even wall-to-wall carpeting made with nontoxic compounds (a rare product) poses a potential health hazard since it is extremely difficult to keep clean. Especially when it is thick or high-pile, wall-to-wall carpeting quickly builds up significant quantities of food particles, dander (dead, shedded skin), and all sorts of microorganisms such as dust mites (a common allergy trigger). Researchers who have studied the "sea of microorganisms" in carpets say that they often harbor millions of germs per square foot.

Frequent shampooing or steam cleaning can marginally improve how clean a carpet is, though it has little effect on outgassing since most carpet chemicals are not water soluble. Cleaning products may themselves contain toxic pesticides or other chemicals. Routine vacuuming, on the other hand, may actually worsen carpet-related health conditions since it often pulls organisms up from the base of the carpet to surface layers, where they are more easily kicked up into the air and inhaled.

Wall-to-wall carpeting in children's bedrooms presents an added health concern. Crawling infants and small children are much closer to the floor, where there are likely to be higher levels of lead (tracked in from outdoor soil), microorganisms, and disintegrated carpet particles. Children with allergies or asthma should especially avoid playing on carpeting.

Spray a natural and nontoxic sealant on a wall-to-wall carpet that can't be removed. For instance, Carpet Guard by AFM of Riverside, California, inhibits outgassing and blocks a significant percentage of the chemical fumes emanating from the carpet. It is available by mail order (see "For More Information").

There are a variety of healthful alternatives to wall-to-wall carpeting, including natural-fiber area and throw rugs, oriental carpets, and reed mats. Look for floor coverings without a strong odor from a potentially toxic dye or a chemical treatment such as mothproofing. Keep in mind that some natural-fiber rugs may be made from cotton that has been heavily sprayed with pesticides. A throw rug can be effectively cleaned by bringing it outside, hanging it over a line, and beating it.

Hardwood and other types of floors are admittedly more expensive to install than wall-to-wall carpeting, but over the long run you may save thousands of dollars in health costs. Consider taking steps to avoid toxic glues and finishes if you do install a new floor.

Identify other potential sources of indoor pollution in your bedroom and replace toxic materials with natural alternatives. In addition to wall-to-wall carpeting, common sources of bedroom pollutants include

❑ Pressed-wood furniture. Plywood, particleboard, and other low-quality wood products are typically made using glues or resins that off-gas formaldehyde. If your bedroom contains desks, beds, or chairs that are veneer-covered, they may be giving off formaldehyde.

❑ Polyester and permanent-press blankets, sheets, and curtains. These fabrics are made wrinkle-free by a process that incorporates formaldehyde into the final product.

❑ Dry-cleaned clothes. Dry cleaners remove dirt and stains from fabric by applying toxic solvents such as carbon tetrachloride, trichloroethylene, or perchloroethylene. Exposure to these chemicals has been linked with such symptoms as dizziness, headaches, nausea, and fatigue, as well as major health problems such as liver cancer and permanent nervous-system damage. EPA studies indicate that indoor air does contain higher levels of such chemicals after being exposed to dry-cleaned clothes.

Don't dry-clean clothes unless you must, and if you do, hang the clothes outside or on a porch for a few days before bringing them into the bedroom.

❑ Mothballs and commercial room deodorizers. Mothballs emit a constant supply of toxic vapor. Though mothballs used to be made with natural camphor, most are now produced using either naphthalene or paradichlorobenzene (PDB), both of which are potent synthetic chemicals capable of causing harm to the liver, kidneys, and nervous system. Instead of mothballs you can protect woolen garments by regularly brushing (or wearing) them. Or you can put in your closets containers or cheesecloth sacks of cedar chips or lavender flowers.

PDB is also an ingredient in some commercial room deodorizers. Herbal sachets made from rosemary, mint, or thyme, can be used both as moth repellents and as room deodorizers.

❑ Toxic body-care, office, and art supplies. If your bedroom doubles as a dressing room, office, or art studio, take steps to reduce your use of potentially toxic products like nail-polish remover, typewriter correction fluid, cleaning products, and colored markers. Nontoxic or low-toxic plant-based alternatives exist for virtually every product you may need. See mail-order sources in "For More Information."

Reduce your risk of exposure to high levels of electromagnetic radiation. Within the past decade a number of studies have demonstrated that exposure to electromagnetic fields poses small but measurable health risks. Exactly how much risk is associated with various levels of exposure is controversial. It is easy to get lost in a discussion of complex technical details, but in essence you need to be concerned about three factors:

❑ The field's strength. Scientists have conflicting opinions, but consumer advocates such as Louis Slesin, publisher of the widely respected newsletter *VDT News,* says that in general you want to limit your exposure to fields that measure more than one to three milligauss (mG, a measure of the field's strength).

❑ Your distance from the source of the field. The intensity of electromagnetic fields falls off rapidly as you move away from the generating source. Most small household appliances such as clocks will usually register under 1 mG if you're at least three feet away. Larger appliances such as refrigerators, electric stoves, and televisions may generate a magnetic field that extends eight to ten feet before falling below 1 mG in strength.

❑ How long you spend within the field. Most scientists think that being exposed to a strong field for only a minute or two (as when you blow-dry your hair or use an electric shaver, which may expose the brain to a field that measures 100 mG or stronger) probably poses minimal risks. Most of the studies that have shown adverse health effects have linked leukemia, brain tumors, or miscarriages to long-term (eight hours per day) exposure to lower-strength but longer-lasting fields, such as those that people who sleep under electric blankets are exposed to.

Take a few minutes to survey your bedroom. Do you see any of the following potential sources of strong magnetic fields?

❑ Water bed heaters. These pose a triple whammy: strong fields, in close proximity to the body, for extended periods of time. Unlike electric blankets they're used year-round, too. As if these three strikes against water bed heaters are not enough, these devices also have thermostats that switch the current on and off all night, causing magnetic-field surges that add to the health risk. As an alternative, try covering the water bed with a layer of insulation such as a thick mattress pad so that you don't have to heat the water.

❑ Electric blankets and heating pads. Electric blankets have been measured to have field strengths of 15–50 mG close to the body. Since they're typically used for several hours at a time, they pose more of a risk than most other electrical appliances. As an alternative, use natural-fiber blankets or quilts, or heat the bed with the electric blanket and then unplug the blanket before getting under it. (Don't merely turn it off, since some blankets can maintain a field even while off but plugged in.) Some new electric blankets have the heating wires running in opposite directions to cancel out and thus minimize the magnetic field.

❑ Electric space heaters and electric baseboard heat. In general any device that uses electric coils to produce heat generates a strong magnetic field in the immediate vicinity. This includes blow-dryers, electric ovens or burners, and electric heaters. Don't place a space heater right up against your bed, or your baby's crib. At even a foot away the field can measure 8 mG.

❑ Nightstand clocks. The small motors that run the hands on most electric clocks can give off a significant magnetic field. Switch to digital clocks or battery-operated clocks, which have a negligible field, or move your electric clock to at least five feet away from your head.

❑ Televisions and cathode-ray tube (CRT) video display terminals (VDTs). Both of these electrical devices create a picture by shooting a beam of electrons toward the back of the picture screen—in other words, toward the face of the watcher or user. The electrons strike phosphors, releasing visible light used to create pictures or letters. Visible light, however, is not the only form of electromagnetic radiation released. The technology may also give off not only small amounts of X rays but also a variety of nonionizing radiation frequencies. The radiation disperses in all directions, too, and EM fields go through wood and other building materials, so consider moving a TV or computer on the other side of a wall if it is routinely on when you or children are in bed.

★ ★ ★

Appliances like the above can often be easily moved or re-arranged to lower exposures. If you want to take the next step and check ambient background levels, you'll need to buy a monitor (see "For More Information") or hire an electrician or other specially trained person to take measurements. They may find other sources of electromagnetic fields in the bedroom, including

❏ The electrical-service drop. This is where your home's main electric supply line comes from the street into your home. If the electric-service drop is located directly outside a bedroom wall, you may have high field readings near the area in the bedroom. In that case either move the bed to the opposite side of the room, or don't use the room as a bedroom. You might also consider getting the field measured to make sure even that distance is safe.

❏ Wires running under the bed. Move the bed or have an electrician move the wires.

High ambient levels may also result from improper wall wiring, erroneous electrical grounding, or nearby distribution lines or pole-mounted step-down transformers.

Help to harmonize the natural flow of energy through your bedroom by using the oriental art and science of fêng shui. Literally "wind" and "water," fêng shui is the ancient practice of situating buildings, rooms, and furniture in ways that encourage harmony with nature. The Chinese and other oriental peoples have long believed that life and nature are imbued with currents of subtle energy they call *qi*. Acupuncture is a way to direct and control the *qi* flowing through the body's channels, or meridians. Fêng shui is acupuncture on home and nature: a way to allow the free and harmonious flow of *qi* through and around buildings and rooms.

For interior design, the principal tools of fêng shui are placement of furniture within the room, and the use of mirrors and wind chimes to deflect or redirect energy as it flows through a room.

Sarah Rossbach, a fêng shui consultant and author of *Interior Design with Feng Shui,* notes that a harmoniously arranged bedroom is particularly advantageous to the health of the inhabitant. The chief way to ensure a smooth and balanced flow of *qi* throughout the bedroom is to ideally situate the bed relative to the door. The bed should be positioned such that the person lying on it has a wide perspective and clear view of the door. Fêng shui has a solid base in common sense: having a door at one's back, whether in a bedroom or an office, allows persons to enter the room without your knowledge and thus startle you. The long-term effect is to make you continually uneasy and jumpy.

An ideal bed placement is catercorner, or opposite and facing the door. Windows are also a consideration, since it's best not to locate the bed directly under a window. When the bed can't be situated to afford a good view of the door, hang a mirror in a place that allows you to see from the bed directly to the door. On the other hand, don't put a mirror directly facing (or on the ceiling over) the bed such that you can see your reflection while lying in bed, since fêng shui masters contend that is disturbing to the spirit. Also try not to situate the bed directly under a beam or a ceiling that slopes down toward the bed, both of which create oppressive feelings in the sleeping person.

Short Tips for a Natural Bedroom

❏ As a safety measure, keep radios, stereos, phones, answering machines, and other electric appliances in the bedroom at least five feet away from the bed.

❏ Remove your shoes before entering your home to track fewer pollutants onto your carpeting.

❏ Keep some houseplants in your bedroom as living air filters. According to studies, spider plants, philodendrons, peace lilies, and orchids do remove such pollutants from household air. Houseplants are not as efficient as mechanical air filters, but they're a lot quieter, cheaper to run, and more attractive.

For More Information

Mail-order sources for nontoxic building and cleaning products include:

AFM Enterprises
1960 Chicago Ave., E7
Riverside, CA 92507
(909) 781-6860
Sells Carpet Guard to reduce off-gassing of toxic carpet fumes.

The Natural Choice
1365 Rufina Circle
Santa Fe, NM 87502
(505) 438-3448

Mail-order sources for natural bed products include:

Dona Designs
1611 Bent Tree St.
Seagoville, TX 75159
(214) 287-7834

Janice Corporation
198 U. S. Highway 46
Budd Lake, NJ 07828
(800) 526-4237

The Cotton Place
P. O. Box 59721
Dallas, TX 75229
(214) 243-4149

Better Bed
4760 Grand Ave. S.
Minneapolis, MN 55409
(612) 822-9604

Bean Products, Inc.
5338 N. Winthrop
Chicago, IL 60640
(800) 726-8365

The following books offer advice on how to identify, avoid, or minimize indoor pollutants:

A Consumer's Dictionary of Household, Yard and Office Chemicals by Ruth Winter (New York: Crown Publishers, 1992)

The Healthy House by John Bower (New York: Lyle Stuart, 1989)

The Nontoxic Home & Office by Debra Lynn Dadd (Los Angeles: Jeremy P. Tarcher, Inc., 1992)

Nontoxic & Natural by Debra Lynn Dadd (Los Angeles: Jeremy P. Tarcher, Inc., 1984)

The following books offer background on electromagnetic fields:

Warning: The Electricity Around You May Be Hazardous to Your Health by Ellen Sugarman (New York: Fireside, 1992)

Cross Currents: The Perils of Electropollution, The Promise of Electromedicine by Robert O. Becker, M.D. (Los Angeles: Jeremy P. Tarcher, Inc., 1990)

Books on fêng shui include:

The Feng Shui Handbook by Derek Walters (London: The Aquarian Press, 1991)

Interior Design with Feng Shui by Sarah Rossbach (New York: E. P. Dutton, 1987)

The following is a mail-order source for EM-field monitors and other environmental detection equipment:

The Cutting Edge Catalog
P. O. Box 5034
Southampton, NY 11969
(800) 497-9516
(516) 287-3813

19

MAKE YOUR
WORKPLACE SAFE

It's important that your office or workplace be conducive to better health since, like your bedroom, you're likely to spend one-third of your life there. Indoor environments with even low levels of some pollutants can cause sick-building syndrome, in which workers suffer from headaches, sinus infections, dizziness, allergic reactions, and other conditions. In effect, the building is sick from exposure to toxins and not being able to breathe properly, and it contagiously passes on the illness to those it shelters. One estimate by the World Health Organization is that almost one in three new or remodeled buildings have unusually high worker complaints.

The problem has become especially acute in recent years as the need for greater energy conservation has caused architects to design structures that are almost airtight and are totally dependent on mechanical ventilation for fresh air. Since windows no longer open, if air filters and cleaners wear out or become clogged, pollutants, microorganisms, molds, and spores fill the indoor air. A detailed investigation may be needed to determine the source of the pollution.

Improving the ventilation in your workplace is often a necessary first step toward better health on the job. If you work in a building with nonfunctioning windows, identify the vents in your area and if possible clear the space around them. Hold a piece of tissue paper in front of the vent to see if it is working. If it's not, talk to a

151

supervisor or the building manager about the system. Dirty air-conditioning and humidifying units are common problems. An office or desktop air filter is a last-resort solution to polluted indoor air.

Everyday Steps to Natural Health

Even if you work in a drafty old building with plenty of fresh air, you can do much to ensure a healthful work environment.

Take steps to eliminate secondhand smoke at your workplace. By now there can be no doubt that the health risks associated with inhaling the drug nicotine into the lungs—from smoke out of either end of a cigarette—include such major killers as lung cancer and heart attack. At least thirty major scientific studies, many done within the past five years, support the evidence for major health risks from secondhand smoke. A recent Environmental Protection Agency (EPA) report estimates that passive smoking—inhaling the secondhand smoke from other people's cigarettes—kills three thousand nonsmoking Americans annually from lung cancer alone. If you're being constantly exposed to cigarette smoke as you work, it is possible that it poses a greater risk to your future health than any other indoor pollutant.

If your office is not smoke-free, organize to make it so. Increasingly, local, state, and federal regulations and court decisions are on your side. Inform company management that employers who refuse to offer a smoke-free working environment may subsequently be sued by employees who develop smoke-related illnesses. "Any employer that permits unrestricted smoking is asking for it, just as if they had particles of asbestos leaking from the ceiling," says John Banzhaf, executive director of the Washington, D. C.–based citizens' group Action on Smoking and Health.

Form a coalition of like-minded coworkers, present a plan to the company, and don't settle for anything less than smoke-free conditions.

Improve your lighting. Working all day in dim, uneven, or flickering light is sure to take a toll on your eyes. Many people now work in offices whose sole illumination is from overhead fluorescents, which often give off a harsh light concentrated in the yellow band of the light spectrum. The pioneering light and health researcher John Ott, Ph. D., author of *Light, Radiation, & You*, says that such light causes the body to release higher levels of certain metabolic hormones related to stress. His research has also tied "mal-illumination" to behavioral conditions, vision problems, and fatigue. Along with the other advocates of natural light, he says that full-spectrum light is best for keeping the body healthy. Light affects bodily functions ranging from calcium absorption and hormone secretion to emotional stability. Consider taking some of the following steps to improve your workplace's light environment.

❏ Switch to color-corrected incandescent bulbs, or better yet to full-spectrum fluorescent lamps such as the Vita-Lite, which has spectral characteristics similar to natural sunlight. If your light diet is seriously deficient, you might consider a high-tech multibulb system such as those that have been developed for use by sufferers of seasonal affective disorder, or SAD, which is common in light-deprived areas of the world like Scandinavia.

❏ Wash your windows and take other steps to unblock the light from natural sources. Natural light is usually many times brighter than anything from an artificial light source.

❏ Cross-illuminate your desktop and computer screen. Adjustable-neck lights placed three to four feet from the desk work well to diffuse light over your work area and reduce stressful glare. Light levels should be consistent around your work area. Avoid making your eyes repeatedly adjust from a bright computer screen to a dim piece of paper on your desk, for instance. Also avoid placing fluorescent light fixtures and lamps right next to your head, since fluorescents emit stronger electromagnetic fields than do conventional incandescent bulbs.

Reduce your exposure to toxic substances commonly found in the workplace. Some of the most common toxins in offices include those found in homes, including building materials that off-gas formaldehyde and other toxic substances.

As it is in bedrooms (see Step 18), synthetic carpeting is a major source of indoor pollution in offices. This was dramatically illustrated by the 1987 incident in which the EPA created a "sick building"—and sick employees—when it installed new carpeting at its headquarters offices in Washington, D. C. Some ten percent of the EPA employees in the building began to suffer from a variety of health problems, including burning eyes, memory problems, light-headedness, nervousness, and depression. Congressional pressure recently forced carpet manufacturers to agree to put warning labels on new carpets to alert consumers to the side effects carpet chemicals cause.

Some of the other most common sources of office toxins include

➤ copying machines, laser printers, and plain-paper fax machines, which may allow ozone and other fumes to accumulate if not properly maintained and well ventilated
➤ room dividers, bookcases, and desks made from particleboard and plywood, which off-gas formaldehyde
➤ upholstered chairs that use polyurethane foam for padding and are covered with acrylic or polyester that is coated with formaldehyde to resist stains
➤ office supplies including typewriter correction fluid, epoxy, rubber cement, and permanent-ink pens and markers (water-based correction fluid and markers are less toxic)

Interrupt your workday for frequent brief stretching sessions. Here are a few you can try without even getting up from your chair. Try to hold each for thirty to sixty seconds, at a point where you feel the stretch but don't have actual pain.

❏ To help improve your posture and relieve tension in your upper body, roll your shoulders by rotating them five to ten times in a forward direction then an equal number of times backward.
❏ Stretch deltoids and other shoulder muscles by raising one arm and lowering the other so that you grasp your fingers behind your back. Hold the position for thirty seconds, and then reverse sides.
❏ Interlock your fingers and then stretch your arms out in front of you, pushing your palms away from your body. Keeping the fingers interlocked and the arms straight, raise your hands so that the palms are facing the ceiling.
❏ To help keep wrists and hands supple, extend your arms in front of you, grab the tops of the fingers of one hand with the other hand, and pull back the hand to flex your wrist. Reverse hands and repeat.
❏ Interlock your fingers and place the palms of your hands on the back of your head. Pull your elbows up and back to stretch the chest muscles.

Short Tips for a Safer Workplace

❏ Reduce your exposure to hazardous electromagnetic pollution generated by computers. Since magnetic fields can be generated from the side and back of computers, adjust your desk so that a coworker's computer is not within two to three feet of you.

❏ Substitute safer herbs for coffee (see Step 38). Caffeine is the most commonly abused office drug, used by virtually the entire American workforce. Drinking coffee, tea, and cola to excess may cause various health problems, including nervousness, insomnia, stomach and bladder irritations, indigestion, and urinary problems.

❏ Help to harmonize the natural flow of energy through your office by using the ancient oriental art and science of fêng shui, which shows how to situate buildings, room, and furniture in ways that encourage harmony with nature (see Step 18). Just as the position of your bed is the most important consideration in the bedroom, in your office the proper positioning of the desk relative to the door is crucial. The desk should be positioned such that the person sitting at it has a wide perspective and a clear view of the door. This prevents persons from entering your office without your knowledge, thus possibly startling you and keeping you continually "on edge." An ideal desk placement is catercorner, or opposite and facing, the door. When the desk can't be situated to afford a good view of the door, hang a mirror in a place that allows you to see the door from your desk.

For More Information

(See Step 18 for mail-order sources for nontoxic building and cleaning products and for books with useful discussions of indoor pollutants and fêng shui.)

Mail-order sources of full-spectrum lights include:

Bob Corey and Associates
P. O. Box 73
Merrick, NY 11566
(516) 485-5544

Duro-Test Corporation
9 Law Dr.
Fairfield, NJ 07004
(800) 289-3876

Ott BioLightSystems, Inc.
28 Parker Way
Santa Barbara, CA 93101
(800) 234-3724

For further information on computer health and electromagnetic fields:

Computer Health Hazards by Marija Matich Hughes (Washington, D. C.: Hughes Press, 1990)

Contact the following organization for more information on secondhand smoke:

Action on Smoking and Health
2013 H St., N. W.
Washington, DC 20006
(202) 659-4310

20

HERE COMES THE SUN

Sunlight has taken a beating from health authorities in recent years. It is now being blamed for a long list of human ills, including wrinkling of the skin, premature aging, and vision defects. In addition, more Americans suffer from cancers of the skin than any other type of cancer, and according to the Skin Cancer Foundation sunlight is the cause of at least 90 percent of skin cancers. Scientists point to findings like the following to support their contention that sunlight constitutes a major health hazard:

❑ Australia, a sunny area where many fair-skinned northern peoples have settled, has the highest rate of skin cancer in the world. In the U.S., an American's lifetime risk of developing a melanoma has increased in the past fifty years from one in 1,500 to one in 120.

❑ More and more ultraviolet radiation (UVR), a part of the sunlight energy spectrum that most scientists cite as especially hazardous to health, is reaching the earth's surface now than in the past. That's because the ozone layer of the earth's atmosphere, which blocks some UVR, is being depleted by chlorofluorocarbon pollution.

❑ Animal studies suggest that UVR is a factor in causing macular degeneration, a vision disease involving the area of the retina responsible for central vision.

Such findings have led an increasing number of health authorities to take the position that virtually all exposure to the sun is detrimental. Many dermatologists say flatly that children should always wear sunscreen when outdoors, contending that a powerful sunscreen with an SPF (sun protection factor) of at least fifteen should be applied to children's skin routinely every morning. These doctors speak of sunscreen as an essential daily hygiene product, like toothpaste. The UCLA School of Public Health doctors who wrote *50 Simple Things You Can Do to Save Your Life* have nary a positive word about sunlight, noting only that "'soaking up some rays,' even in everyday activities, could be costly." Among their recommendations: "Use sunscreen, even if you're not at the beach."

"There is no question," says optometrist Jacob Liberman, Ph.D., author of *Light: Medicine of the Future,* that UVR light "in large amounts is harmful; in trace amounts, as in natural sunlight, it acts . . . as a 'life-supporting nutrient' that is highly beneficial. Is it possible that science has gone too far?"

Despite the recent antisun hysteria, there are two important reasons why you should regularly expose yourself to some sun and avoid habitual use of sunscreen:

1. Some sunlight is necessary and even beneficial to health. Sunlight's many health benefits are well documented. Researchers now know that ultraviolet rays from sunlight strike the skin and produce vitamin D_3, a hormonelike substance that helps the body absorb calcium and other minerals from the diet. (Vitamin D occurs naturally in only a few foods, such as egg yolks.) Too little sunlight leads to rickets in children and osteomalacia in adults, characterized by weak and porous bones that become misshapen or break easily. Sunlight also plays a major role in maintaining the body's biological rhythms and secreting of essential hormones. Without sufficient sunlight a person may suffer from depression or frequent mood swings.

2. Sunlight may actually prevent some cancers, including, surprisingly enough, melanoma. A number of scientists have explored the role of sunlight, vitamin D, and calcium in preventing cancer. Some of the most striking work in the field has been done by two scientists, Cedric and Frank Garland, brothers in the San Diego area. Cedric is director of the epidemiology program at the UC San Diego Cancer Center, and Frank is head of occupational medicine at the Naval Health Research Center. Over the past twenty years they've

published their findings in *The Lancet,* the *International Journal of Epidemiology,* and other major medical journals. In a study they published in 1990, they described their findings related to U. S. sailors who had contracted melanoma, the second most common malignancy among sailors (after cancer of testicles). The Garlands expected to find that sailors who spent the most time outdoors in the sun would have the highest rates of melanoma; and that melanomas would be more likely to appear on parts of the body with the most exposure to the sun, such as the head and arms.

To their surprise, neither of these expectations was supported by the data. Rather, sailors with the highest rates of melanoma were those whose jobs required them to work indoors and thus had the least exposure to sun. Sailors who worked outdoors had fewer melanomas. But those who worked both indoors and outdoors, and thus got brief but regular sun, had the lowest rate. Also, melanomas were more common on the trunk of the body than on the head and arms.

Another set of studies supporting a cancer-preventive role for moderate sunlight found that, both in the U. S. and the former U. S. S. R., women living in northern climes suffer from higher rates of fatal breast cancers. Some researchers believe that the extra cancers are due to lower average levels of sunlight.

Everyday Steps to Natural Health

Here are some suggestions for optimizing your exposure to natural sunlight.

As a general guideline, try to get outside and expose yourself to thirty to sixty minutes of natural light each day. Most health experts agree that approximately fifteen to twenty minutes of direct exposure to the sun, on your face, arms, and hands, every day is sufficient to confer sunlight's various benefits. In addition, it is worthwhile to try to spend an hour or so outside being exposed to natural light, even if in the shade. Remove your glasses or contacts to allow your eyes to absorb some full-spectrum light, including UVR.

While sitting or working indoors, try to spend some time under a skylight or next to an open window. Artificial indoor light is no substitute for sunlight, for a number of reasons:

❏ The light in even a well-lit indoor room is only one-tenth as bright as outdoor light, and glass blocks most UVR.

❏ The spectrum of artificial lights does not closely match that of sunlight. With the exception of some special light systems used to prevent seasonal affective disorder or "the winter blues," most bulbs have little UVR and an unbalanced color spectrum.

Elderly shut-ins and nursing-home residents are not the only people who may routinely be getting insufficient regular exposure to natural light. Office workers who spend the whole day indoors and work in windowless, artificially lit rooms may not be getting enough sunlight, for instance. (When those workers then go on a three-week winter vacation to sunny Jamaica and expose themselves every day to eight to ten hours of intense sun, they're compounding the risk of suffering adverse effects.) In addition, some 25 million U. S. workers are employed during night shifts and thus often get insufficient full-spectrum light.

Avoid excessive use of sunglasses and tinted contacts. Sunglasses reduce glare and brightness but also block certain portions of the light spectrum from entering through the eyes, including some UVR. The latest models block nearly all the UVR; light researcher John Ott, Ph. D., recommends models that meet only the minimum FDA standards for transmission of UVR. Even if you're getting plenty of UVR, overuse of sunglasses can make your eyes light sensitive. When a bright day, high altitudes, or other conditions do call for sunglasses, choose lenses colored a neutral gray, which reduces light intensity in a balanced manner, rather than pink, blue, or some other fashionable color. It's also a good idea to avoid overuse of contacts tinted in various shades that allow the eyes to receive unbalanced light.

Watch out for the midday sun, when its rays are the strongest. Scientists distinguish two types of burning rays: ultraviolet A (UVA) and B (UVB). The shorter UVB rays are strongest between ten A.M. and two P.M. and cause most cases of sunburn. Longer UVA rays predominate in early morning and late afternoon. Though less frequently the main cause of a skin injury, they can burn and they can cause photosensitivity reactions as well. Since ultraviolet rays can pass through clouds, certain conditions call for extra caution:

❑ People with delicate skin, red or blond hair, and blue eyes burn more easily than do darker-skinned people. Dermatologists say that fair-skinned people can damage their skin even while slowly getting tan.

❑ High altitudes allow for greater exposure to burning rays. At six thousand feet the skin burns twice as fast as at sea level.

❑ Certain substances can increase your susceptibility to sunburning. These include some prescription drugs (tetracycline and certain oral contraceptives, antihistamines, and tranquilizers); food additives (including saccharine); some sunscreens; and skin contact with certain plants and essential oils (including lemon and bergamot).

Some of the photosensitizing agents can not only make sunburn worse, they may cause a type of allergic reaction known as photoallergy.

If you have overdosed on sunlight, use natural remedies to treat a sunburn. Like any burn, sunburn should be immediately treated to cool the skin and prevent ongoing damage. Some natural remedies that work especially well for sunburn include the following:

❑ Spread on soothing fresh aloe. Most natural practitioners agree that fresh aloe is best. Aloe requires little more than occasional watering to grow, so it's an easy houseplant to keep around. To use it, first clean and cool the burn with water. Break a few inches off one of the older, lower leaves of the aloe plant, slice it lengthwise, squeeze its gel onto the burn, and allow it to dry. It is especially effective to use as soon as possible on first-or second-degree burns. Reapply four to six times a day.

Fresh aloe is safe to use on broken skin, and it can also be applied after healing begins. Allergic reactions are uncommon, but discontinue use if one does occur. Aloe gel should not be taken internally for a burn.

Though some bottled aloe products may not contain the healing ingredients of fresh aloe, others do and can be effective. Look for juices or gels of 96–100 percent pure aloe, without mineral oil, paraffin waxes, or coloring, and that haven't been "stabilized" or preserved with alcohol, which will neutralize aloe's skin-healing properties.

A plant in the lily family, aloe has been used to treat burns and wounds for thousands of years. Scientific studies done over the past fifty years support its power to speed the healing of burns and help prevent infection. Most dramatically, a recent animal study reported in the medical journal *Plastic and Reconstructive Surgery* showed that aloe-treated burns healed in an average of thirty days while untreated burns took fifty.

❏ Apply vitamin E to the burn. Vitamin E oil is available in capsules or bottles at drugstores, supermarkets, and natural-food stores. For a small burn, simply puncture a vitamin E capsule and gently cover the burned area with the oil. Some brands of vitamin E may sting, so you should test it first on a small area. To apply to a larger area, spray on vitamin E using an oil atomizer. Repeat every one to four hours. Also consume 400–800 IU of the vitamin daily.

This topical vitamin therapy is one of the most popular and effective home treatments for minor burns. Vitamin E can help promote healing and prevent scars from forming even for third-degree burns. Vitamin E oil can be combined with other substances, too. For instance, you can squeeze some aloe from a leaf and mix it with vitamin E out of a capsule.

❏ Apply chamomile cream that's been mixed with five to six drops of the essential oil of peppermint. Herbalist Christopher Hobbs notes that this has an immediate cooling and anti-inflammatory effect.

❏ Splash some vinegar onto the burn, or apply cool compresses soaked in whole milk. Exactly why these folk remedies seem to soothe a sunburn is a mystery, though many people swear they're effective treatments.

Help protect your skin after a sunburn by taking extra antioxidants. Antioxidants protect the body against the effects of free radicals, reactive and unstable atoms or molecules (from UVR, chemicals, smoke, fatty foods, and other sources) that are damaging to living cells. Antioxidant nutrients such as vitamins A, C, and E, and herbs such as ginkgo, can combine with and neutralize free radicals without themselves becoming unstable, thus defending the body against harmful effects that may range from cancer to aging.

Take vitamin A in the form of beta carotene (10,000–20,000 IU daily), vitamin C (500–1,500 mg), vitamin E (400–800 IU daily), and the herb ginkgo (*Ginkgo biloba,* an ancient Chinese herb; take 40 mg three times per day of a standardized extract containing 24 percent ginkgo heterosides). These will help control free radicals formed by the sun's burning rays. (See Step 29 on cancer prevention for more information about antioxidants.)

Short Tips for Optimizing Your Light Exposure

❑ Limit your exposure to sunlight using clothing, hats, and shade rather than sunscreen. Creating or using shade is one of the simplest and easiest ways to block out excessive sunlight. Wide-brimmed hats and loose, light-colored cotton clothes can keep you cool even in direct sunlight. (UVR can penetrate some light clothing.)

❑ Avoid overusing sunscreens. According to a number of scientists, including sunlight researchers Frank and Cedric Garland, sunscreens may block healthful portions of the light spectrum and even promote skin cancer. Liberman says, "My first recommendation for sunbathing is to gradually build up your time in the sun and to use no sunscreens if you have moderate to dark skin."

❑ If you do need a sunscreen and have fair skin and burn easily, choose one with a rating of twelve to fifteen. If you sometimes tan lightly, you can use six to twelve, while if you burn infrequently or almost never (even black skin can burn sometimes), try a sunscreen rated two to six.

For More Information

Books with useful discussions of natural light include:

The Light Book: How Natural and Artificial Light Affect Our Health, Mood, and Behavior by Jane Wegscheider Hyman (Los Angeles: Jeremy P. Tarcher, Inc., 1990)

Light: Medicine of the Future by Jacob Liberman, O. D., Ph. D. (Santa Fe, N. M.: Bear & Company, 1991)

Cancer Therapy: The Independent Consumer's Guide to Non-Toxic Treatment and Prevention by Ralph W. Moss, Ph. D. (New York: Equinox Press, 1992)

The following organization provides general information about therapeutic treatments using light. Send an SASE to:

Society for Light Treatment and Biological Rhythms
P. O. Box 478
Wilsonville, OR 97070
(503) 694–2404

The following is a mail-order source for bulbs and fixtures for full-spectrum lighting, books on light and health, UV-transparent sunglasses, and more (see Step 19 for mail-order sources of full-spectrum lights):

The Cutting Edge Catalog
P. O. Box 5034
Southamptom, NY 11969
(800) 497–9516
(516) 287–3813

SIMPLE STEPS
TO
NATURAL HEALTH

THE HEALING
TOUCH

21

DIAGNOSE YOURSELF

As medical costs continue to spiral out of control, more and more people are attempting to treat their minor illnesses with natural medicines and home remedies. People are also increasingly concerned that they become aware of degenerative diseases at the earliest possible moment. Two unique medical approaches offer help to such people: the Eastern art of "visual diagnosis" or "body reading" and the Western science of do-it-yourself testing. Using either or both allows anyone safely and accurately to gain important insights into his or her state of health.

Perhaps because their culture and technology emphasized an approach to the body and illness based on subtle energies, traditional healers in the Orient became expert at examining the body. Both in China and Japan, visual appraisal of the face, hands, tongue, hair, and other body parts played an important role in diagnosis. For traditional oriental healers, internal health is reflected externally. Looking closely at a person's lines, features, posture, and so forth can reveal both constitution (a person's inherent physical strengths and weaknesses) and his or her current condition, whether healthy or ill. For instance, from the Eastern perspective close-set eyes point to an intellectually and emotionally sharp character, but also one who may have trouble with the liver, pancreas, spleen, and kidneys. Oriental healers also say that a bulbous, red nose reflects stress on the heart and is possibly a sign of a heart condition. Western scientists have begun to confirm some of the surprising connections made between visual diagnosis and states of health. A certain type of crease on the earlobe, for example, is now accepted by conventional doctors as a warning sign of heart disease.

In the West, the tools of diagnosis are scientific lab tests, an estimated 150 of which can now be done by the layperson at home, to diagnose pregnancy, blood pressure, allergies, and more. Three trends in the past decade have spurred the growth of the home lab-test industry, according to Michael Castleman, coauthor of *Before You Call the Doctor:*

> ➤ the upsurge of interest in self-care
> ➤ technological developments such as microelectronics and monoclonal antibodies that have allowed devices to become smaller, lower priced, and more accurate
> ➤ the pace of modern life. "Who has time to make the trip to the doctor's office?" Castleman asks. "At a time when millions of Americans put such a premium on their leisure time, it's no wonder that they avoid time-consuming trips to the doctor if possible."

A fourth trend might be added: the growing number of people without health insurance. People who pay each time they visit a doctor will often choose to use a $15 home pregnancy test than spend $50–100 to get the news from a doctor.

Women have long been using self-diagnosis and examination to predict ovulation and thus either avoid or become pregnant. Today, new developments in home testing make this form of fertility control even easier and more reliable. Along with pregnancy tests and blood-glucose monitors for diabetics, home lab tests now represent a half-billion-dollar-per-year industry. Other home-diagnosis tools that have recently become available include those that can monitor your heart rate and test your body fat. In the near future these may be joined by home tests for strep throat, AIDS, and vitamin and mineral levels.

Self-diagnosis is not without its perils—simply being wrong chief among them. Recognize your limitations as a diagnostician. Don't ignore or misread signs of serious illness. Some symptoms are so serious (difficulty breathing, sudden loss of coordination or slurred speech, poisoning, and unexpected loss of consciousness, among others) that if you experience them, you should immediately call your health-care practitioner or go to the emergency room. If you are diagnosing your child, keep in mind that some conditions that adults recover from quickly (diarrhea or sore throat, for instance) can be more difficult to diagnose and treat in a child or infant. If a physical sign or a home-diagnosis test conflicts with obvious symptoms, test again or see your health-care practitioner. Self-diagnosis ideally allows you to work more closely with your health-care practitioner, rather than to drop him or her.

Everyday Steps to Natural Health

Your body offers insight into what is happening inside it through a variety of physical and emotional clues. Becoming more astute at reading these clues can be the difference between a short illness and a protracted one, or even between life and death.

Learn how to use the growing number of simple lab tests that can be done in your home. The most popular home lab tests include those that assist diagnosis of the following conditions:

❑ Pregnancy. Women put a few drops of early-morning urine onto a dot containing monoclonal antibodies. The antibodies detect a hormone that shows up in the urine shortly after becoming pregnant. The test takes only a few minutes and costs about $15.

❑ Urinary tract infection (UTI). The user soaks a tiny dipstick in urine to detect nitrites that increase when you have a UTI. The test is about 90 percent accurate; a pack of twelve strips cost $12–15.

❑ Cholesterol. Two types of tests are now available, using either a test strip or a thermometerlike gauge. You need to prick your finger and draw a few drops of blood. The tests take about fifteen minutes and approach laboratory tests in accuracy, though the home tests do not distinguish between so-called good and bad cholesterol. The strips cost about $10–15 per test while the gauge runs about $50 and is good for three uses.

❑ Colorectal cancer. This test can be a lifesaver, since more Americans die from colorectal cancer than any other cancer with the exception of lung cancer (among nonsmokers colorectal is the leading cause of cancer death). If colorectal cancer is detected early, however, it has a relatively high survival rate. Health authorities encourage people over the age of fifty to be tested for colorectal cancer annually.

The most popular home lab test makes use of a chemically impregnated toilet paper to detect tiny amounts of blood in the stool. It costs only $5 per test. Unfortunately, recent studies indicate this is one of the least accurate home lab tests, yielding a high rate of false negatives (the test fails to detect an existing tumor) and false positives (since blood in the stools may be due to conditions other than cancer). You can raise the accuracy rate by closely following test instructions.

❏ Kidney disorders. The user dips special color-coded strips into his or her urine to detect protein or blood, signs of possible kidney problems. A packet of a dozen strips costs $12–15.

❏ Blood-sugar disorders. Specially formulated urine dip strips can also be used to detect diabetes. The strips measure microglycosuria in the urine and are virtually 100 percent accurate. A container of a dozen strips costs approximately $15. Confirmed diabetics often use home lab tests to monitor their blood-sugar, or glucose, levels. This allows them to take steps to control their blood-sugar levels, whether by taking insulin or eating certain foods. Home lab tests that cost $50–100 can measure glucose levels in blood.

Put together a personalized doctor kit to help you diagnose simple conditions in you and your family. These tools might include the familiar thermometer as well as the following tools previously reserved for medical doctors:

❏ Blood-pressure monitors. Many people who are obese or have a personal or family history of heart disease are purchasing their own blood-pressure monitors. Chronic high blood pressure increases your risk of heart disease. Home monitors allow periodic testing and may be more accurate than readings taken in doctors' offices (where you are more likely to be tense and anxious).

There are various types of home blood-pressure monitors. The most popular is similar to the devices used by doctors, in which a cuff is slipped around the upper arm or the wrist and slightly inflated by pumping on a small bulb. A newer technology allows you to slip a finger into a hand-sized computerized device. Both types provide systolic-diastolic pressures and your pulse rate and don't require the use of a stethoscope. Finger blood-pressure monitors are not as accurate as arm-cuff monitors, according to an analysis by *Consumer Reports* in May 1992. Costs range from $60–150, depending upon options such as automatic pressurization and digital readouts.

❑ Earscopes, or otoscopes. Parents with young children can, with some study and practice, use an earscope to diagnose ear infections before they become acute. Earscopes cost $25–75.

❑ Breathing, or peak-flow, monitors. Asthma sufferers can use breathing monitors, which measure the force of exhalation, to predict when an asthma attack may become serious.

Hone your skills at observing your body's subtle external signs of illness. Some illnesses at their height will cause dramatic, observable physical symptoms, such as skin rashes. Yet how often do you hear about the person who was supposedly healthy until he or she suddenly dropped dead from a heart attack or was diagnosed with an advanced cancer? Were there really no early signs of illness, or were the victims unaware of what signs there were?

Becoming expert at the oriental form of visual diagnosis is a lifelong undertaking, but there are some basic signs that anyone can watch for as early indicators of ill health. Look closely at your face for the following:

➤ vertical lines or deep furrows above the nose and between the eyes: this is traditionally seen as a sign of liver trouble
➤ dark circles under the eyes: may indicate kidney problems
➤ sores on the mouth and lips: from the oriental perspective the mouth and lips correspond to the digestive system, so these could indicate disorders of the stomach, pancreas, or intestines

A person's hands can be as revealing as the face. "Although modern medical experts have routinely scoffed at palm reading," says Rita Robinson, author of *The Palm: A Guide to Your Hidden Potential,* "scientific studies at leading research universities in the past few years indicate that some signs of impending illnesses, genetic abnormalities, and psychological problems may appear in the hands long before more noticeable signs become evident. The new studies, under the heading *dermatoglyphics,* go beyond the frontiers of palmistry yet bear resemblance to that ancient art."

Some of the most dramatic correspondences between external signs on the hands and internal conditions, notes Robinson, involve fingerprint patterns. Studies have shown that specific arches and whorls can indicate gastrointestinal disorders, an inherited predisposition to constipation, or Down's syndrome. More easily observed aspects of the hands are also revealing. According to Richard Lee, M. D., professor of medicine at the State University of New York at Buffalo, if your palms are

➤ reddish, as from dilation of blood vessels, this is a possible sign of alcoholism and cirrhosis of the liver
➤ tinted blue, it may be from poor circulation or problems with the lungs
➤ yellow, it can signal jaundice, intake of certain toxic chemicals, or high blood-fat levels

According to Eugune Scheimann, M. D., a medical doctor who has been studying palmistry since the 1940s, if your hands

➤ have a swelling of the knuckles at the base of the fingers, it may be an early sign of arthritis
➤ are dry and doughy with thin, brittle nails, you may have a thyroid disorder

Nails are also worth examining closely. Look for

➤ red streaks around the cuticle, which may indicate lupus; if the streaks are under the fingernails, it could be due to circulating parasites such as trichinosis, a parasite from eating undercooked pork
➤ bluish nails, which suggest circulation problems or metal poisoning
➤ small, round pits in the nails, which show psoriasis
➤ spoon shapes; nails that have reverse curvature could be a sign of an iron deficiency, thyroid disorder, or rheumatic fever

Learn from your body's waste products. One of the traditional practices of medicine from antiquity until recent times was to examine closely a patient's urine. Doctors would look at its color and density and even smell it to help diagnose the patient's condition. Though their diagnoses were often wrong and their treatments, such as bloodletting, harmful, their methodology had a rational basis. Urine can offer important clues about the body's health. That's one of the reasons so many home lab tests rely on urine samples. To some extent, modern lab methods have supplanted the need to examine urine with your senses. Nevertheless, you can gain some insights into your health by becoming more aware of what your urine reveals. For instance, if your urine is

➤ copious and straw-colored: you're healthy
➤ dark yellow to orange and diminished in quantity: this may signal that you should be drinking more water, or that you are suffering from a fever, kidney disorder, jaundice, or diarrhea
➤ greenish: this is often a normal reaction from taking certain vitamins or medicines and is not worrisome
➤ cloudy or milky looking: may be from loss of weight, depression, or consuming too many phosphates
➤ cloudy with long, thin, white threads: in men may indicate a disorder of the prostate gland
➤ strong or foul smelling: may be a sign of urinary-tract infection
➤ sweet and fruity smelling: possibly an indication of diabetes
➤ pink or reddish: can be insignificant if it is from eating certain red foods (such as beets or foods artificially dyed red) or taking aspirin derivatives; if it indicates blood in the urine, however, it could be a sign of serious conditions of the bladder, kidneys, or urethra

Likewise your stools are significant. They can be affected by factors including diet, emotions, water intake, drug consumption, and of course illnesses. Here are some common possibilities. If your stools are

➤ loose and runny (diarrhea): this can signal numerous conditions, including food poisoning, flu, and allergies; of most concern is chronic diarrhea, which could be from an infection of the small intestine or other serious condition
➤ too hard: this may be from a fever or a lack of fluid
➤ reddish, as from blood in the stools: if red streaks are on the outside of the stool, it is probably from minor bleeding of hemorrhoids; more worrisome is red mixed into the stool, which could indicate ulcerative colitis or a growth on the colon or rectum

➤ full of undigested food: in children this could be due to over-feeding; in adults it may signal a digestive disorder or pancreatic trouble

➤ full of worms: in children these are usually pinworms; in adults they may be roundworms, tapeworms, or others picked up as parasites from a trip to a tropical area

Short Tips for Self-Diagnosis

❑ Pain is your body's principal way of calling attention to an imbalance. Listen to it. Learn from it.

For More Information

Two excellent books on home lab tests and oriental diagnosis are:

The People's Book of Medical Tests by Tom Ferguson, M. D., and David Sobel, M. D. (New York: Summit Books, 1985)

Reading the Body by Waturo Ohashi with Tom Monte (New York: Viking/ Penguin, 1991)

A useful mail-order resource for home lab tests and other self-care tools is:

SelfCare Catalog
5850 Shellmound St.
Emeryville, CA 94662
(800) 345-3371

22

FIND THE THERAPIES
THAT SUIT YOU

If you're ill and have decided to use a natural therapy, there are many to choose from. Herbalists prescribe plant medicines, acupressurists press on energy points on your body, chiropractors adjust your spinal column, and nutritionists recommend supplements, to name just a few. What natural therapists share is an emphasis on finding the right aids and tools that will help your body to heal itself. But how do you know what will work best for you and for your illness? Among the key factors to consider are what type of therapy you prefer and what health problems you are experiencing.

Breaking natural therapies into four broad categories sheds some light on these factors. These categories include

❑ Holistic Medicine. This category includes holistic physicians, naturopaths, and practitioners of the traditional medicines of other cultures, particularly those in the Orient. This category includes many of the general practitioners of the natural-health field, since they use an eclectic array of tools and techniques that include therapies from the other three categories of bodywork, remedies, and movement disciplines.

❑ Bodywork. This encompasses many hands-on therapies that touch, stroke, or manipulate a person's muscles, bones, joints, and other deep tissues. The purpose may simply be to improve relaxation, to restructure the body's alignment, or to promote the body's natural flow of energy and thus prevent or treat illnesses.

❑ Remedy Therapies. These are similar to conventional medicine in that they rely upon the patient's ingesting a medicinal substance to remedy an illness. Instead of synthetic drugs, however, the emphasis is on natural substances such as herbs, homeopathic remedies, essential oils, flower essences, and nutritional supplements. Many of the best remedy therapists will not limit their recommendations to a prescription—they will also question the patient about his or her diet, lifestyle, and emotional well-being. This helps to avoid a common pitfall to the remedy approach: the patient can come to rely on the medicine to "fix" problems that often require more of a commitment from the person. For instance, the herb white-willow bark may be safer and as effective as aspirin in relieving the pain of a headache, but unless the person addresses the condition that is causing the headache, neither remedy will provide more than temporary symptomatic relief. With some study most people can learn to self-prescribe natural remedies.

❑ Movement Disciplines. These teach you to hold and move your body in new ways. They tend to be best for health conditions that can be traced to postural and musculoskeletal problems, including backaches and muscle injuries (strains, sprains, and tears), though frequently movement disciplines have positive effects on various bodily systems. Movement disciplines generally require a series of visits over weeks or months to a practitioner trained in the subtleties of the various techniques.

Everyday Steps to Natural Health

Let's take a closer look at some of the most popular practices among the four main categories of natural therapies, answering the questions: *What is it? How did it develop? Who can do it?* and *What does it do best?* See "For More Information" for addresses and to find practitioners.

Holistic Medicine

NATUROPATHY

What is it? Naturopathy emphasizes harnessing the body's innate healing powers to prevent and reverse illness. The best naturopathic doctors (N. D.'s) are well versed in herbalism, nutrition, bodywork, homeopathy, and a few less common techniques such as hydrotherapy (using water to heal). Naturopaths can even do minor surgeries, though they cannot prescribe pharmaceutical drugs.

How did it develop? Naturopathy drew from hydrotherapy and a number of other mostly European traditions as it developed in the nineteenth century. In the U. S., the writings and lectures of the German-born physician Benedict Lust in the early 1900s focused the movement and helped to popularize the practice.

Who can do it? Naturopaths' training and licensing varies. Some have a correspondence degree while others are trained at one of the two accredited schools (John Bastyr in Seattle and the National College of Naturopathic Medicine in Portland, Oregon), where the course work rivals that of many medical schools in depth and rigor.

What does it do best? Naturopaths can treat virtually any illness, though on occasion they'll refer patients to a conventional physician. A naturopathic examination touches upon all aspects of your health (diet, emotions, work) and can set the stage for an excellent disease-preventive lifestyle.

ORIENTAL MEDICINE

What is it? Oriental medicine includes a number of practices, ranging from acupuncture to shiatsu (a bodywork) to Chinese herbalism to tai chi (a movement discipline). What these techniques share is a view of the body as an energy vessel, with treatments aimed at preventing or removing blockages of vital energy (*qi* in Chinese, *ki* in Japanese), thus establishing harmony or balance between the person and the natural world.

How did it develop? Most oriental medical practices go back thousands of years and are based on the traditional philosophies of China, Japan, Tibet, and other cultures.

Who can do it? Training varies considerably and may have been obtained in the Orient or at one of a number of schools that have opened in recent years in the U. S. Practitioners may be a doctor of oriental medicine (O. M. D.), an acupuncturist (an "L. A." is a licensed acupuncturist), an acupressure practitioner, or some other type of healer. Many of the techniques of self-diagnosis and self-care can be learned by the interested layperson.

What does it do best? Oriental medicine excels at preventing disease, reducing chronic pain, and rejuvenating the body; skilled practitioners can also treat a wide array of illnesses.

AYURVEDA

What is it? *Ayurveda* is a Sanskrit word that translates as "knowledge of life." It is the traditional healing practice of India, originating some three thousand years ago. Like Chinese medicine, it is based on an ancient system of thought encompassing universal forces and life energies. Ayurveda posits three forces, or *doshas* (termed *vata, pitta,* and *kapha*) that affect life energy *(prana)* and help to determine a person's body type, constitution, favorite foods and activities, and even overall health. Practitioners of ayurveda use a number of therapeutic approaches, including diet, massage, acupuncture, and herbalism, to balance these forces and maintain or restore harmony to the body, mind, and spirit.

How did it develop? Indian sages developed ayurveda as a method for living a long and healthy life in harmony with the cosmos. Ayurveda is still widely practiced in India alongside Western, conventional medicine. Author Deepak Chopra, M. D., and the Maharishi organization (which teaches transcendental meditation) have been major popularizers of the practice in the U. S. in recent years.

Who can do it? There are a limited number of practitioners of ayurveda in the U. S. today, some of whom have extensive training in India comparable to Western medical education. (Ayurveda is not a licensed medical practice, however, anywhere in the U. S.) Many of the principles and practices of ayurveda can be learned by interested laypeople and used for disease prevention and self-care.

What does it do best? Although ayurvedic physicians can treat a wide variety of conditions, in the U. S. ayurveda is primarily used as a general program of internal cleansing and rejuvenation.

Bodywork

CHIROPRACTIC

What is it? Chiropractors manipulate the spine and adjust the body's joints to align its parts and allow the free flow of vital energy. Because the spine carries so many nerves and is central to the body's neuromuscular system, chiropractors believe that misalignments (what they term "subluxations") there can eventually cause illnesses elsewhere in the body. By manipulating and pressing on the vertebrae, chiropractors enhance the body's natural healing abilities.

How did it develop? Chiropractic is a century-old discipline founded by a self-taught Iowa healer named Daniel Palmer (1845–

1913). Seeking an alternative to harmful drug therapy, he combined his knowledge of traditional bodywork and his experience working on people's spines to cure various diseases. Palmer's son continued his work and helped make chiropractic one of America's most widely accepted natural therapies.

Who can do it? There are thousands of doctors of chiropractic (D. C.'s) licensed to practice medicine by all fifty states. The chief division in the field is between "straights," who focus almost exclusively on spinal adjustments, and "mixers," who include other natural therapies and techniques in their practice. Because of the potential for causing harm by inexpert pressing on the back, chiropractic is not a self-care therapy (though chiropractors do make numerous self-care suggestions about exercises and health habits).

What does it do best? Any pain or malfunction of the neck, back, or spine is likely to improve from a series of sessions with a chiropractor. By aligning the spine, chiropractors can also often promote overall health and relieve common illnesses.

OSTEOPATHY

What is it? Osteopaths manipulate and palpate the muscles, bones, joints, spinal column, and nerves (craniosacral osteopaths focus on the head and neck) to remove structural imbalances and restore the body's natural ability to heal itself. Doctors of osteopathy (D. O.'s) are fully trained and licensed physicians, equivalent to M. D.'s, and many also use conventional medical procedures including drugs and surgery to diagnose and treat.

How did it develop? Osteopathy was founded over a century ago by Andrew Taylor Still (1828–1917), a Virginia country doctor who sought a more effective alternative to the toxic drugs and questionable surgeries of conventional medicine of the time. He coined the term *osteopathy* because it focused in part on manipulating bones (from the Greek *osteo*) to relieve suffering or disease (from the Greek *pathos*).

Who can do it? There are about thirty thousand osteopaths practicing in the U. S. today. Of these, perhaps 5–10 percent adhere to the classical school of osteopathy that focuses primarily on manipulation and hands-on treatment, and lifestyle advice about diet, stress, and emotions, rather than conventional practices.

What does it do best? Osteopaths can treat almost any condition, although backaches and injuries or diseases of the neuromusculoskeletal system respond particularly well.

ROLFING

What is it? Rolfing, or "structural integration," is a type of deep massage that reorganizes the body's structure by manipulating the protective sheaths that surround muscles and the connective tissue around joints. The therapist uses her fingers, knuckles, and elbows to apply deep, sometimes "pleasantly painful" pressure that can help realign the head, neck, torso, legs, and feet.

How did it develop? The practice was founded by New Yorker Ida Rolf (1896–1979), an organic chemist who developed the approach after studying yoga, chiropractic, and osteopathy.

Who can do it? There are about seven hundred trained Rolfers worldwide. They typically work on clients for a series of ten sessions, each an hour or more, over a few months time. Each session focuses on one area of the body. After you've been aligned, you may need periodic readjustments. Some Rolfers can teach techniques for proper body use that can help you retain the proper alignment.

What does it do best? It is especially effective at aligning the body, improving posture, increasing flexibility and range of movement, relieving stiffness and chronic fatigue, and eliminating structural aches and pains as well as any condition that may be aggravated by poor bodily use or the effects of an earlier injury to the bones or muscles.

ACUPRESSURE

What is it? Acupressure works on the same principle as acupuncture—freeing the flow of vital energy in the body's meridians, or energy channels—except that acupressure uses finger pressure rather than the ultrathin needles of acupuncture. Acupressurists say that balancing or improving the flow of *qi* can alleviate pain, prevent disease, and promote healing. Acupressurists typically use the tip of the thump to apply deep penetrating pressure to a specific bodily point for one to two minutes.

How did it develop? Acupressure evolved thousands of years ago as part of traditional Chinese medicine.

Who can do it? While acupuncture is not a self-care technique, acupressure is. Laypeople who take the time to study the body's meridians and learn the location of a dozen or so of the hundreds of energy points can use acupressure on themselves and others. A number of schools in the U. S. teach acupressure, though few natural-health practitioners practice it exclusively.

What does it do best? Acupressure may be used to relieve various conditions or as a complementary therapy to promote healing. It also has important first-aid applications.

MASSAGE

What is it? *Massage* is a broad term for practices that use the hands to touch and rub the body. Western approaches to massage, such as Swedish massage, generally focus on the body's musculoskeletal system, while oriental approaches, such as shiatsu, focus on the body's system of energy channels.

How did it develop? Humans have no doubt been using forms of massage for tens of thousands of years, with the first systematic approach to healing massage going back about five thousand years to traditional Chinese practitioners.

Who can do it? There are at least fifty thousand massage therapists in the U. S. today, with varying degrees of licensure and certification. Basic massage techniques are easy to learn and apply (see Step 24).

What does it do best? Massage is widely used to promote relaxation and reduce overall bodily tension. Some types also have important therapeutic properties.

Remedy Therapies

HERBALISM

What is it? Herbalists use plant remedies, either singly or in combination, to cure ailments or promote overall vitality. The split between Western and Eastern herbal traditions is similar to that between Western and Eastern bodywork traditions, with Western practitioners focusing on herbs' effects on the body's organs and systems and Eastern herbalists focusing on herbs' effects on the body's energy flow.

How did it develop? The use of plant remedies probably goes back tens of thousands of years, with the first written record being a five-thousand-year-old Chinese reference. Herbalism is a common traditional medical practice throughout the world, with various cultures using the plants found in their environment.

Who can do it? Trained herbalists are widespread, although self-care is more common. Herbs are generally safe and nontoxic, but should be used with knowledge and caution to prevent side effects.

What does it do best? Herbs can be used for most of the same effects as pharmaceutical drugs—to relieve pain, reduce inflammation, lower a fever, soothe nerves, promote sleep, and so forth.

HOMEOPATHY

What is it? The Greek-derived name of this practice indicates its goal: treating *pathos* (suffering or disease) with *homoio* substances—those that elicit the same, or similar, reactions when the person is healthy. This idea that "like cures like" requires that the practitioners question and observe the patient closely to match his or her symptoms with the right remedy from among hundreds of possibilities. The remedies are typically tiny pellets made from extremely dilute herbs, minerals, or animal substances; they're considered over-the-counter drugs by the federal government.

How did it develop? The therapy was founded almost two hundred years ago by Samuel Hahnemann (1755–1843), a German physician who was unhappy with his practice of conventional medicine (or "allopathy," from the Greek *allos,* "other").

Who can do it? There are an estimated fifteen hundred M. D.'s in the U. S. who are trained in homeopathy and treat patients at least in part with homeopathic remedies. Practitioners with training in homeopathy may also be practicing and licensed as naturopaths or other types of healers. Homeopathic remedies are widely available in natural-foods stores and some conventional pharmacies. Because homeopathic remedies are extremely dilute, they are probably the safest oral medications known to humanity.

What does it do best? Homeopathy can address virtually any illness or condition, though many homeopaths use conventional medicine or complementary techniques to treat acute conditions.

AROMATHERAPY

What is it? Aromatherapists use essential oils, which are aromatic liquids derived (mostly by steam distillation) from the leaves, bark, roots, or other parts of plants. Essential oils may be dispersed into the air and inhaled through the mouth or smelled through the nose, applied topically, or added to a bath to cure ailments or change moods. The oils are usually not taken orally, since they are extremely concentrated (typically sold by the ounce and used by the drop) and can be quite toxic.

How did it develop? Essential oils have been widely used in cooking and cosmetics since ancient times. Medicinal uses go back to the

Middle Ages at least. The term *aromatherapy* was only recently coined by the French cosmetic chemist Dr. René-Maurice Gattefossé in the late 1920s. The practice is extremely popular in France and Europe and is making inroads in the U. S.

Who can do it? Aromatherapists are few in number and vary widely in training and experience. Most people use aromatherapy as a self-care approach, though in general it requires more caution than herbalism because essential oils are so potent.

What does it do best? Aromatherapy is most commonly used to affect mood and emotions or increase relaxation or even sexual desire. Essential oils can also have pronounced effects on respiratory conditions when inhaled and on skin conditions when applied locally.

FLOWER ESSENCES

What is it? These are homeopathically dilute liquid remedies made from nonpoisonous wildflower blossoms that are put in a bowl of spring water and exposed to sunlight, thus extracting the essence of the flower. Flower-essence remedies are used to heal the body indirectly by addressing moods, attitudes, and emotions such as fear, anxiety, and restlessness. The FDA considers flower essences over-the-counter homeopathic drugs.

How did it develop? The British physician Edward Bach first developed flower essences into a healing system in the late 1920s. He was reacting in part against toxic substances used as drugs both by conventional and homeopathic physicians.

Who can do it? Some homeopaths use flower essences and there are a limited number of flower-essence practitioners. Self-care is common. Natural-foods stores sell Bach Remedies and other flower essences as single-flower and combination-flower remedies. They are typically liquid preparations meant to be taken in small doses of three to four drops.

What does it do best? Flower essences can help alleviate emotional states such as anger, fear, and despair that are predisposing the individual to illness.

THERAPEUTIC NUTRITION

What is it? This is the practice of preventing or treating illnesses using diet as well as vitamins, minerals, amino acids, and other nutritional supplements, often in dosages well above average daily consumption levels.

How did it develop? Using foods to heal ailments goes back to the ancient Greeks at least. The pioneering "father of medicine," Hippocrates (circa 460–370 B.C.) said, "Let thy food be thy medicine." Scientific confirmation began after the mid-eighteenth century when the Scottish physician Dr. James Lind discovered that citrus fruit could prevent scurvy.

Who can do it? Supplements don't require a doctor's prescription to buy and are widely available over the counter in drugstores, natural-foods stores, and by mail order. They are relatively safe, though some should be used with caution by pregnant women, and many nutrients become toxic when taken in extremely large doses.

What does it do best? Nutritionists and other practitioners now use a wide array of nutrients to prevent or help treat heart disease, diabetes, arthritis, skin disorders, and a host of less common conditions, from carpal tunnel syndrome to Crohn's disease. Food choices and dietary changes play primarily a preventive role, while more concentrated nutrient supplements are used for disease prevention and treatment.

Movement Disciplines

FELDENKRAIS METHOD

What is it? Feldenkrais method, or "functional integration," uses gentle touch and guided movements while the person lies relaxed on a massage table. "A Feldenkrais lesson communicates to the brain precise movements that change habitual holding patterns and provide new information to the neuromuscular system," says practitioner Victoria Ahrensdorf of Northampton, Massachusetts. This reeducates people and helps them become more aware "of how they move and how they might move differently," allowing more fluid and effective patterns of action.

How did it develop? The system was developed in England during the 1940s by Russian-born Israeli physicist Moshe Feldenkrais (1904–84) after he found that conventional physical therapy could not improve his chronic knee problem. Feldenkrais drew upon the work of other pioneers in movement disciplines, including F. M. Alexander.

Who can do it? There are about five hundred certified Feldenkrais practitioners in North America. Their sessions typically last one-half to one hour. Practitioners also teach movement exercises to be done at home that can supplement table sessions.

What does it do best? Feldenkrais method helps to eliminate poor physical habits, improve posture, increase relaxation, remove musculoskeletal tension, and prevent or cure chronic stiffening resulting from an injury.

ALEXANDER TECHNIQUE

What is it? Alexander practitioners help clients become more aware of how they can improve their routine movements and postures. Teachers work with students on a table, at chairs, and doing common tasks to identify habitual, improper uses of the body and to suggest easy, graceful ways of moving.

How did it develop? The technique was founded at the turn of the century by F. Mathias Alexander (1869–1956), an Australian actor who cured his chronic vocal problem by eliminating stress and tension in his head, neck, and body.

Who can do it? There are about three hundred trained teachers in North America. They often need about twenty one-half-to-one-hour lessons to impart the basic instruction to students.

What does it do best? Alexander technique improves posture and alignment, increases relaxation, reduces chronic muscular tension, and restores people to the natural grace and poise they possessed as children. It relieves many musculoskeletal problems and often resolves seemingly intractable physical illnesses.

TRAGERWORK

What is it? Tragerwork, or "Trager psychophysical integration," promotes a feeling of lightness and well-being while addressing the subconscious roots of muscular tension. The technique uses "light, gentle, nonintrusive movements," says Betty Fuller, cofounder of the Trager Institute, while the person falls into a deeply relaxed state. According to system developer Milton Trager, M. D., rotating, rocking, and bouncing body parts breaks up "sensory and mental patterns which inhibit free movement and cause pain and disruption of normal function."

How did it develop? The technique was founded by Trager, a former acrobat and dancer now in his mid eighties who has been refining his practice of physical rehabilitation, bodywork, and movement therapy for over fifty years.

Who can do it? There are over a thousand Trager practitioners worldwide. They have been trained to get into a "hook-up" state of harmony with the client, who lies on the table for an hour or longer while the practitioner guides his movements and performs light tissue manipulation. Practitioners can also teach clients a set of dance-like exercises called Mentastics, or "mental gymnastics," that can be done at home.

What does it do best? Tragering is especially effective at relieving muscle tension and bodily stiffness, promoting relaxation, increasing range of motion, and improving flexibility and coordinated movement.

Short Tips for Finding the Right Therapies

❑ Whatever type of therapy you choose, find a practitioner you can feel comfortable with (see Step 23).

For More Information

For practitioner referrals and further background information contact the following professional organizations:

HOLISTIC MEDICINE

American Association of Naturopathic Physicians
2366 Eastlake Ave. E., #322
Seattle, WA 98102

American Association of Acupuncture and Oriental Medicine
433 Front St.
Catasauqua, PA 18032
(610) 433-2448

American Holistic Medical Association
American Holistic Nursing Association
4101 Lake Boone Trail, #201
Raleigh, NC 27607
(919) 787-5146

Maharishi Ayurveda Health Center for Stress Management and Behavioral Medicine
679 George Hill Rd.
P. O. Box 344
Lancaster, MA 01523
(508) 365-4549

BODYWORK

Acupressure Institute
1533 Shattuck Ave.
Berkeley, CA 94709
(510) 845-1059

American Chiropractic Association
1701 Clarendon Blvd.
Arlington, VA 22209
(703) 276-8800

American Massage Therapy Association
820 Davis St., #100
Evanston, IL 60201
(708) 864-0123

American Osteopathic Association
142 E. Ontario St.
Chicago, IL 60611
(312) 280-5800
(800) 621-1773

Rolf Institute of Structural Integration
205 Canyon Blvd.
P. O. Box 1868
Boulder, CO 80306
(800) 530-8875
(303) 449-5903

The Upledger Institute (for craniosacral therapy)
11211 Prosperity Farms Rd.
Palm Beach Gardens, FL 33410
(407) 622-4334

REMEDY THERAPIES

American Botanical Council
P. O. Box 201660
Austin, TX 78720
(512) 331–8868

Flower Essence Society
P. O. Box 459
Nevada City, CA 95959
(800) 548–0075

National Association for Holistic Aromatherapy
P. O. Box 17622
Boulder, CO 80308

National Center for Homeopathy
801 N. Fairfax St., #306
Alexandria, VA 22314
(703) 548–7790

MOVEMENT THERAPIES

Feldenkrais Guild
706 Ellsworth St., Box 489
Albany, OR 97321
(800) 775–2118
(503) 926–0981

North American Society of Teachers of the Alexander Technique
P. O. Box 517
Urbana, IL 61801
(800) 473–0620

Trager Institute
33 Millwood St.
Mill Valley, CA 94941
(415) 388–2688

23

TEAM UP WITH YOUR
HEALTH PRACTITIONER

The healing process should be one of joint effort, communication, and discovery between patient and practitioner. If you go in expecting a practitioner, whether doctor or herbalist, to "fix you" without having to participate actively in the process, you are likely to be disillusioned. Indeed, if you tell some practitioners, "I know I can't breathe but I don't want to give up smoking," you may well find that he or she doesn't want you as a patient.

Finding the right natural practitioner can be more difficult than finding the right conventional doctor, since the variety of natural therapies can be confusing. Should you see an herbalist or homeopath or bodyworker or nutritionist for your headache? Frequently, all will be able to offer some help so you must decide based on your preferences and prior experiences.

Of course, it is not necessary to limit your partners in health to a single practitioner. Many people like to have a "family doctor" they see exclusively; others enlist the aid of a holistic physician for serious illnesses, a chiropractor for back problems, and an herbalist for everyday complaints. Your expectations and qualifications for each will differ accordingly. For the physician whom you see infrequently, you may be willing to put up with a gruff bedside manner because you believe her understanding of recent research is outstanding. For the bodyworker who is helping you to deal with your stress-induced headaches, a healing touch and understanding demeanor is of paramount importance.

Everyday Steps to Natural Health

Referring to acupuncturists, Ted Kaptchuk, author of *The Web That Has No Weaver: Understanding Chinese Medicine,* noted that "the ultimate definition of the benefits the patient receives during treatment is determined by the relationship created by the practitioner and the patient." Here's how to create a mutually beneficial relationship.

Shop around. If you take the time to go to the library and check *Consumer Reports,* talk to friends, and compare retailers before you buy a new television, don't you think you should put at least as much time and effort into finding the right health-care practitioner? Yet how many people become a patient of a healer based on a single recommendation, or even an ad in a local magazine?

Do your practitioner shopping when you are well rather than ill. There are numerous avenues to explore for suggestions—the more the better. Talk to friends and associates with beliefs similar to your own and ask with whom they are successfully working. Check with other health practitioners, since they may know who the good people in related fields are. For instance, if you have established a good relationship with a nutritionist and you decide you want to see a chiropractor for your neck pain, check with the nutritionist. She may have heard from her clients who is an effective practitioner and who is not. Professional organizations can also be helpful (see "For More Information").

Once you have a practitioner's name, speak to a receptionist or office manager about the practice. Ask for any relevant brochures or printed information about the practitioner. Find out how long he or she has been practicing. Ask whether you can speak to a current patient or two. The office employee is likely to give out names of satisfied customers, but sometimes you'll get unexpected information. You can also ask about the practitioner's training and his experience in dealing with the types of health problems you've had in the past or expect to experience in the future.

Since money is an issue for most people, address the issue early on. How much does the practitioner charge for office visits and how many treatments are likely to be necessary? Of course, the latter often depends on the condition being treated, but an honest response to the question is helpful. Also, does the practice accept your health insurance and handle billing?

Interview your candidates. If the preliminary information about a practitioner sounds good, the next step should be to schedule a short, 15-minute interview. You may have to pay a partial-hour charge, but it will be worth it. Here are the important factors to consider and compare:

❑ Qualifications and training. In many states natural-health practices are loosely regulated, if at all. For many popular types of practice (such as herbalism, naturopathy, and nutritional therapy) there may be neither laws against the practice nor any laws protecting or regulating it. Thus, for instance, in some states anyone may decide to call himself an herbalist and start practicing. It is up to you to determine whether a practitioner's education, training, and experience warrant your trust.

What type of school the practitioner attended for her training can be revealing. For example, a naturopath may have received his training through a correspondence school thirty years ago or be a recent graduate of one of the two accredited, four-year naturopathic medical schools (John Bastyr in Seattle and the National College of Naturopathic Medicine (NCNM) in Portland, Oregon). If you're not familiar with the practitioner's education, ask about hours of classroom instruction and time spent doing internships and training.

If the practitioner lists confusing initials after his name, ask what they mean. Terms such as *certified, licensed,* and *registered* can be either enlightening or mystifying, since definitions vary and qualifications even for the same term differ from state to state.

Does the practitioner have any supplemental training in specialized techniques she uses?

Of course there are superbly trained and high credentialed practitioners who nevertheless make lousy healers, just as there are minimally trained practitioners with remarkable healing powers. Other aspects such as those that follow need to be considered along with training.

❑ Personality. Sometimes it will be obvious even within 15 minutes that your personality either clashes or harmonizes with the practitioner's. You may also want to consider culture and even gender—if you're a woman who has been sexually abused by male practitioners, you will probably be more successful by limiting your search for a healing partner to female practitioners.

"The most important thing is to get a sense of who this person is, what they have to offer, as well as their credentials. You are an individual. So choose someone who fits you," says Dr. Jared Zeff, dean of the NCNM.

❏ Commitment to partnership. Determine whether the practitioner will be a partner with you in the health process. Ask the practitioner directly whether he would feel comfortable in a situation where you would respect what he had to say, but ultimately you and not he would be making the decision. If he expresses an attitude that he's in charge and your role is to follow instructions, keep looking. Some physicians will balk at the cooperative approach. In some, their training and experience has imbued a godlike sense of self-importance and infallibility. They are too accustomed to reigning as a king to join a democratic partnership. They may also fear that you'll sue them when *your* choice doesn't bring the expected result.

❏ Average time spent with you during office visits. If a practitioner seems uncomfortable even spending fifteen minutes talking with you, find out if she is overly hurried. Ask how many patients she sees in an average day. Divide the number by eight hours to get an average visit time.

Above all, match your choice of practitioner with your own healing beliefs. The role of belief in healing is extremely important. The attitudes and beliefs held by both the practitioner and the patient can be as crucial to a treatment's success as any drug or manipulation.

Beliefs are responsible for causing new drugs to work better when they are first introduced than ten years later, notes Andrew Weil, M.D., in *Health and Healing*. Studies have shown that drugs' greater effectiveness when first prescribed can be traced to the fact that doctors believe in the drug and instill their positive thoughts in patients. As doctors become less enthusiastic about a drug, its effectiveness lessens. By the same token, if you have little faith in your doctor's ideas and methods, he will have little effectiveness treating you.

"Any treatment—whether allopathic drugs and surgery, homeopathic remedies, chiropractic manipulations, shamanistic rituals, or Chinese acupuncture—includes two distinct elements: the direct effect of the treatment itself (if any) and the belief it elicits in both practitioner and patient," Weil says.

Bernie Siegel, M.D., author of *Peace, Love and Healing,* concurs: "Having confidence in your doctor manifests physically, because feelings create positive chemical reactions that promote healing."

Natural medicine offers a broad range of options, including bodywork, holistic physicians, nutritionists, acupuncturists, chiropractors, herbalists, naturopaths, and others. Do you pay close attention to foods and the effects of vitamins and nutritional supplements on your health? If so, in general you'll stay healthier working with a nutritionist or a naturopath than a chiropractor or acupuncturist (though many chiropractors, acupuncturists, and other natural practitioners do offer nutritional guidance). If you are still skeptical of natural medicine, you may want to start with a holistic physician or an osteopath because their basic training is similar to that of conventional physicians'. The variation among holistic physicians and osteopaths, as within other fields, is tremendous. You should still interview the person to see whether you share values and beliefs.

Larry Dossey, M.D., author of *Meaning and Medicine,* says, "This is certainly not a situation for hidden agendas. To play a yes game with a doctor when you believe the total opposite of what the doctor believes poisons the power of a potentially healing relationship right off. Many patients are afraid of offending the doctor by stating their beliefs. Better to do it in the first fifteen minutes than the fourth day after surgery."

Become an active but patient patient. "The greatest gift you can take to a healing interaction is your own progress toward a multifaceted, healthy lifestyle," claims Patch Adams, M. D., founder and medical director of a forty-bed free hospital in West Virginia. Adams says that in his experience the ideal patient is above all involved with her health and has a "genuine, compassionate, loving, and joyous feeling" for herself. He recommends a variety of natural steps for achieving and maintaining health, including deep friendships, play and creativity, regular exercise, and a healthful diet.

"Seek out health-care professionals who love eye contact, touching, and friendship, hopefully through empathy and shared vulnerability. If a healer acts in a way that bothers you, speak up gently but firmly about your concerns," Adams recommends. He also says that if you want attentiveness and thoroughness, expect and accept some waiting. "Medicine is not like fast food where all the needs and solutions are clear and quickly met," he notes.

Short Tips for Teamwork

❑ Find a healer who knows how to listen. Any partnership benefits when this basic communication skill is mutually employed. "A patient should feel listened to, paid attention to, and have had their life and their pain empathetically witnessed," says Ted Kaptchuk.

❑ Being forthcoming with your practitioner establishes trust and provides her with the information she needs to make recommendations. It is always best to be honest about existing conditions—if a massage therapist works on you and you haven't told him you have an infectious skin condition, you may be spreading it to him and to others.

For More Information

See "For More Information" after Step 22 for addresses of the following organizations that can help you find qualified practitioners in your area:

American Association of Acupuncture and Oriental Medicine
American Association of Naturopathic Physicians
American Chiropractic Association
American Holistic Medical Association
American Holistic Nursing Association
American Osteopathic Association

Two helpful books include:

Love, Medicine and Miracles by Bernie S. Siegel, M.D. (New York: Harper & Row, 1986)

Peace, Love and Healing by Bernie S. Siegel, M.D. (New York: Harper & Row, 1989)

24

MASSAGE WORKS

Massage is an ancient form of touch therapy that is experiencing a renaissance in modern times. In the past decade it has made inroads into settings as diverse as offices (including those at the State Department), health clubs, and medical centers. Those who have benefited from it range from Olympic athletes to disaster victims. For instance, in 1989 some two hundred fifty massage therapists gave over eight thousand free massages in the aftermath of the devastating San Francisco earthquake. An estimated one hundred thousand people are practicing some form of bodywork in the U. S. today, many of them trained by one of the nation's more than three hundred massage schools.

Though humans have no doubt been using for millennia the basic technique of holding an injured body part, the origins of a systematic approach to healing bodywork go back about five thousand years to traditional Chinese practitioners. They developed various forms of energy-based massage. These types of massage focus on manipulating points along the body's channels, or meridians, that direct the flow of energy, called *qi* (or *chi*) by the Chinese and *ki* by the Japanese. For instance, shiatsu is a Japanese massage that emphasizes stretching movements and gentle pressure applied by fingers and other body parts. Acupressure uses primarily the thumb to apply deep pressure to energy points on the body.

Western massage derives from more recent European traditions, although the benefits of massage have been recognized since the time of Hippocrates, the Greek medical pioneer. He said, "The physician must be experienced in many things, but assuredly in rubbing." Unlike energy-based Eastern traditions, Western forms of massage are structural, focusing on the body's muscles, bones, and joints. The most popular is Swedish massage, developed by Per Henrik Ling at the beginning of the nineteenth century to complement a type of gymnastics popular at the time.

In the U. S. today massage encompasses an ever-growing variety of practices. What they have in common is the use of the fingers, hands, elbows, knees, and other body parts to touch and rub either one's own or another person's body. Many massage therapists combine techniques and strokes from both Western and Eastern traditions.

Massage has a number of demonstrable physical effects on the body. It can increase the circulation of blood and lymph, the intercellular fluid that transports substances from the muscles to the blood. Massage slows the pulse rate and promotes relaxed breathing. It helps prevent cramps by lowering levels of the metabolic waste product lactic acid in muscles. Massage stretches and relaxes constricted muscles, increases range of motion, and promotes flexibility.

Bodywork has long been recognized even by conventional Western medicine as an important part of physical therapy and an aid to recovery from bone injuries. In recent years touch has gained recognition as a basic human need. Withholding touch has profound physical effects, a fact recognized even in hospitals, where premature babies are now routinely held and touched. Studies show that premature babies thrive and gain weight much more quickly if touched than if left alone in incubators.

Massage offers significant emotional and spiritual benefits. Many people find that massage reduces anxiety, calms the nerves, and even improves self-esteem. A recent study at the Touch Research Institute at the University of Miami Medical School found that a thirty-minute neck and back massage reduced depression in a variety of subjects, including some who were not touch-starved but whose depression arose from trauma. Researchers found that people who had just been massaged had lower levels of stress-related hormones and were more alert, less restless, and better able to sleep.

Massage can also relieve various conditions that are caused by musculoskeletal problems. For instance, massaging the neck, face, and scalp can often relieve a tension headache. An experienced massage therapist can treat muscle cramps, backache, arthritis, digestive disorders such as constipation, temporomandibular joint dysfunction, and sometimes even asthma and breathing problems. Don't wait, however, until you are ill to experience massage. "Massage is the premier wellness modality," says David Palmer, a former director of the Amma Institute of Traditional Japanese Massage in San Francisco. "I would hate to see it restricted only to people who are sick," he says.

Everyday Steps to Natural Health

Massage benefits both the giver and receiver. Here are some ways to bring it into your life.

Set the scene for a successful massage. Create a relaxing environment for giving a massage. This isn't crucial, of course, when you give a quick shoulder massage to a coworker, but in general providing massage in a relaxed atmosphere heightens its effects. The room should be quiet or filled with soft music. The room should also be warm, especially if the receiver is only partly clothed. Keep covered those parts of the body you're not massaging.

If you want to work only on a person's neck, upper back, shoulders, arms, or feet, the person can sit in a chair. To work on most of the rest of the body, the subject needs to lie down on a firm but comfortable surface. Massage tables are ideal, but massage can also be done on a carpeted floor or on a sturdy table cushioned with a few layers of towels. Beds are usually too soft and the wrong height for performing massage.

The person doing the massage should wash his or her hands and briskly rub them together to warm them. Both the giver and receiver of massage should relax, get in a comfortable position, and concentrate on the breath. The receiver should be passive and allow the massager to lift and move limbs. If sitting, the subject should maintain proper, erect posture (see Step 16). The person doing the massage also needs to watch his or her posture and to avoid lifting or leaning over in a way that will cause aches and pains.

Using an oil allows the hands to glide easily over the skin. It also heightens sensations for the receiver. Massage oil can be lightly sponged off after the massage, but if it is inconvenient, don't use it.

You can use a lightly scented vegetable oil or a specially formulated massage oil (with essential oils added) sold in natural-foods stores.

Learn the basic strokes of Western massage. Anyone can perform massage in a way that will provide at least the benefit of touch. To offer the full range of potential benefits, however, you need to know some strokes beyond mere rubbing. Here are the four most common strokes of Western massage:

❏ Gliding, also known as effleurage, is usually one of the first strokes used during a massage. Gliding stretches and relaxes the long muscles of the calves, thighs, and back. It can be done with the pads of your thumbs or the whole hand with your fingers together and extended. Keep your hands relaxed and mold them to the shape of the muscle being worked. Do gliding strokes toward the person's heart with more pressure, then circle away from the heart with a lighter stroke using just the palms or tips of the fingers.

❏ Kneading is working muscles as if handling bread dough: rolling, squeezing, and compressing them to loosen individual fibers. Kneading is a deeper, more penetrating stroke than gliding and is generally done on the large muscles of the back, buttocks, and legs. Use your whole hand including the heel to push and pull and the fingers to pick up and squeeze muscles. Work with circular movements from the depths of the muscle to the surface, being careful not to pinch the skin.

❏ Friction is similar to the technique of acupressure, in which you use your thumb pads or fingertips to apply deep, penetrating pressure to certain points. Apply the pressure slowly and then make circular or rotating movements for ten seconds or so before releasing outward. Friction can be done anywhere but is most often used on the back. It shouldn't be done to the point that it causes pain. Use gliding strokes afterward to relax the area that received friction.

❏ Chopping and cupping are quick percussive movements done in an alternating rhythm with the hands. Chopping uses the outer edge of the palms and little fingers. Cupping uses the hollowed palms of hands shaped as if to swim freestyle. Keep the wrists loose. Striking and tapping strokes invigorate muscles and are usually done after using the more relaxing gliding and kneading strokes. Chopping and cupping are most appropriate for use on the calves, upper legs, buttocks, and the back.

Give and ye shall receive. You can be assured of both by practicing on yourself. With the exception of your upper back, you can
reach most of the places on your body to do self-massage. You won't
gain all of the benefits of receiving a massage, since you have to be
active and can't relax as much, but self-massage can still be an effective way to loosen tense muscles.

Your lower body is the easiest part to self-massage, since it affords you the best leverage. The legs are a good place to start,
especially the front and inside of the thighs and the calves. Sit with
one leg fully extended and the other bent with the knee up. Do the
following steps on the bent leg and then repeat on the other leg.

❑ Mold your hands to the shape of your upper leg and do gliding
strokes from the knee to the upper thigh. Apply deeper pressure as
you stroke toward the heart and lighter away. Reach under the knee
to do similar gliding strokes up the calf.

❑ Place a hand on each side of the thigh just above the knee. Roll
the muscles back and forth, move the hands farther up the leg, and
repeat until you reach the groin.

❑ Use both hands to knead the outside of the hip from the knee
to the upper thigh.

❑ Grasp the inside of the thigh with the hand on the opposite
side of the body from the bent leg and roll out the muscle with
your thumb.

❑ Use your thumbs to do circular friction around the knee and
ankle joints.

Become the most popular person in your office. How?
Easy—give a coworker an occasional upper-back, shoulder, and
neck massage. These areas of the body are easy to work on while
the person is sitting at a desk. They're also areas of the body that
frequently develop aches or become tense from hours of sitting.
Work while standing behind the seated person, who remains fully
clothed. Here's a basic routine.

❑ Start by doing some gentle gliding strokes across the tops of
the shoulders toward the neck. Wrap the fingers of each hand lightly
over the edges of the shoulders and sink your palms into the muscles
as you glide. Then do some gliding strokes using your thumbs. Lay
your thumbs flat on each side of the spine and push them toward

the edges of the back. Start at the base of the neck and work down to the lower back.

❏ Knead the large muscles of the upper back, neck, and shoulder, picking up the muscle with each hand and rolling and compressing.

❏ Knead the biceps muscle from shoulder to elbow by holding the person's arm slightly away from the body, putting your hands on the upper arm with the thumbs next to each other and pointing up, and wrapping the fingers around the inside of the upper arm. Do both arms.

❏ Do friction strokes along the shoulders and base of the neck. Put a hand on top of each shoulder and use the flat tips of your fingers to make slow circles down the edge of the cervical spine and then out toward the shoulders. Use your thumbs to make tiny circles in the area between the spine and the shoulder blade. Feel for tight spots in the muscles and spend a few extra moments massaging out any tension that you discover.

❏ Finish with some chopping strokes along the upper back. Use a rapid, alternating rhythm to lightly strike the muscles of the back and shoulders, taking care to avoid hitting the spine, shoulder blade, and other bones.

Feet first. Feet are ideal for massage, for beginners and others. Since feet are sensitive and have many nerve endings, receiving a foot massage can be extremely relaxing and pleasurable. According to practitioners of a specialized type of Eastern massage called reflexology, various points on the bottom of the feet (as well as the hands) correspond to internal organs and other parts of the body. Thus reflexologists say that working on the feet can have therapeutic effects by harmonizing energy flow throughout the body. Feet are also small enough that giving the massage is not tiring. The feet are good for practicing self-massage, since they're easy to reach and work on. Finally, foot massage works well with people who are not comfortable receiving massage on other parts of the body—shoes and socks are the only clothes that need to be removed.

The person receiving the foot massage should sit comfortably and place her feet on a stool or chair at the same level as your lap. Alternatively, the subject can lie down on her back with heels extended slightly over the edge of the table. Sit or stand so that you can easily handle the feet without strain. Work on one foot at a time but do both feet. Here are some suggestions for a quick and easy foot massage.

❑ Start with some gentle rubbing of the top and bottom of the foot, the toes, and the ankle. Be careful not to tickle the person since that can cause tension.

❑ Do some simple range-of-motion steps. Place one hand on top and the other on the bottom of the foot. Move the top half of the foot forward and backward. Now support the ankle with one hand, grasp the top of the foot with the other, and gently rotate the foot five times in each direction. Next hold the sole with one hand, grasp one toe at a time, and do five rotations in each direction for each toe.

❑ Place your palms on the top and bottom of the foot and do firm gliding strokes, using a milking action to first pull on the top of the foot and then the bottom.

❑ Raise the foot and gently massage the sole. A technique that reflexologists use is to bend your thumb so that the top joint forms a right angle. Use the tip of the thumb (not the fingernail) to apply deep friction pressure, slowly increasing and releasing it. First work the crease and ridge across the foot under the toes. Points there correspond to the neck and shoulders and are effective at inducing relaxation. Now work your way to the heel, first along the inside of the heel (corresponding to the spine), back up the center of the foot (site of the internal organs), and down the outside to the heel.

❑ Lay both thumbs flat on the center of the sole. Use a gliding stroke to work the bottom of the foot from the center to the edges and then back again.

❑ Do tiny circles with the pad of the thumb on the top of the foot, from toes to ankle. You don't need to be as thorough on the top of the foot since it has fewer energy points than the bottom.

❑ Pull on each toe in succession, then run your fingers along the inside of each toe.

❑ Finish by doing gentle kneading movements over the whole foot and around the ankle. Grasp the foot in different areas and apply a squeezing pressure.

You don't have to do all of these steps, nor do you have to do them in a specific order. Experiment with the four basic strokes and see what works for you and the person being massaged.

Short Tips on Massage

❑ To do a total body massage, start with the person lying face-down and work from the neck to the feet. When you reach the feet, have your partner turn over and start back up at the neck again.

❑ A golden rule of massage is to do no harm. Done properly, massage is safe and causes no side effects. There are, however, some restrictions. You shouldn't press directly on injured, burned, or infected areas. Avoid touching an area with a malignant tumor or a contagious skin condition. Always stop or use less pressure if the treatment is causing severe pain or is aggravating the injury. Consult with a knowledgeable practitioner or a medical professional before performing massage on a pregnant woman or a seriously ill person.

For More Information

An excellent general work on massage is:

Massageworks: A Practical Encyclopedia of Massage Techniques by D. Baloti Lawrence and Lewis Harrison (New York: Perigee Books, 1983)

For further information or to locate a massage therapist in your area, contact the organizations listed under "Bodywork" in "For More Information" of Step 22.

25

TRY NATURAL REMEDIES

Most natural-foods stores now carry extensive lines of herbs, homeopathic medicines, nutritional supplements, essential oils, and other natural remedies. Until you begin to learn more about these natural medicines, the overwhelming choice can be bewildering. Still, it is possible to start off with a dozen or so basic natural medicines that can be used to treat the most common medical conditions and injuries you're likely to face.

Natural medicines have a number of advantages over their commercial, over-the-counter (OTC) alternatives. Though there are exceptions, natural medicines tend to be less toxic and have fewer side effects than synthetic drugs. Also, rather than being narrowly formulated specifically to alleviate one or two symptoms, natural medicines are often produced with the purpose of boosting the body's own healing potential.

Ready to start a new natural-medicine chest? The following ten natural remedies can take the place of your aspirin, Tylenol, Ben-Gay, Alka-Seltzer, Dramamine, Valium, Polysporin ointment, Mylanta, No Doz, Maalox, NyQuil, Advil, Nuprin, Sominex, Solarcaine, Desenex, Benzedrine, and Contac. You may even find that using some of the following natural medicines can help you begin to lower your intake of mind-altering drugs such as alcohol, caffeine, and nicotine.

• **Activated charcoal.** Pharmaceutical companies process pure carbon in a special way to make activated charcoal, which is used to relieve gas pains, reduce flatulence, and absorb and excrete from the body poisons and other toxins. Activated charcoal may also lower blood cholesterol levels, reduce uric-acid levels and thus treat gout, and alleviate the pain and itching from insect bites and bee stings.

Taken internally (an average dose for gas is 500–1,000 mg) or applied to the skin (in a paste), activated charcoal works by catching and trapping the large molecules of most toxic substances (the same effect it has when used in air and water filters). It absorbs poisons and drugs in the stomach and intestines, then is excreted along with them by the body. It further prevents toxins from being absorbed into the bloodstream by coating intestinal walls. It doesn't work for all toxic substances, however, and should be used as a poison remedy only after you've checked with a poison-control center.

Activated charcoal is available at natural-foods stores and pharmacies. It comes in a powder, liquid, and capsules. The capsules can be broken open to use the powder for making a paste.

• **Arnica.** Both herbalists and homeopaths make prominent use of this plant (*Arnica montana*, also known as leopard's-bane) to alleviate the effects of shock and trauma, especially the bruising, swelling, and local tenderness that comes from a fall or being hit by a blunt object. Arnica can also help heal strains, sprains, and muscle aches. Recent research has determined that certain of arnica's chemical compounds (such as the lactone helenalin) have anti-inflammatory and pain relieving properties.

Herbalists favor arnica tincture (an extract made with alcohol) or an oil of arnica (sometimes labeled "arnicated oil"). These are for external application only, to unbroken skin. There are a wider variety of homeopathic preparations of the plant (which we'll designate *Arnica*, to distinguish from herbal preparations), including lotions and ointments for external application (though, again, not to broken skin), and even tablets for internal consumption.

• **Calendula.** An ancient herb that originated in Egypt, calendula *(Calendula officinalis)* is one of the most versatile and widely used topical herbs, popularly recommended by herbalists, homeopaths, and aromatherapists to treat small cuts and abrasions, inflammations, skin irritations, bruises, strains and sprains, minor burns and scalds, and hemorrhoids. Calendula stimulates blood circulation and can ease cramps. It is also used as a mouthwash to fight gum infections and as a remedy to fight bacterial, viral, and even fungal infections like athlete's foot.

Herbal calendula is widely available as a tincture or concentrated extract. The herb is frequently combined with other herbs such as goldenseal and myrrh to produce all-purpose healing salves. Homeopaths also use diluted homeopathic *Calendula* preparations (including ointments, tinctures, and lotions) for many of the same purposes that herbalists use the plant—to promote the healing of minor wounds, burns, and skin irritations, help stop bleeding, and inhibit infection.

• **Echinacea.** Herbalists recommend echinacea *(Echinacea angustifolia, E. purpurea)* to treat a variety of injuries and illnesses. You can apply it externally to cuts, bites, and stings to help promote healing, as well as take it internally to fight bacterial and viral infections and boost the immune system. Studies have shown that when used on injuries, echinacea promotes the body's power to regenerate healthy cells and maintain the structure of connective tissue. It is also taken internally to lower fever, calm allergic reactions, and reduce inflammation. Natural-foods stores carry a variety of echinacea-containing salves, lotions, tinctures, and tablets.

There is no known level of toxicity associated with taking echinacea, and it can be taken internally in relatively large quantities. For instance, many herbalists suggest that patients with infections take two to three droppersful of the tincture three times daily as a general immune stimulant. For acute conditions, patients may take a dropperful of tincture every half hour. "It's not toxic, and you need a high dose to quickly activate the immune system," says herbalist Christopher Hobbs, author of *Echinacea: The Immune Herb!*

• **Ginger.** This herb *(Zingiber officinale)* has a noted calming effect on the digestive system and is the premier natural remedy for nausea from morning sickness, upset stomach, and motion sickness. The Chinese and others have used ginger for thousands of years, both as a flavoring and as an herbal folk remedy. Ginger helps expel gas from the intestines and relaxes and soothes the intestinal tract. A number of recent studies have confirmed ginger's effectiveness against seasickness, including a 1982 report in the British medical journal *Lancet* that concluded that powdered ginger was an even more effective motion-sickness remedy than the conventional OTC remedy Dramamine.

Ginger is widely available in capsules, concentrated extracts, and the like. Kids can be given ginger in the form of ginger tea, or even non-artificially-flavored ginger-snap cookies or ginger ale.

• **Goldenseal.** The root of this plant *(Hydrastis canadensis)* is one of the most widely used herbs, with both internal and external applications. Taken internally it alleviates some of the effects of colds, fevers, digestive ailments, and food allergies, eases constipation, and reduces excessive menstrual flow. Topically it is used for its anti-inflammatory, antibiotic, and antiseptic actions. Herbalists prescribe it for hemorrhoids and various skin infections or sores, including ringworm, athlete's foot, and itching.

Avoid using goldenseal if you have high blood pressure or are pregnant, or in large amounts every day for weeks or months. An average dose is one to two dropperfuls of the tincture twice a day.

Goldenseal has been overforaged in some areas. It is thus a relatively expensive herb and is sometimes adulterated, so be sure to buy from a reputable source.

• **Siberian ginseng.** This plant *(Eleutherococcus senticosus,* sometimes referred to as eleuthero) is a versatile "tonifying" herb that has been used for over four thousand years by the Chinese to increase longevity and improve overall health. Like the similar herb Chinese ginseng *(Panax ginseng),* Siberian ginseng is an "adaptogen" that normalizes and regulates all of the body's systems. In particular it supports the working of the adrenal gland and thus prevents the most debilitating effects of stress. It also helps you to fight off fatigue by increasing your energy and endurance. Studies indicate that the herb may help to normalize blood pressure by preventing both postural hypotension (the dizziness from temporary low blood pressure upon quickly standing) and hypertension or high blood pressure.

Siberian ginseng is safer for daily consumption than most other energy-boosting herbs, including those that contain caffeine (coffee, tea) or ephedrine (ma huang). Siberian ginseng is widely available in tincture and capsules. It is often combined with other adaptogen herbs such as schisandra.

• **Tea tree.** The pale yellow essential oil made from the aromatic leaves of this Australian tree *(Melaleuca alternifolia)* has numerous healing powers. Tea-tree oil is a premier natural remedy for bacterial, viral, and fungal skin conditions, including athlete's foot, nail infections, and mouth sores. It is also effective for treating injuries, including burns, cuts and scrapes, and bites and stings. According to Cynthia Olsen, author of *Australian Tea Tree Oil Guide*, some hospitals in Switzerland use tea-tree oil to control infections. It's also an effective insect repellent.

Natural-foods stores carry a burgeoning variety of tea-tree products, including the pure oil (look for oils that are 100 percent *Melaleuca alternifolia*), skin creams, shampoos, throat lozenges, toothpastes, deodorants, and more. The essential oil is nontoxic and, unlike most essential oils, can safely be applied directly to the skin without being diluted (avoid getting it in the eyes, though).

• **Valerian.** The root of this plant *(Valeriana officinalis)* serves as the source for a type of "natural Valium" that can relax the mind and body and thereby help provide temporary relief from stress and anxiety. Valerian is frequently taken to prevent insomnia and provide a deeper sleep. Its calming and quieting effect on nerves can also help relieve headaches, stomach and menstrual cramps, and constipation or indigestion from nervous tension.

Valerian is sometimes combined with other sedating herbs, such as skullcap *(Scutellaria laterifolia)*, to make insomnia remedies. An average dose is a gram of the powder, a teaspoon of the tincture, or 250 mg of the liquid or solid extract. Valerian is safer than Valium but should nevertheless not be taken in large doses or for an extended period of time.

• **White willow.** The bark of this tree *(Salix alba)* has long been used for its pain-relieving and fever-reducing properties. The Greeks used willow-bark remedies two thousand years ago, and willow was a popular herb for fever among colonial Americans. Like the herb meadowsweet *(Filipendula ulmaria)* it is a natural source of salicin, a chemical relative of salicylic acid, which is used to make aspirin (acetylsalicylic acid). Aspirin was first synthesized from salicin by German scientists in the early 1850s, though the new drug was ignored for fifty years until the folks at the German Bayer company decided it had potential as an arthritis remedy. In the early decades of this century aspirin skyrocketed in popularity and quickly replaced natural sources of salicin.

Natural willow preparations have made something of a comeback in recent years. They act like aspirin to reduce pain, inflammation, and fever. Natural pharmacies carry a number of willow-based remedies. The fresh or dried herb can be used to make a somewhat unpleasant-tasting tea. Many herbalists instead recommend products that are marketed as willow-based aspirin substitutes, some of which are standardized for the salicin content.

Since white-willow-bark preparations are close chemical relatives to aspirin, it is best to err on the side of safety and not give this herb to children who have a fever that may be due to certain viral illnesses, because of the risk of Reye's syndrome.

Everyday Steps to Natural Health

Most of the above top ten natural remedies have multiple uses. Here are simple ways to use them for twenty common conditions and injuries.

Bites and stings. Rinse and clean a bite using a natural antibacterial solution. Dilute echinacea or calendula 5:1 in water, or add three to four drops of tea-tree oil per half cup of water. Cover a clean bite with a natural dressing and a bandage. You can make a natural dressing from a goldenseal-root powder mixed with some water, a calendula lotion or salve, or a cotton pad saturated with echinacea tincture.

To reduce the pain and inflammation of stings from insects and bees, apply a cotton pad saturated with echinacea or calendula, dab on a paste made by mixing a little water with some activated charcoal, or apply a few drops of undiluted tea-tree oil.

Also take one to two dropperfuls of echinacea, either directly onto the tongue or diluted in a few ounces of water, internally for two to three days following any kind of bite or sting.

Bruises, strains, and sprains. Use arnica tincture or oil. Dilute the tincture before applying to the skin by mixing approximately one dropperful of tincture per cup of cold water. Soak a cotton towel or cloth in the dilution and apply as a compress to the bruise three or four times per day.

You can also use homeopathic *Arnica* both externally and internally. Spread some of the ointment or lotion on the site as soon as possible after an injury. Dilute a tincture in water as you would for an herbal preparation, and apply with a cold compress. A typical oral dose of *Arnica* for a minor bruise would be two to five tablets of 6X or 12X potency (the X refers to number of dilutions; a 1X dilution is one part in ten, 2X one part in a hundred, and so forth) at the time of injury and the same dose once daily for two or three days. For more severe contusions, supplement the first-day dose by taking two or three more tablets every three to four hours for the next two or three days.

You can also apply a calendula tincture, lotion, or salve on a bruise, sprain or strain.

Burns. Cool a minor burn by running cold water over it. Then apply a calendula tincture, lotion, or salve.

Other remedies that help heal burns include a gel from the aloe plant and vitamin-E oil.

Colds. Take one to two dropperfuls of tincture of echinacea two or three times per day at the first sign of a cold.

You can also take ginger in the form of a hot ginger lemonade. Grate a two-inch piece of gingerroot, add it to two cups of boiling water, simmer in a covered pot for five minutes, and add two table-spoons of lemon juice, one tablespoon honey, and a pinch of cayenne if you have it.

Other natural remedies to help limit a cold's stay include vitamin C (take one to two grams daily), zinc lozenges (23 mg of elemental zinc every two hours for up to twelve hours, for up to a week), and garlic (1,250–2,500 mg of fresh garlic equivalent daily).

Constipation. Goldenseal root or ginger may be helpful to treat constipation due to weak muscular activity in the gut, while valerian may play a role if the condition is due to bowels that are overtense and need to relax. Take one-half dropperful of tincture, concentrate, or extract directly onto the tongue or diluted in a few ounces of water.

Regular constipation is often a sign of a poor, fiber-deficient diet. There are herbal laxatives, such as yellow dock, that are less harsh than conventional OTC and strong herbal (such as aloe and senna) laxatives, but long-term use of any laxative should be avoided. Natural remedies should not take the place of commonsense steps such as eating more fiber (plant sources include psyllium seed and pectin), getting more exercise, and lowering stress levels.

Cuts and abrasions. Use direct pressure to stop any bleeding. Then apply a dressing made by taking a cotton pad and saturating it with tincture of echinacea, calendula, or tea-tree. Tape it on the wound and change the dressing frequently. You can also make a natural dressing from goldenseal-root powder mixed with some water.

Fatigue. Take one dropperful of Siberian ginseng up to three times per day to combat fatigue.

Fever. Take one-half dropperful of white-willow-bark tincture or extract. Also take one to two dropperfuls daily of echinacea.

Keep in mind that a fever is your body's way of reestablishing health and balance. Unless the body temperature is uncomfortably or dangerously high, it is best not to reduce a fever, either with herbs or OTC drugs like aspirin.

Flatulence. Take two or three capsules of activated charcoal.

Hay Fever. Take one-half to one dropperful of goldenseal or echinacea tincture. You can also use one dropperful of Siberian ginseng up to three times per day for its adaptogenic effects.

Headache. Take one-half to one dropperful of tincture or concentrate of white-willow bark for pain relief, or a similar dosage of valerian to reduce tension.

Hemorrhoids. Dab onto the painful area a calendula lotion or salve, or goldenseal powder or paste.

Indigestion. Take two to three capsules of activated charcoal. Or use ginger, in the form of one to two grams or two to three capsules of the powder, or one to two dropperfuls of liquid tincture or concentrate.

Insomnia or anxiety. Drink a cup of valerian tea or take one dropperful of the tincture, concentrate, or extract about an hour before bedtime.

Nausea. Take ginger in relatively large doses to counter motion sickness, morning sickness, or vomiting. Use one to two grams, or two to three capsules, of the powdered herb, or one to two dropperfuls of liquid tincture or concentrate.

Sinus infections. Take one-half dropperful of echinacea plus one-quarter dropperful of goldenseal tincture two or three times per day. You can also put a few drops of tea-tree oil in some hot water and inhale it to relieve nasal congestion.

Skin rashes. Apply a lotion, salve, or ointment made with calendula, echinacea, or tea-tree oil. Make a tea or paste from goldenseal powder mixed with a few drops of water and rub on the skin.

Sore throat. A popular remedy among herbalists is to make a solution by adding one-quarter teaspoon salt and one-half teaspoon goldenseal-root powder to one cup of warm water. Gargle with this solution every half hour until symptoms abate. You can also take tea-tree oil lozenges.

Stomachache. Take one capsule or one-half to one dropperful of liquid or concentrate of ginger up to three times daily.

Stress. Drink a cup of valerian tea or take one-half to one dropperful of the tincture, concentrate, or extract. You can also use one dropperful of Siberian ginseng up to three times per day.

For More Information

There are numerous books on natural remedies, but here are two that cover a wide variety of substances:

Encyclopedia of Natural Medicine by Michael Murray, N.D., and Joseph Pizzorno, N.D. (Rocklin, Calif.: Prima Publishing, 1991)

The Natural Health First-Aid Guide by Mark Mayell and the Editors of *Natural Health* (New York: Pocket Books, 1994)

SIMPLE STEPS
TO
NATURAL HEALTH

YOUR BODY

YES!

Send FREE FACTS about how I can train at home for the career I have chosen. **CHECK ONE BOX ONLY!**

ASSOCIATE IN SPECIALIZED BUSINESS DEGREE PROGRAMS

- ☐ 60 Business Management
- ☐ 61 Accounting
- ☐ 80 Bus. Mgmt.—Marketing option
- ☐ 81 Bus. Mgmt.—Finance option
- ☐ 64 Applied Computer Science
- ☐ 68 Hospitality Management

ASSOCIATE IN SPECIALIZED TECHNOLOGY DEGREE PROGRAMS

- ☐ 62 Mechanical Engineering Technology
- ☐ 65 Electrical Engineering Technology
- ☐ 63 Civil Engineering Technology
- ☐ 66 Industrial Engineering Technology
- ☐ 67 Electronics Technology

- ☐ 07 High School
- ☐ 18 Bookkeeping
- ☐ 13 Secretary
- ☐ 23 Medical Office Assistant
- ☐ 24 Dental Office Assistant
- ☐ 04 Auto Mechanics
- ☐ 05 Hotel/Restaurant Mgmt.
- ☐ 52 Surveying and Mapping
- ☐ 85 Drafting
- ☐ 14 Air Conditioning & Refrig.
- ☐ 22 Travel Agent
- ☐ Wildlife/Forestry Conservation
- ☐ 32 Art
- ☐ 47 Animal Care Specialist
- ☐ 55 Diesel Mechanics
- ☐ 06 Electrician
- ☐ 70 Small Business Mgmt.
- ☐ 02 Electronics

CAREER DIPLOMA COURSES

- ☐ 01 Computer Programming
- ☐ 69 Computer Programming/COBOL
- ☐ 38 Personal Computer Specialist
- ☐ 48 Computer-Assisted Bookkeeping
- ☐ 27 PC Repair
- ☐ 53 Desktop Publishing & Design
- ☐ Secretary with Computer
- ☐ 09 Legal Secretary
- ☐ 59 Catering/Gourmet Cooking
- ☐ 94 Fitness & Nutrition
- ☐ 33 Motorcycle Repair
- ☐ 87 TV/VCR Repair
- ☐ 08 Legal Assistant
- ☐ 03 Child Day Care
- ☐ 29 Police Sciences

- ☐ 10 Private Security Officer
- ☐ 12 Interior Decorating
- ☐ 25 Gun Repair
- ☐ Fashion Merchandising
- ☐ 41 Journalism/Short Story Writing
- ☐ 40 Photography
- ☐ 42 Dressmaking & Design
- ☐ 30 Florist
- ☐ 26 Teacher Aide
- ☐ 15 Home Inspector
- ☐ 39 Medical Transcriptionist
- ☐ 34 Real Estate Appraiser
- ☐ 31 Professional Locksmithing
- ☐ 72 Appliance Repair

CALL TOLL FREE 1-800-596-5505 Ext. 8192

CALL ANYTIME—24 hours a day, 7 days a week.

OR MAIL THIS CARD TODAY!

No cost or obligation. No salesman will visit.

NAME _____ AGE _____

STREET _____ APT. # _____

CITY/STATE _____ ZIP _____

PHONE ( ) _____

International Correspondence Schools Dept. PVKS758

...bsidiary of National Education Corporation

Woman's Day

758XA

26

BREATHE DEEPLY

Breathing is both a simple, unconscious, everyday operation of the lungs and a complex, voluntary activity of the mind/body. In many cultures the multidimensional nature of breathing is evident in the very word. The word for breath and "spirit" or "life force" is the same in a number of languages, whether it is *prana* in Sanskrit, *pneuma* in Greek, or *spiritus* in Latin. The Latin word provides the same root for the English words *respiration* and *inspiration*. Thus, to breathe is both to inhale and to inspire, to take in air and spirit.

The many links between breathing and mind/body/spirit are well-known to ancient cultures such as those in China and India. The health and spiritual practices of yoga, Buddhism, and Taoism have long made use of specialized breathing techniques to relax and harmonize the body.

Each of the fifteen to twenty thousand breaths you take every day moves air into the lungs. This allows your blood to absorb oxygen and then carry it to cells throughout the body. The cells give up to the blood their waste in the form of carbon dioxide, which is brought back to the lungs for removal. Since your body cannot store oxygen (as it can other sources of energy, such as fat), you must continue to breathe to live. Stop eating and you may live for months; stop breathing and you have about five minutes.

There are two ways you can increase your lungs' ability to deliver oxygen to the blood: breathe faster and breathe more deeply. Ultimately, it is more efficient to breathe more deeply because breathing too quickly allows overly cold, unfiltered air to get into the lungs. It tends to fill only the upper portions of the lungs with air, not allowing you to fully exhale and thus leaving behind residual carbon dioxide. Because it increases filtration, correct, full breathing is preferable to shallow breathing even when you are breathing polluted air.

Poor breathing that goes on for too long may cause biochemical changes in the body's blood and cells, leading to fatigue, anxiety, and possibly a cycle of faster, shallower breathing and increasing anxiety (this is what happens to people who hyperventilate). More serious symptoms may follow, including some, such as chest pains, that mimic those of a heart attack.

Of course, in some cases rapid breathing is appropriate to the circumstances. Your brain will signal the lungs to provide more oxygen when you are physically exerting yourself or experiencing an emotional crisis. For instance, you breathe more rapidly when running or having an argument with your spouse. By increasing your oxygen intake you can increase your energy level. Your brain and endocrine glands also release more endorphins and other natural mood-boosting and painkilling chemicals. The point is that there is no single best way to breathe at all times, and feeling guilty every time you take a shallow breath won't increase your overall health.

Everyday Steps to Natural Health

Fortunately, anyone can learn to break inefficient breathing cycles by consciously controlling his or her breath. You can see and feel the rise and fall of your diaphragm and feel and hear the influx and expulsion of air from your nose and mouth. "We can become conscious of our breath during any and all of the activities of our daily lives and . . . it is greatly empowering to do so," notes Michael Sky, author of *Breathing*. Here are some easy ways to develop better breathing habits.

Use the abdomen. Breathing may come naturally, but many people nevertheless don't breathe fully and efficiently. Such factors as tension and poor posture cause people to take rapid, shallow breaths through the mouth, drawing air only into the upper chest. Dinah Bradley, author of *Hyperventilation Syndrome: A Handbook for Bad Breathers*, identifies four basic steps to becoming a better breather:

➤ become aware of faulty breathing patterns
➤ breathe through your nose (to help warm, humidify, and filter the air) into the area of your diaphragm, expanding your stomach on the inhale
➤ reduce your breathing to a slow, even, rhythmic rate, for adults approximately ten to fourteen breaths per minute
➤ suppress upper-chest movement during normal breathing

Since the lungs themselves have no muscles, you control the expansion and contraction of the lungs by using the muscles in the upper chest and along the ribs. Even more importantly, you use the diaphragm, the partition of muscles between the chest cavity and the abdominal cavity. When you inhale, your diaphragm should move down while your ribs move outward. This fully enlarges the lung-containing chest cavity, allowing the lungs to expand and creating a partial vacuum inside the lungs. Air rushes in to fill the vacuum. When you exhale by pulling the diaphragm in and up and relaxing the chest muscles, air is expelled.

Demonstrate to yourself full, deep, abdominal breathing by first lying on your back. Put one hand on your upper chest and the other on your stomach. Inhale through your nose, checking to make sure the hand on the stomach is rising and the one on the chest is not. Exhale slowly, pushing the abdomen down with the hand on the stomach. Practice this abdominal breathing so that you can do it while sitting, standing, and exercising. When it has become your normal way of breathing, you'll be inhaling and exhaling more fully and will be providing increased levels of oxygen to your body's cells.

People who breathe backward—by sucking in their stomach to inhale—are not taking full advantage of their lungs' size and capacity. Most people when they breathe take in about a pint of air, or 12–15 percent of the lungs' fully expanded capacity of over a gallon. By increasing your breathing efficiency, you turn over all of the air in your lungs more quickly than the seven to eight breaths it takes the average person. (Some dinosaurs needed three hundred breaths to fully replenish their lungs, a factor that may have lead to their demise when oxygen levels in the air fell precipitously.)

Learn from the yogis. Yoga is the ancient movement and posture discipline of India. There are many forms of *pranayama,* which are yogic exercises that focus on controlling the breath. The overall goal is to allow you to breathe more deeply and slowly, paying attention to how the breath affects the mind. Here's a simple yogic breathing exercise even beginners can practice.

Sit in a comfortable position, on the floor or in a chair, or lie down on your back. Keep your spine straight and shoulders back so as not to constrict your upper chest or the movement of your abdomen. Bend the index and middle fingers of either hand onto your palm. Use your thumb and third finger, placed onto the sides of your nose where the bone ends, to regulate how you inhale and exhale, alternating nostrils. Close off the left nostril and inhale to a count of four through the right nostril. Then close off the right nostril and exhale to a count of two through the left. Inhale to a count of four through the left nostril, and exhale to a count of two through the right. Try to establish a breathing pattern of long, smooth inhalations and exhalations. Don't become exhausted or out of breath. Do three to five minutes of this breathing exercise, gradually experimenting with ratios and working up to longer periods of inhalation and exhalation.

The traditional yogis of India believe that by controlling your breath you can control the flow of prana, or vital energy, throughout your body. Yoga practitioners say that regular *pranayama* practice can not only improve your lungs' functioning (studies have confirmed that yoga practices can reduce respiratory problems like mild asthma) and boost your overall physical health, it can help you gain greater control of your mind and reduce mental and emotional disturbances.

Make like a snake. In addition to breathing exercises, yoga practitioners use a basic posture known as the cobra to relax the lung muscles and open the airways. Lie on your stomach with your forehead on the floor, palms down under the shoulders. Inhale deeply as you slowly use your back muscles to raise first your head and then your chest off the floor. Straighten your arms as you tilt your head back as far as possible within your comfort zone. Exhale as you slowly reverse the motion and come back to a prone position. Rest for a few breaths and then repeat.

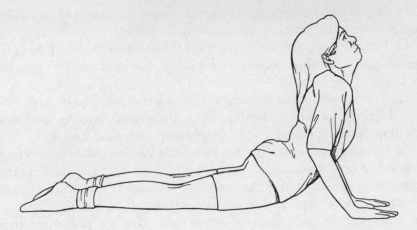

Limit your exposure to airborne pollutants, indoors and out. The American Lung Association estimates that air pollution causes some 120,000 premature deaths in the U. S. each year. Hundreds of common air pollutants that people in urban and industrialized areas face every day can adversely affect the lungs and breathing, including ozone and sulfur dioxide. Athletes who perform in polluted air, and children, because they spend a lot of time outdoors, are especially at risk. Outdoors, avoid any physical activity during an air-pollution alert. If you exercise outdoors, do it early in the morning before rush hour or find wooded areas with fresh air away from urban congestion.

Indoors, avoid airtight rooms with new synthetic furniture and rugs, which may be giving off significant levels of formaldehyde and other toxic chemicals (see Steps 18 and 19). Also avoid smoky rooms. The EPA estimates that secondhand smoke causes three thousand deaths and aggravates at least two hundred thousand cases of childhood asthma each year.

Short Tips for Better Breathing

❑ Do regular aerobic exercise to strengthen your cardiovascular system and help you to breathe easier (see Step 14). Jogging, bicycling, cross-country skiing, and other forms of endurance training force your heart and muscles to work harder. Aerobic exercise thus increases your oxygen uptake and helps you to expel more carbon dioxide. It also helps deliver more oxygen to tissues throughout the body. If you like swimming, the breast stroke is a good exercise for strengthening the lungs and improving breathing.

❑ Laugh. Laughter increases the rate of breathing and oxygen consumption and thus reduces respiratory problems and oxygenates the blood. (See Step 33.)

❑ Take up singing or playing a wind instrument. These are excellent activities for strengthening your abdominal muscles and developing better control of your diaphragm and your breath.

❑ Consume more of the nutrients that improve the functioning of your lungs. Researchers at the University of Maryland, Duke University, and elsewhere have recently found that antioxidants such as vitamins A, C, and E, and the mineral selenium, can help protect the body against the effects of ozone and other air pollutants that act as harmful free radicals in the lungs (see Step 29). Other nutrients that can help keep the lungs healthy include niacin (take 25–300 mg to help protect the tiny alveoli air sacs in the lungs) and garlic (eat regularly as a food or take 1,250–2,500 mg of fresh garlic equivalent in supplement form to improve the lungs' ability to transfer oxygen to the blood and reduce sensitivity to toxins in the air).

❑ Practice pursed-lip breathing for a few minutes each day. This is one of the most popular breathing exercises, used during natural birthing and by people with asthma. To do it, inhale deeply through your nose. Exhale slowly while puckering your lips as if to blow out a candle. Pursed-lip breathing can help open your lungs' airways and strengthen the respiratory system.

❑ Wear loose, comfortable clothing that doesn't restrict your breathing. Blouses, shirts, and pants that are too tight around the abdomen and chest, and collars, ties, and jewelry that constrict the neck, can inhibit natural breathing patterns.

❑ Maintain correct posture to ensure that your rib cage and diaphragm are allowed a full range of movement (see Step 16). Try to take a deep, abdominal breath when you're leaning over with your shoulders hunched forward. This position prevents your lungs from fully expanding and can quickly make you become short of breath. Moshe Feldenkrais, the late human-movement pioneer, once observed, "Good breathing . . . means good posture, just as good posture means good breathing."

For More Information

Books with further breathing exercises include:

Breathing: Expanding Your Power & Energy by Michael Sky (Sante Fe, N.M.: Bear & Company, 1990)

Hyperventilation Syndrome: A Handbook for Bad Breathers by Dinah Bradley (Berkeley, Calif.: Celestial Arts, 1992)

Ways to Better Breathing by Carola Speads (Rochester, Vt.: Healing Arts Press, 1992)

See Step 12 "For More Information" for how to find a yoga teacher in your area.

ALLOW YOUR DIGESTION
TO WORK AS DESIGNED

If, as Charles Townsend Copeland noted, "to eat is human, to digest, divine," it would appear that many Americans are falling far short of godlike satisfaction. Antacids and other over-the-counter (OTC) digestive remedies are a billion-dollar market in the U.S. today. Drugs that prevent stomach acid from forming are the most widely prescribed category of drugs in the world, and there are some seven hundred OTC drugs for constipation alone. An estimated one in ten Americans suffer from daily bouts of heartburn, while almost one in three has it occasionally. Another one in ten suffer from peptic ulcers at some time in their life. Clearly, many people would benefit from a better understanding of how digestion works and what keeps the thirty-foot-long digestive system running smoothly.

Digestion is the process of breaking down food into its component parts so that the body is able to absorb and process them. A popular misconception is that the stomach is the only organ of the digestive system. As important as the stomach is for digestion, it is only one cog in the digestive machinery. Indeed, the stomach plays a limited role in the digestion of whole categories of foods, including carbohydrates and fats.

Digestion begins at the mouth, where the teeth crush food and saliva moistens it. The enzyme amylase in saliva begins the digestion of carbohydrates. The expansion and contraction of muscles in the esophagus then force food down the esophagus, with no help needed from gravity (luckily for astronauts). Food passes through a special muscle, or sphincter, at the end of the esophagus into the stomach. The stomach does some further digestion—gastric acid and enzymes such as pepsin begin the digestion of proteins, and food is also mechanically kneaded—but it is principally a storage tank. More dramatic digestion occurs in the next stop, the twenty-foot-long small intestine.

From the stomach food enters the duodenum, the short first section of the small intestine and the site of the body's most powerful digestive enzymes. The duodenum neutralizes any stomach acid that has entered and provides new enzymes to start the chemical reactions that break down the food particles. The small intestine, with help from the secretions of the gallbladder, liver, and pancreas, digests fats and oils, proteins, and carbohydrates. Nutrients are separated from wastes and absorbed. It is mostly waste matter and undigestible ingredients such as cellulose from raw vegetables that reach the large intestine (or colon) and are excreted from the rectum.

A variety of factors can interfere with the normal flow of nutrients and wastes, resulting in digestive problems such as the following:

❑ Heartburn, also known as acid indigestion, results when the stomach overfills or the sphincter between the stomach and esophagus loosens in a way that allows stomach acid to flow out of the stomach and into the lower esophagus. Since the esophagus lacks the mucous lining that protects the stomach from its own acids, the acid causes a burning pain that sometimes extends up the chest.

❑ Flatulence is gas generated in the stomach and intestines and then expelled from the anus. Some twenty-five to thirty episodes of flatulence a day is considered normal. Flatulence may be caused by talking while eating, insufficient chewing, or eating while feeling anxious or worried. More commonly it is the result of dietary choices. Food that isn't fully digested in the intestines tends to ferment from bacterial action and form methane and other gases. Some people don't have the right digestive enzymes for certain foods, particularly dairy foods. Because of compounds like raffinose in beans, some foods (cucumbers and cabbage among them) are especially gas-producing in almost all people. Excessive flatulence may also result from taking too many bran or vitamin C supplements.

❑ Constipation is difficulty straining while moving bowels. It may be due to a fiber-poor diet, colon problems, pregnancy, prescription drugs, or a lack of water or exercise. Constipation can lead to hemorrhoids, irritable-bowel syndrome, and other health problems if it becomes chronic. Many people rely on laxatives to treat chronic constipation. Unfortunately, the benefits are short-term. Whether conventional or natural, laxatives eventually cause the colon to become lazy and lead to a cycle of relying on stronger and stronger remedies. More appropriate long-term solutions to constipation involve getting more exercise (especially walking), eating a high-fiber diet, drinking plenty of fluids, and taking steps to deal with stress.

❑ Peptic ulcers are erosions in the stomach or duodenum. They result when too much stomach acid breaks down these organs' protective lining. Studies indicate that peptic ulcers are most common in sedentary workers who face frequent deadline pressure and adopt irregular eating habits. Milk was once a popular remedy, but no longer. Studies have shown that it briefly neutralizes stomach acid only to cause it to increase to higher levels, thus preventing long-term healing.

❑ Parasites. Tiny organisms that live in the human gut may cause digestive disturbances as well as immune dysfunctions and other health problems.

Many of these digestive ailments result from similar poor habits: eating too quickly, not chewing your food thoroughly, and overeating. These actions can fill the stomach beyond its normal capacity, cause food to be only partially digested, and disrupt the functioning of the digestive organs.

Everyday Steps to Natural Health

In many cases, simple self-care steps along with the proper dietary and lifestyle choices can render unnecessary the antacids, laxatives, gas-relievers, and other digestive remedies that many people take daily to promote better digestive function.

Eat a balanced, whole-foods diet. This is an essential first step in regulating your digestion. A high-fiber, low-fat, primarily plant-based diet (see Step 1) emphasizes foods that make a speedy transit through the digestive system. Healthful foods allow the body to absorb available nutrients without taking so long that putrefaction occurs. Some complex carbohydrates such as grains and the soybean product tofu may actually help to neutralize excess stomach acid.

Eating healthful foods also entails avoiding the foods that cause digestive-system problems, including heartburn, constipation, and peptic ulcers. Heartburn, for instance, often results from eating foods that either irritate digestive canals or produce too much stomach acid. Fresh vegetables require less stomach acid to digest than do fatty, greasy, and fried foods, which slow digestion. Caffeine and chocolate can irritate the esophagus, while alcoholic beverages, refined sugar, and the drugs tobacco and aspirin increase stomach acids.

The native people of developing countries rarely suffer from constipation, especially if they still follow a traditional diet, since a primary cause of constipation is insufficient fiber in the diet. Fiber absorbs water in the intestines, thereby bulking up the stool, lubricating it, and making it softer and easier to expel. Constipation that is due to a fiber-poor diet will usually start to disappear by cutting back on refined flour and sugar products, and fatty, low-fiber foods such as red meats, hard cheeses, and fried foods. At the same time the person should eat more high-fiber foods such as whole grains, fresh fruits and vegetables, dried beans, and nuts and seeds. (Fiber helps prevent both constipation and diarrhea).

Supplements that can help treat occasional constipation include

➤ psyllium seeds, one to two teaspoons of seeds or powder in a glass of water, followed by more water, with meals, or pectin, one tablespoon three times per day, both of which are sources of dietary fiber that can add bulk to stools
➤ vitamin B complex, 50 mg twice daily, to prevent nutrient deficiencies (particularly of pantothenic acid and folic acid) that are associated with constipation
➤ acidophilus (naturally occurring live microorganisms that keep the gut populated with "friendly" bacteria; available as tablets, powders, capsules, and liquids in natural-foods stores), 10 billion viable organisms daily (take before breakfast with a cup of water) for a week or longer, to establish balanced intestinal flora

Use natural remedies to control indigestion when you do get it. Millions of people take antacids regularly to temporarily relieve the symptoms of acid indigestion. Conclusive scientific studies, however, are lacking that prove antacids are any better than placebos, or that neutralizing gastric acid provides therapeutic benefit. Antacids also contain high levels of certain minerals, mostly aluminum, sodium, magnesium, or calcium. Repeated use can cause a mineral or acid/alkaline imbalance, while overconsumption of some of these minerals has been linked with health problems (for instance, excess aluminum has been tied to Alzheimer's disease and excess sodium to hypertension).

Nutritional supplements and herbs can help counter indigestion by stimulating digestive enzymes, relaxing muscles and organs, and soothing mucous membranes, thus helping to promote overall digestive health and to balance the digestive system. Supplements that can help include

➤ activated charcoal, which is pure carbon processed to make it highly absorbent of particles and gases in the body's digestive system. Activated charcoal slides through the intestines without being absorbed and is excreted along with the particles and gases. Take 500 mg with meals or at the first sign of indigestion, and again two hours later if needed. Avoid taking activated charcoal for long periods as it also absorbs nutrients.

➤ acidophilus. Take 3–5 billion live microorganisms daily. Acidophilus is safe (though expensive) to take indefinitely.

➤ bromelain or papain, which are protein-digesting enzymes derived from pineapple and unripe papaya fruit, respectively. Take 250–500 mg of bromelain or 500–1,000 mg papain after a meal.

➤ ginger, which prevents nausea and has a calming effect on the digestive system. Take 500–1,000 mg to prevent indigestion.

➤ peppermint leaf, which helps to soothe the digestive tract. To relieve heartburn, indigestion, and bloatedness from overeating, take one dropperful of tincture or concentrate. For more serious chronic digestive problems such as diverticular disease (pouches or inflammation in the walls of the intestinal tract), use enteric-coated capsules of peppermint oil, which pass through the stomach into the intestines before dissolving.

➤ garlic, which aids in digestion and destroys harmful bacteria in the colon. An average daily dose is one-half clove or one tablet with 1,800 mg of allicin, a sulfur-containing garlic compound.

Bitters are better. People have been taking herbal bitters to improve digestion for thousands of years. Bitters are single herbs or combinations of herbs that help to promote complete digestion, stimulate appetite, and reduce flatulence. Herbalists don't completely understand how bitters promote digestion, but a popular explanation is that these herbs activate the bitter-taste receptors on the tongue. This promotes secretion of digestive juices.

The most prominent bitter herbs include gentian, rhubarb, dandelion, goldenseal, and angelica. Gentian is perhaps the most widely used bitter and has been shown to be effective at relieving indigestion by a number of clinical studies. Natural-foods stores offer a number of brands of herbal bitters, such as the popular Swedish Bitters brand. Herbal companies also offer bitter herbs in capsules, though some herbalists believe that bypassing the taste function prevents bitters from working.

Bitters are usually most effective when taken twenty to thirty minutes before meals. Take one teaspoon three times a day. You can swallow the liquid undiluted or mix it with water, carbonated springwater, or herbal tea. Obliterating its taste in a sweet juice is difficult and possibly countereffective.

Turn to mild herbal laxatives when necessary. Numerous herbal laxatives work just like conventional, OTC laxatives. That is, they stimulate bowel contractions by irritating the lining of the intestines. Most herbal stimulant laxatives are less harsh than OTC laxatives, though still strong enough to cause similar side effects, such as intestinal cramps. Like any laxative, even herbal stimulant laxatives should not be used habitually. Herbal stimulant laxatives, which can be taken in capsules (a typical dose is one to three capsules daily), tinctures, and other oral forms for a day or two, include buckthorn, senna, and cascara sagrada.

More gentle herbal laxatives work by stimulating the secretion of digestive juices. Better for chronic constipation than stronger herbs like buckthorn are the aforementioned bitter herbs, such as rhubarb and dandelion root. An average laxative dose is one dropperful of tincture or concentrated drops.

Make eating a relaxing, unhurried event. A recent survey found that one in four Americans eat their breakfast while driving to work. How many people also eat meals while watching television, reading the newspaper, or arguing over money or politics? Eating while anxious or emotionally upset hampers proper digestion. This is because secretion of gastric juices in the stomach is triggered by the vagus nerve, which is easily affected by stress or strong emotions. Some nutritionists go so far as to say that how you feel when you eat may be as important as the actual foods you consume.

The late French scientist René Dubos noted, "The digestion of fats after a meal can be seen as a purely biochemical process . . . but here again the digestive process is affected by the mind. Observations made on a teacher of anatomy in his forties revealed that the mere prospect of having to lecture to medical students slowed down the rate at which [fat particles] disappeared from his bloodstream. More generally, it was found that the digestion of fat particles was retarded by almost any disturbance in the life routines. Thus, mental processes can affect the course of physiological processes as seemingly simple as the digestion of food."

Take your meals at regular times, quietly and without distraction. Your digestive system will thank you.

Short Tips for Better Digestion

❑ If you like homeopathic remedies, try *Carbo vegetabilis* for indigestion and heartburn from even plain foods or *Nux vomica* for indigestion accompanied by constipation resulting from eating overly rich and fatty foods.

❑ Foods to eat occasionally for a positive effect on digestion include figs (which nourish and tone the intestines), prunes (which have a mild laxative effect), and dandelion greens (which promote both digestion and liver function).

❑ The twelve-step yoga routine known as the sun exercise (see Step 12 for a description) is a calming set of stretches that can help prevent hyperacidity if done shortly before or after a meal.

❑ Soak beans overnight before cooking to allow them to be more easily digested.

❑ A twelve-to-twenty-four-hour fast will relieve many digestive troubles (see Step 5 for more information on fasting).

❑ Drinking ten to twelve ounces of water at the first sign of heartburn may relieve the condition by washing food and stomach acid from the lower esophagus back into the stomach.

❑ Do something restful after a meal. Your body responds to food in the stomach by diverting blood and energy toward the digestive organs. Allow this natural process to happen rather than jogging, swimming, or doing something else that requires blood and energy in the major muscles of the legs and arms. On the other hand, you may find your digestion benefits when you take a leisurely walk after a large meal. Whatever you do, avoid lying down since that may worsen heartburn by allowing acid to seep into the esophagus.

For More Information

The following book offers a unique cross-cultural perspective on the organs of the digestive system, as well as the rest of the human body:

World Medicine: The East West Guide to Healing Your Body by Tom Monte and the Editors of *Natural Health* (New York: Jeremy P. Tarcher/Perigee, 1993)

28

BOOST YOUR
IMMUNE SYSTEM

Your body's immune system is central to your overall health. It detects invaders and protects you from them, whether they be toxins or disease-causing agents such as bacteria and viruses. When it is working well, your immune system prevents chronic diseases, fights infections, and increases your longevity. When it doesn't work as it should, even if the rest of your body is humming along, trouble lies ahead.

The immune system can malfunction in two ways. First, it can overreact to a substance that normally isn't a dangerous threat (for instance, to pollen, thus causing an allergic reaction, or to other substances, thus causing arthritis or lupus). Second, it can weaken and fail to react when it should, thus allowing the growth of cancerous cells, the spread of herpes viruses, or the development of conditions such as chronic fatigue syndrome. A weakened immune system also makes you more susceptible to less serious conditions, such as colds and the flu.

Immunology is a relatively new field. Popular medical books written before 1960 don't even mention the existence of an immune system when discussing the nervous, circulatory, and other bodily systems. Medical scientists identified the first immune deficiency diseases in the 1950s; the most well-known, acquired immune deficiency syndrome, or AIDS, appeared on the national scene only within the past fifteen years.

The major organs of the immune system are dispersed through-out the body. They include the lymph nodes (grouped along lym-phatic vessels), bone marrow (in the core of bones), the thymus (in the upper part of the chest), and the spleen (on the left side of the abdomen). These and other organs produce and store an array of white blood cells and specialized immune cells that go by names such as T cells (*T* for thymus), lymphocytes, neutrophils, mast cells, macrophages, and B cells (*B* for bone). These cells variously help the body to identify invading agents, produce antibodies that neu-tralize or destroy them, turn off the immune reaction when it is no longer needed, and remember the whole process for future reference.

Everyday Steps to Natural Health

Some immune problems are inherited, but many are due to other factors. Your immune system can be depressed by the effects of radiation, toxic chemicals, legal and illegal drugs (from tobacco to marijuana), prolonged stress, nutritional deficiencies, and depressed emotional states. Here are some suggestions to keep your immune system working well in the face of such challenges.

Develop an immune-positive personality. Research in the new field of psychoneuroimmunology (PNI) shows that people can influence their immune systems through emotions, thoughts, beliefs, and attitudes. Within the past two decades studies have consistently confirmed that body and mind are not two separate systems, each acting independently of the other. Rather, the brain, the nervous system, and the various organs of the immune system communicate with each other and with other parts of the body. Studies have shown that even physical responses of the body that seem to be purely automatic can be influenced by the mind and emotions.

For instance, in *Recovering the Soul*, Larry Dossey, M.D., re-counts studies done by British scientists in the early 1960s. They suggested to subjects under hypnosis that their positive skin reac-tions to a tuberculosis test (which if positive normally stays positive for life) would disappear. After administering further tests, the re-searchers found that skin reactions could indeed be markedly inhibited. In other works, suggestions and subjects' expectations could be used to boost or inhibit the body's immune response. These early experiments proved that "the mind can penetrate to the cellular level of the body and modify 'mindless' bodily processes," according to Dossey.

How do you harness the positive effects of mind on body to improve your immunity? Try the following techniques.

❑ Stay positive in outlook and mood. A number of studies have found that people who are frequently depressed, angry, or hostile have weakened immune systems. For instance, many people carry the herpes virus in their bodies for long periods of time without experiencing an outbreak of symptoms. Yet clinicians have noticed that among people who carry the herpes virus, those who are depressed, hostile, unable to handle stress, and prone to anger have more outbreaks of the condition than others. Many doctors and health practitioners have also noticed that people who react to the news that they have a serious illness with resignation and fatalism are less likely to get well than those who see the illness as a challenge worth confronting.

❑ Recognize and assert your needs. While it is a good idea to avoid constant states of depression and hostility, on the other hand you don't want to become so other-directed and Mr. Nice Guy that you ignore your own needs.

The importance of assertiveness was demonstrated by a recent study performed by psychiatrist George F. Solomon, M.D., and colleagues. They studied eighteen gay men with AIDS, including a number who were long-term survivors. According to Henry Dreher, author of *Your Defense Against Cancer*, "The patients with the most helper T cells—key defenders against disease—showed less anxiety, depression, fatigue, and stress related to their illness. Among the long-term survivors, however, the most surprising correlation with strong immune function was a 'yes' answer to a single question: Could you say 'no' to a request for a favor?" Solomon, a pioneer in PNI, says that this reflects "assertiveness, and the ability to resist becoming a self-sacrificing martyr. It also demonstrates the capacity to monitor and take care of your own needs, psychologically and physically." Studies such as this one and others indicate that some people have an "immune-competent" personality, an important aspect of which is being able to recognize and assert one's deepest needs.

Solomon is quick to point out that other aspects beyond self-assertion come into play, including coping skills that allow you to ward off depression, being able to ask for and accept support from loved ones, having a sense of meaning in your daily life, and maintaining your capacity for pleasure and play. Solomon says that being overly nice won't necessarily make you sick, but you may be sacrificing your immune system if your sense of duty causes you to neglect important personal needs.

Take nutritional supplements that boost immunity. Researchers have found that a number of nutrients can enhance immune function. Principal among these are the antioxidant nutrients, especially vitamins A, C, and E, and the mineral selenium, which protect the immune system by neutralizing free radicals before they damage cells and organs, particularly the oxidant-sensitive thymus (see Step 29 for more information on antioxidants). By the same token, a deficiency in almost any essential nutrient has a negative effect on the immune system. The most effective supplements to take to stimulate immunity include the following (recommended dosages are daily amounts):

➤ vitamin A (10,000–20,000 IU in the form of beta carotene). Beta carotene is especially effective at protecting the thymus from damage, boosting the effectiveness of immune-system mediators such as interferon (a protein that protects the body from viruses), and increasing the number of immune cells such as T-helper cells.
➤ vitamin C (500–1,500 mg), vitamin E (400–800 IU), and selenium (100–150 mcg). These nutrients enhance the production and function of white blood cells or stimulate the activity of antibodies.
➤ vitamin B complex (50–100 mg). Among the individual B vitamins that are most important for promoting immunity are pyridoxine, or B₆ (25–100 mg), and folic acid (400–1,000 mcg).
➤ the major mineral magnesium (450–650 mg) and the trace elements zinc (17–25 mg), which is crucial to the proper functioning of the thymus gland, and copper (2–4 mg).
➤ organic germanium (150–200 mg), a synthetic compound developed by Japanese researchers from the trace mineral and natural element germanium found in soil and some foods.

Add immune-boosting medicinal mushrooms to your daily diet. Although most Americans consider mushrooms merely an occasional gourmet food, in the Orient and other parts of the world various mushrooms are heralded for their remarkable medicinal effects. "Mushrooms have unique and highly varied chemistries, producing an array of novel compounds not found elsewhere in nature," says Andrew Weil, M.D., an expert on the healing effects of plants. He notes that one of the greatest successes of modern pharmacology is the isolation of antibiotics from fungi or molds, which are related to mushrooms.

Researchers are also now finding that medicinal mushrooms can have dramatic effects on the immune system. Weil says, "Some of the food mushrooms and most of the hard, woody medicinal mushrooms from China and Japan contain large molecules, called polysaccharides, that may have antiviral and antitumor properties as a result of their ability to stimulate cells that affect immune responses. Because they are structural components of all organisms, polysaccharides have never excited much interest among pharmacologists as possible medicines, but it now appears that some of them can act as immunomodulators [agents that change the function and activity of the immune system] in animals and humans. . . . It almost goes without saying that nontoxic compounds with these properties would be valuable, given the inability of conventional medicine to do much about viral infections and depressed immunity."

The most well-known medicinal mushroom is known by its Japanese name shiitake *(Lentinus edodes)*. It has long been used in the Orient for its positive effects on aging and sexual dysfunction. A number of scientific studies conducted by Japanese researchers and others indicate that the polysaccharide lentinan found in shiitake helps stimulate the immune system and may shrink tumors. Shiitake is sold whole, fresh, dried, and as a concentrate. As a food, add shiitake to a soup with green leafy vegetables or use it in a stew, stir-fry, or any other dish that calls for mushrooms. As a supplement take one to three capsules daily.

Other medicinal mushrooms of the Orient that may also have immune-boosting and antitumor properties include enokidake *(Flammulina velutipes*, a gourmet-food mushroom that grows wild in North America), maitake *(Grifola frondosa*, a delicious edible mushroom also known as hen of the woods in the U.S.), and *zhu ling* *(Polyporus umbellatus* or *Grifola umbellata*, which grows only rarely in North America). Enokidake, maitake, and zhu ling are sometimes found as ingredients in prepared Chinese herbal medicines.

Take herbs for the immune system. A number of herbs have polysaccharides, like those found in medicinal mushrooms, or other compounds with positive effects on the immune system. The most important of the immune-boosting herbs include

❑ Echinacea *(Echinacea angustifolia, E. purpurea)*, a favorite herb among some Native American tribes, has been "rediscovered" by American herbalists over the past twenty years and is now recognized as a powerful healer and immune booster. The plant contains a broad range of chemical compounds with potential medicinal effects, including the polysaccharide inulin. Echinacea is sold fresh, dried, and in concentrates, tinctures, and extracts. To stimulate immunity take one dropperful of tincture or concentrated drops three to four times daily. Echinacea seems to be most effective when it is not taken regularly. Rather, use it for seven to ten days when you think you've been exposed to an infection-causing agent or at the first signs of symptoms.

❑ Garlic, the popular food and nutritional supplement, is a natural antibiotic, antifungal, and antiviral. It also has antioxidant properties and several of its many compounds have been shown to increase immunity. Eat fresh, raw garlic, use it in your cooking (though heat inactivates its enzymes and significantly reduces its medicinal effects), or take supplements that contain 1,250–2,500 mg of fresh garlic equivalent. Garlic can be taken every day.

❑ Astragalus is a famous Chinese herb derived from the root of a plant *(Astragalus membranaceous)* in the pea family. It is also known as milk-vetch root (astragalus species grow in the U.S.) and *huangqi*. Astragalus is used by practitioners of traditional Chinese medicine to strengthen (or "tonify") the body's overall vitality and support the spleen. Studies confirm that the herb contains medicinally active compounds, including a polysaccharide that stimulates the immune system by increasing the action of antibodies and certain immune cells. Herbal companies offer astragalus fresh or dried and in capsules, concentrated drops, tinctures, and extracts. An average dose is one dropperful of tincture or concentrate two to three times daily or 500–1,000 mg of the powered herb in capsules. It is safe to take on a daily basis.

Relate to others. Various studies have confirmed that loneliness and isolation over long periods of time tend to depress immunity. There are a number of ways beyond getting married or staying in touch with your immediate family to increase your sense of connection with others. For instance, have a long-term relationship with a partner with whom you can share intimacy, establish a network of close friends from work or a favorite sport or activity, or become a member of a support group. Social relationships are increasingly being recognized as a major determinant of not only immune competence but overall health (see Step 46).

One study of caged macaque monkeys found that those animals put into stable groups of forty had stronger immune systems than monkeys put into "shifting" groups of the same size that had new monkeys added each month. Furthermore, those monkeys in the shifting groups that showed more ability to affiliate and were friendlier to newcomers, and those who touched, groomed, and sat closer to their cage mates, were found to have stronger immune systems than those who displayed more dominant behavior.

Particularly if you are suffering from a disease, such as cancer or AIDS, that requires a strong immune response, joining a support group of people facing a similar challenge can be immensely helpful. Studies of people suffering from breast cancer show that those in active support groups live longer.

Eat more of the foods that support the immune system and fewer of those that damage it. The same foods that support the immune system also increase the overall health of the body (see Step 1). These include

➤ leafy green vegetables, vegetables in the cabbage family (broccoli, cauliflower), sea vegetables, whole grains, legumes, and others rich in nutrients and high in fiber
➤ foods with high concentrations of the antioxidants beta carotene (such as carrots and squash), vitamin C (such as citrus fruits), and vitamin E (nuts and seeds)
➤ foods rich in flavonoids (especially any of the dark red or purple berries)

Juicing is an excellent way to include more immune-boosting nutrients in your diet (see Step 5 for more information).

Dietary habits that weaken the immune system include consuming large amounts of foods high in refined sugar, fat, and cholesterol. Sugar reduces the ability of white blood cells to engulf and destroy bacteria. Researchers have found that children are more prone to infection after consuming high levels of sugar. Eating fatty foods can lead to obesity, a condition that impairs immune function, or have other adverse effects. "Increased blood levels of cholesterol, free fatty acids, triglycerides, and bile acids inhibit various immune functions, including the ability of white blood cells to produce antibodies and to migrate to areas of infections where they can engulf and destroy infectious organisms or cancer cells," according to Michael Murray, a naturopathic doctor and the author of *The Healing Power of Foods*.

Short Tips for Boosting Immunity

❑ Avoid regularly turning to antibiotics during the first stages of an infection. The immune system is like a muscle: if you never use it, you're in danger of losing it. Frequent use of antibiotics over an extended period of time can harm white blood cells and weaken the immune system, leaving you more vulnerable to bacterial infections.

❑ Deal with stress (see Step 41). During stressful activities the adrenal glands produce more of certain chemicals that may depress immune function.

❑ Don't stay tired. Studies have shown that less fatigue is associated with increased numbers of various immune cells, including helper T cells, cytotoxic "killer" T cells, and virus-killing cells.

❑ Retain your tonsils and appendix. These two organs are deemed "vestigial," or no longer functioning, by conventional medicine, but they are possibly useful for the full operation of the immune system. Don't allow a surgeon to remove these organs if they're healthy just because he or she happens to be in the bodily neighborhood with scalpel handy.

For More Information

Mail-order sources of medicinal mushrooms include:

Fungi Perfecti
P.O. Box 7634
Olympia, WA 98507
(206) 426-9292

Maitake Products
P.O. Box 1354
Paramus, NJ 07653
(800) 747-7418

Some helpful books on the immune system include:

Immune Power by Jon D. Kaiser, M.D. (New York: St. Martin's Press, 1993)

Maximum Immunity by Michael A. Weiner (Boston: Houghton Mifflin, 1986)

29

REDUCE YOUR CANCER RISK
WITH FOODS AND NUTRIENTS

If recent U.S. surgeons general had been trained at West Point rather than at top medical schools, they might well have already surrendered in the two-decade-old war on cancer. After all, this country has now spent over $1 trillion to fight the disease, including $100 billion in 1992, a figure that represents 10 percent of the nation's entire health-care bill. Cancer is now the cause of 50 million doctor visits and a million surgical operations every year.

Yet, despite the medical weaponry arrayed against it, cancer remains a common disease and a major killer in the United States. The odds that an American will get cancer during his or her lifetime are one in three. In 1990 an estimated 5 million Americans had some form of the disease. By the decade's end twice that number will be diagnosed with new cancers, or three times if you include nonmalignant skin cancers. Cancer kills over half a million Americans annually. It causes more deaths in the United States than any other illness with the exception of cardiovascular disease.

Everyday Steps to Natural Health

The overwhelming presence of cancer in modern industrial society would be less depressing if treatments were safe and reliable. Unfortunately, conventional treatment with drugs and surgery are debilitating, and five-year survival rates for all types of cancers hover around 50 percent, a figure that has not risen appreciably since the early 1970s. It is in your best interests to avoid getting this disease in the first place, and diet and nutrients can help you do just that.

Take antioxidants. Antioxidants protect the body against the damaging effects of free radicals, which are reactive and unstable atoms or molecules derived from exposure to chemicals, smoke, fatty foods, and other sources. The following antioxidant nutrients can combine with and neutralize free radicals without themselves becoming unstable, thus defending your body against harmful effects that include cancer.

If you want to use antioxidant supplements, you don't have to take all of the following vitamins and herbs to lower your cancer risk. Each is beneficial by itself. Another option is to take one of the popular new antioxidant formulas vitamin producers now offer. Many are known as ACES formulas because they contain vitamins A, C, and E and selenium. A typical ACES supplement contains 25,000 IU of vitamin A/beta carotene, 1,000 mg of C, 100 IU of E, and 25 mcg of selenium in each tablet or capsule.

❑ Beta carotene, the plant-based precursor to vitamin A, is a safer source of the nutrient since taking high doses of animal-based vitamin A can be toxic. Orange or dark green leafy vegetables are good sources of beta carotene, or take 10,000–20,000 IU daily of a beta-carotene supplement.

❑ Vitamin C is found in many foods, with the highest levels in leafy green vegetables, broccoli, brussels sprouts, strawberries, and citrus fruit and juice. Oranges have a reputation as the premier vitamin C food; they are a good source of C (50 mg of C per 3.5-ounce serving) but are surpassed by leafy green vegetables (186 mg of C per 3.5-ounces of kale leaves, for instance). Supplements are inexpensive, widely available, and nontoxic. An optimal supplement level is 500–1,500 mg daily.

❑ Vitamin E is common in vegetable oils, wheat-germ oil, dark green leafy vegetables, and whole grains and legumes. Meat and dairy products usually have low amounts. In supplement form take 400–800 IU daily.

❑ Selenium is found in foods such as radishes, carrots, and cabbage (if they're grown in selenium-rich soil), and in fish and sea vegetables (also known as seaweeds). A number of studies have found that areas where people have the highest blood selenium levels have the lowest rates of cancer deaths. Most nutritionists say that a selenium deficiency probably does not directly cause cancer, but that consuming too little selenium may lower the body's cancer defenses. For instance, the enzyme glutathione peroxidase needs selenium to help protect cell walls from carcinogens. As a supplement take 100–150 mcg daily.

❑ Coenzyme Q10 (coQ10) is a natural, vitaminlike nutrient found in salmon and many other foods. Natural-foods stores carry a variety of coQ10 supplements in tablet sizes ranging from 10 to 50 mg. An optimal supplement level is 15–30 mg daily.

❑ Ginkgo (*Ginkgo biloba*), the world's most ancient tree species, has been used by the Chinese for thousands of years to treat asthma and coughs. A standardized extract of ginkgo leaves has also been shown to prevent damage from free radicals in the body and to benefit circulation and immune function. Ginkgo is available in tablets, capsules, or liquids at most natural-foods stores. An average dose of a common powdered form known as a "standardized extract containing 24 percent ginkgo heterosides" is 40 mg three times per day.

In addition to being an effective antioxidant, milk thistle (*Silybum marianum*) has been used as a liver remedy for thousands of years. Recent research done mainly in Germany confirms that silymarin, a complex compound extracted from milk-thistle seeds, helps liver cells regenerate and boosts the organ's ability to filter blood and break down toxins. Milk-thistle-seed products are available as concentrated herbal drops and capsulated extract products. A typical capsule contains 200 mg of milk-thistle extract, standardized for a flavonoid content of 70 percent silymarin (140 mg). Take one capsule three times daily.

Eat foods and herbs that contain the cancer-fighting compounds known as complex polysaccharides. These inhibit the growth of cancer cells and tumors by increasing your body's natural killer-cell activity and strengthening your immune system. Reliable sources of complex polysaccharides include the following:

❑ Sea vegetables are one of nature's most nutritionally dense foods. They have some of the same healing properties as land-based greens such as broccoli and cabbage. Seaside peoples the world over have long eaten sea vegetables, and some varieties were even used by the ancient Egyptians and Chinese to treat cancer. Sea vegetables are high in minerals like selenium and low in fat. Many contain sodium alginate, a compound that has been found to reduce tumors and limit the body's absorption of radioactive contaminants and heavy-metal pollutants. In your local natural-foods store look for noodlelike and mild-tasting arame; thick, fat kombu; bright green and leafy wakame; crispy, sheetlike nori (which is used to wrap the seafood and rice rolls known as sushi); and dark, rich hijiki. These can be used as condiments, in soups and salads, or as side dishes.

❏ Certain medicinal mushrooms have demonstrated anticancer properties. These include shiitake, which has a polysaccharide that may shrink tumors (use in any dish that calls for mushrooms or take as a supplement one to three capsules daily), and the more exotic enokidake, maitake, and zhu ling, which are sometimes found as ingredients in prepared Chinese herbal medicines (see Step 28 for more information).

❏ Ligustrum *(Ligustrum lucidum)* or "Chinese privet" is a fruit-bearing evergreen shrub that grows widely in China, where traditional herbalists dry and powder the fruits for use in products to tonify the liver and kidney. Recent studies both in China and the United States indicate that it boosts the immune system and enhances white-blood-cell counts after cancer treatments such as chemotherapy or radiotherapy. Ligustrum is also an ingredient in a number of herbal combination products sold in the U.S. A typical dose is one dropperful of tincture or concentrate two to three times daily.

❏ Echinacea contains a number of chemical compounds with potential anticancer effects, including polysaccharides such as inulin. Take one dropperful of tincture or concentrate three to four times daily for up to ten days. (See Step 28 for more information).

Eat a high-fiber, cancer-fighting diet. An overall dietary approach to limiting your cancer risk should include generous helpings of whole grains such as wheat, rice, rye, and corn. These are high in various cancer-preventing nutrients, such as fiber, which speeds food's transit time through the digestive system and thus lessens contact with potential carcinogens. Eating high-fiber whole foods also helps you to avoid obesity, which is directly correlated with breast, endometrial, and other cancers. Other anticancer foods include

❏ Cruciferous vegetables such as cabbage, broccoli, cauliflower, and brussels sprouts. These are high in fiber as well as compounds known as indoles, which act as antioxidants in the body.

❏ Soybean products such as tofu and tempeh. These are rich in phytoestrogens, which inhibit hormone-dependent cancers of the breast, uterus, and ovaries.

❏ Garlic and onions. These and other foods from the large allium family (including leek, shallot, and chives) contain sulfur compounds that medical researchers believe have potent antitumor effects. For instance, a Chinese study suggests garlic may reduce the risk of stomach cancer. Garlic also provides vitamins A and C and trace minerals that have antioxidant properties. Garlic and onions can be used in myriad ways in your everyday cooking, or take garlic supplements (1,250–2,500 mg of fresh garlic equivalent daily).

Avoid eating too many fatty foods and other cancer-promoting agents. By following a healthful diet, you also avoid consuming too many of the types of foods that promote cancer. These include foods high in fat, whether of the polyunsaturated or saturated variety. In the body, fats oxidize and create the free radicals that are precursors of cancer cells. Saturated fats also promote obesity and stimulate hormone production, which increases the incidence of hormone-dependent cancers. Other foods and drinks to avoid consuming too much of because they increase your risk of developing cancer include

❏ Salted, pickled, or smoked foods, especially animal foods. These have been tied to higher rates of stomach and gastric cancers in the Orient and Scandinavia.

❏ Peanuts and peanut products. Excessive amounts of these are risky due to the natural contaminant aflatoxin (from a fungus), which causes liver cancer.

❏ Meats like bacon and hot dogs cured with nitrite preservatives. In the stomach these may lead to the formation of carcinogenic nitrosamines.

❏ Meats, fish, and other foods that are barbecued or grilled to the point of becoming charred. Smoke deposits carcinogenic molecules known as polycyclic aromatic hydrocarbons (PAHs) onto the food. Cancer scientists estimate that eating a single charbroiled steak causes you to consume as many PAHs as does smoking six-hundred cigarettes.

❑ Alcohol. Booze can cause cancers of the esophagus, stomach, and liver when consumed to excess.

❑ Coffee. Some studies indicate coffee addicts experience higher rates of cancers of the bladder and lower urinary tract.

Short Tips for Preventing Cancer

❑ Do regular aerobic activities or exercise. By stimulating the immune system and elevating your mood, aerobic exercise increases the effectiveness of white blood cells and your body's other natural defenders against cancer. Some studies indicate that exercise may protect women from breast, uterine, and cervical cancer by lowering levels of circulating estrogen.

❑ Become more expressive and assertive. Mind-body researchers have firmly established that holding in anger and grief suppresses the immune system and decreases white-blood-cell activity. One way that you can become comfortable expressing so-called negative emotions is by tuning in to your bodily sensations when you are upset or angry. Ask yourself why you are feeling this way and what you can do to address your needs.

❑ Practice safe sex. To lower their risk of cancers of the cervix and sexual organs, women should limit the number of sexual partners they have, particularly before the age of sixteen. Early and long-term use of oral contraceptives may increase a woman's risk of breast and liver cancer. Heterosexuals as well as homosexuals should use condoms and take other steps to prevent contracting AIDS, the deadly immune disease that often kills by causing Kaposi's sarcoma, a cancer of the skin, mucous membranes, and lymph nodes.

❑ Relax and quiet your mind on a regular basis. Meditation and other forms of deep relaxation have been found to alleviate chronic fight-or-flight stress patterns, which depress the immune system and prevent the body from defending itself against cancer cells. (See Step 41.)

❑ Avoid exposure to cancer-causing chemicals used in your workplace, particularly if you work in industries that make rubber, chemicals, paints, furniture and cabinets, shoes, and textiles. Other high-risk industries include radiology and mining. An estimated one in ten cancers result from exposure on the job.

❑ Limit your exposure to home and yard carcinogens including toxic chemicals from common household solvents, cleansers, paints, pesticides, and herbicides.

For More Information

Some excellent books on the cancer-and-diet connection are:

Cancer & Nutrition by Charles B. Simone, M.D. (Garden City Park, N.Y.: Avery Publishing Group, 1992)

Healing Through Nutrition by Melvyn Werbach, M.D. (New York: Harper Collins Publishers, 1993)

Your Defense Against Cancer by Henry Dreher (New York: Harper & Row, 1989)

Mail-order sources of traditional Chinese herbs and prepared medicines include the following:

East Earth Trade Winds
P.O. Box 493151
Redding, CA 96049
(916) 241-6878
(800) 258-6878

Meridian Traditional Herbal Products
26 McGirr St.
Cumberland, RI 02864
(401) 728-0650
(800) 356-6003

Roots & Legends
38 Miller Ave.
Mill Valley, CA 94941
(415) 381-5631

30

SHARPEN YOUR VISION

Vision correction—prescribing eyeglasses and contact lenses to sharpen eyesight—is a booming industry in the U.S. An estimated 134 million Americans, more than half the population, wears corrective lenses. Vision services and products represented a $15 billion industry in 1990. On the other hand, vision improvement—using techniques such as eye exercises and tools such as nutritional supplements to make your eyes function better—is still a blip on the screen. Only one in eight of the doctors who measure vision errors and prescribe corrective lenses are so-called behavioral optometrists. These professionals show patients how to use computerized optometric activities, eyepatches and special glasses, games and mazes, vision devices, and biofeedback to improve coordination of the entire vision process. Vision improvement takes more time and effort than vision correction, but the payoff is "both optically and emotionally rewarding," says Janet Goodrich, Ph.D., a teacher of natural vision improvement.

"When I began teaching vision improvement in 1968," Goodrich says, "I had watched twenty years flow past from behind thick lenses, and it took me two years and two sets of reduced glasses to 'play' my way out of them completely. Since then thousands of self-motivated vision-improvement students I've worked with have done the same, reading down the eye charts both close and far and bringing new life back to moribund eyes."

The human eye is often compared to a camera or a camcorder. Like these optical machines the eye concentrates light rays and forms a picture of the outside world. But such a comparison does the eye an injustice. The eye is one of the most complex organs of the body, and its estimated billion working parts make light-recording machines seem as simple as a toothpick by comparison.

The eye's multitude of tiny muscles and nerve endings allow it effortlessly to shift focus in a tenth of a second and accommodate changing light levels. It can perceive 10 million gradations of light, distinguish 7 million shades of color, and detect light as dim as a hundred-trillionth of a watt. The eye transforms light into electrical nerve impulses and through the optic nerve transmits visual data to the brain at a rate of a billion messages per second.

Even more importantly than these mechanical advantages the eye has over any camcorder is the human quality of seeing. Mechanical eyes such as those found in some robots, says Deepak Chopra, M.D., "are never bored by what they look at or enthralled by beauty. They do not prefer crimson to scarlet, or vice versa. They do not relish the softness of the shadows in Titian's paintings or the stark melodrama in Caravaggio's. None of the qualities of light that really matter, in a human, personal sense, can be translated into mechanical terms."

Chopra's comment underscores the fact that vision encompasses much more than the eyes. It is a complex activity involving body, mind, and spirit. Vision is often reduced to a single factor, acuity. This is the ability to see a high-contrast object from a certain distance, with the norm determined by discerning a three-eighths-inch-high figure on the Snellen eye chart from twenty feet away (20/20 vision). Yet optimum vision also includes factors such as depth perception (seeing objects in perspective), focusing (bringing images into sharp focus from various distances), shifting (moving the eyes to sweep over the visual field), and fusion (using the eyes as a team that works together).

Most people accept their vision as a given, like their eye color or height. But like any complex system, the eyes need care and attention to keep them functioning at their optimum.

Everyday Steps to Natural Health

"The holistic approach recognizes that our eyes and vision are influenced by all factors in our lives," says Robert Michael Kaplan, O.D., author of *Seeing Beyond 20/20*. "The food we eat, the way we think, our degree of tension or distress, daily visual habits, purpose, intention, breathing, posture, attitudes, and the movement of our eyes collectively play a more powerful role in our vision than any of the individual components are able to achieve alone." Here are some ways to use the holistic approach to improve your vision.

Take vision-boosting nutrients. Vitamins and minerals of special benefit to the eyes include average daily doses of the following:

❏ Vitamin A, 10,000–20,000 IU in the form of beta carotene. Vitamin A levels in the body play an important role in vision, especially night vision. Vitamin A is concentrated in the retina, the thin screen at the back of the eyeball that transforms light into electrical signals for the brain. Specialized light-receiving cells in the retina known as rods release vitamin A when struck by photons of light, a crucial step in the chemistry of vision. A deficiency in vitamin A often results in blurred vision (which can also result from *too much* vitamin A) and an inability to adapt to darkness.

❏ Vitamin B complex, 50–100 mg. A number of the B vitamins are necessary for eye health. For instance, there is some evidence that vitamin B_6 protects the lenses of the eyes from cataracts. Nutritionalists have also noticed that a deficiency in riboflavin (B_2) can cause a sensitivity to light and a worsening of acuity.

❏ Vitamin C, 500–1,500 mg. Vitamin C and other antioxidant nutrients (such as 400–800 IU of vitamin E and 100–150 mcg of selenium) protect the eye from damage by neutralizing free radicals, unstable atoms or molecules (from chemicals, smoke, and other sources) that harm living cells. Researchers have linked vitamin C to a reduced risk of cataracts and other eye diseases. Studies indicate that vitamin C may also promote recovery from cornea burns and help treat glaucoma.

❏ Zinc, 17–25 mg. Researchers have found that zinc can stop progressive loss of vision. Like vitamin A, zinc deficiencies can lead to various eye problems. Zinc is alone among nutrients in also boosting two other senses: taste and smell.

Your eyes use light as a nutrient, too. For glands such as the hypothalamus and the pineal located in the brain, light that enters through the eyes is a vital nutrient. These specialized hormone-control centers use light in part to control the body's biological rhythms, metabolic rate, blood pressure, immune response, and even emotional balance. Limited light over a period of weeks or months causes the pineal to release too little of the hormone melatonin. Lack of melatonin has been linked with seasonal affective disorder (SAD), the depressed state that afflicts an estimated 35 million Americans during the winter. The condition is most common among populations far from the equator.

Human evolution has occurred under natural sunlight, which is at least ten times brighter than even the most well-lit indoor rooms. Sunlight also differs from artificial light in its spectral pattern, the level of various colors and wavelengths that make up light. Some light researchers such as Dr. John Ott, formerly director of the Environmental Health and Light Research Institute in Sarasota, Florida, say that long-term exposure to artificial light with distorted spectral patterns can affect hormone levels in the body. Health problems ranging from headaches to fatigue may result.

Richard Leviton, author of *Seven Steps to Better Vision*, suggests the following practical steps to improve your light diet:

❑ Get outdoors for at least a short period of time every day. "Even during the winter in northern climes, if you dress appropriately and find a sunny spot, you can be comfortable long enough to give the eyes a nice natural-light bath," Leviton says.

❑ Wear sunglasses only when it is overly bright outside. Many people wear sunglasses whenever they go outside, even when it is not particularly bright. Over time this can make the eyes sensitive to normal light. Habitual sunglass wearing may also be depriving you of colors or other parts of the light spectrum (such as ultraviolet) that in tiny amounts are beneficial to health (see Step 20).

❑ Upgrade your indoor lights, especially if you spend almost all of your time indoors (as most of us do!). You can switch some of your fixtures to full-spectrum fluorescent light tubes with a high "color rendering index," a measurement of how closely a light duplicates the visible spectrum of sunlight. A popular brand is the Vita-Lite manufactured by Duro-Test. Incandescent-bulb technology does not allow for such close duplication of sunlight, though so-called "color-corrected" incandescents are a slight improvement on regular incandescent bulbs and fluorescent tubes. If price is no object, consider one of the high-tech multibulb systems that victims of SAD use to create indoor sunlight.

Exercise the vision muscles. Take a few minutes each day to do the following eye exercises. Remove any corrective lenses, sit comfortably with erect posture, and breathe deeply.

❑ Tromboning. This exercise, suggested by Janet Goodrich, helps to restore and maintain proper focusing. Cover one eye with your hand and use the other eye to look at a postcard, photo, or other flat, detailed object you hold in your other hand. Now slowly trombone the postcard back and forth in two-inch intervals, trying to keep it in focus as you bring it to within three to five inches of your nose and then out to arm's length. Look at different parts of the object to prevent staring. (Habitual, excessive staring is a bad habit that can eventually harm your vision.) Try varying your tromboning speed. Work with one eye for two to three minutes and then switch sides.

❑ Edging. This exercise discourages staring and teaches the eyes to shift rapidly over the visual field, allowing you to see with greatest clarity. Look at a detailed object that is just beyond your range of clear seeing. Slowly trace the edges of the object. Rather than keeping your head still, move your head as if your nose is a pointer that directs the eyes' movement. Edge your vision around the object's perimeter first in one direction and then the other.

Your eyes also need to relax. Your eyes are surrounded and controlled by nerves and muscles that benefit from periodic rest and relaxation, as do the nerves and muscles in your legs or arms. For the following relaxation exercises remove any corrective lenses, sit with proper posture, and breathe deeply.

❑ Palming. This exercise was promoted by New York ophthalmologist William H. Bates, M.D., who pioneered vision improvement in the first decades of this century. Palming relaxes the eyes by bathing them in total darkness. The warmth and pressure of the hands also relaxes the eyes' nerves and muscles. Keeping your back straight while sitting, bend over at the waist and rest your elbows on a desk or table. Cover your eyes with your palms by placing the heels of your hands on your cheekbones. Cross the fingers on the forehead to avoid pressing on the nose in a way that restricts breathing. Cup your hands slightly so that you are not directly pressing on the eyeballs. Try to prevent any light from getting through your hands. Close your eyes and direct them slightly downward. Relax your eyes and facial muscles. Breathe deeply and palm for two to three minutes. When you take away your hands and open your eyes, you may find your vision improved.

❑ Blinking. Most people blink automatically about twenty times per minute. People with poor eyesight or vision habits may blink less frequently. This can result in staring or squinting, which will eventually worsen vision. Blinking exercises can also gently stretch the muscles that attach the eye to the socket. The exercise is simple: do a series of forty to fifty blinks for ten to twenty seconds at a time while slowly moving your head from side to side.

Don't let VDT stand for "vision destroying terminal." An estimated 40 million Americans—writers, scientists, salespeople, and office workers of all types—now spend eight hours or more daily working on computers. Detailed near-point work tends to lock the eyes into place and encourage staring. It also frequently promotes postural problems that can contribute to poor vision. Some surveys estimate that as many as two out of every three VDT users experience general eyestrain, fatigue, headaches, a burning sensation in their eyes, or other visual problems related to the work. Eyestrain is "a high-tech health concern of our information society," according to Edward Godnig, O.D., and John Hacunda, authors of *Computers and Visual Stress*. Here are some ways to avoid the worst effects of VDT work.

❑ Every ten to fifteen minutes look away from your computer screen and momentarily focus on a more distant object.

❑ Provide your work area with ample bright but nonglaring light. Underillumination indoors is a common problem. An ideal placement for your work area is next to a window or under a skylight. For a windowless office or at night, use a number of lamps positioned three to four feet away to cross-illuminate your work area. Make your VDT screen approximately the same level of brightness as your desk or work area.

❑ Use a book or manuscript holder to position working materials at approximately the same height and distance from your eyes as is your computer screen.

❑ Sit on your sitting bones and keep your head, neck, and torso aligned (see Step 16).

Short Tips for Better Vision

❑ Help stimulate the eyes and increase local circulation by doing a traditional Chinese acupressure massage. Sitting, put your elbows on a table and make two fists. Bring your eyes to the fists and put the thumbs on the temples. Use the middle joint of the forefinger of each hand to rub points around the perimeter of the eye sockets. Gently rub each point four times counterclockwise and then four times clockwise.

❑ Try the herb bilberry *(Vaccinium myrtillus)* to improve your night vision. Jam made from this European relative of the blueberry was eaten by RAF pilots before night missions during WWII to provide them a tactical advantage. Scientific studies have since identified compounds in bilberry (anthocyanosides) that affect certain enzymes crucial to vision. To temporarily relieve eye fatigue or boost night vision, take 25–50 mg of a concentrated extract containing 15–25 percent anthocyanosides.

❑ Work out emotional imbalances that may be hampering your vision. "Somebody gets myopic for a purpose, as a strategy, as a way of bringing the mind and body into some kind of different balance," says Jacob Liberman, O.D. Many holistic vision therapists agree, citing studies that have found links between personality traits, early emotional traumas, and vision. For instance, some studies have found that nearsighted people tend to be emotionally controlled and analytical. Take steps to express your inner nature and your vision may improve as well.

For More Information

Useful books on vision improvement include:

Natural Vision Improvement by Janet Goodrich, Ph.D. (Berkeley, Calif.: Celestial Arts, 1985)

Seeing Beyond 20/20 by Robert-Michael Kaplan, O.D. (Vancouver, B.C.: Beyond Words Publishing, 1987)

Seven Steps to Better Vision: Easy, Practical and Natural Techniques That Will Improve Your Eyesight by Richard Leviton (Brookline Village, Mass.: East West/Natural Health Books, 1992)

The following organization offers vision products, practitioner referrals, and information on behavioral optometry:

Optometric Extension Program Foundation and Vision Extension
2912 S. Daimler St.
Santa Ana, CA 92705
(714) 250-0846

See "For More Information" in Step 19 for mail-order sources of full-spectrum bulbs.

SIMPLE STEPS
TO
NATURAL HEALTH

AT NIGHT

31

SLEEP SOUNDLY

Sufficient and restful sleep is an often overlooked health factor. Your body needs sleep to work well. One recent study found that when you miss three or more hours of sleep, your immune-system activity decreases by as much as 50 percent. Immunity returns to normal when your sleep pattern does. Not only your immune system but most other bodily systems also undergo major positive changes while you sleep. For example:

- ➤ brain waves slow
- ➤ blood pressure falls
- ➤ muscles relax
- ➤ hormone production from the pituitary increases
- ➤ the rates of activity of the heart and lungs decrease
- ➤ your body repairs damaged tissues and cells
- ➤ you dream, allowing your mind to work on unresolved anxieties and fears

In spite of the many benefits of sleep, the average American gets 20 percent less nighttime sleep than Americans of a century ago, and scientists estimate that one in four Americans are sleep deprived. Being deprived of sufficient sleep can also have more serious consequences than a compromised immune system. The Department of

Transportation estimates that drowsiness or falling asleep at the wheel causes two-hundred thousand auto accidents every year and is the cause of an estimated one in three fatal truck accidents. Sleep deprivation probably played a role in such recent disasters as the *Exxon Valdez* oil spill, the Union Carbide explosion in Bhopal, and the nuclear-power accident at Chernobyl, according to Roger Fritz, Ph.D., author of *Sleep Disorders: America's Hidden Nightmare.* A recent report from the National Commission on Sleep Disorders estimated that the direct costs of sleep disorders are almost $16 billion per year, from accidents and lost or inefficient work time.

Exactly how much sleep you need varies. Infants usually need at least ten hours, children at least eight hours, and most adults seven. Adult ranges depend on the individual, too. "There is actually a range of anywhere from five or six to ten hours a night," says Sanford H. Auerbach, M.D., director of the Sleep Disorders Center at Boston University. He adds that many people do not get as much sleep as they need to function optimally.

One reason for widespread sleep deprivation is that getting by on only five to six hours of sleep has become a badge of honor among workaholics. Viewing sleep as an indulgence or luxury instead of as a requirement for better health is a sign of time sickness. In addition to the long-term health costs, insufficient sleep may also lead to chronic underalertness, lower creativity levels, poorer language skills, and an increased risk of depression.

The quality of your sleep is as important as the quantity. Recent studies have shown that many people suffer from sleep that is restless and frequently interrupted, whether from the results of daytime stress or because of external factors like loud noise. You can improve your sleep quality by being more relaxed at bedtime. The ultimate arbiter of whether you've gotten sleep of sufficient quality and quantity is awakening refreshed and energized, ready to enjoy the day.

If your sleep is less than perfect, you're in good company. At least 40 million Americans suffer from some type of chronic sleep disorder. The most common sleep disorder is insomnia, which is characterized by difficulty falling asleep (takes an hour or more) and waking in the night without being able to get back to sleep. Insomniacs often awaken too early, anxious and tired from not sleeping.

Common causes of insomnia include caffeinated or alcoholic beverages in the evening (alcohol is deceptive because it may make you drowsy but later in the night interferes with sound sleep), nervous tension and anxiety, PMS or menopause, lack of exercise, vitamin deficiencies, and food allergies. Cigarette smokers take longer to fall asleep, as do workers who change shifts frequently. Insomnia may also result from taking various medications, including those for asthma (such as theophylline) and headaches (some pain relievers such as Anacin and Vanquish contain caffeine). More serious conditions ranging from chronic fatigue syndrome to viral infections may also cause insomnia in adults.

Everyday Steps to Natural Health

Everybody suffers from sleep problems once in a while. If your sleeplessness is habitual, you should consult a health practitioner for advice. For many people, though, the following suggestions are all that are needed to help them get a good night's sleep.

Develop a series of personal nighttime rituals and regular daily practices for facilitating sleep. Sleep can't be willed; it must be coaxed. One trick for courting sleep is to work up to it every night by following a nighttime ritual. The ritual can be any of various steps that you take to signal your body that sleep is next. This allows you to start to relax before you actually go to bed. Include your family or mate in your regular bedtime routine. Your ritual may involve a warm bath, meditation, light stretching, stargazing, or just brushing your teeth. Whatever the series of acts, when a ritual becomes regular, most people find that it allows sleep to come much more easily.

Your ritual should be customized for your personality and tastes, but some steps are more appropriate than others. For instance, don't do things right before bedtime that increase alertness. Many people find too stimulating such things as watching television news, reading scary literature, and performing aerobic exercise. Exercise earlier in the day, on the other hand, promotes restful sleep. Relaxing activities may include reading, needlepoint or other repetitious hobbies, or playing a musical instrument.

Do your ritual activities *before* getting into bed. Most sleep experts agree that it is best to use your bed only for sleeping, so that your body associates lying in bed with slumber, not watching television or reading. Also, lie down to sleep only when you are actually sleepy.

Finally, extend your sleep ritual to the morning by getting up at the same time each morning regardless of how much sleep you got at night. Likewise, try to eat dinner at the same time each night to help regulate the body's internal clock. Over time these steps will help your sleep to become more regular.

If you still can't sleep, use simple relaxation techniques for dealing with stress and anxiety. Occasional insomnia strikes almost everyone at some point in life. A frequent cause is stress or nervous tension associated with work, money, or a family problem. There are numerous steps for dealing with stress on a daily basis (see Step 41). You can also help to relax shortly before bed by doing either the abdominal breathing technique described in Step 26 or some of the light stretches suggested in Step 12. The relaxing yoga pose aptly labeled "the corpse" is a stress-relieving technique you can use while tossing and turning in bed.

Lying on your back in bed, put your arms at your side, palms up. Stretch your legs out and allow your feet to fall open. Maintain a deep and even breathing pattern, inhaling and exhaling through the nose. Consciously tell each part of the body to relax, starting at the top of the head and proceeding to the scalp, eyes, face, neck, and so on down the body. After you've relaxed all of the major muscle groups, follow your breathing. Your mind will naturally wander, but try to keep it from dwelling on personal problems or your work, which may cause sleep-preventing anxiety. Rather, think about pleasant things that happened to you during the day, or anytime in the past. Avoid concentrating, whether on your breath or your problems. Concentration has a stimulating, anxiety-causing effect. Rather, let your attention dwell lightly on your breathing or some pleasant subject. Identify any muscle tension that creeps back into your body and gently release it.

When necessary, use natural remedies to help you get to sleep rather than alcohol or sleeping pills. Faced with an inability to sleep well, many people turn to sleep-inducing drugs. Sleeping pills are among the most frequently used drugs in the world. American physicians write out an estimated 24 million prescriptions every year for sleep disorders. Millions of Americans also attempt to cure their insomnia by taking over-the-counter, nonbarbiturate sedatives like Excedrin P.M. or the antihistamine Benadryl. Barbiturates should never be used more than occasionally. If used regularly for more than three to four weeks, they become ineffective at inducing sleep and may actually cause insomnia instead of relieving it. They also cause addiction and harmful side effects, alter normal sleeping cycles, and suppress dreaming.

Fortunately a number of herbs as well as other natural remedies are effective at inducing sleep. Compared to sleeping pills, these remedies are generally milder, safer, and less addictive. Herbs and nutrients also don't cause adverse reactions with alcohol. In addition, most herbs used for insomnia also have bitter properties that improve digestion and liver function. In some cases they help improve a person's overall health. Even so, herbs should not be used on a regular basis to fall asleep since they don't directly address whatever is causing the insomnia.

The most popular natural sleep aid is the herb valerian. Derived from the root of a European plant *(Valeriana officianalis)* now spread throughout the northeastern U.S., valerian helps relieve anxiety and nervous tension. Researchers have found that valerian extracts depress the central nervous system and relax the smooth muscle tissue that controls the intestines, blood vessels, and other body parts. Studies have found it as effective as some barbiturates for reducing the time needed to fall asleep. Valerian also improves sleep quality. For instance, a recent Swedish study found that 45 percent of subjects reported improved sleep after taking valerian.

Valerian's action is somewhat slower than that of antianxiety drugs like Valium, according to Rob McCaleb, president of the Herb Research Foundation in Boulder, Colorado, "Take valerian thirty minutes to one hour before you want to sleep," he says. It is safe even when taken in moderate doses (a gram of the powder, a teaspoon of the tincture, or 250 mg of the liquid or solid extract) but should not be used for an extended period of time.

For unknown reasons, a small percentage of people who take valerian find it stimulating instead of calming. If valerian doesn't work for you, choose from among the following four herbs. Like valerian they are generally recognized as effective sleep-inducers and relaxants.

Herbs to help induce sleep are frequently taken about thirty to forty-five minutes before bedtime. Alternatively, try one dose about one to two hours before bedtime and another dose right at bedtime. All of the following herbs come in capsules, tablets, extracts, tinctures, and concentrated drops. A warm herbal tea is relaxing, though the dose of active ingredients is limited. A common dosage for the tincture or concentrated drops is one dropperful.

❏ California poppy is a flowering plant *(Eschscholtzia californica)* that produces a calming and quieting effect on the central nervous system. It is not as widely known as other herbal sedatives like valerian, but is increasing in popularity.

❏ Hops is derived from the conelike fruits of a climbing plant *(Humulus lupulus)* best known for giving beer its bitter flavor. It works particularly well at relieving muscle tension that is preventing sleep.

❏ Passionflower preparations are made from the leaves of a climbing vine *(Passiflora incarnata)*. It was used as a sedative by the Aztecs and is still taken today for its mild calming effects.

❏ Chamomile is an ancient and widely used herb made from the flowers of either of two annual plants (German chamomile, or *Matricaria recutita,* and Roman chamomile, or *Anthemis nobilis*). It is usually taken as a tea to treat anxiety and insomnia as well as digestive problems. It is among the mildest of the herbal sedatives and a good choice for children.

The following three nutritional supplements can be used either instead of or along with herbs to help induce sleep:

❏ Melatonin is a pineal-gland hormone that helps regulate sleep. An average dose is 3 mg before bedtime.

❏ Calcium and magnesium are usually taken in a 2:1 ratio, such as 800 mg calcium and 400 magnesium, at bedtime for their relaxing effect.

❏ Tryptophan is an essential amino acid found in various protein foods such as turkey, tuna, and nut butter. It is used by the body as a precursor to the neurotransmitter serotonin, which has a calming effect that can help some people to fall asleep. It has not been available in supplement form since 1989, when the FDA recalled all tryptophan products after three dozen deaths were tied to a contaminated batch from Japan. Numerous studies performed prior to then had confirmed that tryptophan is an effective sleep remedy.

Tryptophan is present in some protein foods at amounts of up to 200 mg per serving. Nutritionists disagree, however, whether eating tryptophan-rich foods is sleep-inducing. That is because other amino acids in protein foods compete with tryptophan for uptake by the brain and may prevent the tryptophan from having much effect. Some researchers say that an indirect route is more effective: eat a serving of complex carbohydrates like pasta, bread, or potatoes right before bed. The carbohydrates raise insulin levels in the blood, and this lowers all amino-acid levels with the exception of tryptophan. More tryptophan is then available to become serotonin and produce a calming effect.

Try a helping of either protein-rich or complex-carbohydrate-rich foods about an hour before bedtime to see whether either work for you.

Short Tips for Better Sleep

❏ A warm bath is often relaxing, possibly because it temporarily raises your body temperature. The subsequent lowering of your temperature is accompanied by a feeling of fatigue. Boost the bath's relaxing effects by adding four to five drops of the calming essential oil of lavender or chamomile.

❏ Put a sachet of dried lavender in your pillowcase.

❏ Cut back on the late-in-the-day consumption of caffeine-containing drinks like coffee, tea, colas, and foods such as chocolate with related compounds.

❏ If a mate's snoring is the cause of your insomnia, spray his or her throat with a saline nasal-spray lubricant that is free of other active ingredients. The spray lubricates the nasal passages and discourages congestion, a common cause of snoring.

❏ *Coffea,* the homeopathic medicine made from dilutions of coffee, is an effective remedy for insomnia from excitement or joy, an overactive mind, or drinking too much coffee.

❏ If you anticipate increased stress levels (you're changing jobs, for instance), prevent it from affecting your sleep by taking extra vitamin B complex (50 mg twice a day) and calcium/magnesium (800/400 mg daily). A deficiency of these nutrients is associated with insomnia.

❏ Lower your exposure to disturbing levels of nighttime noise and artificial light. Researchers have found that even lights not bright enough and sounds not loud enough to awaken you can still disrupt normal patterns of sleeping and dreaming. Relatively low levels of intermittent light and noise can cause you to sleep fitfully and awaken feeling tired and anxious. Nighttime lighting can be more than merely annoying or bothersome: it can desynchronize your body's internal clock.

❑ Increase your nighttime sleep if you find yourself nodding off during the day or napping frequently, signs of sleep deficiency.

For More Information

The following book offers a wide range of effective suggestions for improving sleep:

Natural Sleep by Philip Goldberg and Daniel Kaufman (New York: Bantam Books, 1980)

The following organization refers patients to accredited sleep-disorder centers and provides information on sleep-disorder medicine and research:

National Sleep Foundation
122 S. Robertson Blvd., 3rd Fl.-L
Los Angeles, CA 90048

32

LET DREAMS BE
YOUR GUIDE

If you're like most people, you give your dreams a few fleeting thoughts upon awakening in the morning but otherwise mostly ignore them. This dismissive attitude results in part from Western cultures' scientific and materialistic bent—what can't be easily measured and controlled is often relegated to the fringes. Some mechanistically oriented scientists, such as Nobel Prize-winner Francis Crick, now even say that dreams are random images, life's little typos that the brain/computer has no need to put into its long-term storage banks. By Crick's perspective (one based on speculation, incidentally, not dream research), dreams are either totally meaningless or best forgotten.

Therapists, counselors, and people who actually work with dreams, on the other hand, have a diametrically opposed view. Building upon the work started by the publication of Sigmund Freud's *The Interpretation of Dreams* in 1899, they contend that dreams are not only pregnant with meaning but a potential source of deep insight into character and action. In their experience, dreams reflect reality and offer hidden clues about waking life. Modern dream researchers such as Rosalind Cartwright, Ph.D., have demonstrated in numerous studies that dreams provide direct access to the key emotional issues of our lives. "Most everyone who seriously studies their own dreams . . . finds them personally meaningful," says psychiatrist Gordon Globus, author of *Dream Life, Wake Life.*

Exactly how dreams work and what they represent are not known. Theories abound from followers of Freud, the Swiss psychiatrist Carl Jung, and others. Among the most popular explanations of dreams are

➤ they represent the working out of unconscious wishes and repressed impulses, desires, fears, and emotions
➤ they review the happenings of the day, consolidating memory and assimilating traumatic experiences
➤ they represent images from humanity's vast "collective unconscious"
➤ they are metaphors for our emotions; "Dream images . . . are a kind of picture language for how we feel," according to psychologist and dream authority Patricia Garfield, Ph.D.
➤ they are a release valve for insecurities and neuroses; "Dreaming permits each and every one of us to be quietly and safely insane every night of our lives," notes dream researcher Charles William Dement

While there is disagreement about interpretation, sleeping patterns and the mechanics of dreaming have been more clearly outlined in the past forty years, thus providing a foundation for learning how to benefit from your dreams. Scientists divide sleep into five main stages. Stages I through IV are progressively deeper states of sleep, from stage I in which the person is easily awakened to stage IV in which the person is aroused with difficulty. During these stages the body gradually slows its metabolism and lowers its blood pressure, heart rate, and temperature. It takes about ninety minutes for the body to progress through stages I–IV.

The fifth stage of sleep is known as REM sleep, for the bursts of rapid-eye movements that the sleeper makes while in it. First identified in the early 1950s, REM sleep is markedly different from the non-REM sleep that precedes it. During REM sleep, your blood pressure, pulse, and breathing become irregular. Brain waves also become irregular, resembling those common while awake. Body temperature rises slightly and the sex organs become aroused. The parts of the brain responsible for processing visual and sensory data are stimulated. Some studies indicate the REM periods allow the mind to work on retaining information and boosting recent memory. Most importantly, REM sleep is characterized by your most vivid and frequent dreaming.

While it is a myth that dreams occur only during REM sleep, dreams that occur during stages I–IV tend to be shorter, more thoughtlike, and less elaborate then REM dreams. Approximately 25 percent of most people's sleep time is spent during the REM stage—two hours if you get eight hours of sleep (infants' sleep is 50 percent REM, declining gradually to 25 percent by age ten). Various factors can, however, cause you to experience shorter periods of deep stage IV sleep and REM sleep, including

- ➤ smoking
- ➤ consuming excessive amounts of alcohol
- ➤ taking sleeping pills on a regular basis

(See Step 31 for how to improve your sleep).

Everyday Steps to Natural Health

There are three basic steps to take to begin to benefit from a greater understanding of your dreams: remembering them, recording them, and interpreting them.

Develop your ability to recall your dreams. Not being able to remember the previous night's dreams is a common complaint among newcomers to dreamwork. From one perspective, not remembering a lot of dreams is a sign of getting full, healthy sleep. The relaxed, calm person who does not awaken numerous times during the night will usually be able to recall only his or her last dream, while the tense and anxious person who awakens repeatedly during the night may remember a number of dreams. Here are some suggestions for any type of sleeper to develop better dream recall.

❑ The first step in promoting dream recall is simply to decide that your dreams hold meanings that are valuable to you and you want to remember them. As you ready yourself for bed, make a mental note that you'll recall your dreams upon wakening.

❑ Put a pad and pen, or a tape recorder, next to your bed to ease dream reporting.

❑ If you awaken during the night with a dream memory, lie still as you try to recall it. During REM sleep your muscles become slightly paralyzed. Prolong the stillness upon awakening, keeping your eyes closed, and review what you can of the dream in your mind. Let your mind wander to prevent outside images from distracting you from the dream. If stillness is not working, try shifting sleep positions to see if that jogs a memory.

❏ Try to awaken naturally in the morning rather than using an alarm. On occasion an alarm will disrupt your sleep at an opportune moment for remembering a dream (that is, during the dream's last moments), but more frequently an alarm has a sudden, jarring effect that jerks you into full consciousness. Dream recall is enhanced, however, by lingering in the twilight period between sleep and total wakefulness.

❏ Jot down a few key words about the dream or tape a few sentences into a recorder. Use a lighted pen or a tiny night spotlight so as not to disturb your ability to get back to sleep. A voice-activated tape recorder allows you to record without moving about, thus promoting better dream recall.

❏ Reconstruct what dreams you remember backward: from the end to the beginning. The end will be more fresh in your memory and each episode in the dream may prompt memories of those that preceded.

❏ If you can't seem to recall much of what happened in a dream, try focusing on the feelings and emotions.

❏ Don't get discouraged if you can't remember much on any given awakening. Dreams that contain strong emotions and vivid images and sensory experiences are easier to remember than other dreams, and many dreams involve little more than you talking with another person. You won't frequently have dreams like the one in which you're falling naked down a twisting green tube while the "Star Spangled Banner" plays in the background.

Keep a dream journal as well as a day journal to help you understand your dreams. Writing down your dreams establishes a record and eases analysis. Some people who feel that they haven't the time to write out their dreams on a daily basis do so only on weekends. Others just keep a journal of especially noteworthy dreams. Start with a time commitment you're comfortable with and make adjustments as necessary.

Create your journals in whatever manner you prefer. Write your dreams out longhand in a notebook or enter them into your computer files. You can also draw pictures if you are artistically inclined or if drawing seems to help you reconstruct the dream. Give each dream a pithy title and provide a short summary of its events, characters, and feelings. Write up your dreams as close as possible to the time you experienced them. Use the rough notes you took in the morning or during the night. Writing the dream in the present tense seems to promote better recall.

You will probably find it easier to make sense of your dreams if you keep a day journal in addition to your dream journal. Before you go to sleep at night take a few moments to record thoughts and feelings about your day's experiences. Make a note of major events, strong emotions, and interactions with family, friends, or coworkers. A number of studies indicate that dreams often comment upon and attempt to resolve the most noteworthy emotions you experienced during the previous day. Keeping a day journal facilitates comparisons between real life and dream events. As Aristotle commented, "The most skillful interpreter of dreams is he who has the faculty of observing resemblances." The day journal can be particularly useful because current events in your life may not show up in your dreams for weeks or months.

Explore the dream text to find meanings useful to your everyday life. The French writer Michel de Montaigne commented, "Dreams are the true interpreters of our inclinations, but art is required to sort them out." Time and experience also help. After you've studied your dreams for some time, you'll probably recognize images and themes that reoccur. Soon you will more quickly realize how these familiar dream events relate to your everyday life.

An easy way to start is to explore the aspects of the dream that most intrigue you. Beginners to dreamwork are often intimidated by a dream's sheer strangeness. Don't try to do a full analysis or get discouraged if even an apparently simple dream does not yield to analysis. A dream's meaning may become apparent to you over time.

It is also best to immediately focus on your own role in the dream drama. One study of over 600 dreams from 250 normal subjects found that 95 percent of dreams are first-person narratives in which the dreamer plays a starring (or at least prominent) role. In the one dream in twenty that you are not a star, you are likely to be the person observing the dream events. In these cases, consider whether one of the objects, or another person, in the dream is a symbol for you.

An overall strategy is to become a dream detective. One of the things detectives do to reconstruct events is to ask questions. Upon arriving at the scene of a crime a good detective will immediately want to find out the "five Ws and H":

❑ Who are the main characters? Who are you in the dream? Are some parts of you similar to other dream characters?

❑ What are the major objects, events, and actions and how are they used in the dream? What do they remind you of from your recent life?

❑ Where is the action occurring?

❑ Why are you having this dream now?

❑ When is the dream set—past, present, or future?

❑ How old are you in the dream? How do you feel in the dream? Do the experiences and feelings of the dream remind you of anything that has happened to you recently?

It is crucial to consider the feelings and emotions of the dream, not just the objects and the story. According to psychoanalyst Walter Bonime, "An emotion experienced in a dream never symbolizes anything. It is always an authentic response to something in the dreamer's life." Dream researchers agree that emotions and feelings are often the key to understanding the dream's meaning.

Don't be discouraged by the seemingly negative content of most of your dreams. Even more so than women, men's typical dreams feature characters acting in unsocial ways. Aggression, violence, anger, and other hostile emotions are more common than loving ones. One dream researcher who studied ten thousand dreams of normal people found that two-thirds of the dreams were not enjoyable by waking standards. Having dreams in which you behave poorly by real-life standards does not mean you're crazy.

If possible, work with your mate, a close friend, or a dream group. Telling other people about your dreams on a regular basis can be a risky affair. As the English satirist Max Beerbohm commented, "People who insist on telling their dreams are among the terrors of the breakfast table." If you are not interested in your own dreams, it is likely that you are even less interested in another person's. So find someone who is interested in dreamwork to share your own exploration. The sharing will reinforce your efforts and even promote dream recall.

A good way to begin dream interpretation is to develop a basic understanding of common dreams and their potential meanings. For instance, one extremely common dream involves taking a test for which you haven't studied. Typically this may mean one of two things. One, you're not prepared to face a problem you're grappling with and need to prepare in some way. Or, two, ready or not, you've passed tests before and will somehow pass this one. Other common dream situations involve falling (these often come at times of threats to your security, from a job loss for instance) and flying (often a sign that you're proud or pleased with yourself). A number of widely available dream and symbol dictionaries and popular books on dreamwork offer insights into common dreams.

Short Tips for Better Dreaming

❑ Take 50 mg twice a day of B complex. For some people the B vitamins play a role in the chemistry of dream memory. In addition, studies indicate that one of the B vitamins (B_3) can prolong REM sleep by 20–40 percent.

❑ Take steps during the day to relax and deal with recurrent stress (see Step 41). One study showed that subjects exposed to stressful situations experienced measurably disturbed REM sleep. Stress results in the body releasing hormones that make the body alert and poised for action, not ready to sleep.

❑ If you are having trouble recalling any dreams, try getting a little more sleep. The REM periods of vivid dreaming increase in length throughout the night. If you sleep eight hours and have four REM stages, for instance, the first one may last only ten minutes, the second fifteen, the third thirty, and the final one forty-five minutes. If instead of getting eight hours of sleep you are getting only six, you may be depriving yourself entirely of the longest and most intense period of dreaming.

❑ It is not necessary to try to remember and record every dream of the night. Dream researchers have discovered that the first dream of the sleeping period often establishes a theme. The subsequent, longer dreams become increasingly complex, characterized by stronger emotions and more vivid images, often from periods in your past. The last dream is like a feature film compared to the one-scene first dream.

❏ Take a nap to promote dream recall. An afternoon nap usually lasts through only one sleep cycle, giving you an opportunity to recall the brief REM cycle that usually concludes the nap.

For More Information

The following are excellent general books on dreams:

Crisis Dreaming: Using Your Dreams to Solve Your Problems by Rosalind Cartwright, Ph.D., and Lynne Lamberg, M.A. (New York: HarperCollins Publishers, 1992)

The Healing Power of Dreams by Patricia Garfield, Ph.D. (New York: Simon & Schuster, 1991)

A valuable dictionary of dream symbols is:

A Dictionary of Symbols by J. E. Cirlot (New York: Philosophical Library, 1962)

The following organization provides information on dreamworkers and dream research through a newsletter, professional journal, conferences, and dream-related books and tapes.

Association for the Study of Dreams
P.O. Box 1600
Vienna, VA 22183
(703) 242-8888

SIMPLE STEPS
TO
NATURAL HEALTH

TAKE IT EASY

33

LAUGH

Some are so disenchanted with modern medicine that they say it's a joke. Ah, if only it were! People might be getting better faster than they do with drugs, surgery, and hospital stays. As Dr. Thomas Sydenham, the seventeenth-century physician, once said, "The arrival of a good clown exercises more beneficial influence upon the health of a town than of twenty asses laden with drugs."

Laughter and humor have been hailed for their health-enhancing powers since at least the time of the ancient Greeks. The idea is recognized in the Bible as well: "A merry heart doeth good like a medicine." Robert Burton, the author of the early-seventeenth-century *Anatomy of Melancholy*, said that the three "doctors" who cure all disease are "Dr. Merryman, Dr. Diet, and Dr. Quiet."

The late Norman Cousins is often credited with inspiring modern medicine to take a deeper look at the potential therapeutic use of humor. He reported, in his now famous "Anatomy of an Illness as Perceived by the Patient" article for a 1976 issue of the *New England Journal of Medicine*, on his successful cure of an illness that had caused severe inflammation of his spine and joints. He said, "I made the joyous discovery that ten minutes of genuine belly laughter had an anesthetic effect and would give me at least two hours of pain-free sleep." Subsequent blood tests confirmed that laughter was causing a physiological response in his body that had a cumulative

275

and positive effect in reducing his illness. Laughter alone did not cure his disease (he also applied other therapies, including taking megadoses of vitamin C), but for Cousins and others it confirmed "the ancient theory that laughter is good medicine."

Since Cousins's publication of the article (and a book by the same title in 1979), researchers worldwide have made humor, laughter, and health a burgeoning field of study. Cousins came to refer to laughter as "internal jogging," since it had so many diverse and positive effects on bodily systems and organs. Recent medical research has confirmed that laughter

➤ enhances the flow of blood to the body's extremities and thus seems to have a positive effect on many cardiovascular problems
➤ increases the number of disease-fighting immune cells and thus boosts the functioning of the immune system
➤ briefly speeds up the heart rate (twenty seconds of laughter can double the heart rate for three to five minutes) and raises blood pressure, before relaxing the arteries and allowing heart rate and blood pressure to fall
➤ increases the rate of breathing and oxygen consumption and thus reduces respiratory problems and oxygenates the blood
➤ plays a part in activating the body's release of endorphins and other natural mood-boosting and pain-killing chemicals
➤ relaxes muscles not involved in laughter
➤ stimulates digestion
➤ massages internal organs and muscles such as the diaphragm, thorax, abdomen, heart, lungs, and even the liver

By laughing frequently and taking a basically humorous approach to life, you can more easily deal with high levels of stress, since researchers have determined that humor is as effective as biofeedback in reducing stress. You can also help prevent many common debilitating diseases and become more relaxed, creative, and flexible in how you solve personal and emotional problems.

Research into the connections between humor and well-being is increasingly causing the medical community to recognize the truth in humorist Josh Billings's statement, "There ain't much fun in medicine, but there's a heck of a lot of medicine in fun." Hospitals, nursing homes, and other medical institutions are beginning to implement programs that help people benefit from the positive effects that humor and laughter have on illness. Duke University Hospital as well as others around the country are now using carts or "laughter wagons" that transport humorous videos, books, toys, and games from room to room, providing laughter to those who need it most. Nurses have been seen wearing buttons that say, "Warning: Humor may be hazardous to your illness." Doctors are telling patients to "take two aspirins and call me with a joke in the morning."

In no doubt the most ambitious merging of humor and medicine, Patch Adams, a self-professed clown/doctor and social revolutionary, is building in West Virginia (with the help of a wide circle of friends and volunteers) a community and a forty-bed free hospital that will be devoted to healing, fun, and play. The Gesundheit Institute (currently located in Arlington, Virginia), Adams says, "will be a new, fun, home-style hospital . . . that embodies to the extreme the philosophy that art, fun, and connectedness are as important to health as CAT scans and IVs."

"The best therapy is being happy," Adams, who usually wears a bulbous red clown's nose as he sees his patients, told *Natural Health*. "All the other things doctors can do—acupuncture, surgery, homeopathy—are, at best, aids." As thousands of patients who have experienced his unique brand of healing can attest, a daily diet of laughter can go a long way toward restoring health and happiness.

Everyday Steps to Natural Health

What is the best way to develop and expand the role humor plays in your life? After all, not everyone can reel off a string of jokes like Dennis Miller, or mug like Steve Martin. The key, says humor-monger Adams, is to "strive for goofiness and fun, not an infinite string of jokes . . . jokes die quickly, and we found that for an atmosphere of humor to thrive, we had to *live* funny."

Try to integrate some of the following suggestions into your weekly routine. Remember, it's important to actively become more humorous and inspire more humor in those around you, rather than just passively expose yourself to funny books or movies.

Laugh at yourself. Become your own best audience. The point is not to tell jokes to yourself in the mirror (unless by all means this cracks you up) but to recognize the humor implicit in your foibles, mistakes, and shortcomings. For instance, if you're a typical guy, when you say something like "I *always* empty the dishwasher" to your wife, recognize it immediately for the whopper it is and laugh at yourself.

When something does strike you as funny, don't fight the urge to laugh out loud. People often think that injecting humor, or reacting to it with a hearty laugh, is out of place at a business meeting or on an elevator full of strangers. Sure, there are times when you should trust your better judgment and maintain a serious demeanor (you've been pulled over for speeding, let's say, and the policeman's voice sounds like Peewee Herman's). But for the most part humor and laughter are great social icebreakers, personal mood boosters, and tension defusers. Indulge to your heart's content.

Determine what makes you laugh and seek it out. Humor can be as personal as culinary taste. One person's gourmet feast is another's cause for permanent fasting. The important thing is to discover what tickles you and seek out more. Yuppie Republicans who like to golf (don't they all?) will probably laugh at the humorous writings of P. J. O'Rourke but may remain unaffected by the prose of Molly Ivins. As with food, cultivate what you like, whether it is Russell Baker columns, Gary Larson cartoons, or *I Love Lucy* reruns, while being open to the new and untried.

Films are a ready, if uneven, source of laughs, from classics like the Marx brothers, Charlie Chaplin, and Laurel and Hardy to newer hits like the takeoffs on police movies (the *Naked Gun* series) and the *National Lampoon* movies. Try setting aside one night a week or so to view a funny film with family or friends. Even television sitcoms can be a source for increasing your weekly humor quotient—try taping the show and then viewing it while fast-forwarding through the commercials to keep the laughs coming.

Going to nightspots that feature stand-up comedy is another option. Call ahead to find out whether the comedians are likely to reflect your particular sense of humor. (Some people also like to inquire about the club's state of ventilation, since secondhand smoke may be a problem).

Build humor into your life. "Put cartoons and jokes on the refrigerator at home, or on a bulletin board at work," says Joel Goodman, founder and director of The Humor Project, a laughter catalog and resource center in Saratoga Springs, New York. "You can also write spoof memos or use funny props. Frequently almost by osmosis the humor seeps into other individuals and sometimes even the corporation." Goodman also suggests putting together a "humor first-aid kit," full of books, tapes, games, and other funny stuff for whenever you're feeling particularly solemn.

By the same token, look for ways to tie humor into your life. Books, movies, comedy routines, and the like are much funnier when they have some relevance to your immediate life. For instance, if you've just bought a house in desperate need of repairs, by all means rent tapes of movies like *The Money Pit* and *Mr. Blandings Builds His Dream House.* When the inevitable happens and you spring a leak while repairing that old sink, you'll be better able to laugh rather than curse at your situation.

"My wife found a Dave Barry column on moving," says a friend of ours, "while researching a pending move. We couldn't stop laughing at his outrageous but true comments. For instance, his first law of moving is that it's impossible to empty a house—the more you take out the more is left behind. To someone getting ready to move this was a frightening, and funny, insight."

Short Tips for Cultivating Humor

❑ Inject humor into mothers' meetings, after-tennis get-togethers, and the like. Feel free to act silly, tell jokes, or laugh about the funniest parts of a book everyone has read.

❑ Listen to comedy audiotapes in your car while commuting. A lot of funny material is available on cassettes and compact discs, whether you prefer Rodney Dangerfield or Paula Poundstone or tales from Lake Wobegone. Check your local record or book store, video store, and library for recorded comedy routines and readings of popular humor books.

❑ Learn to laugh with rather that at others. Raymond Moody, Jr., M.D., author of *Laugh After Laugh: The Healing Power of Humor,* notes that it is within the context of the "network of human relationships that the distinction between *laughing with* and *laughing at* acquires its meaning and becomes so important. In cruel laughter, in laughing at someone, we exclude him from the network of love, understanding, and support; in laughing with someone, we enfold him within it."

❑ Play with kids. They're often doing funny things, plus they're easy to get laughing. "Jollytologist" Allen Klein, owner of the

Whole Mirth Catalog, notes that adults average about a laugh an hour while children laugh many times that. Somewhere between childhood and adulthood, we lose a lot of laughs a day, he says. Laughing along with children is one way to regain some of those lost laughs.

❑ Reframe reality. At odd moments, ask yourself the following question: "What would Robin Williams do if he were here now?"

❑ When you visit an ill person, bring a funny novel, humor anthology, or audiotape rather than flowers. Tell the person jokes and funny stories (unless the person has just had abdominal surgery, in which case the humor should be smile-inducing but not laugh-inducing) and help him or her seek out caretakers with a sense of humor.

For More Information

For more information on humor and health contact:

American Association of Therapeutic Humor
222 S. Meramec, #303
St. Louis, MO 63105
(314) 863-6232

Books that provide summaries of laughter's positive effects on health:

Anatomy of an Illness as Perceived by the Patient by Norman Cousins (New York: W. W. Norton and Co., 1979)

Gesundheit! by Patch Adams, M.D., with Maureen Mylander (Rochester, Vt.: Healing Arts Press, 1993)

Head First: The Biology of Hope by Norman Cousins (New York: E. P. Dutton, 1989)

Laugh After Laugh: The Healing Power of Humor by Raymond A. Moody, Jr., M.D. (Jacksonville, Fla.: Headwaters Press, 1978)

The following are excellent resources for humor-related books, gags, recordings, performers, and more.

The Whole Mirth Catalog
1034 Page St.
San Francisco, CA 94117
(415) 431-1913

The Humor Project
110 Spring St.
Saratoga Springs, NY 12866
(518) 587-8770

To help support Patch Adams and his friends build the world's first humor-oriented hospital, contact him at:

Gesundheit Institute
6877 Washington Blvd.
Arlington, VA 22213
(703) 525-8169

34

DON'T RUSH

"We watch time, we are fixated by it. It can even be said that most of us are dominated by it," maintains Larry Dossey, M.D., the author of numerous books on the effects of emotion and attitude on health. Dossey devoted his first book, *Space, Time and Medicine,* to exploring how an individual's (and a culture's) perception of time influences personal health. Dossey says that modern industrial society's arbitrary carving up of time into minutes and seconds, its fascination with clocks and watches ("symbols of death," he calls them), is responsible for widespread cases of "time sickness" or "hurry sickness."

"Time for these people," Dossey told *Natural Health,* "is constantly running out; this is their felt sense of time . . . The immune system is affected by our time sense or the level of stress in our lives and thus cannot withstand or fight off insults from without. I don't know of any illness that is not affected by our sense of time passage."

Dossey describes time sickness in some of the same terms used by cardiologists Meyer Friedman and Ray Rosenman, who in the late 1950s started to study what they termed *type A* and *type B* personalities. They identified a type A person as someone who is overly aggressive, competitive, and controlling. He or she is often impatient and is easily provoked, angered, and made tense. Such persons have a sense of time urgency, which may be evident in their restless behavior and inability to sit still for more than a moment. By contrast, type B personalities are more relaxed, friendly, and open. Friedman and Rosenman found that people with type A personalities suffer from significantly higher rates of heart disease than do type Bs.

Social critic Jeremy Rifkin is another voice warning about the adverse effects of time awareness. In *Time Wars*, he decries the effect that clocks and schedules, and now computers and programs, have had on modern society. He says, "The modern time world is fast-paced, future-directed, and rigorously planned. The artificial time worlds we have constructed have been accompanied by a radical new temporal value: efficiency . . . Today efficiency pervades every facet of life: it is the primary way we organize our time and has burrowed its way into our economic life, our social and cultural life, and even our personal and religious life."

Rifkin's comments underline the importance of developing a more harmonious relationship to time. The point is not merely to reorganize your schedule to allow you to do more, to work longer hours—to become more efficient in your use of time—but to free yourself entirely of the "time as resource" model, which is in any case just a version of the type A mantra, "time is money."

Everyday Steps to Natural Health

Dossey, Rifkin, and others say that the goal is to reinsert time into the context of the natural world, as reflected by the body's circadian rhythms, the daily rise and fall of the sun, the changing of the seasons, and the "eternal returns" associated with birth, life, and death. What follows are some suggestions for developing a more harmonious relationship to time.

Recognize the symptoms of time sickness in your life. Answer the following dozen questions:

❑ Are you frequently late and worried about it?
❑ Do you constantly try to take over a task from someone who is doing it too slowly for your tastes?
❑ Do you constantly interrupt people who seem to talk too slowly or say things like "Yes, yes" to try to speed them up?
❑ Do you often look at your watch reflexively or at inappropriate

times (as President Bush did during the middle of one of his debates with Clinton)?

❑ Do you feel guilty whenever you find yourself sitting and relaxing without doing anything in particular?

❑ Do you frequently sacrifice sleep to finish a project or undertaking?

❑ Do you look forward to the day when you can cross off as finished every task on your long "to do" list?

❑ Are you frequently pulled over for speeding or rolling through stop signs? Do you make elaborate attempts at shortcuts to avoid traffic jams?

❑ Do you walk faster than anyone else on the sidewalk?

❑ Do you fidget, tap your fingers, or squeeze a tennis ball even while sitting and working or doing some other task?

❑ Do you eat meals while driving, brush your teeth while showering, read a magazine while talking on the phone, or otherwise combine two or more activities to save time?

❑ Would you rather have a tooth pulled without anesthesia than wait in a long line?

If you answer yes to more than a few of these questions, it is likely that your personal and family life, as well as your overall health, could be improved by developing a more calm and balanced approach to time.

Determine how you spend your time. Without changing your usual daily schedule, keep track of how much time you spend doing various activities. Make a table and every night for a week estimate how much time, to the nearest half hour, you've spent that day preparing meals, eating, exercising, sleeping, working, commuting, walking, reading, drinking, meditating, watching television, playing a musical instrument, conversing, and so forth. After a week, total your hours for each activity. If you're like most people, the results will offer some surprises. You may find, for instance, that you're much closer to the national average of four and a half hours per day watching television than you thought.

Use these weekly totals to establish stronger commitments to those activities that support your health. If you want to exercise more, don't cut back on your hours sleeping (if you average seven or eight hours per night) or eating (rushing through meals is seldom healthful). Try to resist the temptation as well to "make more time" by combining activities. For instance, don't continue to watch as much television by putting an exercise cycle in front of it. If you're a typical type A, you want to break this habit of doing multiple tasks at once without really focusing on any. Rather, look for ways to adjust your time spent on those things that are not bringing you fulfillment and pleasure, and to make space in your daily schedule for exercising, talking, cooking, or whatever.

Diet and exercise advocate John McDougall, M.D., says in his book *The McDougall Program*, "You say your life is overcrowded? I say, straighten out your priorities." He notes that most people spend about seventeen hours per weekday with the basics of sleeping, eating, and working. That leaves about seven hours per day of uncommitted time. "Do you really think it's impossible to fit a mere thirty minutes for exercise into that span each day?" he asks.

Learn how to stretch your perception of time by overcoming an obsession with numbers and quantities. There's never enough time for people with hurry sickness, partly because of their compressed sense of how time flows. They tend to become obsessed with time as defined by quantities such as bits per second, calls per minute, or dollars per hour. They measure the success of their lives by quantities such as patients treated, money earned, and hours billed. (Is there a better candidate for a future heart attack, or a barren, lonely life, than *The Firm*–type superlawyers who brag about billing 120 hours per week?)

Such time- and quantity-obsessed people benefit by taking steps to think in terms of the quality of life. They need to be reminded that life is more than a series of tasks to be completed or transactions made. Life is enriched by experiences that activate the senses and broaden the mind, whether it be a stroll through a rose garden or immersion in a rich novel.

Those who need to can also begin to stretch their perception of time by using techniques such as meditation (see Step 41) and biofeedback. Medical researchers have found that pain and time sense are related. Pain contracts time, while a drug, relaxation, or other tool to control pain acts to expand a person's awareness of time. Dossey notes that when a person with a hurried attitude begins to learn biofeedback, he or she will think a minute is up after a mere fifteen seconds. After becoming proficient at biofeedback, however, the same person is likely to think a minute is up after a minute and a half or two minutes. In other words, the perception of time is stretched. This stretching of time, Dossey says, is associated with a lower incidence of diseases such as peptic ulcers, angina, and high blood pressure.

Biofeedback training is done with any of a number of devices that monitor subtle bodily functions, such as changes in brain waves, hand temperature, or electrical skin resistance. The subject learns how to stay in an "awake and aware" state, during which he or she can recognize and control feelings of tension. Usually it takes about ten weekly, hour-long sessions to learn biofeedback. Eventually the subject can dispense with the machine and still consciously induce a relaxation response. (See "For More Information" for how to find a biofeedback practitioner in your area).

Pace yourself. A person with an extreme case of hurry sickness will often employ two strategies to try to cram more into his or her life: perform everyday activities faster and do more than one thing at a time. Thus, slowing down or pacing yourself can help reduce stress levels and increase enjoyment of life. People with hurry sickness should make a conscious effort to recognize unnecessary speediness in their speaking and eating. They should intersperse short breaks or periods of quiet time into their daily schedule to allow for periods of calmness or stretching. Hurry-sick people are often guilty of trying to impose their sense of no-time onto those around them and will thus interrupt or try to speed up slow speakers. Parents in a continual hurry can damage their children's self-esteem by repeatedly taking over from them tasks that they are doing "too slowly."

Listening quietly without breaking in every ten seconds is an invaluable exercise for type A's. So are steps such as eliminating clocks and watches when they're unnecessary, and every once in a while doing nothing but relaxing and listening to music.

Become comfortable about "wasting" time. People with a compressed sense of time often become highly agitated when forced to wait, whether for a salesclerk, bank teller, or traffic light. Any time spent alone with one's thoughts is deemed "wasted"—that is, not used to earn money, build muscles, or make or consume products. By becoming more comfortable and intrigued by your inner life and what you can do while waiting, however, you can transform this perception of "wasted" time to "free" time.

A journalist we know says, "I used to fret every time I'd approach a streetcar station and see a train pull away. 'What bad luck,' I'd say. 'Now I have to waste ten minutes waiting for the next one." Then I'd stand there in an impatient funk, no doubt with higher blood pressure and increased levels of acid in my stomach than a few minutes before. This happened so frequently I realized that I had to make a change.

"I started to look upon time spent waiting for the next train as relaxing time, during which I could read. Now, if a train approaches the station and I'm a block away, I not only won't make a mad rush to fling myself into the train at the last possible moment, I'll positively dawdle to make sure I miss it and have a chance to spend some time with Dick Francis's characters."

Anybody can make this simple change in perspective. If reading is not on your list of favorite activities, do what is. If you're outgoing, maybe you like to strike up conversations. You could also study local plants or the architecture of surrounding buildings, make up stories about the lives of nearby people, do isometric exercises, listen to music on a headset, write, knit, bird-watch, or hum. The point is, see the time spent waiting as a relaxing opportunity rather than as a nerve-wrenching waste. Your body will respond accordingly.

Experience the present moment fully. "Be here now" was a popular catch phrase of the 1960s. Though somewhat shopworn, this advice nevertheless conveys a timeless health message: focus on the present moment to gain the most from what life has to offer. Vietnamese Zen master Thich Nhat Hanh says, "The most basic precept of all is to be aware of what we do, what we are, in each minute . . . We practice to get back to the present moment. You must transform the present moment into the best moment of your life." As do many spiritual teachers, Nhat Hanh recommends becoming aware of your breathing (see Step 26 for better breathing techniques) and your body as techniques for fixing your awareness in the present moment.

At moments throughout the day, stop and take stock of your body. Are your face, neck, shoulders tense? Is your posture poor, with your body slumped or crouched over? If so, relax, straighten up, and take a deep breath. Return to the present. Smile.

Allow yourself more time. Frequent lateness is often a cause or symptom of time sickness. You cram meetings and appointments too closely together and end up being late for one after another, despite a series of headlong rushes between obligations. The solution is to bite the bullet: make fewer appointments, allowing more time than you think you will need both for the meeting and for getting to your next destination. If necessary, make adjustments such as rising fifteen minutes earlier each day so that you don't have to rush to shower, eat breakfast, and get to work.

You can also avoid artificial deadlines by scheduling within parameters. Thus, tell a friend, "Let's meet at the restaurant between six and six-twenty," rather than, "I'll be there at six o'clock sharp no matter what." When you are late and hopelessly stuck in traffic, breathe deeply and relax. You won't get where you're going any faster by tensing your neck and facial muscles, squirming in your seat, and swearing at yourself and others.

Short Tips for Making Friends With Time

❑ If you're a type A, resist the temptation to do multiple tasks at once. Heart researchers who have studied hurry sickness report that type A's take some unusual steps to save time. High-powered male executive type A's have been known to brag about how they shave with two electric razors at once or read a trade journal, carry on a telephone conversation, exercise, and sign checks simultaneously. Such flurries of activity are impressive, but so is the circus bear that can ride a unicycle while balancing a ball on its nose. The difference is that the bear is not likely to die of a premature heart attack. Instead of doing many things quickly and casually, cultivate the ability to do one thing at a time really well. Practice by taking on tasks, such as reading a thoughtful book, performing yoga, meditating, or carrying on a heartfelt conversation, that demand your full attention and concentration.

❑ Commit only to what you can really put your heart—and time—into. Many people who are constantly feeling time pressure simply have too much on their plate. Even those who are well organized and proficient at time-budgeting can try to undertake too much. Sometimes the problem is that they haven't learned to say no. As a result these "supermoms" and "robodocs" are frequently overwhelmed with more projects than they—or anyone—can accomplish. If you recognize this as a problem that bedevils you, take steps to become more honest with yourself about what you can do and to become more assertive with others. Learn how better to estimate what a project will require of you before saying yes. When necessary, say, "No, I can't do that," or, "I can do that three months from now." Sometimes it is possible to delegate to coworkers, friends, and family members what you can't do but that nevertheless needs to get done. Learning how to say no is an important tool in setting priorities for how you spend your time.

❑ Use stimulants wisely. Many time-obsessed people are major abusers of stimulants such as caffeine and nicotine. Type A people often want to speed up the body's systems to help them get more done in the same amount of time. Caffeine (from coffee, tea, and cola drinks) and nicotine (from tobacco smoke) are, however, powerful drugs that can be addictive and debilitating to your overall health. People who are addicted to stimulants often spend much more time attending to the needs of their habit than they could possibly "save" by working at a faster pace. Stimulants do not, in any case, create more energy in your body. Rather, they allow you to borrow against your chemical and energy reserves. Abusing stimulants can aggravate a distorted relationship with time.

For More Information

The following books offer insight into how time affects health and consciousness.

Space, Time and Medicine by Larry Dossey, M.D. (Boston: Shambhala Publications, 1982)

Time Wars by Jeremy Rifkin (New York: Henry Holt, 1987)

Treating Type A Behavior and Your Heart by Meyer Friedman, M.D., and Diane Ulmer, R.N., M.S. (New York: Alfred A. Knopf, 1984)

Type A Behavior and Your Heart by Meyer Friedman, M.D., and Ray H. Rosenman, M.D., (New York: Fawcett, 1976)

To find a biofeedback practitioner in your area, send a self-addressed, stamped envelope to:

Association for Applied Psychophysiology and Biofeedback
10200 W. 44th Ave., #304
Wheat Ridge, CO 80033

35

OVERCOME EVERYDAY
ADDICTIONS

Addictive substances include not only the obvious drugs (such as alcohol, cocaine, nicotine, and caffeine) but a whole host of activities. The latter might include gambling, having sex, shopping, shoplifting, eating, not eating, working, exercising, making money, spending money, and even praying. Clearly, some addictions are more dangerous than others, with addiction to drugs, legal or illegal, heading the list. (See Step 38 for suggestions on how to gain more control over your use of caffeine and alcohol.) Addictions also vary in degree to include obsessions, compulsions, and cravings. So-called codependent behavior results from being in a close relationship with an addicted person.

Addictive behaviors are often most visible as a lack of balance in your life. While the person who indulges in overeating, too much drinking, or constant sex may experience short-term pleasures, he or she soon realizes that the long-term effects are constricting. Ultimately, the addict fails to address emotional needs and ends up lonely, isolated, and unloved. Addictions limit your freedom by restricting you in some way from pursuing life in its fullness, notes Andrew Weil, M.D., an authority on psychoactive drugs and natural health.

There are no easy answers to the riddle of addiction. At the heart of any treatment program, however, must be a willingness to confront the behavior and recognize it as a harmful force in your life. "Addiction is not a psychological or pharmacological problem and cannot be solved by the methods of psychology or pharmacology. It is at root a spiritual concern because it represents a misdirected attempt to achieve wholeness, to experience inner completeness and satisfaction," says Weil.

Twelve-step programs such as Alcoholics Anonymous are among the most popular approaches to addiction. They have diversified wildly beyond alcoholism to include such activities as gambling and even shopping. What they have in common is group support and the requirement that the individual admit to a powerlessness to control the addiction.

Despite these programs' overall success, theirs is not the only approach to addiction. There are now secular programs based on the twelve-step model that don't require the individual to "give up control to a Higher Power." Critics of the disease model of addiction and spiritual recovery programs such as Wendy Kaminer, author of *I'm Dysfunctional, You're Dysfunctional: The Recovery Movement and Other Self-Help Fashions*, contend that some people are actively discouraged from actually helping themselves. "Addiction is considered a disease of the will; believing in self-control is one of its symptoms," she says.

You needn't adopt a religious viewpoint or admit to a serious spiritual weakness to address areas of addiction in your life, even though many addictions do have an emotional component. Nor do you need to consider twelve-step programs for all of the everyday activities you do that have an addictive element to them. There are many types and degrees of addiction and obsession, and each individual needs to consider what works best for him or her.

Everyday Steps to Natural Health

"Addiction is not going to disappear overnight," says Linda Leonard, a Jungian analyst and the author of *Witness to the Fire: Creativity and the Veil of Addiction*. "But the more we look at it—and the only way is to look within—the more possibilities we have of leading creative rather than addictive lives." Here are some ways to transform your addictive or obsessive relationships to work, love and sex, and food.

Watch for the signs of addictive behavior. Few people are completely free of any addictive behavior, and some addictions have more profound effects on your health and well-being than others. Still, it is worthwhile to become familiar with the basic elements of addiction and to recognize when your behavior slips into its realm.

Addictions usually alter your awareness or consciousness such that while under the effects of the substance or activity you feel powerful, in control, or "high." This effect is most noticeable during the beginning stages of the addiction. As the addiction takes a firmer grip on your life, you rely more and more on it, typically needing a fix one or more times per day. You may come to use the addiction to relax or to counter the effects of stress. You become less interested in other activities and interests as the addictive activity takes on supreme importance. Eventually the addiction may require most of your resources to feed it, including much of your time and money. By then the addiction colors all of your experience, including emotions, feelings, and energy levels.

Over time you build up a tolerance and need larger and larger doses of the substance or activity to obtain pleasure, numbness, or satisfaction. You feel as if you cannot start the day or achieve a "normal" mental state without it. When you try to do without your addiction, you feel depressed and unhappy. Frequently there are physical withdrawal symptoms as well, such as headaches and dizziness.

Most people know which addictions cast the greatest spell over them. Examine your habits and routine behaviors and honestly evaluate whether there are substances or activities you indulge in so frequently and wantonly that you are sacrificing your best long-term interests, particularly as they affect your health, relationships, and emotional well-being.

All work and no play is no fun. Being addicted to work often escapes social condemnation or even garners encouragement. Many use the term *workaholic* in a positive sense to convey the image of industriousness and dedication to job. Likewise, our market-economy society sees an obsession with making money as an unalloyed good, putting it above almost all other values.

Despite these views, many people who spend twelve hours a day, seven days a week at their job are addicted to work. While hours worked is an important determining factor, it is not the only criterion, notes Bryan E. Robinson, Ph.D., a recovered work addict, the author of *Work Addiction*, and one of the foremost national authorities on the subject. "The major difference between abusive (or addictive) work and healthy (or constructive) work is the degree to which excessive work interferes with physical health, personal happiness, and intimate and social relationships," Robinson says. "Work abusers cannot control their compulsive work habits and even use different words that reflect their true feelings about 'the great divide': work responsibilities and family obligations."

People who are addicted to work use work as a drug that makes them feel better and more powerful. The addiction increases self-esteem and becomes the defining activity in the person's life. Like other addicts, the work addict may go on binges and suffer withdrawal symptoms such as irritability and anxiety when deprived of the activity. The addiction masks the same feeling of inner emptiness that lies at the heart of other addictions. "Work abusers can never be fully happy, self-content, and peaceful until they face their neglected inner feelings without the medication of work," says Robinson.

Of course, everyone must work, so treating a work addiction involves not total abstinence but a balance between work and other activities, such as leisure and spending time with family. Among the suggestions that Robinson offers for recovering from work addiction are

❏ Make friends outside of work and cultivate them.

❏ Develop creative interests or hobbies in fields other than those of your work.

❏ Slow down your pace and live in the present moment.

❏ Take long weekends and frequent vacations, but only if you can resist the temptation to bring your work with you.

❏ Make a point of celebrating family birthdays, anniversaries, holidays, and other special days. "Rituals, family celebrations, and traditions are the glue that cement a family together. [They] help us appreciate the here and now—'what is' rather than 'what will be,'" says Robinson.

❏ Make forty hours a week your norm for working. Delegate, learn to say no, and schedule projects over a longer period of time. Avoid bingeing on work.

Keep love and sex free of addictive traits. Love and sex offer fertile ground for the seeds of addiction. The pleasures and stimulations associated with romance, relationships, and sexual activity can be sublime. Like work, cultural norms often reinforce a positive perception toward the unbridled pursuit of love and sex. For men, it is acceptable or even admirable to seek unlimited sexual experiences. People perceive the same behavior in a woman, however, as a sign of moral decay. Women, in any case, are more likely to suffer from addictive behavior in the context of a relationship. For example, they might become emotionally numb when someone is caring or loving or use sex as a means to prevent a partner from leaving.

Unfortunately, the addictive pursuit of "sexual conquests" or orgasms reduces sex to a merely physical act. It also transforms a lover or partner to an object, preventing the kind of closeness and intimacy that leads to communication and possibly a level of spiritual understanding or insight. "Touching, caressing, and caring are extremely healing and nourishing actions. But addictive or codependent sex can bury the spirit and soul," according to Charlotte Davis Kasl, Ph.D., author of *Women, Sex, and Addiction.*

Addictive relationships can also curtail personal freedom and responsibility. Kasl says that women can avoid addictive relationships by committing themselves to living their own life, taking responsibility for themselves financially, creating excitement and passion in their lives from the things they do for themselves, and being involved in an active support system. Women, she says, also need to maintain a separate identity from their partner and know that they can survive without the relationship—even as they do everything they can to make it work. "Without self-awareness, a strong support system, and a sense of personal responsibility, a person is far more susceptible to addictive or codependent sexual relationships," Kasl says.

Avoid emotional eating. Addictions or obsessions with food, dieting, weight control, body size, calories, and body-fat levels are common in the U.S., particularly among young women. Some authorities estimate that as many as one in five college-age women suffer from bulimia, a condition in which the person first binges and then vomits. Bulimics may also suffer from an addiction to exercise as a means for burning calories. Anorexia nervosa, from not eating to the point of extreme thinness, is less common but strikes an estimated 1–2 percent of teenage girls. Females constitute 95 percent of the victims of anorexia nervosa. Many other people, women and men, experience emotionally based eating disorders that lead to obesity and other health problems.

Why American women are more likely than men to suffer from addictive eating patterns and other eating disorders is unclear. One potential reason relates to the aesthetic norms imposed on women by the basically male power structure of Hollywood and Madison Avenue. Some elements of society view fat men as powerful but fat women as unattractive. Women today identify fatness as an obstacle to having loving relationships with men, a fear with more than an element of truth since many men as well think that women should look like full-size Barbie dolls.

For whatever underlying reasons, some people invest food with the presumed power to bring happiness and "fullness"—physical and emotional. Eating becomes a way to disguise an underlying emotional problem. "Food is precisely the effort to fill that existential howling, to give yourself as a woman something, desperately and urgently, that will make your terrible hunger for your Self go away," says Kim Chernin, author of *The Hungry Self.* "The eating disorder is like a Band-aid placed over this enormous spiritual yearning . . . what's raging and roaring inside women is this hunger for an authentic female spiritual and cultural tradition."

Chernin and others who have worked with people who have eating disorders and food addictions say that people must come to recognize food as the substitute for their spiritual hunger. They need to seek to fulfill that hunger in ways more likely to bring spiritual growth, whether that be through bonding with other women, coming to terms with your mother, or accepting your power as a woman. Women in particular also need to work on accepting their bodies. A woman's body, Chernin says, should be defined by her, not by cultural norms or the men in her life. Women need "a body that tells her how it wants to be, rather than a body she's constantly trying to prune and pare back and reduce to match a cultural ideal," as Chernin puts it.

While working on the personal and emotional levels to eliminate an eating disorder, you should also at least try to switch to more healthful foods (see Step 1) if you are compulsively eating such high-fat foods as chocolate, ice cream, or cookies. Also take steps to connect to your food (see Step 2), such as by eating more slowly and actually tasting each bite, so that you break the pattern of eating with your emotions instead of your senses.

Short Tips for Overcoming Everyday Addictions

❏ Find friends or other people who have fought and overcome the addiction you are seeking to beat. Their example and positive support can inspire your own efforts. Support groups for a wide variety of addictive activities can be found throughout the country.

For More Information

Useful books include the following:

The Hungry Self: Women, Eating & Identity by Kim Chernin (New York: Harper & Row, 1985)

Women, Sex and Addiction by Charlotte Davis Kasl, Ph.D. (New York: Ticknor & Fields, 1989)

Work Addiction by Bryan E. Robinson, Ph.D. (Deerfield Beach, Fla.: Health Communications, 1989)

STAY HEALTHY
WHILE TRAVELING

One in every three people who fly, vacation, or travel to new places is likely to fall ill or suffer an injury, according to the National Institutes of Health. This statistic is less surprising when you consider some of the immediate effects of travel. Travel causes people to go off healthful diets, eat more fast food, and drink more alcohol and coffee. Various types of travel cause jet lag and motion sickness. Foreign travel exposes people to new and unusual foods and liquids, which may contain new and unusual microorganisms that can cause all sorts of digestive upsets and diseases.

Travel can also be supremely stressful. Who has not experienced the dread of unexpected airport delays, the confusion associated with being lost in a strange place, the anxiety that comes with being questioned by a border official or stopped by a small-town cop?

When you're away from home, you are probably more likely to change your sleeping, eating, and exercising patterns. Those well-thought-out plans for getting seven hours of sleep, cutting back on junk foods, and staying active go by the wayside as more immediate concerns take over, such as "Where should I get my next meal?" and "Have I been credited with my frequent-flier mileage?" The keys to staying healthy while traveling are similar to those while at home: set priorities and goals, schedule time for the important stuff, and stick to your commitments.

Everyday Steps to Natural Health

The health challenges of travel can be met, but it does take some forethought. Here are some ways to keep you going while on the road.

Make plans to exercise. It isn't always possible to do your favorite activity on the road—finding a court and a partner to play tennis can be time-consuming in an unknown city. It is often easier to concentrate on solo activities, such as stretching and strengthening exercises. Many large hotels have exercise rooms with free weights or resistance machines, and some have swimming pools. Schedule the activity into your day just as you would at home to make sure you don't skip it.

Here are some other road-worthy exercise alternatives to consider:

❑ Bring a jump rope with weighted handles. A jump rope is easy to pack and can be used anywhere you can find sufficient headroom. Jumping rope is an excellent exercise for upper-body strength, endurance, and coordination.

❑ Pack a five pound weight and some ankle weights if your luggage can bear it and do some basic strengthening exercises (see Step 13).

❑ Jogging and walking are excellent aerobic exercises while traveling because of the excitement of exploring new paths and routes.

❑ If you belong to a health club, before you leave home check to see whether it has temporary membership privileges at other clubs around the country.

Take extra nutrients to counter the effects of travel. A number of vitamins and minerals can play a role in safeguarding your health while traveling. For instance, travel often exposes the body to higher levels of radiation (from flying at high altitudes), stress, and pollution. Certain nutrients can help counter these agents by boosting your immunity and protecting you from free radicals. The so-called antioxidant nutrients combine with and neutralize free radicals without themselves becoming unstable, thus defending your body against harmful effects that include cancer (see Step 29).

Take some or all of the following nutrients. They will be most effective if taken seven to ten days before traveling as well as during the trip. Suggested dosages are optimal daily amounts (see Step 3):

➤ vitamin A in the form of beta carotene, 10,000–20,000 IU
➤ vitamin C plus bioflavonoids, 500–1,500 mg
➤ vitamin E, 400–800 IU
➤ vitamin B complex, 50–100 mg
➤ selenium, 100–150 mcg
➤ zinc, 17–25 mg
➤ coenzyme Q10, 15–30 mg

If your traveling exposes you to new foods, you might also consider taking acidophilus, live bacteria that populate your intestines and help to prevent unwanted microorganisms from setting up shop there. Take 10 billion viable organisms daily.

Keep supplements in their original containers if you're going through customs to prevent any question about the pills' identity.

Prevent jet lag. Flying across time zones disrupts your body's internal clock, located in a section of the brain connected by the optic nerve to the retina at the back of the eye. This biological clock sets the ebb and flow of body temperature, blood pressure, breathing and heart rate, and sleeping and waking patterns. When jet travel throws these functions out of sync, you develop the common symptoms of fatigue, insomnia, and irritability.

Instead of relying on dangerous, habit-forming sleeping pills to relieve jet lag, use some of the following commonsense steps and natural remedies:

❑ Take 3 mg of the supplement melatonin when you arrive in a new time zone approximately an hour before you go to sleep.

Light is crucial to setting the body's clock. Along with factors such as body temperature, light regulates the secretion of melatonin, a hormone produced by the tiny pineal gland in the center of the brain. Melatonin affects mood and fatigue; it also plays an important role in maintaining regular sleep patterns and biological rhythms. Recent research confirms that it counters the effects of jet lag. For instance, an endocrinologist in England found that melatonin pills significantly decreased the symptoms of jet lag among sixty-one people tested.

Taken orally, melatonin is rapidly absorbed into the bloodstream, metabolized, and eliminated from the body. Studies indicate that side effects from taking melatonin are negligible.

Melatonin is classified as a food supplement and is available in some natural-food stores.

❑ Fly during the day and arrive in the evening to avoid disrupting normal sleep patterns.

❑ Wear earplugs while flying. Many people find that the loud, high-pitched whine of nearby jet engines is disruptive to the nervous system. Holly Eagle, a doctor of oriental medicine who practices at Ancient Roots Medical in Santa Cruz, California, says, "I know a musician who had a terrible jet-lag problem and flew quite frequently because of his career. Finally he was told to wear earplugs or ear-covering headphones to protect his ears while flying. He's told us that since using a heavy set of headphones he's had absolutely no jet lag. None."

❑ Avoid extensive napping on arrival. This just delays adjustment to your new schedule.

Relax. Even when you're taking a vacation, travel can be more stressful than your daily routine. Traffic problems, weather-related changes in plans, waiting in lines—the possibilities for tense moments are frequent. You may be dealing with unknown customs and languages. You may also be fighting the urge to do more and see it all while you can. Travel-related stress can lead to headaches, backaches, insomnia, and a host of other emotion-induced ailments. Hurry and anxiety may also make you more accident–or illness–prone.

It is important to make realistic plans for your time on the road. Whether you are working or playing, don't overschedule. Try to set aside some time each day for activities you find relaxing, such as exercise, napping, hobbies, reading, or whatever. Also try to maintain your normal practice for dealing with stress, whether it is through meditation, biofeedback, or other methods of relaxation (see Step 41).

Stick to your healthy eating habits. It is sometimes tempting to use travel time as an excuse to eat foods you'd rarely eat at home. Eating what's offered on airlines and stopping at fast-food places while driving is all right every once in a while. If you travel frequently or for long periods, however, eating their typical high-fat fare can harm your health. With a minimum of extra effort you can maintain your healthy diet away from home:

❑ When making your ticket reservations, ask the airline to serve you a vegetarian meal or a plate of fresh fruit.

❑ However you travel, bring some healthy foods of your own. Pack fresh fruit, whole-grain breads or crackers and a natural nut spread, prewashed baby carrots, raisins and seeds, high-fiber muffins, and other healthful foods.

❑ Eat out but don't pig out. Most restaurants serve dishes for the health-conscious, including pasta, fish, salads, and vegetarian entrées. Some will prepare foods not on the menu, such as steamed vegetables. When you're in a new locale, the clerks at natural-food stores can usually tell you about restaurants in the area that serve fresh, whole foods.

❑ Drink healthy fluids (see Step 6). Carry a water container with you. It is especially important to drink plenty of fluids before and during a flight, since pressurized cabins increase the risk of dehydration. Bring some herbal tea bags with you and limit your intake of alcohol and caffeine, which cause you to lose fluid.

Prevent traveler's diarrhea. If you're a frequent overseas flier as well as an indiscriminate eater, you've probably experienced the inconvenient condition known as traveler's diarrhea, turista, and a host of place-specific names ("L.A. belly" when you're a Mexican visiting the U.S., "Montezuma's revenge" when vice versa). The condition is often limited to few days of loose and frequent stools, though warning signs of a more serious condition include severe abdominal cramps and blood in the stools.

Traveler's diarrhea is usually caused by bacteria (such a *E. coli*) or parasites *(Giardia lablia)* that you consume in food or water. People in the native area who eat the same substances don't get the condition because their digestive systems have adapted over time to the microorganisms. In your intestines, the microorganisms cause water to pass through without being absorbed, giving you diarrhea.

Especially when you are traveling in a developing area or a country that has poor water quality or sanitation, you should take steps to keep your food and water free of contamination. According to Stephen Bezruchka, M.D., author of *The Pocket Doctor: Your Ticket to Good Health While Traveling,* "Your mantra for food is: 'Boil it, cook it, peel it, or forget it.'" Drink clear fruit juices from sealed cans or bottles, or water that has been properly treated (such as with iodine tablets) or boiled for twenty minutes.

Treat traveler's diarrhea by drinking plenty of pure water to prevent dehydration and taking natural-fiber supplements such as pectin or psyllium to add bulk to stools. Supplements that may promote recovery include garlic, goldenseal, and acidophilus. All of these are also potentially beneficial preventive agents. Garlic and goldenseal have antibacterial and immune-boosting powers while acidophilus is a "friendly" bacteria that inhibits the growth of unwanted microorganisms in the intestines. Take these on a daily basis starting one week prior to leaving and ending one week following your return from a developing country. An average daily dose of garlic is one tablet of 1,800 mcg allicin content; of goldenseal, one to two dropperfuls of the liquid extract or concentrated drops (pregnant women should not take goldenseal); and of acidophilus, 10 billion viable organisms.

Don't let motion sickness ruin your trip. Also known as seasickness and car sickness, motion sickness is the nausea and vomiting brought on by riding in a boat, car, or plane. It can strike anyone, including at times the most sea-encrusted sailor. It's caused when your brain receives a confusion of data from your eyes, your inner ears, and nerve cells in your skin and muscles about your body's motion and orientation in space. For instance, in a pitching boat, your eyes tell the brain that the body is standing still on the deck, while the touch sense organs and the ears relay a jumble of reports indicating movement. The brain and nervous system tell the gastrointestinal system to deal with the problem, which it does by unloading the contents of your stomach.

Conventional drugs for motion sickness generally cause considerable drowsiness. Here are two tried-and-true natural methods with no side effects.

❏ Take one to two grams of dried ginger. This herb is even more effective at preventing motion sickness than Dramamine, a popular over-the-counter remedy, according to a study published in the British medical journal *Lancet*. Even eating cookies or drinking ginger ale made with real ginger may be helpful.

❏ Wear a special acupressure wrist strap that presses on an acupressure point located in the middle of the inner wrist. "This is the most famous point for relieving nausea, motion sickness, and even the morning sickness of early pregnancy," notes Michael Reed Gach, author of *Acupressure's Potent Points*. Gach notes that studies have confirmed the antinausea effects of manipulating the point. A number of manufacturers make cloth wristbands with a slightly protruding knob that stimulates the point as the band is worn on the wrist. (See "For More Information" for a mail-order source.)

Short Tips for Healthy Travel

❑ Take care of your most vulnerable organ—the skin. Don't get sunburned. Flying into a sunny climate during the winter, or vacationing at the beach anytime, exposes your skin to higher levels of burning ultraviolet rays. Cover up with hats and light clothing, or use a natural sunscreen, until your skin adjusts to the new environment.

❑ Bring a small natural-remedy kit with you when you travel. Include first-aid supplies such as bandages, sterile gauze pads, and elastic bandages, and first-aid remedies such as homeopathic *Arnica* for bruises, the herb calendula for minor cuts and scrapes, and herbal aloe for burns. You may also want to pack some useful remedies for everyday ailments, such as ginger for nausea, willow bark for pain, ipecac for poisoning, echinacea as an immune booster, tea-tree oil as an antiviral, valerian as a sedative, zinc lozenges to forestall a cold, and bromelain or papain for indigestion.

For More Information

A useful and compact book on healthy travel is:

The Pocket Doctor: Your Ticket to Good Health While Traveling by Stephen Bezruchka, M.D. (Seattle, Wash.: The Mountaineers, 2nd ed., 1992)

The AcuBand acupressure wrist strap is available from:

Lifestyle Enterprises
P.O. Box 156
Little Silver, NJ 07739
(800) 831-8777

SIMPLE STEPS
TO
NATURAL HEALTH

────

MIND
AND SPIRIT

37

TAKE GENUINE RISKS

It should not be surprising that a society founded by people willing to settle unknown lands by crossing an ocean in crude ships, or two centuries later by traversing a wilderness in covered wagons, values risk taking. Americans still pay more than lip service to the willingness to take a chance on a risky endeavor. Advertisers that encourage consumers to "go for it" or "just do it" promote risk taking as a positive trait. Mental-health counselors and cultural pundits rarely offer the advice to "play it safe." Risk equals movement, and growth, while not risking is seen as stagnation. Thus, "take more risks" is a common prescription for effecting change, getting ahead, and gaining personal satisfaction.

On the other hand, risk taking also has a negative connotation, especially when it is expressed through outlets such as thrill-seeking sports, gambling, or adventurous sexual encounters. A number of locales have banned hazardous stunts such as bungee-jumping and parachuting from towers. Many psychologists label as immature or even suicidal persons who repeatedly take foolish or dangerous bodily risks.

This ambivalent view of risk is due in part to varying perceptions of what is meant by risk. Some risks are primarily emotional, such as making a long-term commitment, getting married, or switching jobs. Other risks are primarily physical—racing motorcycles or climbing a mountain. Compared to emotional risks, physical ones present obvious negative outcomes (injury, death) and more elusive benefits. Dictionary definitions of risk reinforce this latter impression. *Webster's* defines *risk* as "the chance of injury, damage, or loss; dangerous chance; hazard."

Risk is difficult to pin down because, like beauty, it exists primarily in the eye of the beholder, observes Ralph Keyes, author of *Chancing It: Why We Take Risks*. His definitive work on the topic defines risk as "an act involving fear of possible loss." For the risk to be real, the potential loss must be tangible. He says that the advent in America of risk substitutes such as simulated adventure vacations, lifelike computer games, and totally controlled theme parks can't provide the one thing that real risk does: stakes.

Moreover, because risk is such a subjective concept and varies so much with temperament, time, and circumstances, Keyes says, "only the risk taker can determine what's genuinely risky. In such a determination, *authenticity* is a far better criterion than objective danger. Someone who crosses the street despite being afraid of getting hit by a car is taking a bigger risk than someone else who leaps from an airplane with a parachute, sure of floating safely to the ground. If risk involves challenging fear, then the street crosser has done so more bravely than the sky diver."

Surveys on risks and fears also reflect subjective, ambivalent attitudes. For example, one survey found that the type of risk that is identified by the largest group of people (37 percent) as the hardest to take is physical risk. On the other hand, a noted survey of three thousand Americans found that most people's major fear—public speaking—does not relate to a predominantly physical act. Almost twice as many people (41 percent) identified speaking before a group as their major fear as the next-highest-rated fear (of heights, cited by 22 percent). What many would presume to be the most-feared consequence of physical risk-taking—death—didn't even make the top five major fears.

Clearly, risk taking and facing your fears are highly personal matters. For some, it could mean finding the courage to risk asking for help, facing the possibility of failing to achieve a specific goal, or being honest in expressing your feelings. Taking on a challenge means that you must be willing to give something up. Depending on the risk, you could lose security, affection, control, money, autonomy, self-esteem, or a stable job.

The nature of risk taking is that you don't know for sure you will gain something from your efforts. The rewards may be great, whether in the form of love, strength of character, wealth, or happiness. The willingness to take some risks allows you to challenge yourself to your full capacity. Instead of lamenting that you have few opportunities in your everyday life to take risks, set high goals and use your innate confidence and motivation to meet your challenges. "The fun is often in playing the game," says C. Norman Shealy, M.D., Ph.D., founder of the American Holistic Medical Association. "Every day you take risks—in breathing, eating, driving, walking. Choose your risks wisely. Use you intuition to help you select the risks worth pursuing. Actually, you never lose by trying, for you gain new skill, knowledge, courage, and strength when you take responsibility for attempting your dream."

Everyday Steps to Natural Health

"The policy of being too cautious is the greatest risk of all," noted Jawaharlal Nehru. Here are some ways to avoid that greatest risk.

Identify what type of risk taker you are. In *Chancing It,* Keyes identifies two distinct types of risks, which he calls Level I and Level II. Level I risks are over quickly but are highly stimulating, exciting, and dangerous. Thrill sports such as parachuting or activities such as performing in public are Level I risks. Level II risks are less dramatic, take longer to experience, and are more reassuring. They are usually more challenging to the mind, emotions, or spirit than to the body. Examples include starting a family, getting married, building a career, developing self-knowledge, and beginning a creative endeavor.

Keyes notes that Level I risks are more readily identified as risks by the average person. An overemphasis on taking Level I risks, however, can stunt personal growth rather than promote it. In the extreme, "physical derring-do" and an overemphasis on action is a concept of risk best suited to a seventeen-year-old boy. Taking Level I risks may substitute mere novelty and stimulation for real change. Change for the sake of change can also prevent other social values, such as intimacy and community, Keyes notes. Level I risk taking may become compulsive or result from a self-destructive urge. Keyes emphasizes that whether it is Level I or II, it is not a true risk if it is taken with ignorance, carelessness, peer pressure, or a desire to impress.

Balance your risk taking. Most people combine physical and emotional risks in their lives, though many individuals are much more comfortable facing one type or the other. The true risk taker is willing to take those risks he or she is most uncomfortable with. Let's say your are a Level I risk taker whose idea of fun is to join a three-month expedition to climb mountain peaks in the antarctic. On the other hand, your idea of a long-term commitment is a two-night stand. For you, marriage presents a greater risk than any climbing expedition.

Thus, choose your risks with an awareness of your inclinations. The risks that are most challenging and most likely to result in personal growth are those you may be least willing to take. What is necessary is learning how to identify your fears and take action anyway. Whether you face physical danger is not as important as being open to change and adventure.

"Ideally the ability to take both types of risk is balanced within each of us," Keyes says. "We all need a blend of excitement and security, adventure and community. But in recent centuries our ability to substitute anxiety for fear has reduced the need for either response to danger. As a result, both our nervous systems and our social bonds are creaky from disuse. We suffer from risk hunger."

Keyes notes that it is possible to combine risks from both levels, giving the example of the couple that wanted to increase family unity and physically challenge their young son. They hiked the entire Appalachian Trail, a risk that did yield short-term excitement and long-term commitments.

Determine what you want from taking a risk. Discovering your true motives for taking a risk is an important part of assessing its pros and cons. Are you taking up a physically challenging activity such as rock climbing to increase your powers of concentration? To build self-esteem? To relieve boredom? To impress a girlfriend? To achieve self-transcendence? Taking risks can accomplish all of these, and more, though as we've seen, it is hardly necessary to put your body in harm's way to benefit from risk taking.

Having a goal or an objective for your risk allows you to evaluate possible outcomes. It is a risk to drive your car without wearing a seat belt. Is this a risk you are willing to take? If so, you have good company—about half of all Americans don't bother with seat belts. Why? Many people may not bother at all to examine the consequences of this choice. Some offer the reason that not buckling is evidence that they are independent thinkers, rugged individualists, or just "a risk taker." Most people who do buckle up do so because they realize that if they have an accident, they are more likely to survive and not be injured. Is it wrong to presume that if more people took the time to weigh the consequences—an enhanced self-image versus possible death—of the risks of wearing seat belts, more people would buckle up?

"To stay alive and lively we need a steady diet of risk," notes Keyes. "But we're the only ones who can assess what that means. The assessment of others isn't what matters, the size of a risk, or its potential to thrill. All that matters is that a risk be genuine. And no one knows but the risk taker the meaning of genuine risks."

Question routine. Having a routine can serve many useful purposes. Habits such as exercising at the same time every day and brushing your teeth before going to bed allow you to simplify your life and set priorities. Routines can keep you on track—but that same track may be preventing you from wandering down some of life's interesting byways and detours.

When a routine becomes a means for living without making mistakes, it needs to be questioned. Playing it safe by never stepping outside of your habitual actions can lead to loneliness and boredom. A life of slavish devotion to routine is uneventful and possibly one-dimensional. Just like bones that are never stressed, without the strengthening effects of occasional risks you become brittle and unable to adapt to new conditions.

Taking risks can allow you to step outside of your normal self, to see or experience yourself as a new person. Routines that prevent an occasional foray into the wild or offbeat can stifle innovation. Try to break out of your schedules and routines occasionally to do something new and unexpected, something that will open your eyes to a new reality. Let chance be a creative force in your life.

One way to question routine is to cultivate a wide variety of friends and acquaintances. Rather than surrounding yourself only with people who agree with you, find those who will argue, disagree, probe, and challenge you.

The movie *Shadowlands* portrays the short relationship between the American writer Joy Gresham and the renowned British author

C. S. Lewis. Gresham interrupts Lewis's safe routines, at one point by accusing him of surrounding himself with only immature students and like-minded Oxford dons. These people, Gresham challenges Lewis, never force him to deal with strong emotions. The closely circumscribed lifestyle he has fashioned for himself, she contends, is comfortable but ultimately sheltered and without risk. As a result, though Gresham sees Lewis as a concerned, caring person, she also sees him as essentially uninvolved and incapable of having deep feelings. Falling in love with Gresham was a risk Lewis did eventually accept—and one that led to suffering and pain because of her death—but one that he realized was also necessary for his happiness.

Accept that you might fail. The nature of risk taking is such that it exposes you to unpleasant consequences. If you can be certain of avoiding any unwanted effects, you are assured of success and thus are not really taking a risk. The more often you take risks, the more likely that some will not proceed as planned. If your risks are physical, you may suffer discomfort, injury, disease, or even death. If you are more likely to take intellectual or emotional risks, you may experience loss of control, disappointment, rejection, or ridicule. In either case, you should prepare yourself for these consequences. Avoid placing the blame for failure on shortcomings in your character, bad luck, or your dysfunctional family. Rather, accept failure as a learning experience. See it as the natural result of chances you have willingly undertaken as part of your pursuit of growth.

Those who are willing to risk failure are often the most effective agents for social change. Such people stand up for what is right and refuse to play it safe, whether that means refusing to take a seat at the back of the bus or risking a jail sentence to protest an unjust war. Even Abraham Lincoln's life of accomplishments was peppered with failures. He lost his first election to the Illinois legislature, failed as a storekeeper, was not offered a sought-after appointment in Washington in 1849, lost as a vice-presidential candidate in 1856, and was defeated in a senatorial election in 1858. A lesser man would not have risked defeat again in 1860, yet Lincoln did and was elected president.

An obsession with health can be a form of risk aversion. At its extremes you can end up a Howard Hughes-like recluse deathly afraid of germs (he died anyway). Indeed, one of the consequences of risk taking that many people find hardest to accept is ill health.

Yet accepting illness is another aspect of accepting failure, maintains Kat Duff, author of *The Alchemy of Illness*. Duff led a healthy life yet still unexpectedly came down with chronic fatigue immune-deficiency syndrome at thirty-six. While pondering the eternal question of "Why me?" Duff realized that in many ways "perfect health" has become an impossible ideal in our culture. The predominant perception of health defines it in terms of eternal youth and vigor, optimism and strength. Any abnormalities, from small breasts to short height, are increasingly defined as illnesses to be treated with surgery, drugs, or therapy.

"When problems are quickly solved," Duff notes, "and we return to our old selves, the questions illnesses inevitably raise—and the insights and opportunities they offer—are erased and nullified. We have developed so many tools, from visualizations to painkillers, for suppressing symptoms and their accompanying question marks, that we have lost the ability to come to terms with pain and suffering, to be changed, informed, and even illumined by their presence in our lives."

Short Tips for Risk Takers

❑ Take your own risks. Don't be talked into taking a risk, whether it be a hazardous rock climb or a marriage, by someone else who is more interested in, prepared for, or suited to that risk. Always judge for yourself whether a risk is worthwhile. Also, don't hoist your risk taking onto other people. "If you need someone to take your risks, you are gaining no experience, and when the day comes that you will have to risk on your own, you are more likely to be overwhelmed, more likely to fail," says David Viscott, M.D., author of *Risking*.

❑ Update your concept of risk. The chances you are willing to take, or should be considering more seriously, change as you grow older. At nineteen you may have thought marriage was a bigger risk than hitchhiking around Asia. At thirty-nine you have probably reversed this position. Realize that the risks you want and need to take change throughout your life as new challenges present themselves.

❑ Be realistic about what a risk will gain for you. Don't expect any particular risk to solve all of your problems for the rest of your life. Accept that some risk taking and personal growth are lifelong processes that can be embraced throughout your life.

❏ Line up support for your risks. "Even the most venturesome among us need safety zones where we can rehearse and seek support from others before taking important risks. Ideally our families, schools, and churches can serve such a purpose. But too few of them do," says Keyes.

❏ Prepare for a risk, but if you decide to take it, do so fully before it is too late. Endless researching of outcomes and planning for contingencies can smother a risky venture before it is undertaken. Seize the moment when it presents itself and expect to adapt and change with circumstances. William Lloyd George said, "Don't be afraid to take a big step if one is indicated; you can't cross a chasm in two small jumps."

For More Information

For more on the benefits of not playing it safe and the character of risk taking in American society see:

Chancing It: Why We Take Risks by Ralph Keyes (Boston: Little, Brown, 1985)

People of Chance: Gambling in American Society from Jamestown to Las Vegas by John M. Findlay (New York: Oxford University Press, 1986)

Risking: How to Take Chances and Win by David Viscott, M.D. (New York: Simon & Schuster, 1977)

38

JUST SAY MAYBE

If you choose to use drugs, you are in good company. Humans have been using mind-altering substances for thousands of years and will no doubt continue to do so in the foreseeable future regardless of laws or slogans such as "Just say no." Today, the vast majority of Americans use drugs, with the most popular mind-altering substances being legal ones: tobacco, coffee, tea, cola, wine, beer, and spirits. If you are among those who do use these, you should take time to consider how your use is affecting your life and your health. Do you have a positive relationship with these substances? Do they give you more of something you value (energy, pleasure, relaxation) without robbing you of other things you need (self-esteem, health, longevity)? Do you use these substances consciously or habitually? Are drugs controlling and possibly damaging your life?

An important rule suggested by Andrew Weil, M.D., and Winifred Rosen, authors of *From Chocolate to Morphine: Understanding Mind Active Drugs,* is that if you do take mind-altering substances, take them orally so that they enter your bloodstream through the stomach and intestines. This is a much slower ingestion process than taking drugs either by direct injection into the bloodstream, smoking or inhaling substances into the lungs, or snorting drugs through the nasal passages. Taking substances in these ways rushes the drug to the brain in a matter of seconds (as with inhaled nicotine) or minutes. The speed and intensity of the action makes the process addictive—a British study found that young people who smoke more than a single cigarette have less than a one in six chance of remaining a nonsmoker. Non-oral drug use also increases the risk of overdose and long-term damage to the lungs and other tissues.

From this perspective, "Just say no" does make sense if it is applied to tobacco as well as to various illegal substances, such as marijuana, cocaine, and heroin, typically taken by inhaling, snorting, or shooting. Nicotine is an extremely addictive substance, and breaking the smoking habit is difficult. If you're one of the almost 50 million Americans who still smoke, many programs can help, from using self-hypnosis to wearing nicotine patches. If one program doesn't work, try another. The more times you try to quit, the greater your chances of succeeding. Your long-term health depends on saying no to tobacco.

"Just say maybe," on the other hand, is a more realistic policy to apply to the two other principal mind-altering substances widely taken by tens of millions of Americans: caffeine and alcohol. While not necessarily benign just because they are taken orally, many people do drink coffee and alcoholic beverages without compromising their health. Other people may benefit by reexamining their relationship to these drugs.

Everyday Steps to Natural Health

The cultural and social pressures to use caffeine and alcohol are considerable. Coffee and alcohol rank one and two among the foods most often consumed and mentioned on prime-time television, according to a survey done by researchers at the University of Minnesota. Soft drinks—mostly caffeine-containing—rank third. Here are some suggestions for how you can resist the pressures and make your own choices about these substances.

Take a break from coffee. The average American drinks almost three and a half cups of coffee each day, according to the National Coffee Association of America. One in five Americans drinks five or more cups of coffee per day. Some people can't make it to breakfast without a cup, then drink it more or less continually throughout the day—almost four hundred thousand people drink at least ten cups per day. Not surprisingly, average daily caffeine consumption in the U.S. today is a whopping 150–225 mg. In other words, many people consume more caffeine than they do vitamin C.

Drinking even a couple of cups of coffee per day may cause sleeplessness or anxiety in some people. More serious harmful effects have been documented at levels beyond that. Caffeine has an adverse impact on your nervous system, kidneys, and adrenals. It raises cholesterol levels, depletes certain vitamins and minerals, and may cause breast and prostrate problems. Drinking more than five cups per day gives you a three times greater risk of heart disease compared to those who drink no coffee.

In addition to coffee, other common sources of caffeine include tea and most cola soft drinks (as well as a few others, such as Dr Pepper and even some orange sodas) and certain over-the-counter painkillers. Chocolate has relatively low levels of caffeine but higher amounts of a compound called theobromine, a chemical relative of caffeine that has similar effects on the body.

If you need coffee to do your job, whether that means selling, writing, or driving, you may be addicted to caffeine. According to Weil, "I estimate that 80 percent of coffee users are addicted to it. The addiction is physical, with a prominent withdrawal reaction when use is suddenly discontinued." Those who drink coffee steadily at work all week, for instance, may notice a "rebound" headache by noon on Saturday if they haven't fed their habit. Becoming more aware of caffeine's role in your life is a first step toward establishing control over it.

Those who have already made the switch to decaffeinated coffee may be interested in trying one of the dozen or so grain beverages on the market. Even if the caffeine has been removed by a nontoxic water-process, coffee may still lead to digestive, urinary-tract, and other problems. Most grain beverages are mixtures of roasted barley, chicory, acorn, rye, and other healthful ingredients. Some have malted barley, figs, or molasses for sweetness. Grain beverages are brewed and served hot much like coffee and have a similarly pleasing aroma and taste.

"The best reason to choose a good grain beverage over a decaf coffee is flavor," says food writer Craig Weatherby, who recently organized for *Natural Health* a blind taste test of leading grain beverages. Weatherby says, "Although the flavor of grain beverages is distinctly different from that of coffee, even the regular coffee drinkers on our test panel found several grain beverages as flavorful as a popular brand of instant decaf." The grain beverages that ranked highest in overall flavor among the eleven tested were Lima Yannoh, Barley Brew from Sundance Roasting Co., Polish Naturals Inka, and General Foods' Postum.

If you drink alcohol, do so with moderation. Approximately two-thirds of adult Americans drink alcoholic beverages. Alcohol is also the most widely used drug among American youths. It is a leading cause of illness and death not only in the U.S. (through disease and accidents accounting for at least two hundred thousand deaths annually) but throughout much of the world.

Some 8–10 percent of alcohol users can be expected to develop an addiction or drinking-related problem. Excessive consumption can deplete the body of vitamins and nutrients, cause cirrhosis of the liver, increase the risk of heart disease and various cancers, and lead to sexual impotence. Even among casual users it impairs motor skills and thus increases accidents and injuries. Drunken driving is responsible for about half of the fifty thousand highway fatalities in the U.S. annually.

Clearly, only a small minority of moderate drinkers become problem drinkers. But what exactly is moderate drinking? Most health authorities in the U.S. say one to two drinks daily, though some say up to three drinks a day is still moderate. A drink is approximately an ounce of alcohol—about what is found in a mug of beer, a glass of wine, or a shot of whiskey. Such moderate consumption, according to recent studies on alcohol, is not only safe but may actually offer a number of important health benefits, most notably protecting the heart from cardiovascular disease.

Exactly how moderate drinking lowers heart disease is still being studied. Among the possibilities are its ability to promote relaxation and to improve cholesterol levels. The latter theory was given a boost by a recent study done by researchers based at Brigham and Women's Hospital in Boston and published in the *New England Journal of Medicine*. The study of 680 people found that one to two drinks per day raised levels of two forms of high-density lipoprotein (HDL) cholesterol, the "good" cholesterol. Though lead author J. Michael Gaziano said that "we don't recommend that people pick up drinking to prevent heart disease," he noted that the reduction in heart-disease risk was about the same as that from eating a healthful diet.

Red wine may be the most healthful alcoholic beverage. It offers low levels of a few healthful minerals plus, more importantly, some compounds, such as the bioflavonoid quercetin, that may be effective at lowering your risk of cancer. University of California, Berkeley, biochemist Terrance Leighton is studying possible anticarcinogens in wine. With quercetin, Leighton says, "we have a molecule that can inactivate a known human cancer gene and prevent it from exerting its malignant effects on a normal cell." Scientists are also looking into other components of red wine, such as tannins and a compound formed in grapes called resveratrol. One or more of these may be responsible for an association researchers found between moderate drinking of red wine and elevated levels of HDL cholesterol.

Other studies have supported claims that moderate drinking of wine or any other alcoholic beverage can lower mortality rates. The landmark Framingham Heart Study, for instance, found that "men who drank had lower mortality than men who did not, the lowest mortality being for light drinkers." The bottom line, says Eric Rimm, project director of the Health Professionals Followup Study at the Harvard School of Public Health, is that "people who don't drink should not start drinking. There are too many potential detrimental effects. But moderate consumption is okay for people who do enjoy alcohol and know they can control their consumption."

Question your motives for using mind-altering substances. What do you want from drugs such as caffeine and alcohol? From the strictly physiological point of view, caffeine is a central-nervous-system stimulant and alcohol a depressant. These effects can be delivered with comparable or better levels of safety and effectiveness by other natural substances, including some herbs (see below).

For many people, the reasons behind drinking coffee and alcohol go beyond physiology to issues of social acceptance, friendship, and camaraderie. Dean Ornish, M.D., who directed the landmark study that found diet and lifestyle changes could actually reverse heart disease, says that the positive health effects supposedly derived from alcohol may be due not to the substance itself but to how it is used. "The studies that indicate that moderate drinking is beneficial miss the point," he says. The protective effect is from the socializing, relaxation, and unwinding that surround drinking and "happy hour" in our culture. "Although there may be some benefit in the relaxing effects of alcohol, a better approach would be to find ways to relax and manage stress and be with friends and family in ways that don't center around alcohol or high-fat foods."

By the same token, some people depend upon alcohol, if not

caffeine, for more personal effects. Perhaps without realizing it, drinking becomes an attempt to fill emptiness or to satisfy a yearning for wholeness. No drug or natural substance can provide these, which must be found within one's self and through one's relations with others, society, and nature (see Steps 35, 39, and 46 on addiction, developing positive attitudes, and social networks).

Use less toxic herbs and supplements for some of the same effects. If stimulants and depressants are what you want, there are a number of alternatives to caffeine and alcohol. Most natural stimulant products of "herbal uppers" contain ephedra, or ma huang, an herb that is as potent as caffeine in stimulating the central nervous system. Ephedra also shares, however, caffeine's drawbacks, including potentially causing anxiety, insomnia, and other side effects. A better choice as a natural-stimulant herb is ginseng.

Ginseng is a human-shaped root that is one of the most popular healing herbs of East and West. It includes species from Asia (*Panax ginseng,* usually called Chinese or Korean ginseng) and North America (*Panax quinquefolius,* called American ginseng). People take it to boost energy levels as well as to enhance memory, lessen the effects of stress, and improve performance. Most people find ginseng less of a stimulant than caffeine, while others find ginseng to be too strong. Its effects are sometimes cumulative and may become more apparent after using it regularly for weeks or months. It is sold as a whole root, sliced, or powdered, and in capsules, tablets, tea bags, tinctures, and extracts. Follow dosage directions on the label.

If you want a natural sedative, try the herb valerian, derived from the root of a European plant *(Valeriana officinalis)* now spread throughout the northeastern U.S. People take valerian to relax mind and body, provide temporary relief from anxiety, and prevent insomnia. It is sometimes combined with other sedating herbs in insomnia remedies. Studies have found it is as effective as some barbiturates for reducing the time needed to fall asleep. It is safe even when taken in moderate doses (a gram of the powder, a teaspoon of the tincture, or 250 mg of the liquid or solid extract) but should not be used for an extended period of time. It is sold dried and in tablets, capsules, concentrated drops, tinctures, and extracts.

Short Tips

❏ Avoid regularly using one mind-altering drug to cancel the effects of another. In other words, if you drink so much coffee every day that you need to drink alcohol at night to wind down from the caffeine-induced high, you are probably on the road to compromising your long-term health.

❏ Let acupuncture help you to quit smoking. "Since we have proof that acupuncture is successful in treating cocaine and heroin addiction," says naturopath Lyn Patrick of Tucson, Arizona, "it's likely to follow that nicotine addiction can also be successfully treated." Patrick says that 60 percent of the 120 people she has helped to kick the tobacco habit in recent years were still not smoking six months to four years after quitting. A number of other acupuncturists around the country (see "For More Information") are also reporting success rates higher than behavioral programs for quitting smoking.

❏ Take nutritional supplements to help treat alcoholism. "Why do people persist in believing that the damage done by excess ingestion of alcohol can be undone with psychological methods alone?" asks Joan Mathews-Larson, Ph.D., founder and executive director of the Health Recovery Center in Minneapolis, Minnesota. The Center uses nutrients such as vitamin B complex, vitamin C, calcium, magnesium, evening-primrose oil, and amino acids to help alcoholics restore biochemical balance and kick the booze habit. Along with a number of other holistic-oriented alcohol treatment centers, the Center (see "For More Information") reports a success rate dramatically higher than conventional alcohol recovery programs.

❏ Drink grape juice to enjoy the benefits of resveratrol, the cholesterol-lowering substance in red wine, without consuming alcohol. Researchers have found that grape juice is actually a more dependable source of resveratrol than red wine, since inexpensive red wines are processed in a way that removes the compound.

❏ Protect your liver with the herb milk thistle. On those drinking occasions when you do throw moderation to the wind, help your liver to deal with the added stress by taking milk-thistle seeds *(Silybum marianum)*. According to Robert McCaleb, president of the Herb Research Foundation, the herb "has been found to protect liver cells from damage due to viral hepatitis and from liver toxins such as solvents, alcohol, [and] drugs." Milk thistle also "speeds the regeneration of liver cells after damage has occurred," he notes. Look in your natural-foods store for milk-thistle seeds or for silymarin, a standardized extract of one of the herb's complex compounds.

For More Information

By far the best book on mind-altering substances and other drugs is:

From Chocolate to Morphine by Andrew Weil, M.D., and Winifred Rosen
    (New York: Houghton Mifflin, rev. ed., 1993)

The following organization will refer readers to one of their 1,400 members, all of whom are certified acupuncturists treating nicotine and other addictions:

National Acupuncture Detoxification Association
349 E. 140th St.
New York, NY 10454
(718) 993-3100

For more information on nutritional treatment of alcoholism:

Alcoholism: The Biochemical Connection by Joan Mathews-Larson, Ph.D.
    (New York: Villard Books, 1992)

Health Recovery Center
3255 Hennepin Ave., S.
Minneapolis, MN 55408
(612) 827-7800

39

THE GLASS IS HALF-FULL

Developing a healthful approach to everyday stresses by emphasizing positive attitudes and beliefs allows you to live a more
harmonious and rewarding life. Among the many valuable physiological consequences of optimism you can reap are a significant boost
in immunity and a lower risk of killer diseases, including cancer.
For example, a study of cancer patients done by Dr. Lawrence
LeShan found that 76 percent of them suffered from hopelessness
and low self-esteem, compared to only 10 percent of a control group
of noncancer patients. A number of other larger studies have indicated that chronic depression can increase your risk of death from
cancer.

Attitudes, beliefs, and emotions that can adversely affect your
body and increase your chances of developing illness include hopelessness, despair, low self-esteem, isolation, neglect, anger, hostility,
passivity, helplessness, psychic numbness, fear, and sadness. Everyone experiences these states on occasion, but when they become
your everyday outlook, and you have no way to communicate them
to those around you, you are hurting your chances for a long and
healthy life.

On the other hand, mental states that can boost your body's
ability to stay well include optimism, hope, faith, humor, confidence, purposefulness, self-esteem, flexibility, and tolerance. An

ability to find meaning in life, whether through your work, spirituality, or creativity, is another important gauge of physical and emotional health. Again, no one person is perfectly developed in all these attitudes at all times, but to the extent that you can make these your predominant attitudes and beliefs you will enjoy health and longevity.

Everyday Steps to Natural Health

Since overall health is determined by physical, emotional, and spiritual factors, the steps you take in each area have a positive impact on the others. Thus, the efforts you make to develop positive outlooks will have a ripple effect that brings you better bodily fitness and spiritual peace.

Love yourself. Self-esteem is something that comes naturally with better physical and emotional health. Many of the steps in this book can help you to develop in a way that will naturally boost your self-esteem. For instance, as you become more physically fit (see Steps 8–15), break bad habits (see Step 42), increase the depth and variety of your social network (see Step 46), find work that you love (see 47), and become more creative (see Step 51), your self-esteem will naturally float up on the rising tide of your self-improvement.

What you can look forward to is an increased sense of your self-worth, more awareness of who you are and what you like to do, and a greater respect for the value of your contributions to your family, coworkers, and community. Learning how to love yourself and developing self-esteem does not mean you will never be unhappy or that you will have eliminated all weaknesses in body, mind, and character. Rather, it means that you have established a healthy respect for yourself and developed a sense of purpose for your life. It means that you know what your strengths and weaknesses are and can take realistic actions allowing for both. When you love and respect yourself, you trust your judgment about yourself and other people. Your confidence in your self-worth attracts others to you and thus increases your chances of developing healthy, stable relationships. A healthy sense of self-esteem helps you decide what you want from life, establish goals, and pursue them.

Proper self-esteem allows you to feel comfortable about meeting your needs, at times even when other people's needs are clamoring for your attention. Loving and respecting yourself, however, is not the same as being selfish, says Reed C. Moskowitz, M.D., author of *Your Healing Mind*. To treat another person with respect, he notes, you must first be able to treat yourself with kindness and understanding. What you don't have you can't give. "Selfishness is actually the opposite of self-love," Moskowitz writes. "Selfishness arises out of an unfulfilled hunger for self-respect and love. Selfishness occurs when we are feeling empty and need to grab for anything we can get. A starving person is too desperate to share a morsel with others. When we have plenty of love, then we can share the bounty with others."

Communicate positive messages to your body. The mind/body connection is now so well established that few doctors or other health practitioners doubt that attitudes, beliefs, and emotions can either keep you well or contribute to illness. New evidence indicates that mental states can also either extend or shorten your life and help you heal or prevent you from recovering from an illness.

A recent large statistical study of over 28,000 Chinese American adults published in the medical journal *The Lancet* offered dramatic proof that the beliefs you hold about your health can either add or subtract years from your life. Researchers at the University of California at San Diego quizzed subjects about their belief in a tenet of traditional Chinese philosophy: that people tend to get certain diseases depending upon what year they were born.

Some Chinese believe that each year of the lunar calendar can be classified as belonging to one of five "elements" or "phases": Fire, Earth, Metal, Water, and Wood. The five elements are linked to certain illnesses as well as to various aspects of nature, including the seasons, bodily organs, and foods and herbs. Thus, a person born in a Fire year may be most affected by the summer, be prone to problems with her heart, and so forth. The researchers found that when Chinese Americans develop an illness that is associated with their element, they die anywhere from one to five years earlier than would otherwise be expected.

According to sociologist Dr. David P. Phillips, who conducted the study, "When a person contracts a disease that is associated with the phase of his birth year, he may be more likely than others who contract the disease to feel helpless, hopeless, and stoic." These attitudes can significantly shorten survival times. Phillips pinpointed belief as the causative agent by comparing the death certificates of the Chinese Americans with those of over four hundred thousand white Americans with similar statistics (including cause of death, year of birth and death, and sex).

Other researchers recently confirmed and even expanded upon the well-known power of belief when wielded by patient and doctor to act as a healing agent. They demonstrated that the placebo effect, in which a sham surgical procedure or an inert drug such as a sugar pill triggers healing, is more effective than previously thought. Numerous studies have found that placebos are effective from 10–90 percent of the time. The most widely accepted figure is that placebos promote healing in approximately one in three cases. Clinical psychologist Alan Roberts, Ph.D., of the Scripps Clinic and Research Foundation in La Jolla, California, and colleagues found that placebos' effectiveness may be twice that. Roberts analyzed the results from numerous studies in which medical treatments were effective in almost 70 percent of the cases. When the studies were repeated with placebo controls, however, researchers found that placebos were as effective as the treatments. This caused the treatments to lose credibility, while Roberts said of equal importance is the implication that the placebo effect may be much stronger than thought.

In *The Wizdom Within,* authors Dr. Irving Oyle and Susan Jean relate a remarkable anecdote that demonstrates the healing power of suggestion and belief. Oyle and Jean were told by a physician from Calcutta that a farmer came to see him experiencing a moderately severe reaction, characterized by hives and difficulty breathing. Since the farmer refused to be hospitalized, the physician wrote a prescription for the anti-inflammatory drug cortisone. The physician related, "I took great pains to explain that this was very powerful medicine and that he was to take it four times a day without fail." The patient returned in thirty-six hours completely recovered. The physician asked him about the leftover cortisone, but the farmer said that "there was none because he followed my instructions explicitly. 'I tore your medicine paper into four parts and swallowed one on arising, one with lunch, one with the evening meal, and the last after I was in bed,' he said. He had eaten the paper on which the prescription was written, and he was fully recovered. He requested another medicine paper as insurance against the return of the malady. Naturally, I gave him one."

Become more expressive and assertive. Mind-body researchers have firmly established that dwelling on anger and grief suppresses the immune system and decreases white-blood-cell activity. Whether there is a direct link between cancer, attitudes, and emotions is controversial, but recent studies have provided support for a cancer or "type C" personality. Researcher psychologist Lydia Temoshok, Ph.D., says, "Type C behavior is an extreme version of coping methods many of us employ—we appease others, deny our true feelings, and conform to social standards." In *The Type C Connection: The Behavioral Links to Cancer and Your Health,* she and co-author Henry Dreher note that a wealth of data suggests that "type Cs, who lack quality social support, internalize stress, and inhibit emotions, suffer biologically as a consequence of their pattern. In addition, several studies have shown that *people who reverse these behaviors and trends increase their resistance to disease."* (Emphasis in original.)

The point is not to blame the victim for his or her disease, note the authors, but to empower personal change. Among the cancer-prevention strategies they recommend are boosting the immune system (see Step 28) and developing effective social support systems (see Step 46). Another important step is to become comfortable expressing so-called negative emotions so that their hold over the body is of limited duration. For instance, Temoshok and Dreher suggest

❑ Tune in to your bodily sensations when you are upset or angry and ask yourself why you are feeling this way, and what you can do to address your needs.

❑ Don't blame another person for your feelings or try to change him. Rather, tell him how you are feeling and what you want from him.

❑ Avoid passive-aggressive behavior, in which you express your anger in indirect ways. When necessary and appropriate, such as to defend your integrity or your physical/emotional safety, speak and act directly and decisively.

❑ Learn how to say no. Just as aggressive, time-conscious type A's find it hard to refuse new tasks, type Cs often need practice and commitment to recognize when they must refuse demands for their psychic energy.

Experience the moment. A common cause of stress among many people is constant hurry. These so-called type A persons are typically aggressive and hard-charging. They are always imposing deadlines on themselves and trying to get more done in less time. Their personality and attitude can lead to a form of "time sickness." For them, there is never enough time. When you talk to them, they are likely to be thinking about what they'll do next (when they're not interrupting you to try to finish your thoughts). Their preoccupation with the immediate future causes them to frequently try to do many tasks at the same time—brushing their teeth while taking a shower, eating while driving, and so forth.

Such people rarely experience the moment. What they do experience, especially when time sickness is combined with hostility, anger, and cynicism, is an increased risk of heart attack and other stress-related conditions. (See Step 34 for how to develop a more harmonious relationship with time.)

How you view time can be a crucial factor in developing positive attitudes and emotions. A constant preoccupation with the future prevents you from experiencing the moment and instead makes you nervous, distracted, and eternally unsatisfied. Focus your attention on what you have here and now that is valuable, life-enhancing, and pleasurable. Be with the person you are talking to, in the project you are working on. Some people even try pretending that this is their last day alive. This exercise allows you to savor each moment for its specialness, no matter what the circumstances. Meditation and various other relaxation techniques (see Step 41) can also boost your ability to "be here now."

Transform negative thought patterns into positive ones. "Sure I won the lottery, but look at all the extra taxes I'll have to pay." This type of the-glass-is-half-empty attitude is a glaring example of a negative thought pattern that can depress your mood and your state of physical well-being. False assumptions and "dysfunctional thinking" distort reality in a way that prevents growth and healing, according to Michael Antoni, Ph.D. With researcher Susan Lutgendorf and other colleagues at the University of Miami's Division of Behavioral Medicine, Antoni is studying the effects of group therapy, counseling, stress management, and other mind/body approaches to help treat AIDS patients. Antoni says that some of the common negative thought patterns his subjects fall into include:

➤ all–or–nothing thinking: for example, "Why bother to exercise since I'll never look like Jane Fonda anyway?"

➤ overgeneralizing: "If I quite smoking, I'll just gain weight because that's what happens to everybody."

➤ disqualifying the positive: "I'm enjoying this skiing, but to-morrow I'll probably have caught a cold from it."

➤ jumping to conclusions: "My doctor said I'm at risk for colon cancer so I'll die from it eventually."

If you catch yourself indulging in such negative thought patterns, recognize that they can be self-fulfilling. Replace these negative thoughts with constructive ones, such as emphasizing the positive and realizing your uniqueness. Essentially, it is how you react to a person, event, or situation that determines whether the experience is one that promotes health or causes stress and illness. Lutgendorf says, "How you interpret an event will affect your physiological response. If you see something as a huge threat, you're going to have a stress response. If you see the same thing as a piece of cake, you're not. We're trying to cut off our patients' stress levels right at the level of perception."

Antoni notes that cultivating positive thoughts does not mean you should never feel comfortable expressing anger, frustration, and fear. Therapists need to allow for negative feelings, Antoni says. "When a patient displays negative emotion, they shouldn't rush in and say, 'Oh, no. We can take care of that! We'll positivize that!' They've got to let the emotion radiate and let the person feel it, express it. . . . The first step is always awareness."

Short Tips

❏ Get regular aerobic exercise (see Step 14). Dozens of scientific studies have confirmed that being physically fit has a positive impact on your overall outlook. Staying fit can help relieve depression, reduce anxiety, and decrease anger.

❏ Use affirmations, which are encouraging statements that rein-force your positive view of the future. Affirmations can counter negative attitudes by helping you to visualize yourself as happy, powerful, and self-actualized. State your affirmation directly in a short sentence ("I am a creative person whose drawings are unique") and repeat it, out loud or to yourself, a number of times each day.

You can also type it out and post it in a place you'll see it and be reminded of its power.

❏ Smile. Smiling alerts other people to the positive feelings you are having and is infectious in spreading goodwill and reducing stress. And don't forget to smile out loud—laugh—as frequently as possible (see Step 33).

❏ Cut back on your news diet. Let's face it: the type of news that most television stations and newspapers give prominence to can be grim, with its constant focus on disaster, tragedy, death, and mayhem. If you are a news junkie and rarely go more than a few hours without exposing yourself to the news, you may be unnecessarily upsetting your emotions and causing excess stress without realizing any lasting positive effect. Treat a news addiction like any other: cut back slowly and replace it with healthful alternatives.

For More Information

Some excellent books on the role of attitudes and beliefs in health and healing include:

Love, Medicine and Miracles by Bernie S. Siegel, M.D. (New York: Harper & Row, 1986)

Peace, Love and Healing by Bernie S. Siegel, M.D. (New York: Harper & Row, 1989)

Your Healing Mind by Reed C. Moskowitz, M.D. (New York: Avon Books, 1992)

40

MANAGE YOUR ANGER

E veryone loses his or her temper once in a while, but in the U.S. anger control has become a public-health issue. All too often, anger results in physical aggression. According to the FBI's *Crime in the United States,* "In the case of murder, the victim was well-known to the assailant well over 50 percent of the time, and in these cases angry arguments usually preceded the murderous event." Research studies confirm that verbal aggression is related to physical aggression—it's often a short step from yelling at someone to hitting them.

Even when it doesn't cause immediate bodily mayhem to yourself or others, anger may have adverse health consequences. If you are prone to blowing your stack at the slightest provocation, you should know that it's likely your behavior is increasing your risk of heart disease and high blood pressure and probably compromising your immune system as well.

Anger is a feeling of displeasure caused by confrontation, a perceived threat, mistreatment, or provocation. It is not the same as aggression, which is an action or behavior that is one of many possible responses to anger. What anger often shares with aggression, however, is an excited bodily state. As are other emotions, anger is associated with a physiological state of readiness triggered by hormones such as adrenaline. The hormones do not cause anger—that's determined by how your mind and personality (and culture) interpret the specific situation. During an anger episode the extra hormones in your system cause blood vessels in muscles to dilate and heartbeat and breathing to speed up. Your body is readying itself for the perceived confrontation, whether "fight or flight."

Anger thus serves a potentially useful purpose. When a person or an institution acts in a mean and shallow way, your anger arouses you to respond. How you manage that anger determines whether its effect is good or evil, constructive or destructive, useful or meaningless. Anger should not be classified as a "negative" emotion—it is possible that it has been the instigator of as much good as has love (of God, country) been the instigator of tragedy. Anthropologists note that anger is found in all cultures, but that patterns of dealing with it differ dramatically. In one culture to scream in a rage is to be "strong and manly"; in another it is to be shamefully childlike.

It is principally when anger becomes habitual and when it is accompanied by unwarranted aggression that it becomes so unhealthful. Behavioral scientists say that about one in five Americans harbors attitudes and behavioral patterns that are emotionally and physically harmful. In the past few years studies have shown that the typical type A person who is competitive and eternally in a hurry does not necessarily suffer a greater risk of heart disease. Rather, it is a subset of type A's who keep heart surgeons in Mercedeses. These are the aggressive, time-worried people who are also basically hostile, cynical, and easily provoked to anger and aggression.

A recent study demonstrated that anger can physically affect the heart itself. Researchers at Stanford University discovered that test subjects' hearts dropped an average of 5 percent in pumping efficiency when subjects recounted angry memories. According to the researchers, such a drop can cause blood clots that could block arteries. It could also lead to a potentially fatal disturbance of the heart's natural rhythm.

Uncontrolled anger's adverse effects extend to the psyche as well as the body. As behavioral scientist Robert Maurer has said, "The problem with holding on to anger is that it has physical costs, in stress to the body, but it also disturbs people's ability to learn from their mistakes, and it inclines them to cling to their victimhood. Anger may be necessary for a while. But it is at best a detour and at worst a destructive diversion from the healing that needs to occur if one is to learn from experience."

Everyday Steps to Natural Health

If you're among the basically hostile and chronically angry, it's imperative for your heart and your overall health that you learn how to become angry less frequently, break your habitual responses, control your urge to use aggression and violence, and develop new ways for managing anger.

Don't feel you have to express your anger to stay healthy. That's right. It is perfectly acceptable to refrain from punching anyone, pounding on a mattress, or screaming like a newborn when you are angry. Most people are surprised to discover that catharsis, the purging of an emotion through the act of expression, is vastly overrated when it comes to anger. But among anger researchers "the myth of catharsis" is well-known. Studies have shown that aggression is not a natural way to express anger, but rather a learned behavior.

Carol Tavris, Ph.D., author of the authoritative *Anger: The Misunderstood Emotion,* says, "The point is that aggression, in whatever form, is an acquired strategy for dealing with anger, not a biological inevitability. It is no use telling placid, pacifistic, and rational people that they ought to 'let go' and ventilate their rage with a violent display, throwing saucepans or biting pillows. They will only feel worse if they do. Unless, of course, you can guarantee them that aggression will produce the results they want."

Studies have also consistently demonstrated that expressing anger in words doesn't necessarily alleviate it—often it fans the flames of anger. Talking about your anger typically causes you to fixate on it in an unhealthy way. When study subjects are exposed to the same provocation, those who are encouraged to talk about it experience negative health effects for a longer time than those who are not. According to psychologist and anger researcher Edward Murray, "Expressing hostile feelings is not a sufficient condition for the reduction of anger."

Anger researchers note that the presence of certain conditions make it more likely that catharsis will be effective (for instance, you must be able to direct your anger at the target of your anger, and he or she must not retaliate with anger), but these conditions rarely come together in real life.

If you've found that talking through your anger is an effective way to deal with it, at least use language that promotes conciliation rather than confrontation. That is, describe your feelings without casting blame. For instance, say, "I feel angry when you're late and don't call," rather than, "You're such an inconsiderate jerk for being late all the time."

There are various actions to take beyond aggression and talking it out for dealing with anger. For instance:

❏ Think it over. Look at the situation objectively and decide whether a rational person—you—has enough reason to be angry. If you can get that far, decide on a proper response to the anger. Of course, anger is partly determined by cultural norms, and in the U.S. it is all too normal to carry a lot of anger around and be quick to display it in aggressive ways. Self-reflection and thinking things through are more highly valued in other cultures. Tavris notes that the Utku Eskimo are tolerant of their young children's rages, "but not because they think tantrums have much to do with adult character. Just the opposite. The Eskimo accept childhood outbursts because they know that babies and toddlers have no *ihuma* (reason, thought). Anyone who has reason, however, is expected to control his or her anger, and that includes children over the age of three or four. The only adults who are exempt from this expectation are idiots, the insane, the very sick . . . and *kaplunas,* white people."

❏ Will your attention elsewhere. If you are practiced at meditation, use whatever technique you've found helps you to calm your mind. Your body will soon fall in step by slowing the discharge of adrenaline into the bloodstream, thus leading to a reduced heart rate, slower breathing, and a more relaxed attitude. If you're not a meditator, try distracting yourself. For example, if you tend to get angry whenever you have to wait in a line, always have on hand something to read or listen to.

❏ Look for the humor in the situation. If you can find an element of the silly or absurd, your body is more likely to react in a healthy way (see Step 33). Also, you may be able to defuse another person's hostility. The point is not to use ridicule or sarcastic insults as a form of aggression, but to creatively change your perception of the situation itself.

Be aware of signs of an impending explosion. If anger has become a constant in your life, or your habitual response to anger is hostility and aggression, first take steps to recognize its early signs. For instance, your chest may contract or your face flush. If you can see your anger developing, you have a much better chance to deal with it. It allows you to choose from among a number of strategies and use one or more to effect a positive outcome.

Becoming more aware of your feelings in general can help you to anticipate anger. It also helps you to differentiate anger from fear, jealousy, hatred, and other strong emotions. Another tactic is to take a moment after you've lost your temper to reflect on the process. Did your heartbeat speed up or your body become stiff? Most people react consistently to anger, and if you can determine your own "distant early warning" line, you'll be in a much better position to avoid habitual responses.

Recognize your anger and then get on with life. This is the approach of the psychotherapy and practical lifestyle known as constructive living, which traces its roots to the writings of Japanese philosopher Masatake Morita in the first decades of the twentieth century. Constructive living focuses on reality and actions. It advocates doing what needs to be done. Feelings are deemed uncontrollable by the will; since behaviors are controllable, a person can—and should—act regardless of feelings. As David K. Reynolds, Ph.D., the foremost American proponent of constructive living puts it, "Feelings are not acceptable excuses for doing or not doing something."

"Critics assume that the only two possibilities for handling feelings is to express them or to suppress them," Reynolds notes. "The third alternative—recognizing them, acknowledging them without external expression, and getting on with doing what needs doing—isn't considered, although that third alternative is the one we all utilize most of the time."

In other words, recognize and acknowledge your anger without letting it control your actions and behaviors. You cannot control your anger, but you can control your urge to pick up a chair and throw it through a window. To blame your anger for your action is not only to duck responsibility but to deny your very freedom.

Pick your spots. Anger is sometimes justified. It can be a natural and normal response to an insult or an injustice. Anger represents a potential health problem only when it becomes a constant in your life. If you get angry because you can't open a cereal box, and again because the milk has gone sour, and again because the phone rings as you sit down for breakfast, it is likely that your anger has become habitual and unhealthy.

"Hesitation is the best cure for anger," declared the Roman philosopher Seneca. Counting to ten—or one hundred if you need to—is an age-old anger remedy that works for a good reason: it allows you a few moments to determine whether your anger is an appropriate response to the situation. In some cases your anger may be a holdover from an unrelated event. For instance, you're trying to put dinner together for five rambunctious children. The youngest keeps getting underfoot and you get angry and feel like screaming and maybe smacking him. Are you really angry at the child, who is after all mainly expressing his needs as he knows how? Or are you upset at your husband, who has started to stop off at the local bar for a few drinks every night after work, leaving you to deal with the children? In this case, your anger is justified but mistargeted at the child. Delaying a few moments in expressing the anger may allow you to decide on a more appropriate immediate response.

According to Margaret Chesney, M.D., an epidemiologist at the University of California Medical School and one of the researchers in the Stanford study on anger and the heart, "Many of us are carrying around a bag loaded with resentments and angry events that we pull out and talk about with relish. There may be some relief in sharing feelings of anger, but for the most part there's a lot of stress that goes along with catharsis. We're not saying that people shouldn't get angry—sometimes anger is justified. But be selective—don't get angry over every little thing. And for events that happened a long time ago, work on letting the angry feelings go. Practice focusing on the good things that happen in life as well as the things that you perceive as annoyances. I like to think that when we practice compassion towards ourselves and others, we're nourishing our hearts in a healthy way."

In other words, don't sweat the small stuff—and it's almost always small stuff!

Short Tips for Anger

❑ Pretend today is your last day, suggest Redford Williams, M.D., and Virginia Williams, Ph.D., the authors of *Anger Kills*. Would you really work yourself into a state of anger over a perceived slight if you had only another twenty-four hours to live? "Being brought face-to-face with one's own mortality," the Williamses note, "has a way of focusing attention on what's really important."

❑ Developing your ability to listen can be an effective strategy for dealing with anger by forcing you to acknowledge another's point of view.

❑ Identify and deal with the emotions hidden beneath anger. "Under the anger is always fear or pain, or both—the fear that we can't cope; feeling helpless or powerless . . . I try to teach people to accept their anger, uncover it if it's buried, and find out who and what they're angry at," says transpersonal therapist Patricia Henry.

For More Information

Good books on dealing with anger include:

Anger Kills by Redford Williams, M.D., and Virginia Williams, Ph.D. (New York: Times Books, 1993)

Anger: The Misunderstood Emotion by Carol Tavris (New York: Touchstone, rev. ed., 1989)

CONSCIOUSLY RELAX

Ask people what they do to relax and you'll often hear "I watch TV" or "I read a book" or maybe even "I go for a drive." Yet these activities' ability to help you relax relies in part on their being distracting or entertaining. On occasion they can also be challenging or horrifying. They require attention, can be tiring to the eyes and mind, and are often done with little or no concern for the body by being accompanied by addictive eating and poor posture. Consciously relaxing is both easier on the body and more difficult to really do well. It can help you attain a state of apparent opposites: aware yet passive, calm yet alert, relaxed yet focused, resting yet awake.

An important benefit from learning some form of conscious relaxation is an increased ability to deal with the stresses of everyday life. These stresses may be due to factors in the environment that are mostly out of your immediate control (such as noise, insane drivers, a demanding boss, or the death of a loved one). Stress may also result from things you can, but often don't, control, whether that be ingesting stimulating substances such as caffeine or nicotine or harboring negative attitudes and emotions, such as guilt, cynicism, and hostility.

What these assorted "stressors" have in common is an ability to jerk your nervous system into action by flooding the bloodstream with adrenaline and other hormones that prepare you for "fight or flight." Since most of us have the good sense not to constantly react to these stimulations by either punching out another person or running three miles in the opposite direction, the effects of these stressors stay with the body beyond the ending of the immediate stimulus. The immediate effect may be nothing or it may be insomnia, headaches, backaches, and other seemingly unrelated conditions. If a pattern of failing to deal constructively with stress is maintained over years and years, the adverse health effects may be worse, including an increased risk of heart disease, chronic digestive problems, and a weakened immune system.

It is best to remove those causes of stress that you can. You should also work on improving your attitudes and emotions (see Step 39) to prevent unnecessary stress. Still, you can't expect to eliminate stress completely from your life—nor would you enjoy such a dull, uneventful existence. Rather, seek to prevent long-term "distress" by learning how to change your typical reaction to stress. The techniques of conscious relaxation reduce the effects of stress not just for the ten to fifteen minutes that you practice them, but more importantly these techniques can show you how to respond in a healthy way to stressful situations that occur throughout your everyday life.

Many of the simple steps presented elsewhere in this book have a positive effect on reducing distress: you need to get the right amount of sleep, exercise regularly, breathe fully, cultivate humor, and eat a healthful diet. At the same time you can also take the time on a regular basis to fully relax. Unlike simply watching TV, for instance, conscious relaxation techniques provoke a specific "relaxation response." This physical change in the body is characterized by an immediate relaxing of muscles, slowing of breath and heartbeat, lowering of blood pressure, and decreasing of metabolism. These effects are the exact opposite of what happens to the body when it is experiencing stress.

Meditation is a well-known (if sparsely practiced) relaxation method. It is, however, "but one of scores of techniques that will bring about the same physiological state," points out Herbert Benson, M.D., author of *The Relaxation Response* and chief of the Division of Behavioral Medicine at the New England Deaconess Hospital in Boston. Other techniques, he says, "include repetitive prayer, progressive muscular relaxation, autogenic training, Lamaze breathing, yoga, tai chi, and *chi gung*." To this list could be added activities ranging from receiving a massage to gardening to playing a musical instrument.

Everyday Steps to Natural Health

Choose a conscious relaxation technique that is consistent with your culture, beliefs, and lifestyle. Schedule it into your daily routine just like exercise to make it a regular part of your health practice. And stay flexible—if your practice is not working adjust it to fit your needs. Here are some practices to consider.

Take up meditation. Some meditation practices merely aim to achieve temporary relaxation by allowing you to quiet outside distraction, observe your mind, and experience the present moment. Other practices may also emphasize their ability to allow you to attune your attention to a deeper, core self, resolve emotional conflicts, and produce a spiritual awakening. Though these "side effects" can be desirable to some and annoying (or worse) to others, they are not necessary to achieve the relaxation response.

"One of the cardinal principles of meditation is that you're not actually trying to change anything, including your state of mind," notes Jon Kabat-Zinn, director of the University of Massachusetts Medical Center's Stress Reduction Clinic in Worcester, and the teacher of a Buddhist approach called mindfulness meditation. "You're not trying to get from a bad place to a good place, or from a tense, stressful place to a relaxed, pleasurable place. Those things may happen, but they happen far more often when you allow yourself to be completely in the present moment with whatever comes up, including negative thoughts and feelings. If you step back and simply watch with a witnessing-type consciousness, then all the tensions and anxieties tend to dissolve."

Meditation as a relaxation technique grew in popularity in the 1960s when the influence of oriental culture and philosophy took root in young Americans. Most meditators sought to deepen their personal awareness and promote spiritual growth, though now meditators are as likely to use meditation as a tool for reducing stress and promoting physical and mental relaxation.

Techniques from the East that took hold in the sixties and remain popular today include transcendental meditation (TM), Vipassana or "insight meditation," and Zen Buddhist meditation. Various levels of cultural and religious baggage accompany these, depending on the teacher or school. Many Westerners prefer more secularized forms of meditation. John Selby, author of *Kundalini Awakening,* says, "The truth is that you don't have to adopt any new religious orientation in order to embrace these meditative programs in your life. . . . We need no religious symbology dragging us down in our exploration of our deeper spiritual nature. All we need are core meditative techniques that enable us to quiet our thinking minds so we become still and know through immediate personal contact our oneness with God—with whatever name we might give to the infinite and yet intimate spiritual presence that lives deep within us."

Spiritual centers, adult education courses, and individuals teach meditation in all parts of the country. You can also try one of the following basic methods, which use visualizations, sounds, objects, and activities to quiet and focus the mind. Anyone can do these with a minimum of practice.

Meditation generally needs to be done in a quiet place where you won't be interrupted. If you are sitting, sit comfortably with your back straight. Close your eyes and keep still.

❏ A favorite visualization is to imagine filling your body with fiery red, liquid tension. Feel it pass into all parts of your body. Now allow it to run out of the tips of your fingers and toes. Drain your body completely of the liquid and observe the stillness that results. Another form of visualization is to project yourself into an idyllic scene. Depending on what you like, you may visualize yourself on a balmy, isolated ocean beach. Imagine the feel of the warm sun on your skin, the sound of the gently lapping waves, and the aroma of tropical plants. When your mind wanders, re-create the scene and your place in it.

❏ Sounds are repeated over and over, or chanted, to achieve a meditative state. In India sacred sounds such as *om* (drawn out in meditation to sound like *aaah-oh-oooom*) are called mantras. You can use any word, phrase, or sound, although in the Eastern tradition certain sounds have specific effects on your nervous system due to their particular vibration. If a favorite line of poetry works for you, use it. In teaching this form of meditation to subjects participating in his studies, Benson has found that a favorite inspirational phrase seems to work better than a neutral or meaningless word.

❏ Contemplating objects by calmly gazing at them is another popular route to meditative calmness. For example, you can look at a burning candle or a devotional painting. Hindu meditators often contemplate a mandala, the Sanskrit word for a depiction of concentric circles and other shapes or symbols that represent the order of the universe.

❏ Activities that can foster meditation can be as simple as rocking in a chair, although the most popular is probably breathing. Using abdominal breathing (see Step 26) and breathing through the nose, focus your thoughts on your in-breath and out-breath. Notice how the air feels as it enters and leaves your body. Observe as well the pauses between each inhalation and exhalation. If it helps to keep you focused on the moment, count each exhale. Stop your count at five and start over. If you lose count or count higher than five, your focus is wandering and you need to gently bring it back to your breath and your count.

Relax your muscles from toe to head. Progressive muscle relaxation, also known as simply progressive relaxation or whole-body relaxation, is a stress-busting technique that is perfect for beginners. It also works well with people who, for various reasons, resist learning meditation and for those who may not be aware of how tense they are most of the time. Fitness and stress-reduction consultants as well as yoga teachers are now using various forms of progressive muscle relaxation, as are leading medical researchers such as Herbert Benson and Dean Ornish, M.D., author of *Dr. Dean Ornish's Program for Reversing Heart Disease.*

The central tenets of the practice are, one, muscles relax more fully after they have been tensed, and, two, people can more readily experience what relaxation is if they first consciously create tension.

Progressive relaxation can be done seated or, preferably, lying on your back. On your back, put your arms to your sides with your palms up. Your feet should be about eighteen inches apart and rolled outward. Adjust your position to get symmetrical and comfortable. Inhaling through your nose and using abdominal breathing, tense one foot for two to three seconds, then relax it as you exhale. Do the same for the other foot, then take a moment to say to yourself, "My feet are completely relaxed. I feel them sinking into the floor." Proceed to the legs, tensing and relaxing first one and then the other. It may help to raise limbs a few inches off the floor as you tense them and to drop them limply as they are relaxed. Do the legs, buttocks, abdomen, hands, arms, upper chest, shoulders, and neck. Roll your head side to side to relax the neck and squeeze the muscles of your face before relaxing them. Focus on your breathing while watching thoughts come and go without dwelling on them. You can do a series of progressive relaxations, moving from the bottom to the top of the body and back again, finishing with five to ten minutes of complete relaxation. Come out of the practice by slowly stretching while on your back and then rolling over into a sitting position.

Meditate while your exercise. Exercise is one of the most popular ways to deal with stress, according to a survey of *Natural Health* readers. They ranked exercise ahead of meditation, yoga, and talking to a spouse, friend or therapist. While exercise that is competitive or injury-prone is unlikely to elicit the relaxation response, certain types of exercise can be married to meditation to provide some of the body/mind benefits of both of these activities. For example, at The Marsh: A Center for Balance and Fitness in Eden Prairie, Minnesota, owner Ruth Stricker teaches students a series of slow, fluid movements that combine the oriental discipline tai chi with visualizations and attention to the mind. Students may imagine holding and moving their hands around large balls, for instance. Such meditation is now being called "mindful exercise."

Stricker recently helped to test mindful exercise at the university of Massachusetts Medical School. The study was directed by James Rippe, M.D., who heads the Exercise Physiology and Nutrition Center in Shrewsbury, Massachusetts, with the assistance of the Mind/Body Medical Institute at Deaconess Hospital, headed by Benson. The study subjects were divided into five groups. Three groups practiced forms of mindful exercise, such as walking while listening to a relaxation tape that told them to think "step, step" to the rhythm of their footsteps, and doing a combination of tai chi and visualization. Subjects in these groups experienced more enthusiasm, alertness, self-esteem, and feelings of excitement and strength, and less irritability, guilt, fear, and hostility, compared to subjects in the other groups (such as those that read quietly or walked with low intensity).

"Exercise alone provides psychological and physical benefits," according to Rippe. "However, if you also adopt a strategy that engages your mind while you exercise, you can get a whole host of psychological benefits fairly quickly, which makes it easier to keep exercising and allows you to exercise at a less vigorous level. Also, people who feel awkward about practicing meditation often find combining it with exercise to be more acceptable."

Along with tai chi, yoga is another ancient movement discipline that naturally combines exercise and meditation (see Step 12 for a twelve-step yoga stretching routine). Kabat-Zinn has developed a set of meditation instruction tapes (see "For More Information") that guide the listener through a series of gentle, meditative exercises designed to relax both body and mind.

Even without instruction, you can combine exercise and meditation by repeating a mantra while doing any low-intensity, repetitive exercise, such as walking or riding a stationary bicycle. Do the exercise at a pace that raises your heartbeat to about 50–60 percent of your maximum (which is 220 minus your age). Instead of repeating a favorite phrase, you can try listening to specially designed meditation tapes or other peaceful recordings, such as sounds of nature or any music that is soft and rhythmic. Find a place to do mindful exercise that is quiet and free of distraction.

Short Tips for Relaxation

❏ Repetitive activities can be a form of meditation in action. For instance, many people find the repetitive movements and the central focus associated with knitting results in profound relaxation.

❏ Receive a whole body massage. In the right circumstances and environment, the effects of another person's soothing hands working on your body can wash it free of tension. (See Step 24.)

❏ If high tech is your style, look into dissolving your worries in a flotation tank. These are light- and soundproof, human-sized capsules filled with a foot or so of body-temperature, salted water. Floating in one deprives your sense of stimulation and allows for a deep relaxation. "Body/mind centers" around the country feature flotation tanks as well as other high-tech meditation tools, such as biofeedback machines and light-and-sound goggles.

❏ Stop meditating if it is causing harmful side effects, which does occur in a minority of instances. On occasion meditation can actually cause stress by exposing you to subconscious thoughts or deeper levels of awareness. The result can be anxiety, depression, distressing emotional states, or even what meditation researchers call "relaxation-induced panic."

❏ If you are just beginning a meditation program, keep your practice sessions short, suggests meditation teacher Patricia Carrington, Ph.D. Increase the length as you become more comfortable with it. Type A personalities can sometimes adjust to meditation by starting with two-minute "mini-meditations" a number of times each day, Carrington says.

❏ For some people, having sex is a method for relaxing and lowering stress levels. Oriental spiritual practices including Buddhism and Hinduism have developed forms of "tantra" or meditative sexual union in which the partners attain a state of extended bliss during the sexual act.

❏ Take nutritional supplements on a daily basis to promote relaxation and help the body deal with the effects of stress. Important ones to take include vitamin B complex (50–100 mg), particularly for the B_5 and B_6, calcium (800–1,500 mg) and magnesium (450–650 mg), and vitamin C (500–1,500 mg).

❏ Take the herb Siberian ginseng *(Eleutherococcus senticosus)*. Siberian ginseng is noted for its ability to help the body resist the effects of stress. An average daily dose is 500 mg of the dried root.

For More Information

Two informative books on relaxation and meditation are:

Beyond the Relaxation Response by Herbert Benson (New York: Times Books, 1984)

How to Meditate by Lawrence LeShan (Boston: Little, Brown, 1974)

John Kabat-Zinn has developed two tapes with numerous helpful hints on meditation. Send $11 for one or $22 for both to:

Stress Reduction Tapes
Mindfulness Meditation Practice
Box 547
Lexington, MA 02173

42

TAKE CHARGE OF
YOUR HABITS

A habit is a deeply ingrained pattern of behavior. You establish
one by repeating an action so often that it becomes automatic.
After time, the action comes easily, even thoughtlessly. This can be
great if the habit is brushing your teeth after eating, stretching upon
awakening, or listening when someone else is speaking. It is less
rewarding to your health and self-esteem, on the other hand, if the
habit is a negative one such as polishing off a bag of cookies while
watching television, sleeping too little, slouching while reading,
skipping breakfast, procrastinating, or biting your nails. Some habits, too, can be downright deadly, such as smoking cigarettes, consuming excessive alcohol, eating to the point of obesity, or engaging
in indiscriminate, unprotected sex. Taking charge of your habits
allows you to shape them instead of vice versa.

Consciously deciding to take control of some aspect of your
behavior is a first step, but often isn't enough. If a decision to change
and power of will were enough to accomplish the intended result,
fewer people would be constantly struggling to break habits or repeatedly failing to establish positive ones.

One of the most important rules, according to psychiatrist Tom
Rusk, M.D., and D. Patrick Miller, coauthors of *Instead of Therapy:
Help Yourself Change and Change the Help You're Getting,* is to view

your attempt to alter a habit as an experiment, not a test of willpower or character. "Experts mostly agree that the old idea of 'willpower' may be part of the problem," says Miller. Some people are ready to change and others are not, he notes. "We must look at our attempts to change a habit as an ongoing experiment instead of a test of character that we either pass or fail. When an experiment fails, it can always be tried again under different circumstances or in a different way."

Everyday Steps to Natural Health

A number of concrete steps anyone can use will help to bring about desired change.

Increase your awareness of the habit. A habit is no longer a habit if you have to think about it before doing it. Analyzing a bad habit can help to identify why you have it and how you can take control of it.

Experience a habit with your senses when you are doing it. What does it actually feel like to bite a fingernail—what are the sensations on your lips and fingertips? Is the sensation actually enjoyable? Think about the habit and learn from it. Do you bite your nails when you are bored or nervous? Is there some other way you can get through those times without biting your nails?

Consider the reasons you have proposed to yourself in the past for not making a change. Is there something that you get from your habit that could be obtained in some other way? Perhaps most importantly, is the habit distracting you from other concerns, such as that you are lonely or unloved? Repetitive, unconscious behaviors can become so prominent in your life that they can prevent you from growing as a person, according to Susan Thesenga, a psychospiritual counselor and the author of *The Undefended Self*. She says, "What is momentarily gratifying doesn't come close to meeting your real needs. And it's actually less than a stopgap measure; it takes you in the opposite direction of fulfillment because you are ignoring your true needs. That's why habits intensify; what used to work to distract you from your needs eventually doesn't. After a while, an hour of TV won't numb you anymore. So the next time you have to watch two hours—and have a bag of popcorn, too. Sooner or later, your needs must be addressed. They will keep knocking at the door until you pay attention to them."

Try to change one habit at a time and take it slowly. There are two obvious reasons why the half-life of most New Year's resolutions is measured in days rather than months: too many habits, too swift of a change. People typically use the onset of a new year to make up a whole list of habits they will henceforth completely stop: immoderate drinking, habitual TV watching, eating chocolate cake, screaming at the kids, and driving too fast. When you try to tackle so many behaviors at once, your efforts are diffused over too broad an area. Within a few days you've probably broken or forgotten a number of resolutions. When you realize this, you lose confidence in your ability to make any changes. Soon you've given up on the whole list.

Don't try to do it all at once. Focus your concentration on the habit you most want to change first. Make a commitment to changing that behavior, then give yourself time. It is easy to get overwhelmed by a commitment that extends for the rest of your life. Unless the habit is drunken driving or some other palpably dangerous activity, cutting back gradually rather than going cold turkey will increase your chances of succeeding. Presumably the habit has been a part of your everyday life for years, so a few more weeks or months of doing it won't matter in the long run. According to Rusk, "With a long-term habit, you may have to ask yourself whether you're doing less of it this year than last year. . . . Replace 'I am completely giving up junk food today' with 'Today I will try eating a little less junk food and see how I feel afterward. If I succeed at that and I seem to be going in the right direction, I'll try eating even less tomorrow or next week.'"

By the same token, tackle just one day at a time. Convince yourself that if you can make it through today, you've done enough, for today. Tomorrow, renew your commitment to that day.

Supply the motivation. Motivation is the inner drive that you need to accomplish an action. It is the fuel that powers your desire for change. Without clear motivations even the most heartfelt resolutions of today slip into obscurity as life rushes on.

One of the best ways to emphasize the importance of a desired change is to identify explicitly the negative effects of the habitual behavior as well as the expected benefits of your intended action. Take some time to read and research. Memorize the negative effects you'll escape and the benefits you'll embrace. If it is a habit with few obvious adverse health effects (biting your nails, say), list the benefits to your self-esteem and confidence that you'll realize by taking control over it.

Even better than memorizing these effects, write them down in a list. Post the list somewhere you can see it, especially when you are most tempted to indulge a bad habit. For example, if the habit you want to break is eating a pint of ice cream every night, post your list (eating too much ice cream increases my risk of heart disease, makes me gain weight, and causes me to lose self-respect; I will benefit by looking and feeling better, living longer, and setting a better example for my children) on the door of the freezer.

As another example, consider the following list of negatives associated with habitual television viewing, suggested by author Marie Winn in *Unplugging the Plug-In Drug:*

➤ keeps families from doing other things and is a hidden competitor for all other activities
➤ allows kids to grow up less civilized
➤ takes the place of play
➤ makes children less resourceful
➤ has a negative effect on physical fitness and school achievement
➤ may be a serious addiction

A personalized list of expected benefits to go along with this list (I'll play more piano, have more time for tennis, cook with less time urgency, and so forth) can be attached next to the television's on-button. The point is not to feel guilty every time you watch a show, but to watch with greater awareness.

In addition to lists, motivational signs or quotes can boost your resolve. For example, here is a quote relevant to habitual television viewing, from educator Urie Bronfenbrenner: "The primary danger of the television screen lies not so much in the behavior it produces—although there is danger there—as in the behavior it prevents: the talks, the games, the family festivities and arguments through which much of the child's learning takes place and through which his character is formed. Turning on the television set can turn off the process that transforms children into people."

You'll need to change lists, signs, and quotes periodically or they'll drop into the background and go unnoticed. If your habit is one you are not eager to advertise on notes scattered around your home, office, and car, use code words or phrases meaningful only to yourself.

Use goals and rewards to keep you focused and chart your progress. Goals and rewards are especially important in the first few weeks after you've resolved to break a bad habit or to start a positive habit. Having goals allows you to witness your progress in a concrete way. And using rewards reinforces the progress you have made and paves the way for further growth.

Set obtainable goals, taking care to make them easier in the early stages. Unrealistic goals can deep-six a program before it has a chance to take hold. Also allow for setbacks and lapses when you set your goals. Few self-improvement programs follow a smooth, steadily rising success curve. You will experience days when you indulge your old habit to the max, or totally ignore your commitment to a positive change. By planning for such days in your goal-setting, you will be in a better position to acknowledge them for what they are—temporary—and to stay with your program instead of giving up on it at the first sign of failure. Keep your long-term goal in mind and don't expect perfection.

Many people find it helpful to list goals on a calendar or to use a progress chart, with columns for days, goals, and comments. Post the calendar or chart in a place of prominence. You can also post shorter lists of your goals, or notes, words, or colored dots, else-where as reminders.

Personalize the rewards. Treat yourself to something you like for making it through a day or week or meeting some goal. Make the rewards healthful, though, so you don't end up reinforcing a bad habit that is next on your list to tackle. If possible, associate the reward with the habit you are trying to break. For example, if you are trying to give up fast foods and one of your expected benefits is a trimmer body, as you lose weight reward yourself by buying new clothes that reflect your higher level of fitness.

Stay positive. Be patient. Avoid guilt. If you experience a set-back, consider it a shortcoming of the program and change your goals or rewards. If a failure causes you to indulge a tendency to criticize yourself and feel shame, you are giving power to the habit. Recognize the progress you have made, even if only in awareness, and try again.

Short Tips for Habit-Breaking

❑ Celebrate your success. A small party, ritual, or other form of celebration acknowledges your accomplishment and reinforces your commitment to not lapsing.

❑ Replace your bad habit with a more healthful one. If you can't stop overeating while watching television, try busying yourself on an exercise cycle or cross-country machine. Constantly biting your nails when you talk on the phone? Get a hand-exerciser and pump away instead. Sometimes a new activity is all you need to break the old habit's power over you.

❑ Enlist the support of others in your efforts to take charge of your habits. Spouses and family members in particular can help you to stay focused and meet your goals.

For More Information

The following book has numerous helpful suggestions regarding habits:

Instead of Therapy: Help Yourself Change and Change the Help You're Getting by Tom Rusk, M.D., and D. Patrick Miller (Los Angeles: Hay House, 1991)

SIMPLE STEPS
TO
NATURAL HEALTH

LONGEVITY

43

INCREASE YOUR LIFE SPAN

"If I had known I was going to live so long, I'd have taken better care of myself," lament some elderly. Today, a growing number of Americans of all ages are trying to avoid making the same mistake. They want not only to add years to their lives but life to their years. That is, most people agree that it is not enough merely to live longer if your later years are characterized by debilitating illness, lost faculties, and lack of physical mobility. Indeed, so great is the fear of an infirm advanced age that, according to surveys, more than half of Americans don't even want to reach one hundred. Of course, the vast majority of these people have little to worry about in this regard: about one in every twenty-five thousand Americans celebrates a one-hundredth birthday.

Fear of aging results partly from social factors such as the cult of youth perpetuated by Madison Avenue. It is also, however, an accurate reflection of the reality of growing old in America. In the two decades before reaching retirement age of sixty-five, an estimated one in four Americans suffers from arthritis, one in five from hypertension or sinusitis, and one in eight from heart disease. After age sixty-five these numbers rise dramatically.

Yet the aging process is extremely individual. There are remarkable "successful agers" who have lived active, healthy lives beyond 100 years and even beyond 110. While 115–120 years currently looks to be an outside limit to human longevity, that is still some four decades beyond the average life span in America. Many of the factors that determine both longevity and overall health among the elderly are within the control of individuals. "The same factors which determine the quality of life also have a profound influence upon the quantity of life," notes Kenneth Pelletier, Ph.D., author of *Longevity: Fulfilling Our Biological Potential.*

Everyday Steps to Natural Health

All fifty-two steps in this book can have a positive effect on longevity. Here are a few ideas not addressed elsewhere.

Bring your biological age down to lower than your chronological age. Your biological age is a measurement, expressed in years, of how well your body functions and how healthy it is. In a few people this figure may be the same as the chronological age, but for most people it is different. If your biological age is higher than your chronological, you have aged beyond your years. If it is lower, you are young for your years and are likely to enjoy enhanced longevity.

In the effort to determine how aging might be slowed, researchers have developed the concept of biomarkers, physical indicators of age. There are two basic types of biomarkers: those over which you have little or no control and those you can control. A number of large companies own sophisticated computer programs that can determine your biological age by measuring key physiological functions. These functions are primarily those that most researchers say invariably worsen with advancing age: hearing, coordination, reaction time, vision, and memory and learning. Exactly why these and other physical functions collapse with age is still a medical and scientific mystery. Among the theories that scientists have proposed to explain aging are those that relate to DNA repair, how quickly the body produces chemicals that can neutralize harmful free radicals, and how frequently cells can divide before naturally dying.

Researchers have also identified at least two dozen biomarkers that you can control. Some of the most important of these include quantity of air you can take in and breathe out in one breath, how much blood the heart pumps while resting, bone density and rate of bone loss, rate of resting pulse, strength and muscle mass, aerobic capacity, cholesterol level, body fat, and blood pressure. Exercise, activity, and healthful eating habits can all prevent these factors from declining with age. Personal choices can even reverse past losses. Some of these biomarkers are relatively easy for your health practitioner to measure and help you compare to others of your chronological age.

For example, if you are forty years old and exercise regularly, watch your diet, and have a body fat of less than 20 percent, the aerobic capacity and resting metabolic rate of a twenty-five-year-old, and a low ratio of total cholesterol to high-density lipoproteins (HDL, the good cholesterol), your biological age is likely to be much less than forty. All of these factors would reduce your risk of developing chronic conditions such as heart disease, diabetes, and lung cancer, the major killers of older Americans. Thus, you would increase your life expectancy beyond seventy-plus years.

Pelletier has developed a simple personal quiz to test your ability to reach your maximum life span. You start with seventy-five years and either have extra years added on to your longevity potential or subtracted from it, depending upon how you rate according to seventy-five factors. The factors are grouped by family history, lifestyle, nutrition/alcohol/smoking, work and environment, and physical activity and weight. There are also some factors that apply only to women, such as a family history of breast cancer. Among the factors that have the highest positive value are:

➤ being female (plus 4 years)
➤ all four grandparents lived to be eighty or over (+8)
➤ married or living in a long-term relationship (+4)
➤ never smoked (+3)
➤ no alcohol consumption (+3)
➤ over sixty-five and still working (+3)
➤ exercise at a moderate aerobic level at least three times per week for at least thirty minutes per time (+3)

Among the factors that have the highest negative value:

➤ being a nonwhite male (minus five years)
➤ either parent died of a stroke or heart attack before 50 (−4)
➤ sleep more than ten hours per night (−4)
➤ have had a speeding ticket (−4)

➤ smoke one to two packs of cigarettes per day (−6) or more than two packs per day (−8)
➤ women: smoke and use birth-control pills (−5)
➤ women: mother or sister had or has breast cancer (−4)
➤ work regularly with vinyl chloride (−4) or asbestos (−8)
➤ no regular aerobic activity (−5)
➤ 30–40 lbs. over ideal weight (−4); 40–50 lbs. over (−6); over 50 lbs. over (−8)

"Each of the numerical values are estimates based on recent research findings of the determinants of health and longevity," says Pelletier.

Stay thin but healthy. Among the most promising areas of longevity study is calorie restriction. By staying slightly undernourished without becoming malnourished, it is possible that you can add decades to your expected life span. The foremost proponent of this theory is Roy Walford, M.D., a professor of pathology and a widely respected researcher on aging who has published hundreds of scientific articles. By fasting two days a week and eating a low-fat, 2,100-calorie-per-day diet the rest of the week, he hopes to extend his life span by thirty or forty years. "The evidence that it will work is almost overwhelming," he says.

The clinical evidence for dietary restriction affecting maximum life span goes back to the mid-1930s, when Cornell University nutritionist Clive McKay found that he could double the life span of rats by restricting their food intake to 60 percent of normal. He also fed the rats vitamin and mineral supplements. The technique seemed to work only on young rats whose diet was restricted soon after weaning. Adult rats put on restricted diets actually lived less than a normal life span.

Walford reexamined these results in the 1970s. He switched the adult rats to a restricted diet more gradually than McKay had and found that the adult rats also lived longer. So can humans, Walford contends. "The mechanism of aging is certainly the same in all animals," he says. Since restricting calories in children causes smaller than normal development, Walford recommends switching to a low-calorie, nutrient-dense diet at age eighteen to twenty (though not during pregnancy). Weight should be lost gradually over a number of years.

He notes that for an adult on a restricted diet, fat content should be 10–15 percent, protein 16–24 percent, and the rest complex carbohydrates such as vegetables, whole grains, and cereals. He adds that it is crucial to obtain necessary nutrients while restricting calories, a difficult proposition unless you take dietary supplements. "I've computerized the nutritional ingredients of hundreds of foods and found that by combining them the chances are only one in a thousand or so of hitting upon an optimum nutrient mix."

Walford also emphasizes that his maximum-life-span diet preserves health and optimizes intelligence and sexual function in addition to extending life. "When most people think of living to be one hundred and forty, they immediately get the image of being very old, wrinkled, decrepit for a long, long time. That's not the picture at all. It's being younger and middle-aged longer, and being very old for about the same number of years as at present. So it's a big gain in the period of active, vigorous life."

Population studies confirm that being thin in general seems to lower the death rate. A recent report on an ongoing study of twenty-one thousand men who graduated from Harvard University between 1916 and 1950 found that thinner men had lower death rates. Men who weighed an average of 20 percent less than the national average for their height and age had the lowest death rate.

Learn from centenarians, the people who live to one hundred and beyond. While many scientists who study aging focus their research on the cellular level, social scientists and others have begun to look at the lifestyles and habits of "successful agers." These are people who have, for whatever reasons, long outlived the average life span of their compatriots. "Centenarians are our living models for longevity," says Osborn Segerberg, Jr., author of *Living to Be 100*.

What centenarians have to teach us is hardly black and white. Most people know of an individual or two who has somehow defied the odds: he or she has been smoking a pack of cigarettes a day for half a century, never exercises, is always in a foul mood, and is still ticking away at ninety-plus. Such people stand out precisely because they are the exceptions to the rules, say longevity experts such as Segerberg and Pelletier. Their research suggests that if we were to construct a composite individual who possessed many of the characteristics common to centenarians, she might look like this:

➤ has led a stable and orderly life, mostly lived in the same area where she was born
➤ has performed physically active work all of her life and has never retired
➤ has a personality that is low-key, levelheaded, and pragmatic
➤ has been married much of her adult life
➤ doesn't dwell on remorse or guilt
➤ briefly grieves for deceased loved ones but then moves on with her life
➤ takes responsibility and care for her health and rarely sees doctors or other health professionals

Researchers who have studied the lifestyles and health habits of populations with active, lively elderly in their ninth decade and beyond report that positive outlook plays a crucial role in longevity. "Individuals who are withdrawn and disconnected from any social network don't live as long as those who have a positive relationship with others," says Alexander Leaf, M.D., author of *Youth in Old Age*.

Stay active, physically and mentally. One constant among many centenarians is that they are still engaged with life and are consistently interested, enthusiastic, and aware of what is going on around them.

Leaf's reports in the 1970s on three agrarian societies (the village of Vilcabamba in the Andean mountains of Ecuador in South America, the land of Hunza in a section of the Himalayas in Pakistan, and Abkhazia, a former republic of the U.S.S.R. situated in the Caucasus Mountains) arguably started the current explosion of interest in extreme longevity. Leaf eventually became skeptical of the high age claims many individuals made in these areas, but "one does have the impression that there are a lot of vigorous, healthy, elderly people there," he says. Staying active and maintaining feelings of personal and social worth played a large part in their vigor. "As they got older, the chores that they did were diminished in physical requirement, but everybody knew that they were doing things that contributed to the economy and social life in that society, which is in marked contrast to retiring people, putting them on a shelf and indicating very clearly to them that they are not needed. It's terribly important that people get caught up in interests and activities that they enjoy, whether it's something socially useful or not."

Like Leaf, Grace Halsell studied Vilcabamba's *los viejos,* Spanish for the very old. The author of *Los Viejos: Secrets of Long Life from the Sacred Valley,* Halsell was impressed with the unending zest for life among these traditional people. One lesson for longevity, she said, is that "no one retires to inactivity. Among the *viejos* the word does not exist. They stay busy, up until the day they die. We are saying to people in America, with our mandatory retirement: you are old, you are now unfit. Suddenly, many of them, unless they have prepared themselves for other interests, begin to think of themselves as old and useless and unwanted." These negative self-images are counterproductive for health and longevity.

"How did I get so old?" repeated centenarian Jesse Haas to Jim Heynen as he was interviewing her for his book *One Hundred Over 100.* "I don't know. I'm busy."

Short Tips on Longevity

❑ Take daily doses of the antioxidant nutrients vitamins A (10,000–20,000 IU in the form of beta carotene), C (500–1,500 mg), and E (400–800 IU), and the mineral selenium (100–150 mcg). (See Step 29 for more information on antioxidants.)

❑ Wear seat belts. This dramatically reduces your chances of being killed should you be in an auto accident.

❑ Take a walk. You are never too old to benefit from a daily walk. *Los viejos* say that everybody has two good doctors: their right and left legs.

For More Information

Useful books on longevity include the following:

Longevity: Fulfilling Our Biological Potential by Kenneth R. Pelletier (New York: Delacorte and Delta, 1981)

The 120-Year Diet: How to Double Your Vital Years by Roy L. Walford, M.D. (New York: Pocket Books, 1988)

AGE GRACEFULLY

As your journey through life enters its last stages, your body undergoes a natural slowing down. Past your fiftieth year it is no longer as forgiving. You experience distinct biological changes, in part based on shifting hormone levels. For women the cessation of the menses and the decline in the production of sex hormones happens on average between the ages of forty-five to fifty. Some new studies indicate men as well undergo a subtle physical change or "male menopause" due to changing hormone levels. Other physical markers of aging include changes in vision, hearing, bone strength, and reaction time. To some extent these changes may be slowed or even temporarily reversed by exercise or other factors, but ultimately the human body is susceptible to the same natural laws that affect all living things.

Aging also brings notable social and psychological changes. Most people retire from work around age sixty-five or at least experience dramatically declining job opportunities. Parents, spouses, close friends, or siblings may die. Parents whose main activity has been child rearing must shift gears as children move out of the home. New goals and perspectives open up as an older person's focus shifts from education, parenting, career, and accumulating wealth (though these may indeed continue) to other concerns. For some, aging results in a rigidification of habits and ideas. There may be less readiness or ability to accept new information, in some cases leading to an increase in intolerance and conservatism.

Obviously, the changes in body, mind, and spirit that accompany aging affect individuals, and groups within various societies, differently. Roles vary for men and women, the rich and poor, the able-bodied and the ill. This variation has not stopped writers and psychologists from broadly categorizing the senior years as a stage in life, expanding upon Shakespeare's seventh age as he described it in *As You Like It*. Most subsequent descriptions of life's last stage, such as those offered by Jung, Erikson, and others, have been more charitable than Shakespeare's "second childishness and mere oblivion, sans teeth, sans eyes, sans taste, sans everything."

More positively the years beyond fifty-five to sixty can be viewed as a time for continued personal growth. This can also be a stage in life during which you experience high levels of independence, financial security, and leisure time. For some it is a time for self-assessment, a chance to review your achievements as well as failures and to evaluate the results of your life. Your legacy to the future is often established by then, whether it be in the form of children, accomplishments, or creative works. You may be able to open up emotionally, develop deeper personal relationships, or become more intimate with a partner. For many people old age offers the opportunity to turn inward and ponder spiritual questions that go to the heart of life's central mysteries regarding death and the afterlife. It is also the chance to affirm that your life has been a meaningful adventure.

Everyday Steps to Natural Health

When the members of some traditional societies are in need of wisdom, they often turn to the elderly, assuming that their accumulated knowledge has been leavened with observation and experience. Though some doubt this connection (H. L. Mencken said, "The older I grow the more I distrust the familiar doctrine that age brings wisdom"), having a repository of important knowledge and insight can be of immense value to those societies that know how to make best use of it. All too often in Western societies the elderly are shunted aside, retired from public participation. Individuals and the community at large suffer. It needn't be so, and the following suggestions for aging gracefully can help to prevent this sad outcome.

Stay physically active while adjusting to new strengths and weaknesses. An important part of aging gracefully is actually accepting aging. For many, this is difficult. Americans refuse to believe, says Willard Gaylin, that "there are limits to anything—let alone life itself." Gaylin is a psychiatrist and the cofounder of The Hastings Center, an organization that examines ethical issues in medicine and life sciences. He said recently, "Consider the struggle in America to define such terms as *death with dignity* and *growing old gracefully;* the latter, on closer analysis, means living a long time without aging. Dying in one's sleep at ninety-two after having won three sets of tennis from one's forty-year-old grandson that afternoon and having made love to one's wife twice that same evening— this is about the only scenario I have found most American men willing to accept as fulfilling their idea of death with dignity."

Advancing age makes it more difficult for you to do some of the things you've done all your life with nary a thought. Yet even if you are no longer the athlete you once were, there is much that life offers for those open to its riches. Rather than dwelling on your physical limitations, recognize them and strive for new activities, ideas, and ways for expressing yourself.

This is not to suggest that exercise for the elderly is useless and rapid physical decline should be accepted with resignation. If anything, exercise is even more important as you pass middle age than when you were younger, as the aging process can otherwise make your bones brittle, your joints stiff, and even your mental process slow. Staying active in your daily routine (see Step 9) and getting adequate exercise (see Steps 12–15) has a positive effect on your circulation, endurance, strength, and flexibility.

According to Susan Lark, M.D., "As we age, our endocrine glands and digestive systems slow down, and we metabolize food less efficiently. We tend to decrease our level of physical activity as well, and women can find themselves in the unhealthy situation of chronic dieting just to maintain their desired weight." On average, sedentary women between the ages of thirty and forty lose seven pounds of muscle and replace it with fourteen pounds of fat. When that trend extends past middle age into old age, serious health problems are often the result.

While the physical processes of aging can only be slowed, not stopped, through effort you can achieve a high level of fitness at almost any age. Author and martial arts teacher George Leonard says that when he turned fifty, he became "a jock." In an average week he now does several sessions each of aikido (a Japanese martial art), stretching, relaxation, strength training, walking, and endurance training. "I'm in the best muscular shape I've ever been in my entire life, and I'm sixty-nine," he now says. "This is something that can be done by anyone; there's nothing elitist about it."

Adjust your exercise to your changing body, if necessary. Maybe you can't play as much basketball as you used to without getting injured or oversore, but scores of other activities, sports, and exercises can improve fitness and can be done by anybody. One of the most popular among the elderly is walking—work up to a two to three mile walk every other day and you'll stay trim and fit. You can also swim, dance, work out on resistance machines, or lift weights, among others.

People need to find out how to move their bodies in ways that they love, according to herbalist Rosemary Gladstar. She says, "I like the idea of 'life exercise'—creating work and hobbies in your life that get you moving. Arrange your life in such a way that you naturally get a lot of exercise. You can get a pet that you have to walk, take up a new active hobby that has always interested you like hiking or dancing, or volunteer your time to work with small children. The key to staying active is to find a way to live so that moving your body is an integral part of your life."

Stay connected. Three-generation households have dwindled in recent years as family ties have weakened and the elderly are increasingly isolated in nursing homes and sun-belt retirement communities. A strong social network is crucial for overall health (see Step 46) at all ages. If your children have moved out, your friends and neighbors dispersed, and your work connections been severed, you need to take steps to stay connected to other people. If you can maintain the ties you have to the people you love while developing new friendships as well, you may acquire the largest and most varied social network of your life. Take advantage of the opportunity to embrace emotional ties with new neighbors, your children's family, in-laws, and others.

Intergenerational sharing is a new type of volunteer work that brings together children and the elderly. Centers such as the McKinley Life Care Center in Canton, Ohio, have begun to develop programs to provide the support of the extended family that many Americans have lost. In a number of cities elders are being trained to volunteer or work in children's day-care centers and school classrooms. For example, Stride Rite corporate headquarters in Cambridge, Massachusetts, recently began the country's first workplace day care for both children and older adults. Children in turn are being taken to visit the elderly in nursing homes. The Center for Intergenerational Learning at Temple University reports that 70 percent of adults over age sixty-five miss the social contact that was part of their lives before retirement. Studies have found that volunteering in schools also leads to significant increases in elders' self-esteem, ability to function day to day, and mood and memory.

Continue to work or develop a variety of other interests. In industrialized societies people are increasingly living beyond age sixty-five, which in the U.S. since the 1930s has been the accepted age of retirement. As longevity increases and people retain their full mental and physical faculties up to and beyond that point, many are challenging the concept of mandatory retirement and seeking to extend their working years beyond age sixty-five. Without considering economic factors (retirement opens up jobs to younger generations; on the other hand many elderly need the continued income), continued work past sixty-five can be a positive step for those who desire it. The feelings of self-worth that working can reinforce may lead to a longer, more satisfied life (see Step 43).

Feelings of uselessness and loss of self-esteem in the elderly are compounded in the U.S. because of the perception that retirement and loss of a job result in lower status. To some extent this is changing as people live longer and the elderly take on a variety of new roles, as part-time workers, volunteers, and consultants. Senior citizens can also adjust well by embracing their newfound leisure time. Many establish a new and varied range of meaningful activities that allow them to remain satisfied and fulfilled. This may mean new hobbies, skills, interests, sports, crafts, arts, or whatever.

Take the time to ponder the great questions. For some, aging affords the time and inclination to dwell upon what Sam Keen, author of *Fire in the Belly,* calls the great questions. One of the dozen "rules of the road for the spiritual journey" that Keen has found to be most important in his life is to "live the great questions," such as those posed by myth. Myth serves to keep our minds focused on the questions, Keen notes, even though we don't know the answers. He says, "And when we keep these great questions alive—Where did I come from? Where am I going? What is death? How close should men and women be? What's wrong with me? What would heal me? What would I look like if I were healed? Who are my people? What's worth doing? What's worth leaving undone? What can we know? For what may we hope? What ought we to do? Who are the heroes? Who are the heroines?—when we live in these questions, we're going to live openly."

The great questions pertaining to death become increasingly relevant as aging proceeds. With old age comes what may be the first realization of the inevitability of death. Looking inward and finding a meaning and wholeness in one's life is often a prerequisite for accepting death.

How the experience of dying can be approached with dignity and peace may also become an issue of importance as the end of life approaches. Because of the work of researchers such as psychiatrist Elisabeth Kübler-Ross and others, dying is slowly being accepted as a natural stage in life. Efforts to humanize it are being recognized even in the medical profession. In his authoritative new book *How We Die,* surgeon Sherwin B. Nuland says that the ideal death takes place in the comfort of the home or hospice and surrounded by loved ones. This is an ideal that is usually not realized in practice: four out of five elderly Americans die in hospitals. Many of these elderly die while hooked up to life-support machines that temporarily postpone the inevitable without enhancing in any way their experience of this important transition.

"The greatest dignity to be found in death is the dignity of the life that preceded it," Nuland reminds readers.

Stay young in mind no matter how old you get. The body responds to the mind's suggestions, notes Deepak Chopra, M.D., author of *Ageless Body, Timeless Mind.* "The infirmity and inactivity exhibited by many old people is often just dormancy. By renewing their intention to live active, purposeful lives, many elderly people can dramatically improve their motor abilities, strength, agility, and mental responses. . . . By inserting an intention into your thought processes, such as 'I want to improve in energy and vigor every day,' you can begin to assert control over those brain centers that determine how much energy will be expressed in activity."

Your later years can be a time of declining physical powers, increasing illness, and loss of self-esteem. It can also be a time when you congratulate yourself for having reached important goals, however you define them. Researchers have found that maintaining a positive sense of self-worth can be more important than any physical or other social factor in establishing happiness in one's later years. Chopra says, "The decline of vigor in old age is largely the result of people expecting to decline; they have unwittingly implanted a self-defeating intention in the form of a strong belief, and the mind/body connection automatically carries out this intention."

Short Tips for Aging Gracefully

❑ Change your view of leisure from "time not spent working" to time spent doing something valuable in and of itself. Workaholics may have the most difficulty making this transition (see Step 35).

❑ Develop new goals to strive for as old ones are realized.

❑ Remain open to new experiences. Don't let the past determine how you react to new information and new problems.

For More Information

The following organization is a national coalition of intergenerational programs:

Generations United
c/o Child Welfare League of America
440 First St., N.W., Suite 310
Washington, D.C. 20001
(202) 638-2952

SIMPLE STEPS
TO
NATURAL HEALTH

RELATIONSHIPS

NURTURE OTHERS

The word *nurture* shares the same root as *nurse*. It means literally to nourish, both physically in the sense of providing food and emotionally in the sense of providing the love and support necessary for others to grow and develop as fully functioning human beings. The act of nurturing others promotes their optimum well-being. The benefits are mutual, as well. Nurturing enhances your own spirit, and the person who receives the nurturing is also more likely to reciprocate.

Opportunities to nurture those around you present themselves every day. One way is simply to encourage loved ones in their creative endeavors, artistic pursuits, and other activities, primarily by participating and sharing their experiences. Nurturing your partner means doing all of the little things that keep love alive, including touching, expressing feelings, and listening. Nurturing loved ones may also mean being with them and doing what you can to heal them when they are sick, whether with a common cold or a long-term illness.

In cultures throughout the world women have a tendency to be more nurturing than men, a trait that can't be explained entirely as learned behavior, according to anthropologist Helen Fisher, Ph.D., author of *Anatomy of Love*. Fisher says that numerous findings point to a biological foundation for women's nurturing nature. This trait is an aspect "of the feminine psyche that evolved as ancestral females nurtured their young millennia ago," Fisher says. She notes that, compared to infant boys, infant girls are more likely to smile and react to faces than to objects, are more sensitive to touch and voice inflection, and have longer attention spans. "All of these traits are useful to rearing young," Fisher says.

Thus, men may need more help and encouragement to become nurturing to those around them. Any person, however, can become more attuned to the needs of loved ones and nurture their growth. For some men, even the act of recognizing nurturing as a missing aspect of their lives may help them to become more conscious of the importance of feeding others' lives and spirits.

Everyday Steps to Natural Health

Here are some simple ways to nourish those around you.

Share some of your partner's or loved one's interests and activities. Individuals have different preferences for how they exercise, relate to others, and spend their leisure time. Some of this variety may be based on factors such as gender, culture, and age. For example, Fisher notes that men are more likely than women to have well-developed gross motor movements, such as throwing, that require speed and force. Men are also more likely than women to excel at manipulating three-dimensional shapes in space, a talent that allows more men than women to excel at chess and mathematics. On the other hand, in addition to being better nurturers than men, women manipulate language more readily than men. Fisher says that these differences appear to be consistent across cultures and throughout history. Thus, in a heterosexual relationship, how men prefer to share and relate is often distinct from women's preferences. Fisher and others have noticed that many women complain that men do not talk out their problems and share their emotions. Studies indicate, however, that men think of intimacy not in terms of talking face-to-face but being engaged side by side in work, play, or some other close activity. Fisher says, "A woman should probably adopt at least one nonverbal, side-by-side leisure activity that her spouse enjoys, whereas men could improve their home lives if they took time out to sit face-to-face with their mates and engage in talk and 'active listening.'"

With your partner, develop a list of activities and interests you can share. Some may be things neither of you have ever attempted before, while others can be favorite activities you've just never shared. The list might include shopping at garage sales, playing tennis, going to art museums, taking pottery classes, learning how to dance, exploring caves, going out to eat, and so forth. Schedule time together and then each partner can take a turn deciding which activity to share next.

Develop the healing touch. Nursing loved ones back to health is a tradition as old as humanity. Nursing as a technical profession, on the other hand, is only a little more than a century old. Before that healers, wise women, and friends and relatives helped medical professionals as best they could to heal the sick. As technical and complex as modern conventional medicine is, it is easy to lose sight of the fact that the vast majority of illnesses are self-healing with little more than simple, natural medicines and the nurturing presence of another person. For those with the time and inclination, studying the human body and learning the basics of a natural healing method such as herbalism, nutritional therapy, or homeopathy are worthwhile endeavors.

Even if you don't have the skill for diagnosis and treatment, just touching, being with, and listening to an ill person is often enough to boost her spirits and shift her body to a healing state. Offerings of comfort, love, and assistance are appreciated by anyone who is ill. Merely applying your hands to an ache, pain, or bruise, or just holding and stroking a sick person's hand, can have a positive effect on the immune system. Dolores Krieger, Ph.D., developer of "therapeutic touch," says that true healing "aligns with life-affirming forces such as compassion and humane support." Anyone can do it who is willing, Krieger says, to combine compassion, an intention to heal, and a willingness to confront oneself.

This type of nurturance and support is especially necessary when a loved one has cancer or some other serious illness. According to David Spiegel, M.D., author of *Living Beyond Limits: New Hope and Help for Facing Life-Threatening Illness,* "At a time when people need support the most, they often get it the least. Furthermore, they quickly come to feel excluded from the happy, everyday flow of life. Isolation radiates from two directions. Seriously ill people sometimes withdraw from the world of the healthy, and healthy people in turn often do not know how to react appropriately or are frightened by disease and avoid the sick."

Healing a bruised spirit can be as important as healing a bruised body. When a partner or family member is depressed or lonely, offer consolation. By sharing some of the other person's sorrow, you can absorb some of the hurt and thus reduce it in the other. According to therapist Daphne Rose Kingma, author of *True Love,* "We all need to be willing to act as physicians of the spirit for one another during the painful times. For it is when we are assaulted by the visitation of life's sorrows that we most need to feel the presence of the person who loves us. It is when we are brokenhearted that we most need to be ministered to, when we are in grief that we need most to be taken into the arms of love."

Short Tips for Nurturing

❑ Offer affection whenever possible. For love partners, touching on a daily basis that is separate from sex nurtures the relationship and even promotes better sex.

For More Information

Two excellent books for helping someone face a life-threatening illness are:

Living Beyond Limits by David Spiegel, M.D. (New York: Times Books, 1993)

How to Live Between Office Visits by Bernie S. Siegel, M.D. (New York: HarperCollins, 1993)

46

MAKE FRIENDS—
AND MORE FRIENDS

"No man is an island, entire of itself," said poet John Donne. Nor is any woman an island. Humans have evolved over tens of thousands of years in relation to each other, through families, clans, and tribes as well as neighborhoods, churches, and teams. Your mutual interdependence with other people affects how you eat, work, and play. It also intimately affects how well you stay healthy, according to a growing body of social and scientific evidence.

Expanding your family ties and social networks offers a number of health benefits. It can

❏ Lower your risk of chronic disease, particularly heart attacks. "Social isolation has a toll on our health and causes chronic stress, which in turn can lead for many people to illnesses like heart disease," says Dean Ornish, M.D., author of a landmark study that proved dietary and lifestyle changes could reverse heart disease. Other studies that have found a similar connection between heart health and social networks include a 1990 Swedish study. Researchers found that the most important factor determining whether a type A (aggressive, hostile, hurried) man was at risk for a heart attack was not his personality per se but the extent of his social network.

❏ Boost your immune system. Studies by Janice Kiecolt-Glaser at Ohio State University College of Medicine show that loneliness

375

is an important factor in suppressing the immune system. Other studies have found that separated or divorced women suffer from depressed immune systems.

❏ Relieve pain. One study of arthritis patients found that those who received monthly telephone calls reported that they suffered from less pain and could move about more easily than patients who were not called. Researchers at the Indiana University Medical Center in Indianapolis said that the positive effects of social support were nearly as great as would be expected using nonsteroidal anti-inflammatory drugs, with the added bonus that social support is inexpensive, safe, and causes no side effects.

❏ Increase longevity. A twenty-year study of American adults found that those who participated in formal social networks of some type outlived those who didn't, regardless of existing health problems. Social network was found to be the most important predictor of longevity, stronger even than age, health status, or gender.

The longevity/social network connection was confirmed in a comparative review authored by James S. House, Ph.D., et al. and published in *Science* in 1988. House looked at a half dozen studies that tested for the effects of social networks on health. The studies, which involved communities in both the U.S. and Europe, found that people with deep, well-established social contacts had much longer life spans than people who had few human relationships. Overall, people who were lonely, isolated, and friendless were two to four times as likely to die over the next five to nine years.

According to House, "These developments suggest that social relationships, or the relative lack thereof, constitute a major risk factor for health—rivaling the effects of well-established health-risk factors such as cigarette smoking, blood pressure, blood lipids, obesity, and physical activity. Indeed, the theory and evidence on social relationships and health increasingly approximate that available at the time of the U.S. Surgeon General's 1964 report on smoking and health, with similar implications for future research and public policy."

Everyday Steps to Natural Health

So, improve your relationships one at a time while taking steps to grow more branches on your social network. The closer and more intimate your social connections the better, though clearly any social network that is supportive rather than hostile is better than none. Here are some suggestions for expanding your social contacts.

Test your social support. Researchers use a questionnaire called the Perceived Social Support Scale to determine how connected individuals feel to those around them. The survey asks you to rate certain statements from "strongly agree" to "neutral" to "strongly disagree." Those who strongly agree with statements such as the following are rated as having higher levels of social support:

❏ There is a special person who is around when I am in need.
❏ I get the emotional help and support I need from my family.
❏ I can count on my friends when things go wrong.
❏ I can talk about my problems with my family.
❏ I have friends with whom I can share my joys and sorrows.
❏ There is a special person in my life who cares about my feelings.

A survey of readers of *Natural Health* found that roughly half the respondents said that they strongly agree they could count on friends, special persons, and family when things go wrong. Fully 25 percent, however, said that they strongly disagreed that they could get the emotional support they need from their family. If you find yourself strongly disagreeing with most of the questionnaire statements, you would probably benefit dramatically from taking steps to improve your social network.

Maintain close family ties. One of the long-term studies that best demonstrates the remarkable health benefits of close family ties and supportive social networks was done by researchers Stewart Wolf, M.D., and John Bruhn, M.D. They spent decades examining the residents of the town of Roseto in east-central Pennsylvania. The researchers found that during the 1940s and 1950s the residents of Roseto had significantly lower death rates than people in surrounding communities, with whom they shared apparently similar health practices. Furthermore, most of these health practices (such as eating a high-fat diet and smoking) are now recognized as likely to increase the risk of cardiovascular disease. Wolf and Bruhn discovered that what the people of Roseto had that residents of neighboring towns did not were extremely close families, numerous three-generation households, and well-developed social networks tied to neighborhoods, clubs, and churches. When these social ties began to pull apart in the 1960s, the residents of Roseto soon experienced the same high rates of heart disease found in the rest of the state and the country.

Wolf, author of *The Power of Clan: The Influence of Relationships on Heart Disease,* says that the recent declining health in Roseto comes in spite of improvements the people living there made in their diet. "Ironically, although the rate of heart disease and mortality from heart disease increased, their dietary habits had become more like what the American Heart Association recommends. They were eating far fewer dairy products and less animal fats, and using less fat in cooking."

The splintering of family ties and the decline of three-generation families that happened in Roseto has of course also happened to an even greater degree in the rest of the country. "In the last thirty or forty years, America has become for many people a much more isolating place to live," says Dean Ornish. "Less than half of American families are really families, even in the nuclear-family sense. A generation ago it was more a disruption of the extended family, with aunts and uncles and grandparents not living in the same city anymore. But in the last generation, it's the nuclear family that's become disrupted." With half of all marriages ending in divorce, single-parent families are now approaching the norm in many communities.

Andrew Weil, M.D., also laments the decline of the extended family. In *Natural Health, Natural Medicine* he relates the story of an anthropologist he knows who was lecturing on Native American societies and repeatedly referring to their extended families. Weil says that a Native American student finally interrupted the lecturer and told him, "Excuse me, but we don't have extended families. We have families. You have contracted families."

Those who can bring aging parents who are recently widowed or unhappily living in nursing homes back into the family may find unexpected joy as well as health benefits. If the elders are grandparents as well, the benefits are multiplied. "There is a unique relationship between grandparents and grandchildren, an unconditional love," notes psychiatrist Arthur Kornhaber, author of *Grandparents/Grandchildren: The Vital Connection.* "We are genetically, spiritually, psychologically, and physiologically oriented to that system of extended family. Kids need to know they belong to a clan. Elders need a role in the family. This is part of the forty-thousand-year-old fabric of human existence. And it has transformative healing power."

In recent years family extensions have also gone the other way: adult children have moved back in with parents. This is usually done for economic reasons; though unacknowledged, the health benefits may also be considerable.

Even when a family is large and spread out over the country, letters, phone calls, computer networks, joint vacations, and other efforts at communication can renew and refresh family bonds.

Find a partner to share intimacy. More so than women, men suffer higher mortality rates when they lack a "significant other," whether that person be a spouse or lover. The connection between being single and ill health is weaker though still noticeable among women, possibly because women typically develop more close, same-sex friendships. Social scientists have found that marital status is less important in this regard than whether one's partner can openly and freely share personal feelings. Since many marriages are lacking in love and are characterized by tension and hostility, the question comes up, is a bad marriage better than no marriage at all? Many therapists say that unless the relationship is abusive or overtly destructive, there's usually some level of support there that is healthful for both partners.

For some, the most difficult step is finding that special someone whom you feel safe revealing intimate feelings to, touching, and making love to. Others, including many in stagnating marriages, must learn to constantly renew their commitment. There are many small steps anyone can take to nourish intimate relations, such as sharing new discoveries, putting attention into honest communication and listening, fostering each other's self-esteem, playing and working together, and learning how to resolve conflicts fairly and without rancor.

Many people must first learn how to understand and express their own feelings so that they can share them. "If you cannot listen to your own heart, then how are you going to get your wife to understand you?" asks Dr. James J. Lynch, a researcher who has studied the medical consequences of loneliness.

Establish a network of friends or social connections based on shared beliefs, activities, or even illnesses. While intimate connections involving family and lovers seem to have the most positive effects, the connections you make with friends, coworkers, neighbors, and others can also reward you in many ways. Look for opportunities to extend the contacts you make through neighborhood, sports team, fitness center, political party, church or synagogue, and other outlets. Casual acquaintances, someone you smile at and say hi to while passing on the street, don't count. You want friends who play a role in your life, who share interests and actively want to spend time together.

Unfortunately, as Dean Ornish points out, conscious effort is necessary here as well since the places outside the family where people formerly sought a sense of social support are beginning to break down as well. "People often felt a sense of community at work," Ornish notes. "There was a feeling that when they went to a job, it was almost a surrogate family. But in the last decade or two, people don't feel that security. They don't feel that they can be who they are without risking or losing their jobs." Trends in the workplace that have accelerated this loss include the burgeoning use of temporary help and the widespread hiring of freelancers who work out of the home.

Working from home does not have to be a lonely and isolating experience, say Paul and Sarah Edwards, authors of *Working from Home:* "It does mean you have to be active and take initiative to be involved in the world around you." Among the steps that they recommend to help you avoid loneliness and isolation if you work out of your home are

❑ Join community organizations and professional or trade associations that meet regularly.
❑ Attend workshops, seminars, and courses in your field.
❑ Pick up the telephone and call, or hook your home computer to a national networking system and take "electronic coffee breaks."
❑ Invite colleagues and business contacts to your home or arrange luncheon meetings.
❑ "Make new contacts regularly by being interested in others, finding out how you can help them, and staying in touch."

For those suffering from serious illness, support groups can offer not only companionship but increased longevity. In his study of heart patients, Ornish found that support groups were an integral part of any program to reverse heart disease. Participants met in support groups twice a week to talk, share feelings, and open their hearts to others. From Ornish's perspective, illnesses of the heart are rooted in individuals' profound isolation—from feelings, from other people, and from god or a greater force in the universe. (Ornish says that it is important to distinguish between being alone and being isolated: "You can be alone and be peaceful, and you can be with a group and feel isolated.")

Another noted study on the value of support groups was performed by Stanford psychiatrist Dr. David Spiegel. He found that breast-cancer patients who participated in supportive group psychotherapy lived twice as long as those who did not participate. Spiegel says that he encourages participants to cultivate relationships with other members outside the meeting room. He also says, "We encourage members to be more direct, open, and assertive about what they want and what they don't want. Sometimes that involves the people closest to them."

Short Tips for Increasing Your Social Network

❑ If you can't make friends or lovers, at least have a pet, particularly if you are elderly and lonely. Owning and caring for a pet can relieve isolation, reduce family arguments, lead to lower levels of anxiety and depression and fewer illnesses, and even promote a quicker recovery from a heart attack. Pets are undemanding listeners that usually respond with love and affection to attention.

❑ Volunteer your time to help the homeless, battered women, retarded children, and others in need of assistance. Volunteering offers unique opportunities for extending your social contacts while enhancing your own and others' health. One survey of 3,300 volunteers done in 1989 found that those who helped regularly were ten times more likely to report better health than those who volunteered only once a year. One of James House's studies on social relationships and health, done with his colleagues at the University of Michigan's Survey Research Center, followed 2,754 adults in Tecumseh, Michigan, for more than a decade. The researchers found that men engaged in regular volunteer work were two and a half times less likely to die during the research project than those who didn't volunteer.

For More Information

An informative book on social networks and heart disease is the following:

The Power of Clan by Stewart Wolf, M.D. (New Brunswick, N.J.: Transaction Publishers, 1993)

47

DO WORK THAT
MATTERS—TO YOU

D issatisfaction with work extends back in human history to
Neolithic times, Lewis Mumford notes in *Technics and Human
Development*. It was then that humans first began to shape certain
tools by grinding stone on stone, a tedious and laborious process
compared to hunting, fishing, and other daily activities of the time.
According to Mumford, "Our very word to express ennui, *boring*,
derives from—boring. Here was ritual repetition pushed almost beyond endurance." Stone tools were eventually used to grind grain,
leading to another revealing metaphor—*the daily grind*—on the lack
of appeal of repetitive, mindless work.

Humans have been trying to liberate themselves from stultifying
work ever since, with mixed results. Machines and more recently
computers have taken over some of the most repetitive physical
and mental tasks. Exactly how much work "labor-saving devices"
liberate humans from and how much new work such devices create
is an ongoing debate. Some machines have taken over jobs that at
one time offered the opportunity for men and women to employ
skill and craft, elements that make work worthwhile for many people. Also, the manner in which any tool is used in the workplace is
at least as important as the nature of the tool itself. For instance,
when an executive uses her computer to select crucial information
and present it in a new way, she's using the computer in a positive,

creative way and probably making her work more enjoyable. A ticket agent may use the same computer to speed transactions. If at the same time, however, the agent's supervisors are using the computer to enforce and monitor a fifty-transactions-per-hour rule, for the agent the technology is probably perceived negatively as part of the problem that is making the job demeaning and unrewarding.

While labor-saving devices relieve the physical strain of many jobs, modern work is often psychologically demanding and emotionally stressful. Studies have shown that a major cause of stress in the workplace is a feeling that you have no control over major aspects of your job. Boring, repetitive, and poorly designed jobs cause workers to feel passive, helpless, and easily fatigued.

It is possible to instill creative opportunities into work and make it meaningful and healthful. Most people prefer jobs that involve them as active participants in a group effort. Work that is successful provides variety and change and combines active periods with time for reflection. Workers appreciate the opportunity to use their judgment and skills to take control. The ability to make decisions reinforces the feeling that effort and determination make a difference. Workers given a measure of control over what they do are more likely to respond positively to new demands, seeing them as a challenge rather than a stressful work overload. Even when jobs offer tremendous responsibility and potentially high stress levels, as executive positions do, because of the amount of control workers in these positions have, they're likely to report high levels of both job satisfaction and personal health.

Everyday Steps to Natural Health

A 1987 survey of workers in various jobs found that the largest group, 39 percent, said that they believed the most vital element in looking for a job and maintaining interest in it was job satisfaction. Here are some suggestions for making your work more satisfying.

Find out what you really like to do. For any job to yield long-term self-satisfaction, it needs to be closely matched to your personality, goals, and talents. Many people flit from job to job throughout their lives without ever determining what they do best and what most excites them. Whatever line of work you pursue, whether it is doing a craft, raising children, farming, healing, teaching, writing, building, drawing, making wine, selling houses, or serving the public, it should come naturally as an expression of your entire being. You should feel drawn to the activity or pursuit as you are to a loved one, with body and soul, and take responsibility as an individual for nurturing it.

This need to "follow your bliss," as Joseph Campbell put it, has long been seen as a paramount consideration for creative fulfillment and long-term self-satisfaction. The overriding life purpose that everyone needs to find and pursue has variously been called a "ruling love" (by the Swedish philosopher Emanuel Swedenborg), a "rapture," and a "delight." It corresponds to your calling or vocation, suggests Sam Keen, author of *Fire in the Belly*. A calling or vocation is work you feel compelled to do, often from listening to the quiet, persistent inner voice that speaks directly to you. Indeed, the word *vocation* shares the same root as *voice* and *vocal*. Develop and discipline your gifts while listening for your calling, Keen says.

"Following your bliss" is sometimes misinterpreted as an endorsement for hedonism or for pursuit of narrow, egotistic goals. Rather, according to Keen, a true calling connects you to society. "To have a calling means that what you have to give is correlated with something the world needs. There are a lot of people today who are trying to develop a vocation without listening. To have a calling is to discipline a gift that you have so that you do some work well. So that you're effective at it. Don't do everything. Don't try to heal all the world. Consider your gifts. You can be sure that by exercising your gifts you will find your greatest delight and will serve others."

Find work that rewards you in ways beyond money. If you are like most people, you need money—lots of it—to live. And unless you've inherited wealth, won the lottery, or somehow managed to save, you need to work to earn money. A good-paying job affords you material goods, social status, and security.

While monetary rewards can't be denied, many people's search for meaningful work is not limited to those positions that offer the most money. The potential benefits from finding the right job are so much more. Work can keep your mind sharp, provide an avenue for creativity, and put you in contact with a wide circle of friends. The right job increases your self-esteem and enhances personal growth. These nonmonetary values derived from some types of work often overshadow purely economic considerations. In the U.S., this is particularly true among young workers. According to a recent international study of work and values, published jointly by the Public Agenda Foundation and the Aspen Institute and entitled *The World at Work,* workers around the world as well are now placing greater emphasis on transferring social values to the workplace. The researchers termed these values "expressivism" and said that they include "creativity, autonomy, rejection of authority, placing self-expression ahead of status, pleasure seeking, the hunger for new experiences, the quest for community participation in decision making, the desire for adventure, closeness to nature, cultivation of self, and inner growth."

Thus, if you are considering a job, make sure it is a match with your values. If a steady salary and long-term security are most important, the job that is right for you will be different from that if you care most for creativity and self-realization. Don't be willing to ignore the intrinsic satisfaction you can get from work. In some cases, as a popular book title says, you can "do what you love and the money will follow."

Tailor your current job to better fit your interests. Adapting your current job to fit your needs can sometimes be easier than quitting and finding a new job. Some employers are more open than others to changes within a job. Talk to your supervisors and coworkers about how you'd like to change your position. Tell them that the work you are doing is not taking full advantage of your abilities and interests. At least initially you may need to volunteer to take on additional tasks while continuing to do old ones. Hopefully, your enthusiasm and aptitude in the new areas will warrant a permanent shift in your responsibilities.

Keep in mind that you want to find a balance in your work between under- and overstimulation. When your skills are not being challenged, you'll easily get bored and discouraged. Yet too much challenge can also be a problem. When you have to make too many decisions too quickly with too much data, you can easily get overwhelmed. Judgment and job performance suffer. The balancing point for job stimulation is different for each person, so try to get a better sense of your personal needs.

Take this job and shove it. When work ceases to provide essential needs however you define them, and it is not possible to change the job itself, it's time to find different work. If creativity and self-expression are important to you, staying in a boring, unchallenging job can have a ripple effect on other parts of your life. Studies indicate that what you experience at work influences how you spend your leisure time. For example, if you work at a job that stifles you, you have a tendency to become less active in the rest of your life. "The view that workers would be able to compensate for a dull and boring job with stimulating and enriching activities in their free time is being replaced by an understanding of the strong links between a job that is circumscribed and repetitious, and a leisure that is passive and psychologically unrewarding," according to Marianne Frankenhaeuser, Ph.D., professor of psychology at Karolinska Institute in Stockholm.

Working in a boring, repetitive job also causes you to take longer to unwind after you've left work. Your blood pressure and stress hormones remain high for a longer time than when you finish working at a job that you find inspiring. Over years this increased stress response can raise your risk of heart disease.

Before you quit, make sure that you've determined exactly what it is that you can't stand about your current job. Identify as well the elements you want to carry over to your next job.

Especially during tough economic times, leaving a job is a risk. You can help to minimize the potential adverse consequences by developing a plan and setting goals. If you can save money and leave yourself time to job hunt, the process will be less traumatic. The plan may take years and encompass a number of steps. For instance, if you decide to switch fields, you may want to get training or take classes before leaving the old job. You may need to relocate to a new area.

Short Tips for Better Work Satisfaction

❏ Connect to the people you work with, suggest the authors of *Work Is Not a Four-Letter Word*. Developing connections can fulfill many of the social needs that make work more enjoyable. Show an interest in what colleagues are doing, use humor, listen actively, and share resources and ideas.

❏ Volunteer. Volunteering can start you in a field you are interested in yet not overly qualified for. As Ram Dass and Paul Gorman note in *How Can I Help?* the rewards we reap from volunteering or offering "conscious service" include the opportunity "not only to relieve suffering but to grow in wisdom, experience greater unity, and have a good time while we're doing it."

❏ Balance work with other aspects of your life, including family, leisure, and friends. Even the most rewarding work can become addictive and counterproductive if taken to an extreme (see Step 35).

For More Information

An excellent resource for information on organizations and volunteer opportunities in the fields of environmental action, human rights, health, and peace is the following:

What Can I Do to Make a Difference?—A Positive Action Sourcebook by Richard Zimmerman (New York: Plume, 1992)

Books with helpful suggestions for connecting to your work include:

Work Is Not a Four-Letter Word: Improving the Quality of Your Work Life by Stephen Strasser, Ph.D., and John Sena, Ph.D. (Homewood, Ill.: Business One Irwin, 1992)

Dignity at Work edited by Bo Ekman (Stockholm, Sweden: Streiffert and Co., 1985)

The following book, which is regularly updated, is the premier book on the market for instructing you in finding the right job:

What Color Is Your Parachute? by Richard Bolles (Berkeley, Calif.: Ten Speed Press, 1993)

HAVE GREAT SEX

C oming to terms with your sexuality and leading a full and rich sex life offer a wide range of rewards. Most people experience these rewards not so much in the realm of physical health (though one study of middle-aged men found that those who regularly enjoyed sex were less likely to have a heart attack than those who did not) as in the realms of mental and emotional health. This is true in spite of the fact that, for some, sex is purely physical and is divorced from concepts such as love, communication, and commitment.

Yet reducing sex to a merely mechanical act denies its potentially profound effects on the mind, body, and spirit. At its best sexuality can be a reflection of your entire being. It can be a means of expressing, renewing, or discovering your inner self. Sharing sex can reward partners with emotional closeness and intimacy. It can even be a spiritual experience that links you to the divine within each person.

"Like music, sex can be used for utilitarian purposes for entertainment, or for meaningless background filler," notes John Welwood, Ph.D., author of *Journey of the Heart: Intimate Relationships and the Path of Love*. "But it is most powerful when it awakens us to the rich, vital textures and depths of human feeling. Sexual and musical expression both arise from the same place: from the energy flow of the subtle body, which, by animating and shaping gross matter, is the source of all creativity."

Most of the same elements that deepen any interpersonal relationship are also prerequisites for a successful sex life, including a positive sense of self-worth and an ability to express yourself and to listen. Drugs such as alcohol and physical conditions such as diabetes can and do interfere with a healthy sex life. Much more frequently, however, sexual problems can be traced to something that is lacking in the relationship or to emotional problems in one or both of the partners. Accepting your sexuality and liking your own body allow you to develop satisfying sexual relations with others.

At the heart of many satisfying sexual relationships is effective communication. Partly the problem is that men and women speak a different language, according to Jonathan Kramer and Diane Dunaway, the authors of a recent book whose title neatly summarized the issue: *Why Men Don't Get Enough Sex and Women Don't Get Enough Love*. Open communication between partners increases closeness, sharing, and a sense of intimacy. This communication may be through speaking, touching, or other acts (one survey found that men reported the sexiest aspect of a woman is her smile). Sex in turn becomes a further form of communication, a deepening of the connections that two people establish with each other.

Everyday Steps to a Natural Health

Regardless of your marital status or sexual persuasion, there are a number of elements to keep in mind to develop a rewarding sex life.

Touch and be touched. Touching can send mixed signals in Western society. When two men touch, some see it as a sign of an effeminate nature. Certain men and women also interpret touch as a strictly sexual signal: "If you touch me, it must mean you want to have sex with me." As a result many adults either ignore touching or grow uncomfortable with any nonsexual touching. A number of cross-cultural studies have indicated that if this lack of touching is extended to children, when these children grow up, they are more likely to feel alone and isolated. They are also somewhat more likely to become physically aggressive toward each other and engage in violence.

Sometimes, without even realizing it, the devaluing of touching extends to sexual partners. Touching is ignored as a means of expressing love and affection and increasing closeness. If you are having a sexual relation with someone, touching need not be a signal that you want sex. Talk to your partner about what touch means and come to an understanding about when it is intended to be sexual. If one partner is constantly demanding sex, he or she may well be suffering from lack of touch rather than uncontrolled libido. If intercourse has become your only form of touching, your relationship is less than it could be.

Nonsexual touching is an important expression of affection. It is a means of communication that can better attune you to your partner. Make an effort to share touching with your partner every day. Use any and all forms of touching: massage, hugging, kissing, caressing, cuddling, nuzzling, stroking, and so forth.

When it is emphasized during sex, sensuous touching is a means for exploring each other's body. It promotes intimacy and lets you know what your partner likes and dislikes. For women in particular, touching can be the most satisfying part of sex. One study found that about half of all women have difficulty achieving orgasm through intercourse only—they're more likely to experience an orgasm from some combination of touch and manual or oral manipulation.

Let fantasy be your aphrodisiac. Researchers at the University of Vermont who recently surveyed sexually active adults found that fantasy and sex were strongly associated. Fully 84 percent of the respondents admitted to fantasizing about other partners or practices during sex. This fantasizing, however, was not without its emotional costs. One in four of those who fantasized said they felt "significant guilt" about fantasies or thought the practice was harmful to their relationship.

"What a shame to feel guilty about something as normal—and healthy—as sexual fantasies during lovemaking," notes Michael Castleman, author of *Sexual Solutions*. He says that sexual fantasies may be harmful to a relationship only if they pass from the realm of fantasy to obsession. Otherwise, sexual fantasies can play a positive role that should be free of judgment, guilt, or moralizing. When it comes to your inner life, Castleman says, "everything is permitted and nothing is wrong. . . . Lovemaking involves letting yourself go physically and emotionally. It can, without a twinge of guilt, involve letting go mentally as well."

According to Peter Rutter, M.D., a Jungian psychiatrist and author of *Sex in the Forbidden Zone*, sexual fantasies have more in common with dreams than with sex. Thus, fantasies can bring us closer to our inner selves. "Sexual fantasy is in the middle region between our purely inner lives and our outer sexual behavior—a space that can act as a balance to the time pressure and demands of our intrusive and performance-oriented social environment. Like all fantasy, sexual fantasy has the potential to move us in either direction, creatively energizing a relationship with another person or living itself out purely by providing us with a meaningful entrée into deeper aspects of ourselves."

Rutter agrees with the view that fantasies should not be judged in the same way that acts are. He says, "If you can separate yourself from the notion that involvement with your fantasy has anything to do with outer behavior, you will be freer to follow the fantasy, and less likely to judge it as right or wrong, good or bad, healthy or unhealthy. These are judgments that we must apply to behavior that affects another person, but not to the range of inner feelings or parts of oneself that one contacts through the fantasy."

Sexual fantasies can be as varied as your imagination. They can be about people you know, movie stars or models, your first lover, unusual positions, or exotic places.

Keep those sexual flames fanned with your regular partner. It is not uncommon for couples to lose some of their initial sexual excitement over time. After the first few years of marriage or living together, they may be distracted by the daily flow of events. Some couples direct most of their love and attention to their children or work overlapping schedules. Different sleep patterns can reduce sexual opportunities.

One partner's desire for more frequent sexual activity than the other's is a common problem. Among middle-aged heterosexual couples it sometimes stems from nothing more than the myth that women beyond their thirties have lost interest in sex. Yet often women report having more satisfying sex in their middle ages and beyond. Many can reach orgasm then more easily than when they were younger, are more in touch with their bodies, and are able to be more straightforward about expressing what gives them sexual pleasure. Increased self-esteem and fewer inhibitions may also be factors. Finally, middle-aged men are more likely than young men to be able to extend intercourse without ejaculating.

There are a number of ways to keep sexual interest alive over the years:

❑ Talk to your partner about setting aside a special time and place for sex. You want time to be alone together, not just together along with children or friends. You also need to make sure you won't be interrupted by phone calls or other distractions.

❑ Go to bed at the same time. This simple step can be a tremendous boost to a stagnant love life. Waking together in the morning also helps, since this is when some men's sex drive is the highest.

❑ Tell your partner exactly what feels good to you and what you would like him or her to do to help sexually arouse you. Share with your partner how you sexually stimulate yourself. "So often, we expect our partners to know what we like, or we're afraid our partners won't think they're good enough," says Margo Anand, author of *The Art of Sexual Ecstasy*. Taboos and social pressures can make it difficult to be frank with your partner about sex, but the effort at honest communication is worth it. Become selfish concerning your own sexual pleasure. An overemphasis on what your partner needs to gain sexual satisfaction can leave your own desires unfulfilled.

❑ Trade sensual massages with your partner. Dim the lights, put on soft music, and use a fragrant massage oil to awaken touch receptors from head to toe. Giving and receiving a sensual massage can extend your concept of the erogenous zone from merely the genitals to the entire body. It can also transform your idea of the goal of sex from having an orgasm to stimulating the entire body. "The climax of the performance is, of course, orgasm, billed in the words of one popular sex manual as 'the aim, the summit, the end of the sexual act.' However, this tyranny of the orgasm makes sex an effort, creating what sex educators Masters and Johnson singled out as the most common cause of sexual dysfunction in modern times: performance pressure," notes John Welwood.

❑ Take turns initiating sex. This can be a useful strategy when one partner is much more reticent about initiating sex than the other. Though the nonagressive partner may be the male in a heterosexual relationship, women face greater obstacles as sexual initiators because of customs and social pressure. Some men (especially those who are older or have low education levels) feel that women have weaker sex drives than men or that women who initiate sex are somehow bad. Though attitudes have changed somewhat, even recent studies have found that the sexual double standard still exists. Couples may want to try designating one person the sex initiator for one week and then the other person the next week. Just having a discussion about how to initiate sex and what the signals will be is often helpful.

Short Tips for Better Sex

❏ Try some herbal aphrodisiacs on special occasions. The mind is a more powerful aphrodisiac than any substance, but herbs can add spice every once in a while. Two of the most popular ones are the Mexican herb damiana *(Turnera diffusa),* used principally by women an hour or so before intercourse, and yohimbé *(Corynanthe yohimbe),* an African tree bark that is famous for its potent stimulating effects on men.

❏ Make sex safe. Few things can dim sexual ardor as much as anxiety about the consequences of sex, whether these be pregnancy or sexually transmitted diseases. Some of the ways to decrease the risks of sex include limiting the number of your sex partners, when necessary always using a condom, diaphragm, latex dam, or other fluid barrier, and avoiding high-risk sex acts (such as any exchange of bodily fluids with partners who have used intravenous drugs or themselves had multiple casual sex encounters).

❏ Women can boost their sex lives by maintaining muscle tone in the pelvic region. Strengthening the pubococcygeal muscles in particular may help to improve sexual response and increase sensitivity of the vagina (as well as prevent urinary incontinence). An effective exercise is to periodically contract the area of the vagina and anus as if to close them and pull them up toward the navel. Inhale as you tighten the muscles and exhale as you release them. A few minutes of practice daily can strengthen the entire pelvic region.

❏ Stay physically active (see Step 9). Compared to sedentary people, men and women who exercise regularly are more likely to say that they have active, satisfactory sex lives. Fitness may boost sexual response indirectly by elevating mood and improving self-esteem.

❏ Regardless of whether you have a regular sexual partner, if masturbation is a part of your sex life, accept it as normal rather than fretting about it or feeling guilty. A study done during the 1970s found that seven out of ten married people, of both sexes, masturbate regularly. Partners almost always conceal this activity from each other, yet some sex counselors say that masturbation is not necessarily a sign of lack of sexual interest in the partner but rather may be viewed by the masturbator as a separate, additional expression of his or her sexuality.

For More Information

See the following books for more suggestions on leading a healthy sex life:

The Art of Sexual Ecstasy by Margo Anand (Los Angeles: Jeremy P. Tarcher, 1989)

Sexual Solutions: For Men and the Women Who Love Them by Michael Castleman (New York: Simon & Schuster, 1989)

The following is a mail-order bookstore of "accurate, compassionate sexuality material" for men and women, including more than three hundred books, magazines, and videos.

The Sexuality Library
Open Enterprises
938 Howard St., #101
San Francisco, CA 94103
(415) 974-8990

COMMUNICATE
HEART TO HEART

The word *communicate* derives from the same Latin root as do *common* and *commune*. Thus, to communicate is to make common or to share. In the strictest sense, a mere sending and receiving of information is a form of communication. Two computers communicate by exchanging data. Communication in the fullest, most human sense, however, is a more active process. It implies not only a transmission of signals or messages, whether about feelings, plans, or preferences, but an awareness of the intended result: a deepening of understanding between partners in the exchange. In this sense, communication is seen to transcend mere talking and hearing. If the listener is so self-absorbed that what is said has no effect, then genuine communication has not happened.

Lack of effective communication is a common problem in relationships, marriages, and families. It can also be a drawback at work or just playing among friends. While means for communicating more quickly have mushroomed in modern times, from car phones to faxes, the type of person-to-person skills needed for communicating effectively have not kept pace. The distractions and pressures of everyday life (some of which result from the explosion of mass communications) can also have the effect of cutting off communication. When a family routinely watches television while eating meals, certain types of communication (such as transmission of commercial messages) displace others (including heart-to-heart communication between related individuals). The erosion of heart-to-heart communication seems to be well advanced in our society. One study showed that married couples spend on average only seven minutes per week talking to each other.

The key to deep communication with family, friends, and lovers is the willingness to risk revealing some of your inner self. Effective heart-to-heart communication allows the people you love to truly know and understand you. By sharing your innermost feelings and private thoughts, you form deeper connections and closer intimacy with those around you. These bonds can then in turn open you to further personal insights and increase others' love and awareness.

True communication takes time and effort. It also takes courage, since by looking within yourself and honestly expressing what you feel, you open yourself to rejection. True communication in this sense is a risk, but one that pays important long-term dividends in the form of self-knowledge and better understanding of others. Not communicating is also a risk, one that may result in isolation and loneliness.

Being able to talk and impart information verbally is one element of communication, but it is hardly essential. After all, those who use sign language communicate effectively. People also express themselves through actions, gestures, and unspoken communications. These and other communication skills, in particular active listening, can be improved with practice. Heart-to-heart communication does not come naturally to most people. Those who can express authentic feelings, listen to what others have to say, and respond with love and generosity of spirit find that communication is a rich and rewarding experience.

Everyday Steps to Natural Health

The road to better communication is strewn with blockades. Here are some suggestions for avoiding them.

Acknowledge and express your feelings. For men more so than for women, talking about sex, death, love, and other issues of the heart can often be difficult. Given the choice, many people would prefer to stick to the news and other safe topics. Talking about the weather, however, will never deepen a couple's or family members' understanding of one another.

One problem is that the prerequisite for expressing our feelings— observing and recognizing them for what they are—can also be difficult. Social norms and peer pressure may subtly encourage some to hold "negative" feelings in, causing them to resist talking about frustration, shame, or depression. Many men in particular would benefit by learning to listen to and acknowledge the feelings they have. Recognizing your feelings does not mean you lack character or "toughness." People who can accept their feelings without dismissing them as insignificant or labeling them as right or wrong will be much more comfortable sharing them.

Another problem is that many people's language of emotions is limited. A lover rejects your sexual advances and you want to express how that feels, but you find it difficult to get beyond saying "I'm hurt." It is often useful to practice describing your feelings in metaphors or by analogy. Thus, "I feel rejected, not good enough, like I did when no one wanted to go to the senior prom with me." If your lover is more adept at expressing emotions, he or she may be able to pick up the thread, express more feelings, and begin an effective communication.

Any communication from the heart is usually better than none. Relying on actions or facial expressions, or expecting your partner to be a mind reader, often leads to misunderstanding.

Learn to actively listen. Humorist Mark Twain once observed, "A good memory and a tongue tied in the middle is a combination which gives immortality to conversation." The ability to listen and accurately absorb what is being offered is vital for effective communication. Listening is the yin to talking's yang, the wheel to talking's tire. Without both elements, there is no whole—just two useless parts floating in a sea of other unmatched pairs.

Technically, listening is not difficult at all. Humans can listen and comprehend much more rapidly than they can talk (about 650 words per minute for listening compared to about a quarter of that rate for talking). In other words, you have plenty of available thinking capacity to employ when you are listening to anyone but an auctioneer speaking. Unfortunately, what most of us typically do with that extra listening capacity does little to further communication.

Of course, simply not paying attention is the most common habit of poor listening. A variation on this habit is giving a speaker only a part of your attention. Busy executives may try to pretend they can listen to and converse with a person while also reading their mail or listening on the phone to a second person. Other signs of poor listening include

- ➤ frequently interrupting to finish another's thoughts
- ➤ being quick to evaluate, criticize, judge, or advise
- ➤ jumping to conclusions
- ➤ one-upmanship (considering only how you can top what is being said)
- ➤ imposing your own agenda
- ➤ hearing only what you want or expect to hear

All of these are conversation killers. They turn communication into a one-way street, or perhaps more accurately a divided highway with words zooming past each other with hardly a sideways glance. Taking a more active approach to listening requires that you search for the meanings hidden behind and between words. Instead of merely passively hearing the other person while thinking about your next meal or how to respond, you consider each aspect of what is being said and take time to mull it. In addition to your ears, your eyes play a role in active listening by observing the speaker's actions and gestures. Visual signals and cues can sometimes be much more revealing than the words themselves.

Playing such an active role in listening has a number of positive effects. Since you are likely to better understand and remember what is being said, you are more likely to empathize with the person saying it. Empathy encourages a sharing of ideas and feelings and deepens communication. By actively listening, you implicitly admit to at least the possibility that you will be changed by what is being said. This evidence of respect for another's point of view is immensely effective at establishing trust. Active listening also lessens the probability of a mutual misunderstanding. By providing a good example it may foster better listening in others as well.

Attitudes that foster active listening include patience, egolessness, and inquisitiveness. You need to overcome the habit of self-referral and shift your focus to the speaker. Assume that what the speaker is offering comes from her heart and can affect you. Physically demonstrate your interest and attention by maintaining eye contact and using facial expressions. You needn't be silent to be a good listener. Ask questions and make statements, whether to say "Yes, I understand" or "What happened then?" for the purpose of probing what is being said. Nor does being an active listener require that you allow the communication to drift aimlessly. Prompt the speaker to come to conclusions, to ask his own questions, to feel safe that the first moment of silence won't veer the communication to a new subject. Remember, your goal is to foster understanding and empathy rather than merely to exchange information or be entertained.

Argue fairly. Occasional conflicts are unavoidable, whether in a family, between a married couple, or among friends. Like risk, conflict even plays a positive role by provoking change and growth. Also like risk, conflict that goes unchecked or becomes a constant can lead to various unhappy results, from divorce to illness. You cannot escape or avoid all conflict, but how you handle it can play a major role in whether your conflicts resolve themselves, linger, or escalate from a minor squabble into a major, potentially relationship-ending battle.

Studies indicate that happy and unhappy couples have the same numbers and types of problems. Whether couples stay together or grow apart depends more on how they deal with conflicts. Other research indicates that how couples fight can predict with a high degree of accuracy whether they will divorce or still be married within three years. A notable study of two hundred couples done over the past twenty years at the University of Washington by Dr. Daniel Goleman found that the worst conflict habits are criticism, contempt, defensiveness, and stonewalling.

When these tactics become the norm, partners to a conflict typically become agitated and take on a disorganized state of mind, Goleman says. One person becomes fixed in his or her perception of the other. Since the problem is seen as residing in the other person, not in the relationship, no possibility of change can be admitted. Once someone has withdrawn from the relationship, it is almost impossible to reconcile. This "distance and isolation cascade," as Goleman calls it, begins when one of the partners concludes the problems can't be solved.

"Not only to say the right thing in the right place, but far more difficult, to leave unsaid the wrong thing at the tempting moment"— this is one of the most important rules for arguing fairly, says George Sala. It is imperative that an argument not escalate into unrelated nastiness. In the heat of the moment, it can be hard to resist using the most hateful, hurtful types of personal criticisms: "You've always been a lousy lover," "You're fat," "You're totally incompetent." When the argument is over, even a direct apology can't erase the sting of such statements.

Before arguments become a problem, couples should talk about what constitutes a fair fight. Other unfair tactics to avoid include bringing unrelated elements into an argument, interrupting, changing the subject, and using sarcasm, threats, or jokes. Ground rules may also cover such issues as scheduling of arguments and not arguing in front of children. Once fair argument rules are established they can provide a blueprint for keeping fights manageable.

Use first-person messages. This is an important communication tool for anyone in a close relationship. What it means is expressing your feelings, requests, and observations directly, using first-person "I statements" rather than third-person "you statements." For example, let's say you want to express your disappointment that your husband leaves you home twice a week to go to the movies with friends. You could say "You are a jerk for going out with your friends," or, "It makes me feel lonely when you go out with your friends." A better approach is "I feel hurt and lonely when you go out with your friends."

According to Cristy Lane and Dr. Laura Ann Stevens, the authors of *How to Save Your Troubled Marriage,* "An easy way to remember what an 'I' message consists of is to remember the XYZ formula: 'When you do X, in situation Y, I feel Z.'" They suggest that to be effective "I messages" should be direct, immediate, clear, and straight.

Using the third-person statement focuses blame on your partner. He likely feels as if you are criticizing him and accusing him of being at fault. Unless he's a saint (or a wimp), he reacts defensively and puts up resistance. Stating the problem in the first-person takes responsibility rather than places blame. It also encourages you to explore your feelings and put them into accurate words. The "I message" establishes your participation in the action, observes the effect of the action on you, and states a need. Rather than reacting defensively, your partner is likely to respond by acknowledging your feelings and offering a solution. With any luck, over time your use of first-person statements will also show others how to express their feelings in a way that prevents misunderstandings and conflicts.

Short Tips for Better Communication

❏ Appreciate the art of conversation. Hold regular, leisurely, face-to-face talks with friends, coworkers, and others. Allow the conversations to follow thoughts, ideas, and impressions as they come. Resist arguing, trying to prove a point, or covering an agenda. Listen, think out loud, speculate, and confess. Be playful, honest, profound, and silly. Enjoy yourself.

❏ Tell a communication partner what you have just heard. Summarizing an idea you have received can immediately reveal areas of misinterpretation and misunderstanding. Fewer fights would become serious if more arguments contained the statement "What you heard isn't what I meant to say, so let me try again."

❏ Consider your timing in starting an important communication. Telling your partner that you want to discuss the state of your relationship when she is closing a business deal on the phone is a poor way to begin.

❏ Hear the unspoken. Feelings that can't be expressed in words can sometimes be inferred by observing body language, actions, and facial expressions. Gently probe for buried feelings when the other person seems willing to benefit from heart-to-heart communication.

❏ Becoming an active listener tends to improve other people's communication skills, but dealing with the person who is a nonstop talker may tax anyone's patience. When no exchange seems possible, try gently interrupting a motormouth either to provide or ask for a summary. When all else fails, plead a prior engagement.

For More Information

Books with helpful perspectives on communication include:

How to Listen—How to Be Heard by Thomas G. Banville (Chicago: Nelson-Hall, 1978)

How to Save Your Troubled Marriage by Cristy Lane and Dr. Laura Ann Stevens (New York: St. Martin's Press, 1987)

SIMPLE STEPS
TO
NATURAL HEALTH

ENJOY LIFE

CONNECT WITH NATURE

Most Americans spend 90 percent of their lives inside homes and offices that are increasingly airtight and climate controlled. Air-conditioning is now commonplace even in northern climes—it's also standard equipment on most new cars. Not surprisingly, some people's main experience of nature during the summer consists of the hour spent mowing the lawn. During the winter it consists of the short walk from parking garage to office building. Some critics contend that modern peoples are losing their ability to connect to nature, to feel the ground under their bare feet at some place other than the beach, to get off the sidewalks and streets, out of car and home and office and into the woods, fields, or prairie.

So what? Well, connecting with nature provides numerous collective and individual benefits. The collective benefits may be more obvious: people who experience nature are more likely to appreciate it and to value it. They are more likely to work to preserve its diversity and beauty. The benefits to individuals may be less dramatic than, say, the health benefits of regular exercise, yet nature offers much to the person who is willing to commune with it. The benefits accrue to body and mind. For instance, exposing yourself to natural sunlight (more is not necessarily better; see Step 20) and inhaling fresh air affords you vital nutrients. Moving your body to the contours of the earth, whether hiking a trail, climbing a mountain, or jumping from boulder to boulder in a mountain stream, stretches and strengthens muscles you didn't realize you had.

Relaxing to the rhythms and sounds of nature and making contact with other species provides emotional and spiritual sustenance. Getting out into wilderness, or even closely exploring your own backyard, can offer you a new perspective and allow you to see problems in a new light. Emotional problems are forgotten when viewing a mountain range from afar or contemplating the vastness and the incredible fecundity of the ocean.

In *Nature, Man and Woman,* Alan Watts pointed out that the idea of "communing with nature" was given expression by poets East and West for hundred of years but today has acquired "a slightly ridiculous tone," as if it were just another escape from reality. "But perhaps the reason for this love of nonhuman nature," Watts said, "is that communion with it restores to us a level of our own human nature at which we are still sane, free from humbug, and untouched by anxieties about the meaning and purpose of our lives. . . . Rapport with the marvelously purposeless world of nature gives us new eyes for ourselves—eyes in which our very self-importance is not condemned, but seen as something quite other than what it imagines itself to be. In this light all the weirdly abstract and pompous pursuits of men are suddenly transformed into natural marvels of the same order as the immense beaks of the toucans and hornbills, the fabulous tails of the birds of paradise, the towering necks of the giraffes, and the vividly polychromed posteriors of the baboons. Seen thus, neither as something to be condemned nor in its accustomed aspect of serious worth, the self-importance of man dissolves in laughter. His insistent purposefulness and his extraordinary preoccupation with abstractions are, while perfectly natural, overdone—like the vast bodies of the dinosaurs."

Everyday Steps to Natural Health

Connecting with nature can be a joyful part of any healthy lifestyle. Consider some of the following options:

Explore the wilderness. The nation's extensive highway system may have destroyed some natural beauty, but it has also put vast numbers of people within a few hours' drive of wilderness areas. Admittedly, some national parks, with their traffic congestion and RV-jammed campsites, are not much of a retreat from urban areas. But it is still easy to find almost anywhere in the country undeveloped, quiet, and scenic spots that allow you to immerse yourself in nature.

If you want to camp overnight, you need some specialized equipment (tent, sleeping bag, cooking pots, hiking shoes, maps), but once you have these, you can go off for days, weeks, or longer. If you are a newcomer to wilderness hiking or boating, the many guided tours offer various types of treks and expeditions. Touring outfits often take care of lodging, transportation, meals, and other details, generally reducing your concerns to putting one foot in front of the other.

Patch Adams, M.D., who along with friends and colleagues is building Gesundheit Institute, a free hospital in the mountains of West Virginia, says that nature will be a big part of the healing process there. "Nature tops the list of potent tranquilizers and stress reducers," he says. It can help people rekindle wonder and curiosity, explore beauty and inspiration, and relearn humility. "Gesundheit will be an ideal place to find 'power spots': special places for people to go to examine themselves, make important decisions, and relax. . . . We will take a dozen or so people on seven-to-ten-day hikes in the wilderness. They will ford rivers, make camp, cook meals, and experience human bonding, cooperation, self-care, fun, and much more—all thanks to nature."

Find nature in urban areas and your own backyard. "There is a popular belief abroad in this country that holds that the most interesting things in the natural world can only be found in faraway places or specially designated areas," says John Hanson Mitchell, author of *A Field Guide to Your Own Back Yard*. He delights in dispelling this myth, noting that "I have spent some ten to fifteen years in or near the suburbs of North America, and I think I have discovered over the years that in spite of development, in spite of our so-called technological age, the same forces and the same diversity of life that are so evident in the larger wilderness areas of the world are alive and well in the suburban backyard. A watchful eye, a little extra attention to detail, and a sharpened sensitivity to seasonal changes can uncover a veritable Serengeti Park just beyond the bedroom window. All you have to do is learn to see."

Mitchell is referring to the "backyard" in the broad sense, to include vacant lots, adjacent wood, and other natural areas in the immediate neighborhood. Even if your backyard is nothing but a concrete patio, almost assuredly within walking distance there are streams, ponds, small wetlands, thickets, and woodlands that harbor a variety of plant and animal life. If you work in a city, most urban areas have large parks you can escape to for a brief lunch-hour respite.

Practice gardening. Growing flowers, vegetables, herbs, or other plants is a challenging yet rewarding way to experience nature firsthand. Gardening requires that you become a partner with nature. It asks that you observe the seasons and make informed choices regarding the climate and the weather. It calls for you to learn about the soil preferences of plants and the eating habits of insects and mammals. Planting seeds, tending young shoots, reaping a harvest, and preparing food from the fruits of your labor teaches you the cycles of life and death. The best gardening brings you closer to nature than does agribusiness farming, which imposes its rational grid on the natural world, bending and subordinating nature rather than harmonizing with it.

Landscaping, planting trees, and orcharding can also put you in touch with nature, though taking care of your lawn is unlikely to offer the same type of rewards. That's because a lawn is more a denial of nature than a celebration of it, as Michael Pollan notes in *Second Nature:* "Gardening, I had by now come to appreciate, is a painstaking exploration of place; everything that happens in my garden—the thriving and dying of particular plants, the maraudings of various insects and other pests—teaches me to know this patch of land more intimately, its geology and microclimate, the particular ecology of its local weeds and animals and insects. My garden prospers to the extent I grasp these particularities and adapt to them. Lawns work on the opposite principle. They depend for their success on the *overcoming* of local conditions . . . [and on] the tools of twentieth-century industrial civilization: its chemical fertilizers, pesticides, herbicides, machinery, and, often, computerized irrigation systems." The solution that Pollan suggests: turn your lawn into a garden (though there may be a place for your lawn *in* the garden).

Short Tips for Connecting to Nature

❏ Get outdoors whenever you can. Go outside to exercise, meditate, or read. Quiet activities such as walking, running, and cross-country skiing offer an opportunity for the kind of contemplation that promotes communion with nature.

❏ Make friends with another species. Humans are part of nature, but so are dogs, cats, birds, fish, and insects. If keeping a pet is not your style, find some way to observe animals in their wild habitats and come to understand and appreciate their nature.

❏ Put up a bird feeder or two outside windows that provide good viewing from inside your home. Watching the endless feeding, grooming, and interacting among birds can be an interesting and rewarding way to gain a better appreciation of this slice of nature.

❏ Many people buy tapes of nature sounds, such as waterfalls and birds singing, because these sounds are capable of calming the nervous system and lowering blood pressure. The real thing is as effective: check it out.

❏ Bring your garden indoors by growing a variety of houseplants, from ferns to flowers, thus increasing the levels of healthful oxygen in your air, scenting the rooms with a fresh smell, and including a bit of nature where it is otherwise missing.

❏ Use your vacations to reacquaint yourself with nature, whether by traveling to wilderness spots or seeking out the natural world wherever you are.

For More Information

An excellent reference for discovering the nature that is nearby is:

A Field Guide to Your Own Back Yard by John Hanson Mitchell (New York: W. W. Norton & Co., 1985)

51

EXPRESS YOUR CREATIVITY

Creativity is the process of bringing something new into being, of finding new solutions to old problems or new ways of looking at familiar objects. In addition to being just new and different, what is truly creative goes beyond an idea in someone's head—it must be translated into works of usefulness to one's fellow humans.

Creativity is sometimes thought to be the province only of geniuses, the mad, and artists. Indeed, some aspects of creativity may be associated with neurosis, addiction, and special talents. Studies have confirmed that passion, intensity of purpose, and an ability to get deeply lost in one's work are traits that can make it difficult to distinguish talent from creativity. While it is true that people such as the artist van Gogh who, as psychiatrist Rollo May puts it, "do not fit into their culture" may be highly creative, it is a mistake to relegate creativity to the few. As May says in *The Courage to Create,* "The creative process must be explored not as the product of sickness, but as representing the highest degree of emotional health, as the expression of the normal people in the act of actualizing themselves."

John Briggs agrees. He's the author of *Fire in the Crucible: The Alchemy of Creative Genius,* a penetrating look at how the minds of famously creative people work. Briggs concludes that it's possible that everybody possesses what creative genius is based on, a unique

410

perspective and moments of what he calls "omnivalence," when contradictory feelings are experienced not as mere conflict but as potentials, mystery, openness. Briggs says, "But great creators are rare because most of us don't allow a creative self-organizing structure to form. Instead, we permit our omnivalence to fade and our unique perspective to become homogenized into the general cultural perspective. Our ideas, opinions, beliefs, ambitions, are important to us. They're more important than that unique vision, which may at first seem only a subtle difference, a nuance, but can be a door into an immense, ultimately sharable, even universal way of looking."

Creativity can become a more pronounced positive factor in the average person's life. Exploring and expressing your creativity can increase your self-esteem and bolster your confidence in your unique abilities. With some practice most people can become more aware of how creative they are already in their everyday lives. They can also more successfully begin to express creativity through their work, their play, and their relationships. "If we were purists, we would not speak of a 'creative person,' but only of *a creative act,*" affirms May.

Everyday Steps to Natural Health

Here are some ideas for recognizing the creative spirit within you and becoming more receptive to it on a daily basis.

Befriend knowledge but trust your intuition. Intuition is what you know, or what your unconscious mind tells you will work, without first consciously reasoning it out. Intuition is sharpest, however, when it rests on a foundation of knowledge. Your unconscious can draw upon vast stores of knowledge that you're not aware of consciously, but it can't draw upon what's not there.

There are many paths to creativity but most start from the same place: immersing yourself in a project, issue, or subject and becoming knowledgeable about it in depth. It's possible to be creative in music without knowing how to read or write notes, but certainly such a skill can foster creativity in the musical arts by increasing your ability to express yourself to other musicians. Learning how to use the tools of a trade also increases your confidence in your abilities, making you more willing to risk rejection while expressing your creativity. Keep in mind that if you are like most people, you already have vast stores of knowledge about yourself and those who are close to you, especially if you've had the inclination to use such tools as introspection, dream analysis, meditation, and psychological counseling.

On the other hand, it is not possible to gather complete knowledge about any subject or any person, yourself included. Scientific researchers often find that their seemingly narrow field of study is like a well that widens the farther down they go. That is, the deeper you research a subject the further abroad you must search for all of the relevant connections. Your life is too short and your brain too finite to hold all of the possibilities. Thus, at some point you must make decisions and evaluate creative ideas using faculties, including intuition, other than analysis of knowledge and rational reasoning.

Knowledge and intuition work best as partners when relaxing together, such as during periods when you are engaged in active listening or daydreaming. Often these periods follow concentrated terms of work, study, or analysis. Backing off from the work can allow you to put yourself in the right position for the creative solution to come to you. At times you can reexperience what it is like to look at the world as through the eyes of a child, seeing it for the first time and noticing its many wonders.

Writer Arthur Koestler said, "The conscious and unconscious processes underlying creativity are essentially combinatorial activities—the bringing together of previously separate areas of knowledge and experience. The scientist's purpose is to achieve *synthesis;* the artist aims at a *juxtaposition* of the familiar and the eternal; the humorist's game is to contrive a *collision.*"

Silence your inner critic. Creativity at its birth is a fragile infant, easily smothered by a heavy blanket of criticism. Creative people learn to trust an idea's potential before dismissing it because it sounds weird or because "it's never been done that way before." By definition a creative idea is new and unique, so suspending judgment momentarily on its ultimate usefulness is necessary to nurture it. There will be plenty of other people waiting in line to point out your creative idea's shortcomings, to tell you why it won't work or how it looks stupid. Indeed, when others are quick to criticize or dismiss an idea, it is sometimes an indication that the idea is a breakthrough one. Maybe the criticisms from your inner self and from others are right—and maybe they're not. Only by translating your creative ideas into action can you find out. To do that you must recognize when you are withdrawing from action as a result of fear of criticism and courageously overcome this fear.

Allowing creativity to flower in the workplace by restraining immediate criticism is an important step to business success. When new ideas are routinely shot down one step out of the nest, the effect is to discourage creativity, to shatter confidence, and to inhibit risk taking. Daniel Goleman, Paul Kaufman, and Michael Ray, the authors of *The Creative Spirit,* note that the modern workplace must undergo vital changes to encourage creative problem-solving, foremost among them becoming a safe haven for ideas. "This means a willingness to let ideas emerge freely and to be receptive to them. It means curbing cynicism and harsh judgments, so that employees feel free to make iconoclastic suggestions and even to ask what appear to be 'dumb questions,'" they say.

Learn to creatively entertain yourself. The entertainment industry is a major part of most people's lives. Going to movies, watching television, attending sporting events, and listening to music account for a hefty portion of most people's leisure time. Such inherently passive activities, however, can undermine personal creativity. "Creativity works like muscles: the more it is exercised, the greater its tone," says Patch Adams, M.D., a proponent of melding medicine with humor, creativity, and joy. "Just as sitting in front of a television set all day atrophies mental and physical muscles, consistent passive entertainment kills creativity. Passivity can be countered by exploring new ideas and activity, never settling for one point of view. The key here is to be open and spontaneous. Don't catalog hobbies and interests as indulgences; rather, respect them as major medicines."

Assuming responsibility for actively entertaining yourself may take on many forms. You may decide to learn how to play the piano, take up rock climbing or dancing, edit your home movies, carve wood, paint landscapes—or build landscapes. After you've acquired some initial technical expertise, you'll find it easy to begin to express part of yourself through the keyboard, your movements, or your artwork. Don't let your own negative judgments or another person's criticisms of the results discourage you. As Adams says, "The process is more important than the final product."

If you're lucky, during your creative endeavors you may experience a period when everything seems to come together magically. For a time you can be relaxed yet alert, in the moment so totally that you lose sense of time, so open to the flow of the activity that you become one with it. What you are doing seems to come effortlessly. These moments of peak experience or "being in the flow" allow creativity to flourish.

Short Tips for Greater Creativity

❑ **Make mistakes.** Studies indicate that creative people make a lot of mistakes compared to those who are less imaginative. That's because creativity encompasses risk, and those who are not afraid to fail will be more likely to come up with a wide variety of ideas, some of which will succeed.

❑ **Maintain your sense of humor** (see Step 33). Researchers say that brainstorming groups who are willing to laugh and joke about their ideas are more likely to generate new approaches than groups who are deadly serious about their work. That may be because, as Koestler put it, "the jester's riddles provide a convenient back-door entry, as it were, into the inner sanctum of creative originality."

❑ **Gain insight into your dreams** (see Step 32). When you dream, your mind is in a relentless state of free-associating, reversing of logic, and relaxing of normal controls. Dreams thus offer a steady supply of creative ideas, though it is what you do with these ideas when awake that completes the act of creation.

❑ **Nurture your creativity through music.** "Participating in music, whether as performer or listener, brings us into contact with greatness and leaves traces of that greatness as permanent impressions," says psychiatrist Anthony Storr in *Music and the Mind.*

❑ **Observe a Sabbath, a weekly day of rest.** Many people see the weekend as an opportunity to catch up on work, go shopping, or be entertained. Taking a day to rest, play, converse, daydream, and reflect can restore depleted creative energies. Scientists and others note that their most creative insights often occur after periods of intense work, when the mind is free to roam about for new connections.

For More Information

Some excellent books on creativity include:

The Act of Creation by Arthur Koestler (New York: Dell, 1967)

The Creative Spirit by Daniel Goleman, Paul Kaufman, and Michael Ray (New York: Dutton, 1992)

Fire in the Crucible: The Alchemy of Creative Genius by John Briggs (New York: St. Martin's Press, 1988)

52

SIMPLIFY

"To live more simply is to live more purposefully and with a minimum of needless distraction," says Duane Elgin, author of *Voluntary Simplicity*. By stripping away what is superfluous, unnecessary, and distracting, he and other advocates of the simple life claim, individuals can improve themselves, create more harmonious societies, and even save the earth.

Simplifying your life is often thought of in negative terms such as inactivity, isolation or rural living, a rejection of technology, and poverty. This is, however, a misleading reading of a rich cultural tradition. "Simplicity in its essence demands neither a vow of poverty nor a life of rural homesteading," according to David E. Shi, the author of *The Simple Life,* an authoritative examination of the trend throughout American cultural life. Shi says, "As an ethic of self-conscious material moderation, it can be practiced in cities and suburbs, town houses and condominiums. It requires neither a log cabin nor a hair shirt but a deliberate ordering of priorities so as to distinguish between the necessary and superfluous, useful and wasteful, beautiful and vulgar."

While there is no "cosmic guidebook," Shi notes, to follow for leading the simple life, among the priorities that simple-life advocates, from Henry David Thoreau to Scott Nearing to E. F. Schumacher, have cited are the following:

➤ a rejection of rampant materialism and conspicuous consumption
➤ reducing waste and emphasizing conservation
➤ rediscovering the joys of physical work and self-reliance
➤ obtaining satisfaction from family and friends
➤ revering nature and the earth

For modern-day Americans, the simple life means dropping out of the rat race. A recent *Time* magazine survey for its cover story "The Simple Life" found that 69 percent of those surveyed said that they would like to slow down and live a more relaxed life, and 89 percent said that they now placed more importance on spending time with their families. Other surveys have found that only a fraction of Americans—perhaps one in ten—profess to see the ultimate importance of maintaining status or becoming rich as an indication of success.

Questioning the ultimate value of luxury goods and the consumption ethic is an important part of leading the simple life. Another element, which is at the heart of the many movements toward a simpler life, whether espoused by ancient Greeks, nineteenth-century transcendentalists, or modern back-to-the-landers, is a spiritual quest. Seekers of the simple life agree that by somehow simplifying how you live you can become more attuned to the deeper issues regarding humanity's purpose. You can also more easily enrich your inner life, discover your true nature, and be of service to your fellow humans.

"We each know where our lives are unnecessarily complicated," admits Elgin. "We are all painfully aware of the clutter and pretense that weigh upon us and make our passage through the world more cumbersome and awkward. . . . It is to establish a more direct, unpretentious, and unencumbered relationship with all aspects of our lives: the things that we consume, the work that we do, our relationships with others, our connections with nature and the cosmos, and more."

Everyday Steps to Natural Health

"Reduction to essentials is the main art of life," said social critic and urban planner Lewis Mumford. Many if not all of the previous fifty-one simple steps to natural health can be seen as suggestions for reducing your life to its essentials: eat healthful foods, stay active, make friends, relax, connect with nature, find work you love. Rather than repeating these, and keeping in mind the multidimensional aspect of the simple life, we offer here some suggestions for breaking free of hard-core consumerism.

Rid yourself of junk. This is an easy first step on the road to the simpler life. Junk is simply that which you no longer use or has become an encumbrance. Of course, one person's junk may be another person's treasure, so you don't necessarily have to throw away all your junk. You can also give it away, sell it, or recycle it.

Some people find it harder than others to get rid of old clothes, slightly broken appliances, assorted toy parts, and other junk. One evening as he was reading Thoreau's *Walden*, writer Ronald E. Kotzsch says that he was struck by Thoureau's observation that "things are in the saddle and ride mankind." Kotzsch said that this inspired him to start sifting through his possessions. He was soon wantonly discarding dry ink markers, socks without partners, a battered couch, old bicycling magazines, and a set of left-handed golf clubs (since, as Kotzsch admits, "I am a righty and do not play golf").

Kotzsch notes that "junk is a burden on our lives. Storing it requires space. Keeping it in order requires time and energy, as does packing, transporting, and unpacking it when we move. But its greatest negative effect is subtle and insidious. Like all objects junk has a vibrational, energetic aspect as well as a physical, material weight. Junk erodes energy, peace, and clarity of mind. If the junk is dirty, broken, or in disarray, this effect (which can be called junk-itis) is especially great."

Here are a few practical suggestions for identifying and ridding yourself of junk:

❏ Start with that part of your home that is most overwhelmed with unused stuff. This is usually the basement, attic, or garage, although on occasion junk takes over unused bedrooms and closets. If you are like most homeowners, you find yourself subject to a mysterious variation of the physical law that nature abhors a vacuum. Despite your best efforts, you find that houses abhor a vacuum and any empty space is soon filled with all sorts of junk. Clear the space and vow to keep it clear.

❏ Ask yourself whether you have used any particular item in the past two or three years. If not, assume the object's time of need has permanently passed.

❏ Look closest at those possessions you value least. If clothes aren't that important to you, you'll probably quickly be able to fill some boxes with those that you no longer wear.

❏ Files, whether of the oak-panel or floppy-disk variety, are tremendous collectors of junk. Set aside an hour occasionally to sort through what you have and discard what you no longer need.

❏ If you still want it, even if it is old and threadbare, it's not junk, so don't get rid of it. Gandhi observed, "As long as you derive inner help and comfort from anything, you should keep it. If you were to give it up in a mood of self-sacrifice or out of a stern sense of duty, you would continue to want it back, and that unsatisfied want would make trouble for you."

Apply the need test to new purchases. Thoreau observed, "A man is rich in proportion to the number of things which he can afford to let alone." Before you pull out the credit card to make a major new purchase, take a moment to consider whether you can afford to let this particular thing alone. Ask yourself, "Do I need this or do I just want it?" Ask as well, "Will this purchase be stashed away unused (thus becoming 'junk') before it even has a chance to wear out?"

Becoming a conscientious consumer rather than a conspicuous one is essential for simplifying your life. The pressure to buy!buy!buy! in modern society is omnipresent, whether from advertising in the mass media or just keeping up with your neighbors. Holidays are now commercialized to such a great extent that it becomes difficult to observe many without getting caught up in the consumer ethic. For some people material possessions are a means for establishing identity and social position. Keep in mind that when acquisition of wealth becomes a means of self-expression, other values are often sacrificed, whether these be rewarding relationships or personal health.

In addition to questioning whether you really need an object, ask some other questions, such as:

❏ Will this object last?
❏ How difficult and costly will it be to repair if broken?
❏ Does buying it promote my efforts at simplicity?

❑ Is it so expensive that I will need to work excessively, or in a field I don't find rewarding, in order to pay for it?

❑ Will it promote self-reliance or greater dependence on experts and repair people?

❑ Will buying it result in greater connections with other people and with nature or more alienation from them?

Do it yourself. Self-reliance is a traditional American value that has eroded quite a bit in recent years. The everyday skills necessary to take care of basic human needs are not difficult to master, yet modern conveniences have tended to erode their importance. For instance, how many of your acquaintances are proficient at the following activities?

❑ feeding: gardening, cooking, preserving

❑ entertaining: playing a musical instrument, telling a story, drawing

❑ housing: carpentry, plumbing, wiring, landscaping, furniture refinishing

❑ transporting: providing your own power by walking or riding a bicycle, and repairing your own means of transport, whether bicycle or auto

❑ clothing: sewing

Becoming more skilled at these activities can build confidence and self-esteem. It may also save you money, allowing you the flexibility to work fewer hours if that's your choice. Most importantly, it connects you to life's essentials in a way that eating at a fast-food restaurant, watching television, and hiring experts don't.

The computerization of technology is one of the trends that increases reliance on experts. As everything from watches to autos becomes increasingly computerized, it all becomes more difficult to understand and repair. New autos are now beyond the ability of even trained mechanics to repair—simple malfunctions frequently result in entire systems being replaced. On the other hand, with a little perseverance the interested layperson can still understand and sometimes repair many principally mechanical devices and appliances, including bicycles, toasters, toilets, and toys. If you have the aptitude, as well as some manuals or detailed home-repair books, you might be able to take on larger appliances, leaky faucets, and the like. Though they may be complex jobs, such tasks as painting your home, landscaping your yard, and repairing your furniture can be rewarding activities that ultimately simplify your life.

Short Tips for Simplifying

❏ Resist fashions, trends, and fads. You can apply this generalization to clothing, architecture, automobiles, and other products. The truly well-designed and functional objects are those that somehow never go out of style.

❏ Give up some money to obtain more time. The attitude that "time is money" subordinates values such as friendship and personal health to wealth for wealth's sake. Make your motto "money is time" and determine whether you need the money as much as you value the time.

❏ Reduce your waste and recycle most of the waste you do generate. Living lightly and cleanly on the earth allows more people the opportunity to voluntarily choose simplicity, instead of having a debilitating form of the simple life thrust upon them by poverty.

For More Information

Books with excellent suggestions for understanding and living the simple life include:

The Portable Thoreau by Henry David Thoreau, edited by Carl Bode (New York: The Viking Press, rev. ed., 1964)

The Simple Life: Plain Living and High Thinking in American Culture by David E. Shi (New York: Oxford University Press, 1985)

Small Is Beautiful by E. F. Schumacher (New York: Harper & Row, 1973)

Voluntary Simplicity: Toward a Way of Life That Is Outwardly Simple, Inwardly Rich by Duane Elgin (New York: William Morrow, rev. ed. 1993)

CONCLUSION

DO WHAT YOU CAN, MAKE BALANCE, AND HAVE FUN

Take a few moments to think about your life and your health. Every individual has strengths and weaknesses when it comes to doing the things that need to be done in order to stay well, live longer, and enjoy oneself. One person may eat a diet that would be the envy of a macrobiotic, vegetarian, animal-rights Zen master, but has few friends and rarely exercises. Another religiously records and analyzes his dreams and mines tremendous personal insights as a result, but has a hunched-over posture and finds nothing in the world worth laughing at. A third person is a devoted communicator and intent listener, but has no sense of the workings of her body and suffers from a chronically depressed immune system.

The foregoing fifty-two simple steps to natural health represent a comprehensive and sensible plan for taking charge of your life and experiencing better health, happiness, and human development. Which steps are most relevant to your life depends on your particular body, mind, and spirit. If you've been able to follow all of the fifty-two steps and incorporate the suggestions into your life, more power to you. If you've only done some of the steps, that's all right, too. What's important is not keeping score but making the changes you feel comfortable making, and accepting that as long as you are alive, there will always be more opportunities to improve in overall health, inner contentment, and social awareness.

Thus, the steps outlined here represent not so much an end point as a beginning and a process. The process is the lifelong one of growing as an individual and discovering new ideas and new ways of relating. It is also the process of striving for better fitness, knowing that perfect health exists only as a balance between sickness and well-being, activity and sleep, and even life and death. We are all beginners in this process, and should you put this book aside and read it again some years hence, you will read it anew, from the perspective of a different person with new concerns and a changed body. Don't try to carve into marble the changes you've made from these fifty-two simple steps to natural health; incorporate them into your makeup and let them grow and change as you grow and change.

If you have devoted yourself to only a limited number of the fifty-two steps, consider whether there are serious gaps in your health practices that you might still need to address. At the least, you need to break the habits that are most damaging to personal health, including smoking cigarettes, drinking too much alcohol, not getting enough exercise, and being overweight. In addition, try to achieve a balance among the general categories of the fifty-two steps (food and diet, activity and exercise, posture, environment, the healing touch, your body, at night, take it easy, mind and spirit, longevity, relationships, and enjoy life) by at least incorporating into your life the most basic guidelines from each. These include

❏ Eat a low-fat, high-complex-carbohydrate diet of mostly fresh vegetables and fruits, whole grains, legumes, breads and cereals, and fish. Don't diet—change your diet. Make junk foods and fast foods an occasional treat, not a daily routine. Drink water. Take some supplements.

❏ Stay physically active, both by seeking opportunities to use your body in everyday life and by exercising. Balance your exercise to include movements that build muscles, increase flexibility, improve endurance, and increase balance and coordination.

❏ Develop better posture habits, by sitting up straight and carrying yourself in an erect manner when you walk and move. Exercise and stretch to keep your back supple and strong.

❏ Create a natural, nontoxic environment where you live and work. Get some regular sun without overdoing it.

❏ Develop a better sense of how your body works and how you can diagnose it and treat it with natural remedies when it becomes sick. Give and receive massage. Find a health practitioner who shares your overall beliefs and can be a partner in your journey to wellness.

❑ Allow your body to do with efficiency and comfort what it was designed to do: breathe, digest, combat disease, see. Give yourself the best long-term chance you can to avoid major illnesses such as cancer.

❑ Relish your body at rest with sleeping and dreaming. Sufficient sleep is as important to your overall health as sufficient exercise. Gain insights from your dreams that may otherwise be unavailable to your rational mind.

❑ Don't rush through life with the seriousness and punctuality of a Japanese commuter train. Laugh at yourself and with others, seeing humor wherever possible. Question and change your habits and routines to be more open to the unusual or the revealing.

❑ Develop positive outlooks that keep your mind and spirit constantly refreshed. Recognize your need for relaxation. Increase your willingness to take risks and face uncertainty.

❑ You won't live forever, but you can stay active and engaged well into old age.

❑ Take sustenance from friends, coworkers, lovers, and family members. Learn how to express your true self to them and receive in turn their expressions of themselves to you.

❑ Enjoy the simple pleasures, from walking in the woods to drawing a picture. Find out what really matters in life.

To borrow a new-age phrase, do what you can and the rewards will follow. Don't feel guilty because you haven't done everything possible to improve your health. You'll just experience higher levels of anxiety, disappointment, and self-reproach. Rather, congratulate yourself on the improvements you have made and vow to enjoy yourself as you take on new challenges in the future.

INDEX

Bonime, Walter, 270
Boron, 23, 25, 27, 57, 85, 86
Bower, John, 142
Bradley, Dinah, 217
Breathing, 124, 215–21, 287, 425
  in meditation, 342
  and relaxation, 343
  in yoga, 92
Breathing (Sky), 216
Breathing (peak-flow) monitors, 171
Briggs, John, 410–11
Brillat-Savarin, Anthelme, 11
Bromelain, 226, 303
Bronfenbrenner, Urie, 349
Brooks, Svevo, 71
Bruhn, John, 377–78
Bruises, strains, sprains, 208–09
Bulimia, 15, 292
Burns, 209
  see also Sunburn
Burton, Robert, 275

Caffeine, 42, 48, 49, 82, 155, 203, 306,
      225, 289, 290, 301, 316–18
  and insomnia, 258, 263
  motives for using, 319–20
Calcium, 17, 18, 23, 24, 25, 39, 44, 48,
      138, 345
  and bone health, 82, 83, 84, 85, 87
  and cancer, 158
  as sleep aid, 262
  sources of, 84
  and teeth, 56, 57
Calendula, 204–05, 208, 209, 210, 211,
      303
Calhoun, AnneMarie, 110, 111
California poppy, 262
Calorie restriction
  and longevity, 358–59
Calories, 4, 8, 41
  burned in exercise, 66
  from fat, 30, 31
Campbell, Joseph, 385
Cancer(s), 3, 18, 21, 30, 40, 158, 230,
      236, 319, 323, 327
  Colorectal, 169–70
  foods/nutrients and risk of, 239–45
  lung, 152, 357
  skin, 157, 239
  uterine, 81
Cancer-promoting agents, 243–44
Carbohydrates, 55, 222
  see also Complex carbohydrates

Carcinogens, 244–45
Cardiovascular health, 108, 115
Cardiovascular muscles, 99
Carpet Guard, 143
carpeting, toxic, 142–44, 153–54
Carrington, Patricia, 345
Cartwright, Rosalind, 265
Castleman, Michael, 168, 391
Catharsis, 333
Cathode-ray tube (CRT) video display
      terminals (VDTs), 146, 251–52
Cattlemen's Association, 4
Cavities (caries), 51–52
  fillings for, 53–55
Centenarians, 359–60
Chamomile, 162, 262
Chancing It (Keyes), 308, 309
Chemicals, 144, 244
  toxic, 219, 245
Cheraskin, Emanuel, 19
Chernin, Kim, 295
Chesney, Margaret, 336
Chest
  muscle tone, 102–05
  strengthening exercises, 105
  stretching, 90–91, 154
chiropractors, 35, 95, 132, 133, 175,
      178–79, 189, 193
Chocolate, 225, 317
Cholesterol, 4, 8, 32
  "good," 318–19
  home tests, 169
Chopping/cupping, 198
Chopra, Deepak, 178, 247, 367–68
Chromium, 23, 25, 113
Chronic disease, 26–27, 109, 375
Chronic fatigue syndrome, 230, 259
Cobra (yoga posture), 218
Codependent behavior, 290
Coenzyme Q$_{10}$, 26, 57, 241, 299
Coffea, 263
Coffee, 244, 315, 316–18
  see also Caffeine
Cohen, Steve, 118
Colds, 209, 230
Colon, 223, 224
Common Sense Diet and Health (Brooks),
      71
Communication, 396–402
  in sexual relations, 390, 391, 393
Complex carbohydrates, 3, 4, 29, 31, 62,
      65, 225, 263
Complex polysaccharides, 241–42

Ear, 116
Earscopes (otoscopes), 171
Eat More, Weigh Less (Ornish), 64
Eat to Win (Haas), 45
Eating, 11–12, 417
  connecting with food through, 14–16
  and digestion, 227–28
  emotional, 294–95
  for optimum health, 3–10
  and weight loss, 64–65
Eating disorders, 15–16, 295
Eating habits, 8–9, 37
  and aging, 357
  poor, 32–33, 224
  while traveling, 300–01
Echinacea, 205, 208, 209, 210, 211, 303
  and cancer, 242
  and immune system, 235
Echinacea (Hobbs), 205
Edging, 250
Edwards, Paul, 380
Edwards, Sarah, 380
Eicosapentaenoic acid (EPA), 27
Electrolytes, 45
Electromagnetic radiation, 141, 145–47,
  155
Elgin, Duane, 416, 417
Emotional balance/imbalance, 249
  and vision, 252
Emotional risks, 307–08, 310, 312
Emotions, 335
  of dreams, 270
  and health, 323
  and immune system, 327
  language of, 398
  negative, 327
  and stress, 339
  underlying anger, 337
Encyclopedia of Natural Medicine (Murray
  and Pizzorno), 35, 84
End of Nature, The (McKibben), 71
Endurance, 74, 77, 78, 108–14, 115
Endurance exercise, 108–09
  see also Aerobic exercise
Energy, 61, 195
  natural flow of, 147–48, 155
  see also Vital energy
Enokidake, 234
Entertainment, creative, 413–14
Environment, 424
  indoors, 141, 151
Environmental Protection Agency (EPA),
  142, 144, 152, 153, 219

Enzymes, 20, 223, 226
Ephedra, 320
Erikson, Erik, 363
Esophagus, 223, 225, 228, 229
Essential fatty acids (EFAs), 26–27
Essential oils, 162, 176, 182–83, 203,
  206–07, 263
Estrogen, 81, 82, 244
Estrogen-replacement therapy, 81
Evans, William, 100
Exercise, 66–67, 68–69, 209, 424
  and aging, 357, 364, 365
  in back care, 135–36
  and bones, 81–82
  and digestion, 228–29
  frequency of, 111–12
  lack of, and insomnia, 259
  meditation and, 343–44
  and sleep, 259
  tailoring, 74–80
  while traveling, 298
  for vision muscles, 250
  weight-bearing, 82–83, 87
  see also Aerobic exercise
Exercise machines, 74, 111
Exercise programs, 76–79, 89, 109–11
Expressivism, 386
Eye(s), 247, 251
  light as nutrient for, 248–49
Eye exercises, 250–51

Failure, risk of, 312–13
Family, 14–15, 396–97, 417, 425
Family ties, 375, 377–79
Fantasy, sexual, 391–92
Fast/fasting, 16, 34–42, 358
  guidelines for, 39–41
Fat (dietary), 3, 4, 8, 9, 29–30, 64, 65,
  359
  and bone health, 84, 85
  hidden, 31–32
Fat Is a Feminist Issue (Orbach), 64
Fatigue, 210, 237
Fatty foods, 55, 236–37, 243–44
Feelings
  acknowledging and expressing, 379,
  397–98
  of dreams, 270
Feet, 92, 106, 124
  massage, 200–01
Feldenkrais, Moshe, 184, 220
Feldenkrais method, 184–85
Feldenkrais practitioners, 132–33

and ideal weight, 65–67
integrated into daily life, 69–70
posture and, 129
and sex, 394
Physical risks, 307–08, 310, 312
Physicians' Committee for Responsible
Medicine (PCRM), 4–5
Phytoestrogens, 243
Piezoclectric effect, 83
Pineal, 248–49, 299
Pizzorno, Joseph, 35, 84
Play, 72–73, 279–80
Pocket Doctor, The (Bezruchka), 301–02
Pollan, Michael, 408
Pollutants, 151
  airborne, 219, 220
  in bedroom, 141–52
  indoor, 144–45, 153–54
Polycyclic aromatic hydrocarbons
  (PAHs), 243
Polysaccharides, 234, 235
Positive outlook, 232, 323–30, 425
Posture, 90, 95, 123–30, 137, 154, 176,
  424
  and back problems, 132, 133
  and breathing, 216–17, 220
  warning signs of poor, 125–26
Potassium, 23–24
Power of the Clan, The (Wolf), 378
Pranayama, 218
Pregnancy, 40, 56, 132, 184, 202
Pregnancy tests, 168, 169
Progressive relaxation, 342–43
Protein, 8, 41, 48, 82, 223
  and bone health, 84
  tryptophan in, 262–63
Psychoneuroimmunology (PNI), 231,
  232
Psyllium seeds, 225
Pursed-lip breathing, 220
Pyridoxine (B$_6$), 22, 233

Racket sports, 74, 75, 77, 78, 116
Ray, Michael, 413
Recovering the Soul (Dossey), 231–32
Real Vitamin and Mineral Book, The
  (Lieberman), 20
Recommended desirable weights
  (RDWs), 63
Recommended dietary allowances
  (RDAs), 4, 17, 18–19, 20

see also U.S. recommended daily allow-
  ances (US RDAs)
Reflexology, 200
Relationships, 363, 390, 424
  addictive, 294
  first-person messages in, 401
  and immune system, 235–36
Relaxation, 96, 244, 271, 418, 425
  conscious, 338–45
  for eyes, 250–51
  while traveling, 300
Relaxation Response, The (Benson),
  339–40
Relaxation techniques, 132, 133, 260
REM sleep, 266–68, 271
Remedy therapies, 176, 181–84
Resistance exercises, 100–01
Resveratrol, 321
Retirement, 362, 366
Reynolds, David K., 335
Riboflavin (B$_2$), 21, 247
RICE (rest, ice, compression, and eleva-
  tion), 131
Rifkin, Jeremy, 283
Rimm, Eric, 319
Ringsdorf, W. M., 19
Rippe, James, 343–44
Risk taking, 307–14, 387, 397, 400, 425
  and creativity, 414
  motives in, 310–11
  in workplace, 413
Roberts, Alan, 326
Robbins, John, 8
Robinson, Bryan E., 292–93
Robinson, Rita, 171–72
Rock climbing, 75, 117
Rolf, Ida, 180
Rolfing/Rolfers, 96, 133, 180
Root, Leon, 124, 137
Rosen, Winifred, 315
Rosenman, Ray, 282–83
Rossbach, Sarah, 147
Routine(s), 311–12, 425
Running, 74, 77, 83, 125, 409
Rusk, Tom, 346–47
Rutter, Peter, 391–92

Safe Drinking Water Act, 46
Safety concerns
  in endurance exercises, 111
Sala, George, 400
Sarno, John, 132

ABOUT THE AUTHOR

Mark Mayell worked at *Natural Health* for twelve years, including seven years as editor of the magazine and two years as editor of *Natural Health*'s book-publishing division. He has also served as the editor of *Nutrition Action,* the monthly newsletter of the Washington, D.C., nutrition advocacy group Center for Science in the Public Interest. He has written extensively on alternative approaches to health for *Natural Health, Utne Reader,* and other magazines and is on the Board of Advisors of the American Holistic Health Association. Mark has a master's degree in philosophy and social policy from George Washington University. He currently lives with his wife and two children in Wellesley, Massachusetts.

This is his second book for *Natural Health:* Pocket Books recently published *The Natural Health First-Aid Guide: The Definitive Handbook of Natural Remedies for Treating Minor Emergencies.*

ABOUT *NATURAL HEALTH* MAGAZINE

Natural Health: The Guide to Well-Being (formerly *East West Journal*) has been the leading national magazine on alternative health, herbalism, bodywork, personal growth, and natural foods for over two decades. *Natural Health* provides more than half a million readers in the U.S. and around the world with practical information on health and longevity. As a recent magazine review by *USA Today* noted, *Natural Health* "is far too splendid to be confined to a health-food store shelf."

Among the magazine's awards for coverage of issues relating to natural health is the 1989 Alternative Press Award for Service Journalism. *Natural Health* is one of only three magazines listed under the Health and Nutrition Magazines category in *The New York Public Library's Desk Reference* of "the ultimate one-volume collection of the most frequently sought information."

The editors of *Natural Health* have written numerous books on natural healing and whole-foods cooking, including *The Natural Health First-Aid Guide; Quick and Natural Rice Dishes; Meetings with Remarkable Men and Women: Interviews with Leading Thinkers on Health, Medicine, Ecology, Culture, Society, and Spirit; Sweet and Natural Desserts; Shopper's Guide to Natural Foods;* and *Natural Childcare*.

Natural Health is produced bimonthly in Brookline, Massachusetts, by a staff of twenty-five. For subscription information write or call *Natural Health*, 17 Station St., P.O. Box 1200, Brookline Village, MA 02147; (617) 232-1000.